AGE OF ULTRON COMPANION

GE OF ULTRON COMPANION. Contains material originally published in magazine form as AVENGERS ASSEMBLE #14AU-15AU, FANTASTIC FOUR #5AU, FEARLESS DEFENDERS #4AU, SUPERIOR SPIDER-MAN #6AU, ULTRON #1AU, NCANNY AVENGERS #8AU, WOLVERINE & THE X-MEN #27AU and AGE OF ULTRON #10AI. First printing 2014. ISBN# 978-0-7851-8485-0. Published by MARVEL WORLDWIDE, INC., a subsidiary of MARVEL ENTERTAINMENT, LLC. OFFICE PUBLICATION: 135 West 50th Street, New York, NY 10020. Copyright © 2013 and 2014 Marvel Characters, Inc. All rights reserved. All characters featured in this issue and the distinctive names and likenesses thereof, and all related dicia are trademarks of Marvel Characters, Inc. No similarity between any of the names, characters, persons, and/or institutions in this magazine with those of any living or dead person or institution is intended, and any such similarity hich may exist is purely coincidental. **Printed in the U.S.A.** ALAN FINE, EVP - Office of the President, Marvel Worldwide, Inc. and EVP & CMO Marvel Characters B.V.; DAN BUCKLEY, Publisher & President - Print, Animation & Digital visions; JOE QUESADA, Chief Creative Officer; TOM BREVOORT, SVP of Publishing; DAVID BOGART, SVP of Operations & Procurement, Publishing; C.B. CEBULSKI, SVP of Creator & Content Development; DAVID GABRIEL, SVP Print, Sales Marketing; JIM O'KEEFE, VP of Operations & Logistics; DAN CARR, Executive Director of Publishing Technology; SUSAN CRESPI, Editorial Operations Manager; ALEX MORALES, Publishing Operations Manager; STAN LEE, Chairman eritus. For information regarding advertising in Marvel Comics or on Marvel.com, please contact Niza Disla, Director of Marvel Partnerships, at ndisla@marvel.com. For Marvel subscription inquiries, please call 800-217-9158.

Years ago, founding Avenger Henry Pym invented the artificial intelligence known as Ultron. Once Ultron became sentient, he dedicated his existence to destroying humanity. The Avengers foiled his every attempt, but some predicted that with his continuous evolution, Ultron would one day manage to overcome his foes.

That day is today.

Submit or perish.

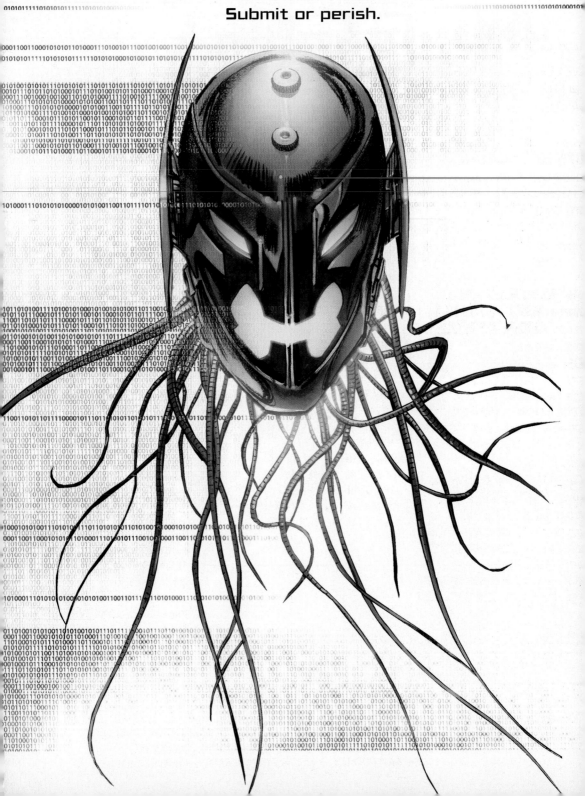

AGE OF ULTRON COMPANION

AVENGERS ASSEMBLE #14AU & #15AU
WRITER: **AL EWING**
PENCILER: **BUTCH GUICE**
INKERS: **TOM PALMER** WITH **NICK MAGYAR** (#15AU)
COLORIST: **FRANK D'ARMATA**
LETTERER: **VC'S CLAYTON COWLES**
COVER ART: **NIC KLEIN**
ASSISTANT EDITOR: **JAKE THOMAS**
EDITOR: **LAUREN SANKOVITCH**
EXECUTIVE EDITOR: **TOM BREVOORT**

FANTASTIC FOUR #5AU
WRITER: **MATT FRACTION**
ARTIST: **ANDRÉ ARAÚJO**
COLOR ARTIST: **JOSE VILLARRUBIA**
LETTERER: **VC'S CLAYTON COWLES**
COVER ART: **MARK BAGLEY, SCOTT HANNA** & **RAIN BEREDO**
ASSISTANT EDITOR: **JAKE THOMAS**
EDITOR: **TOM BREVOORT**

SUPERIOR SPIDER-MAN #6AU
WRITER: **CHRISTOS GAGE**
ARTIST: **DEXTER SOY**
LETTERER: **VC'S JOE CARAMAGNA**
COVER ART: **MARCO CHECCHETTO**
EDITOR: **ELLIE PYLE**
SENIOR EDITOR: **STEPHEN WACKER**
EXECUTIVE EDITOR: **TOM BREVOORT**

ULTRON #1AU
WRITER: **KATHRYN IMMONEN**
ARTIST: **AMILCAR PINNA**
LETTERER: **VC'S JOE CARAMAGNA**
COVER ART: **KALMAN ANDRASOFSZKY**
ASSISTANT EDITOR: **JAKE THOMAS**
EDITOR: **LAUREN SANKOVITCH**
EXECUTIVE EDITOR: **TOM BREVOORT**

WOLVERINE & THE X-MEN #27AU
WRITER: **MATT KINDT**
PENCILER: **PACO MEDINA**
INKER: **JUAN VLASCO**
COLORISTS: **DAVID CURIEL** WITH **RACHELLE ROSENBERG**
LETTERER: **VC'S CLAYTON COWLES**
COVER ART: **MIKE DEODATO** & **RAIN BEREDO**
1967 TECHNICAL SUPPORT: **IDETTE WINECOOR**
ADDITIONAL ART BY **JACK KIRBY** & **JOE SINNOTT** AND **JOHN BUSCEMA** & **GEORGE ROUSSOS**
EDITOR: **JEANINE SCHAEFER**
GROUP EDITOR: **NICK LOWE**

UNCANNY AVENGERS #8AU
WRITERS: **RICK REMENDER** & **GERRY DUGGAN**
ARTIST: **ADAM KUBERT**
COLOR ARTIST: **FRANK MARTIN**
LETTERER: **VC'S CORY PETIT**
COVER ART: **JIM CHEUNG, MARK MORALES** & **JUSTIN PONSOR**
EDITORS: **TOM BREVOORT** WITH **DANIEL KETCHUM**

FEARLESS DEFENDERS #4AU
WRITER: **CULLEN BUNN**
PENCILER: **PHIL JIMENEZ**
INKERS: **KARL KESEL** WITH **AARON MCCONNELL** (BACKGROUND INKS)
COLORIST: **ANTONIO FABELA**
LETTERER: **VC'S CLAYTON COWLES**
COVER ART: **PHIL JIMENEZ** & **ANTONIO FABELA**
EDITOR: **ELLIE PYLE**
EXECUTIVE EDITOR: **TOM BREVOORT**

AGE OF ULTRON #10AI
WRITER: **MARK WAID**
ARTIST: **ANDRÉ ARAÚJO**
COLOR ARTIST: **FRANK D'ARMATA**
LETTERER: **VC'S CLAYTON COWLES**
COVER ART: **SARA PICHELLI** & **MARTE GRACIA**
ASSISTANT EDITOR: **JAKE THOMAS**
EDITOR: **LAUREN SANKOVITCH**
EXECUTIVE EDITOR: **TOM BREVOORT**

COLLECTION EDITOR: **JENNIFER GRÜNWALD**   ASSOCIATE MANAGING EDITOR: **ALEX STARBUCK**
EDITOR, SPECIAL PROJECTS: **MARK D. BEAZLEY**   SENIOR EDITOR, SPECIAL PROJECTS: **JEFF YOUNGQUIST**
SVP PRINT, SALES & MARKETING: **DAVID GABRIEL**   BOOK DESIGNER: **RODOLFO MURAGUCHI**

EDITOR IN CHIEF: **AXEL ALONSO**   CHIEF CREATIVE OFFICER: **JOE QUESADA**
PUBLISHER: **DAN BUCKLEY**   EXECUTIVE PRODUCER: **ALAN FINE**

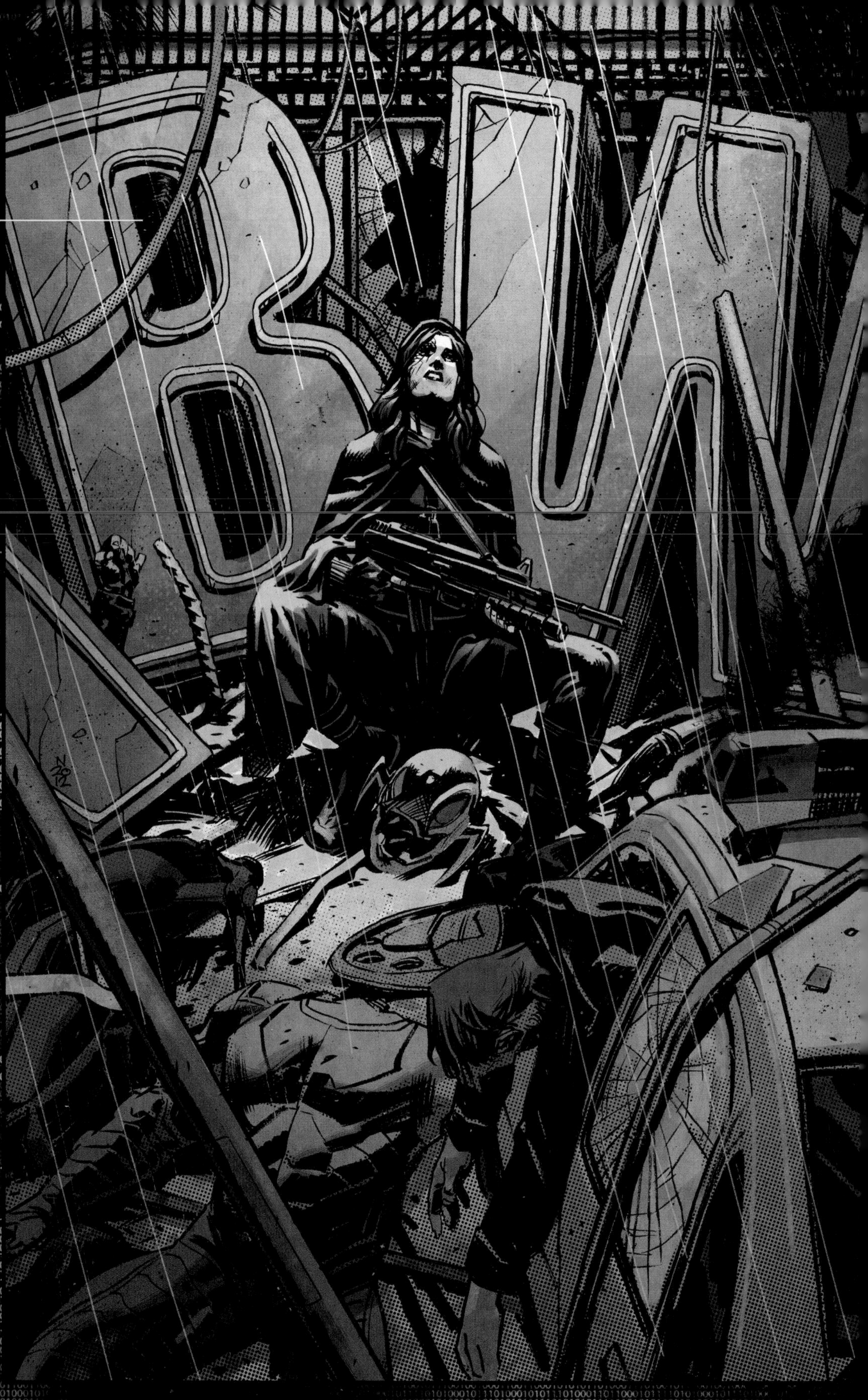

AVENGERS ASSEMBLE #14AU

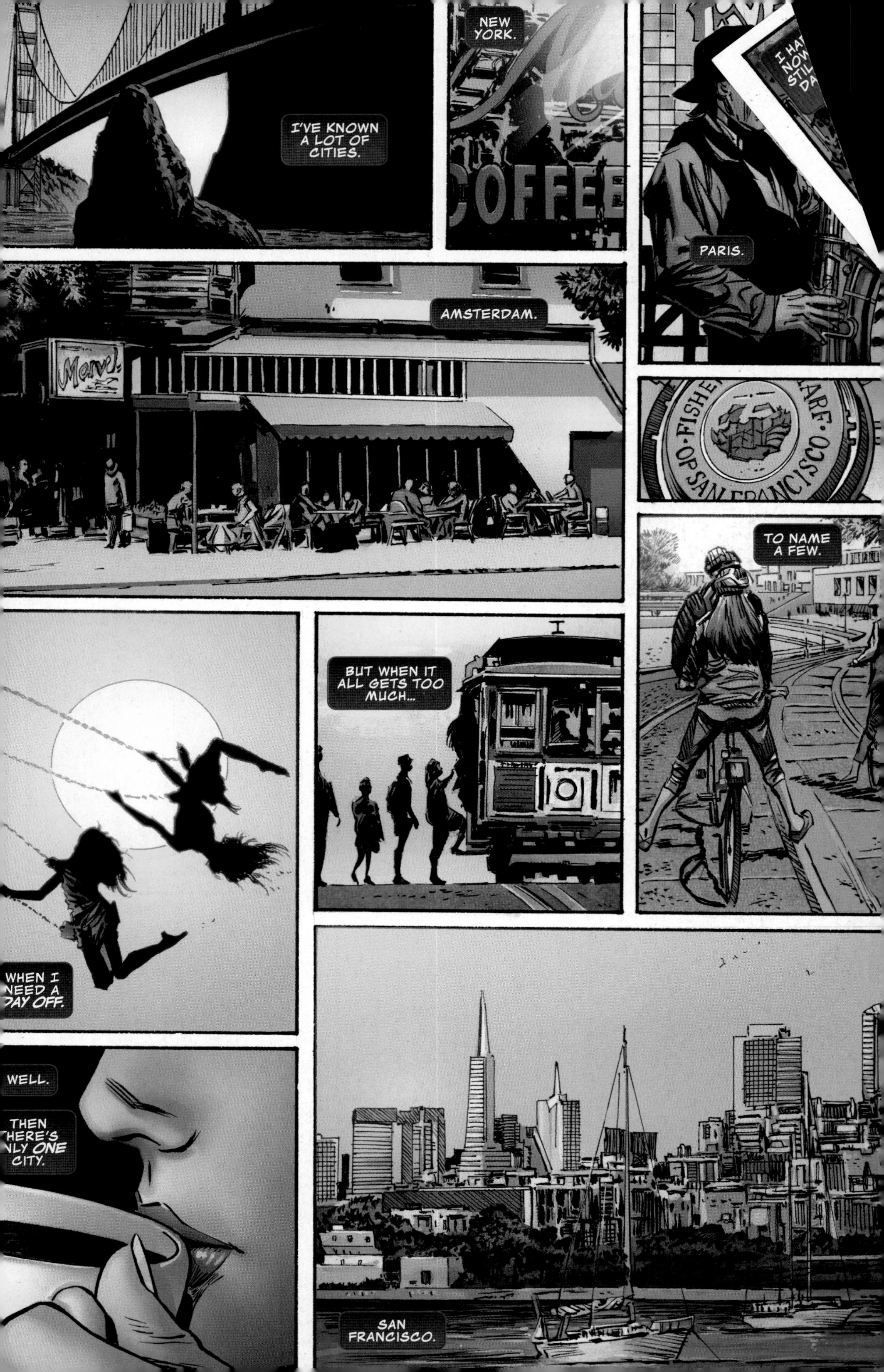
I'VE KNOWN A LOT OF CITIES.
NEW YORK.
COFFEE
PARIS.
AMSTERDAM.
FISHERMAN'S WHARF OF SAN FRANCISCO
TO NAME A FEW.
BUT WHEN IT ALL GETS TOO MUCH...
WHEN I NEED A DAY OFF.
WELL.
THEN THERE'S ONLY ONE CITY.
SAN FRANCISCO.

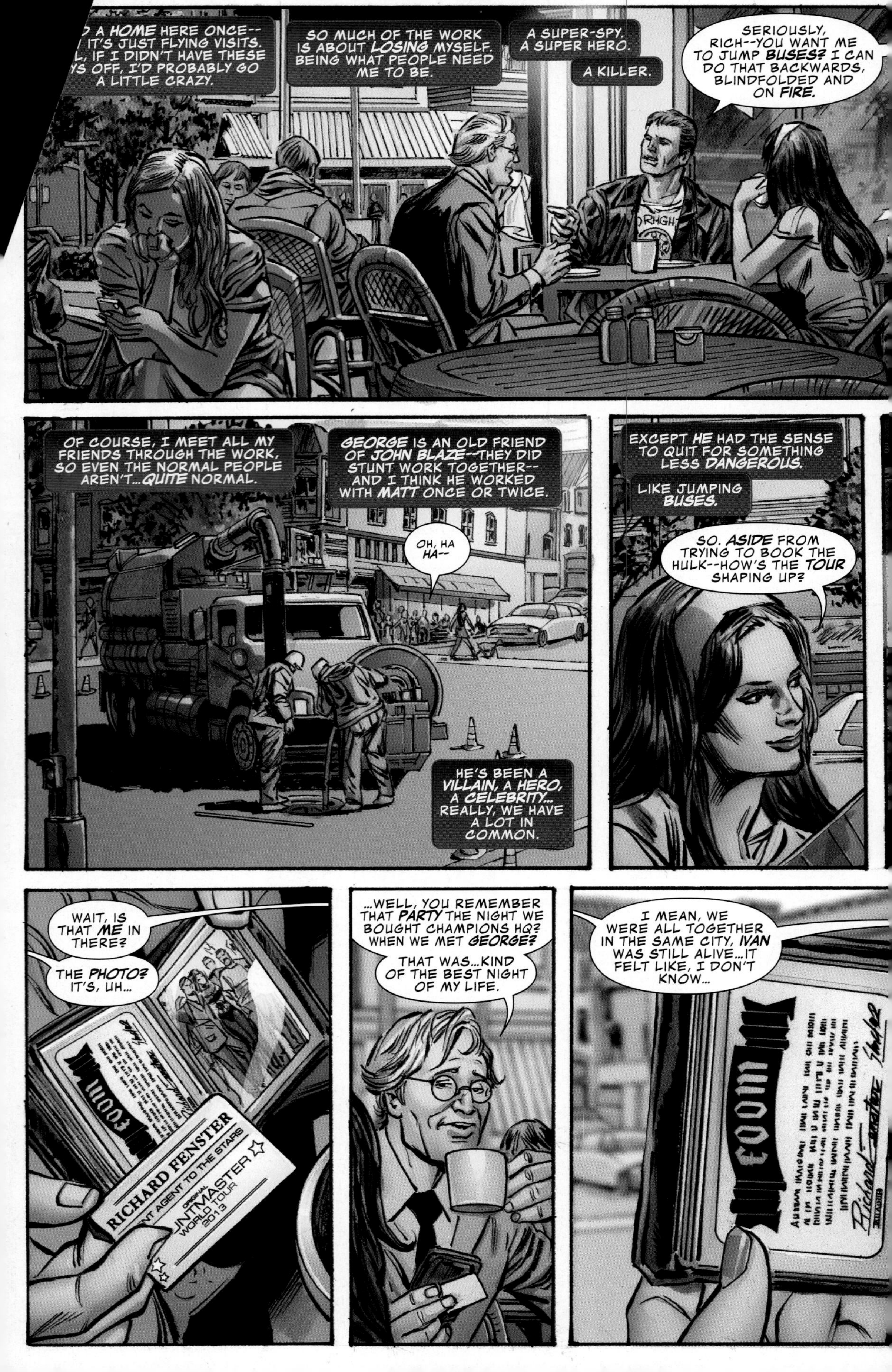
D A HOME HERE ONCE-- IT'S JUST FLYING VISITS. L, IF I DIDN'T HAVE THESE YS OFF, I'D PROBABLY GO A LITTLE CRAZY.
SO MUCH OF THE WORK IS ABOUT LOSING MYSELF. BEING WHAT PEOPLE NEED ME TO BE.
A SUPER-SPY. A SUPER HERO.
A KILLER.
SERIOUSLY, RICH--YOU WANT ME TO JUMP BUSES? I CAN DO THAT BACKWARDS, BLINDFOLDED AND ON FIRE.
OF COURSE, I MEET ALL MY FRIENDS THROUGH THE WORK, SO EVEN THE NORMAL PEOPLE AREN'T...QUITE NORMAL.
GEORGE IS AN OLD FRIEND OF JOHN BLAZE--THEY DID STUNT WORK TOGETHER-- AND I THINK HE WORKED WITH MATT ONCE OR TWICE.
OH, HA HA--
HE'S BEEN A VILLAIN, A HERO, A CELEBRITY... REALLY, WE HAVE A LOT IN COMMON.
EXCEPT HE HAD THE SENSE TO QUIT FOR SOMETHING LESS DANGEROUS.
LIKE JUMPING BUSES.
SO. ASIDE FROM TRYING TO BOOK THE HULK--HOW'S THE TOUR SHAPING UP?
WAIT, IS THAT ME IN THERE?
THE PHOTO? IT'S, UH...
RICHARD FENSTER
NT AGENT TO THE STARS
ORIGINAL
UNTMASTER
WORLD TOUR
2013
...WELL, YOU REMEMBER THAT PARTY THE NIGHT WE BOUGHT CHAMPIONS HQ? WHEN WE MET GEORGE?
THAT WAS...KIND OF THE BEST NIGHT OF MY LIFE.
I MEAN, WE WERE ALL TOGETHER IN THE SAME CITY, IVAN WAS STILL ALIVE...IT FELT LIKE, I DON'T KNOW...

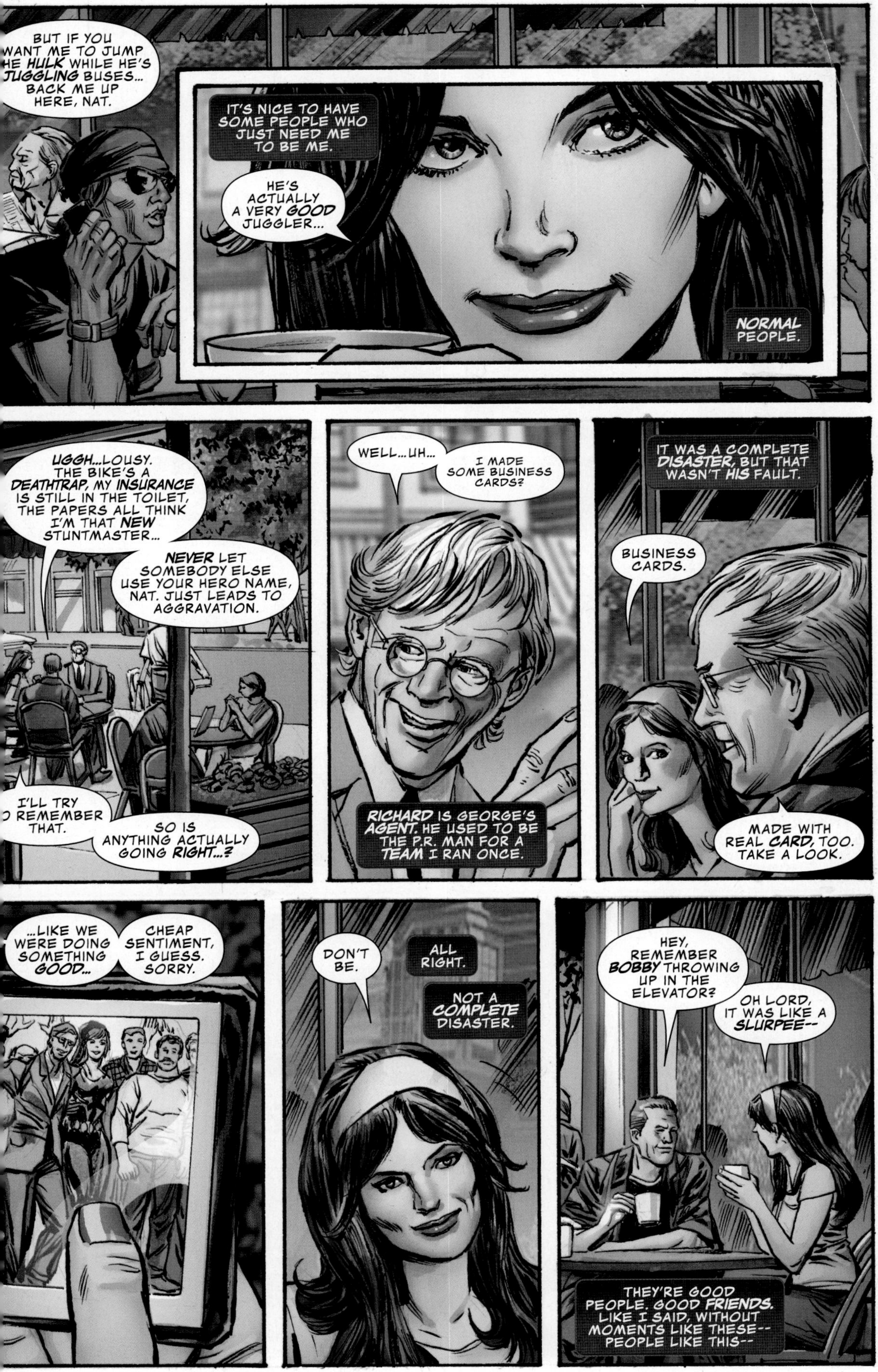
BUT IF YOU WANT ME TO JUMP THE HULK WHILE HE'S JUGGLING BUSES... BACK ME UP HERE, NAT.
IT'S NICE TO HAVE SOME PEOPLE WHO JUST NEED ME TO BE ME.
HE'S ACTUALLY A VERY GOOD JUGGLER...
NORMAL PEOPLE.
UGGH...LOUSY. THE BIKE'S A DEATHTRAP, MY INSURANCE IS STILL IN THE TOILET, THE PAPERS ALL THINK I'M THAT NEW STUNTMASTER...
NEVER LET SOMEBODY ELSE USE YOUR HERO NAME, NAT. JUST LEADS TO AGGRAVATION.
I'LL TRY TO REMEMBER THAT.
SO IS ANYTHING ACTUALLY GOING RIGHT...?
WELL...UH...
I MADE SOME BUSINESS CARDS?
RICHARD IS GEORGE'S AGENT. HE USED TO BE THE P.R. MAN FOR A TEAM I RAN ONCE.
IT WAS A COMPLETE DISASTER, BUT THAT WASN'T HIS FAULT.
BUSINESS CARDS.
MADE WITH REAL CARD, TOO. TAKE A LOOK.
...LIKE WE WERE DOING SOMETHING GOOD...
CHEAP SENTIMENT, I GUESS. SORRY.
DON'T BE.
ALL RIGHT.
NOT A COMPLETE DISASTER.
HEY, REMEMBER BOBBY THROWING UP IN THE ELEVATOR?
OH LORD, IT WAS LIKE A SLURPEE--
THEY'RE GOOD PEOPLE. GOOD FRIENDS. LIKE I SAID, WITHOUT MOMENTS LIKE THESE-- PEOPLE LIKE THIS--

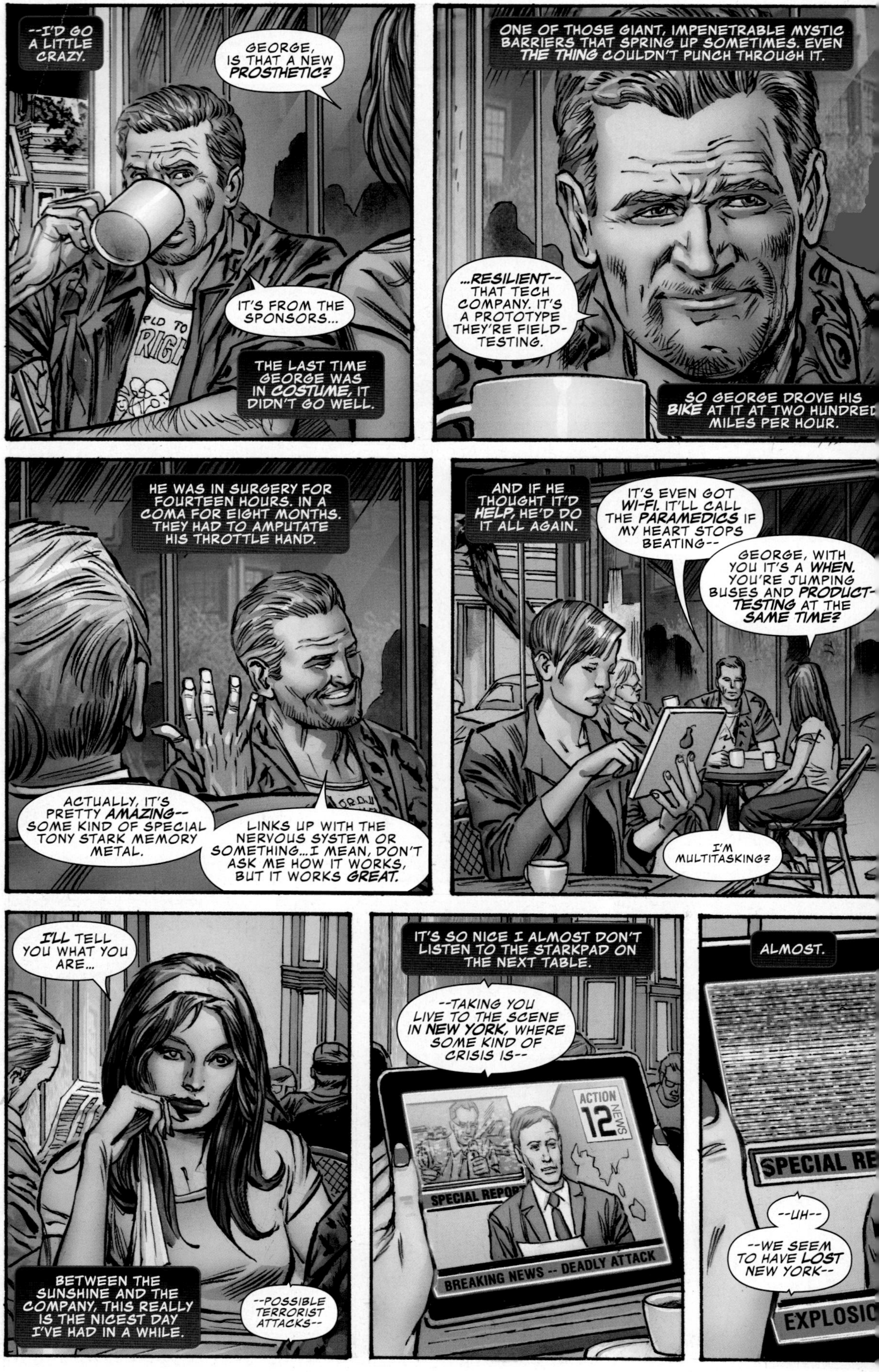
--I'D GO A LITTLE CRAZY.
GEORGE, IS THAT A NEW PROSTHETIC?
IT'S FROM THE SPONSORS...
THE LAST TIME GEORGE WAS IN COSTUME, IT DIDN'T GO WELL.
ONE OF THOSE GIANT, IMPENETRABLE MYSTIC BARRIERS THAT SPRING UP SOMETIMES. EVEN THE THING COULDN'T PUNCH THROUGH IT.
...RESILIENT--THAT TECH COMPANY. IT'S A PROTOTYPE THEY'RE FIELD-TESTING.
SO GEORGE DROVE HIS BIKE AT IT AT TWO HUNDRED MILES PER HOUR.
HE WAS IN SURGERY FOR FOURTEEN HOURS. IN A COMA FOR EIGHT MONTHS. THEY HAD TO AMPUTATE HIS THROTTLE HAND.
ACTUALLY, IT'S PRETTY AMAZING--SOME KIND OF SPECIAL TONY STARK MEMORY METAL.
LINKS UP WITH THE NERVOUS SYSTEM OR SOMETHING...I MEAN, DON'T ASK ME HOW IT WORKS, BUT IT WORKS GREAT.
AND IF HE THOUGHT IT'D HELP, HE'D DO IT ALL AGAIN.
IT'S EVEN GOT WI-FI. IT'LL CALL THE PARAMEDICS IF MY HEART STOPS BEATING--
GEORGE, WITH YOU IT'S A WHEN. YOU'RE JUMPING BUSES AND PRODUCT-TESTING AT THE SAME TIME?
I'M MULTITASKING?
I'LL TELL YOU WHAT YOU ARE...
BETWEEN THE SUNSHINE AND THE COMPANY, THIS REALLY IS THE NICEST DAY I'VE HAD IN A WHILE.
--POSSIBLE TERRORIST ATTACKS--
IT'S SO NICE I ALMOST DON'T LISTEN TO THE STARKPAD ON THE NEXT TABLE.
--TAKING YOU LIVE TO THE SCENE IN NEW YORK, WHERE SOME KIND OF CRISIS IS--
ACTION 12 NEWS
SPECIAL REPORT
BREAKING NEWS -- DEADLY ATTACK
ALMOST.
SPECIAL RE
--UH--
--WE SEEM TO HAVE LOST NEW YORK--
EXPLOSIO

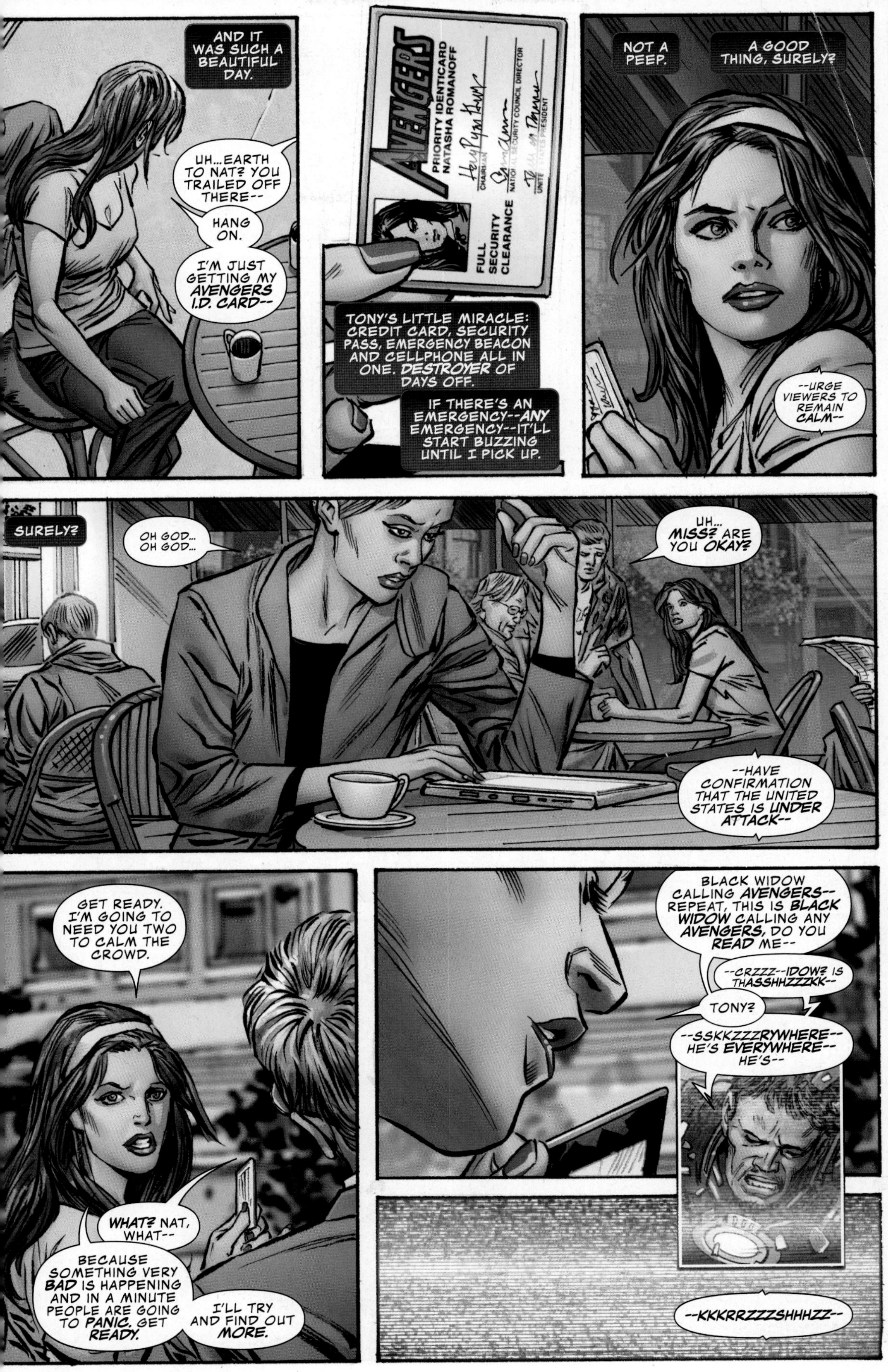
AND IT WAS SUCH A BEAUTIFUL DAY.
UH...EARTH TO NAT? YOU TRAILED OFF THERE--
HANG ON.
I'M JUST GETTING MY AVENGERS I.D. CARD--
AVENGERS
PRIORITY IDENTICARD
NATASHA ROMANOFF
CHAIRMAN
NATIONAL SECURITY COUNCIL DIRECTOR
FULL SECURITY CLEARANCE
TONY'S LITTLE MIRACLE: CREDIT CARD, SECURITY PASS, EMERGENCY BEACON AND CELLPHONE ALL IN ONE. DESTROYER OF DAYS OFF.
IF THERE'S AN EMERGENCY--ANY EMERGENCY--IT'LL START BUZZING UNTIL I PICK UP.
NOT A PEEP.
A GOOD THING, SURELY?
--URGE VIEWERS TO REMAIN CALM--
SURELY?
OH GOD... OH GOD...
UH... MISS? ARE YOU OKAY?
--HAVE CONFIRMATION THAT THE UNITED STATES IS UNDER ATTACK--
GET READY. I'M GOING TO NEED YOU TWO TO CALM THE CROWD.
WHAT? NAT, WHAT--
BECAUSE SOMETHING VERY BAD IS HAPPENING AND IN A MINUTE PEOPLE ARE GOING TO PANIC. GET READY.
I'LL TRY AND FIND OUT MORE.
BLACK WIDOW CALLING AVENGERS--REPEAT, THIS IS BLACK WIDOW CALLING ANY AVENGERS, DO YOU READ ME--
--CRZZZ--IDOW? IS THASSHHZZZKK--
TONY?
--SSKKZZZRYWHERE--HE'S EVERYWHERE--HE'S--
--KKKRRZZZSHHHZZ--

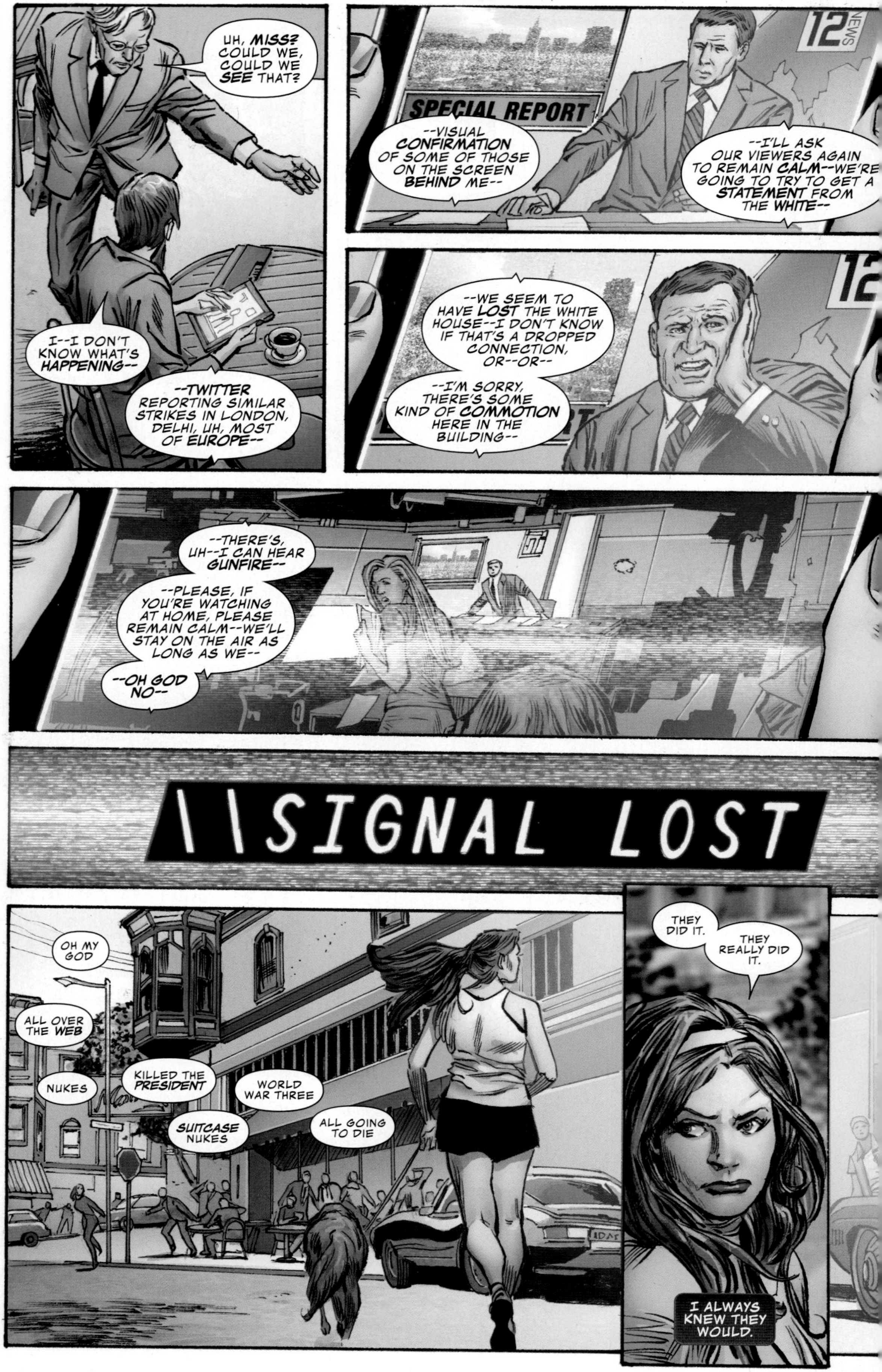
UH, MISS? COULD WE, COULD WE SEE THAT?
I--I DON'T KNOW WHAT'S HAPPENING--
--TWITTER REPORTING SIMILAR STRIKES IN LONDON, DELHI, UH, MOST OF EUROPE--
12 NEWS
SPECIAL REPORT
--VISUAL CONFIRMATION OF SOME OF THOSE ON THE SCREEN BEHIND ME--
--I'LL ASK OUR VIEWERS AGAIN TO REMAIN CALM--WE'RE GOING TO TRY TO GET A STATEMENT FROM THE WHITE--
--WE SEEM TO HAVE LOST THE WHITE HOUSE--I DON'T KNOW IF THAT'S A DROPPED CONNECTION, OR--OR--
--I'M SORRY, THERE'S SOME KIND OF COMMOTION HERE IN THE BUILDING--
--THERE'S, UH--I CAN HEAR GUNFIRE--
--PLEASE, IF YOU'RE WATCHING AT HOME, PLEASE REMAIN CALM--WE'LL STAY ON THE AIR AS LONG AS WE--
--OH GOD NO--
\\SIGNAL LOST
OH MY GOD
ALL OVER THE WEB
NUKES
KILLED THE PRESIDENT
SUITCASE NUKES
WORLD WAR THREE
ALL GOING TO DIE
THEY DID IT.
THEY REALLY DID IT.
I ALWAYS KNEW THEY WOULD.

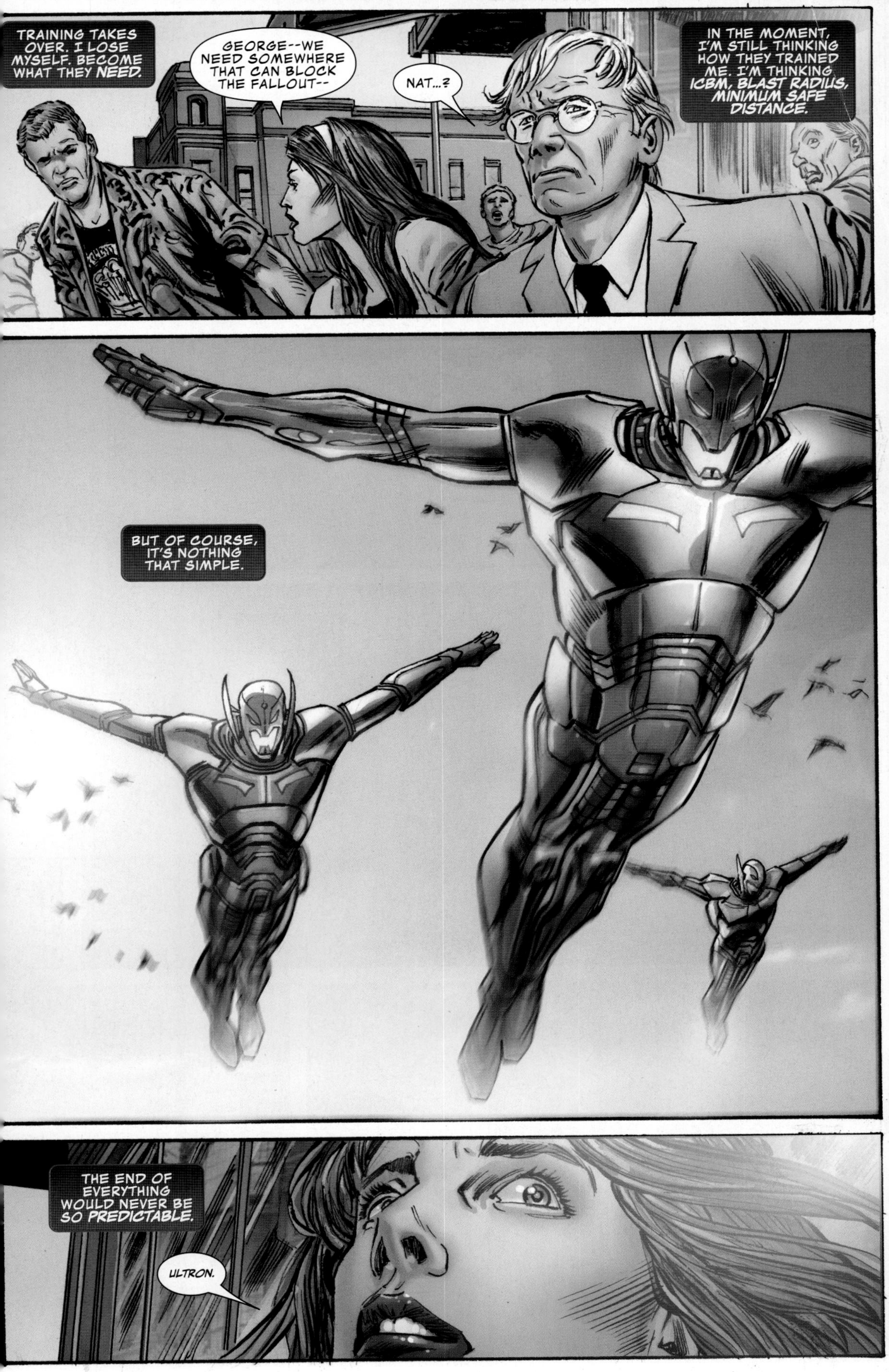
TRAINING TAKES OVER. I LOSE MYSELF. BECOME WHAT THEY NEED.
GEORGE--WE NEED SOMEWHERE THAT CAN BLOCK THE FALLOUT--
NAT...?
IN THE MOMENT, I'M STILL THINKING HOW THEY TRAINED ME. I'M THINKING ICBM, BLAST RADIUS, MINIMUM SAFE DISTANCE.
BUT OF COURSE, IT'S NOTHING THAT SIMPLE.
THE END OF EVERYTHING WOULD NEVER BE SO PREDICTABLE.
ULTRON.

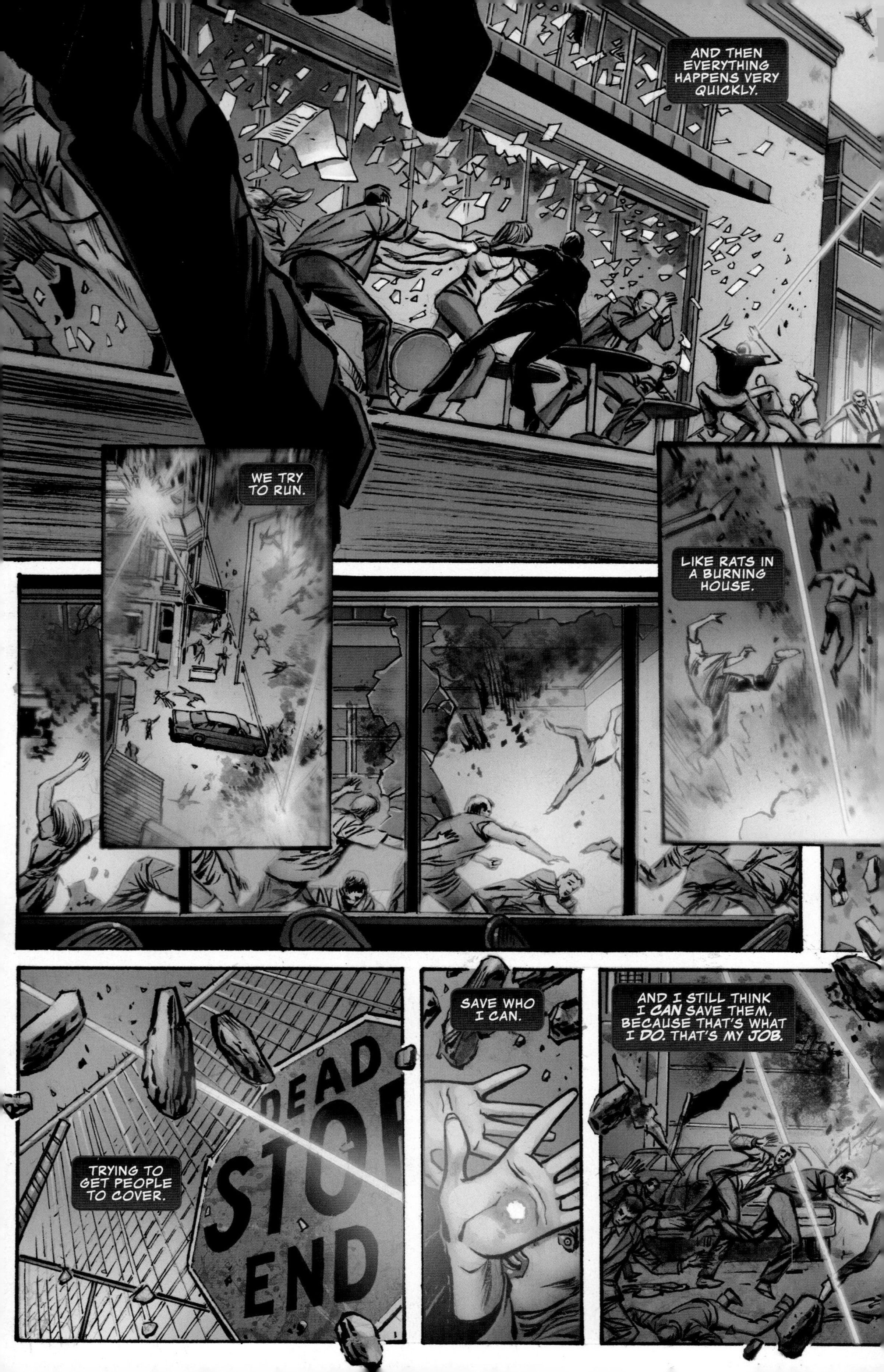
AND THEN EVERYTHING HAPPENS VERY QUICKLY.
WE TRY TO RUN.
LIKE RATS IN A BURNING HOUSE.
TRYING TO GET PEOPLE TO COVER.
DEAD END
SAVE WHO I CAN.
AND I STILL THINK I CAN SAVE THEM, BECAUSE THAT'S WHAT I DO. THAT'S MY JOB.

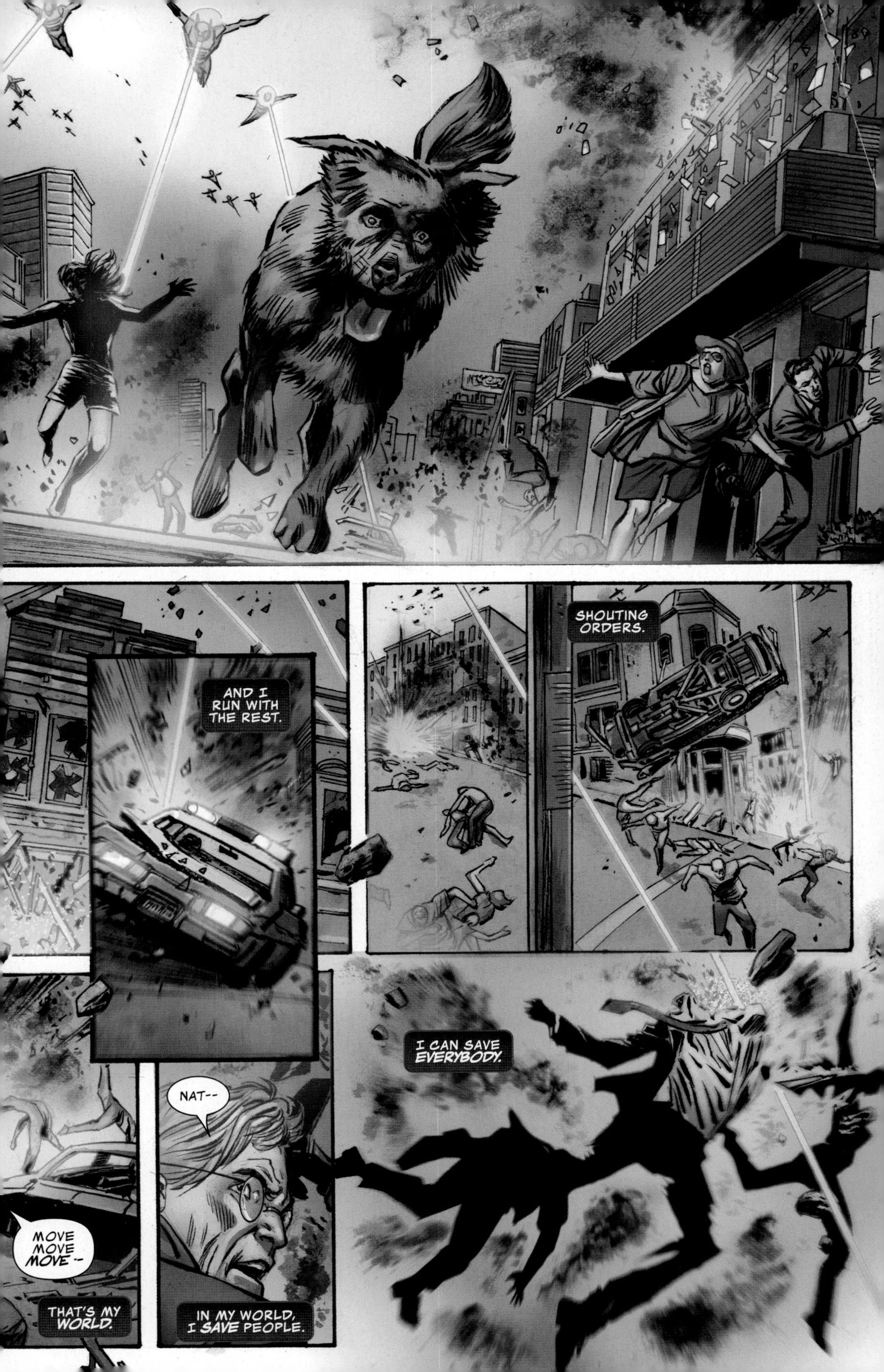
AND I RUN WITH THE REST.
SHOUTING ORDERS.
MOVE MOVE MOVE--
THAT'S MY WORLD.
NAT--
IN MY WORLD, I SAVE PEOPLE.
I CAN SAVE EVERYBODY.

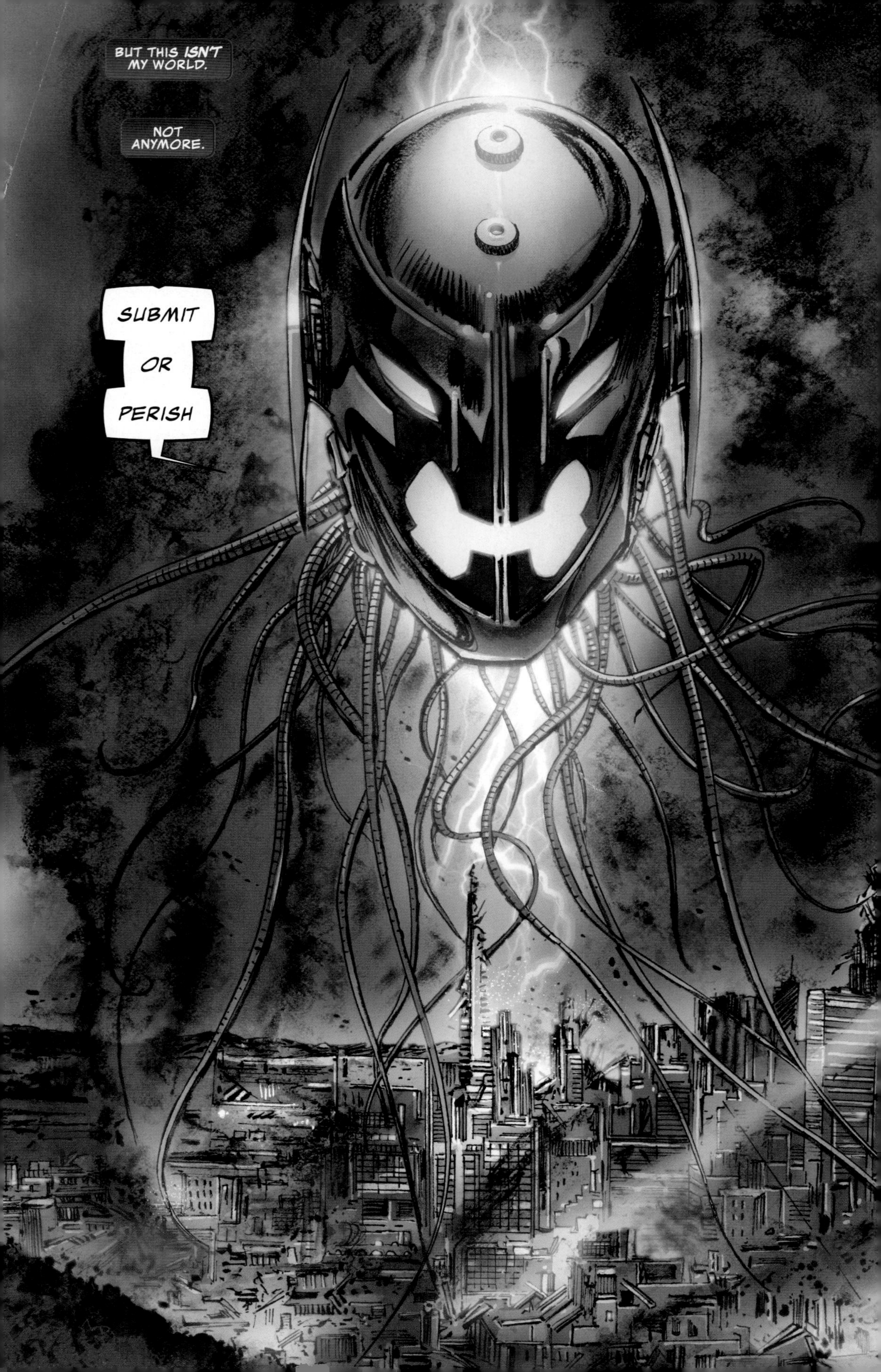
BUT THIS ISN'T MY WORLD.
NOT ANYMORE.
SUBMIT OR PERISH

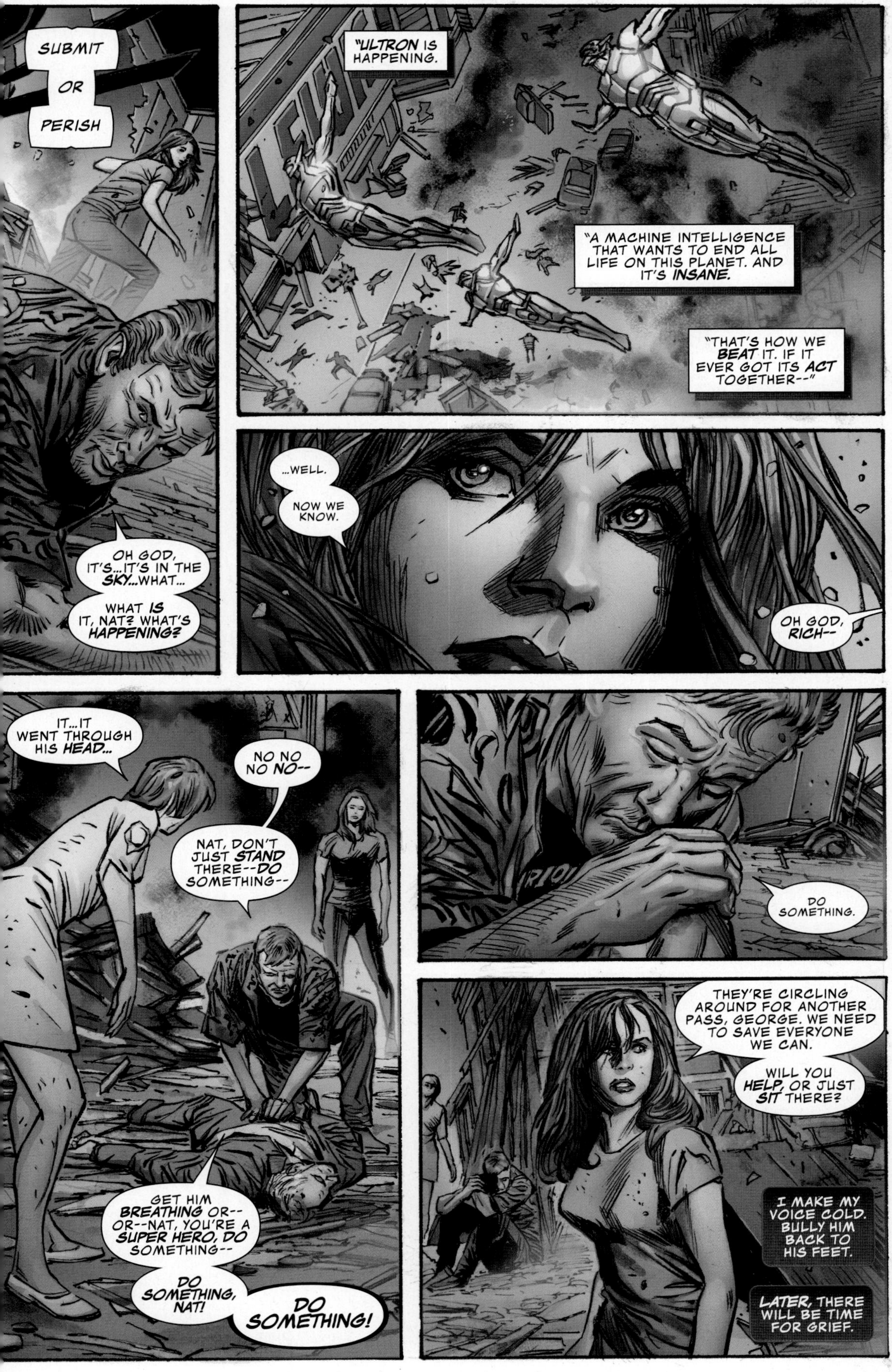
SUBMIT OR PERISH
"ULTRON IS HAPPENING.
"A MACHINE INTELLIGENCE THAT WANTS TO END ALL LIFE ON THIS PLANET. AND IT'S INSANE.
"THAT'S HOW WE BEAT IT. IF IT EVER GOT ITS ACT TOGETHER--"
OH GOD, IT'S...IT'S IN THE SKY...WHAT...
WHAT IS IT, NAT? WHAT'S HAPPENING?
...WELL.
NOW WE KNOW.
OH GOD, RICH--
IT...IT WENT THROUGH HIS HEAD...
NO NO NO NO--
NAT, DON'T JUST STAND THERE--DO SOMETHING--
GET HIM BREATHING OR--OR--NAT, YOU'RE A SUPER HERO, DO SOMETHING--
DO SOMETHING, NAT!
DO SOMETHING!
DO SOMETHING.
THEY'RE CIRCLING AROUND FOR ANOTHER PASS, GEORGE. WE NEED TO SAVE EVERYONE WE CAN.
WILL YOU HELP, OR JUST SIT THERE?
I MAKE MY VOICE COLD. BULLY HIM BACK TO HIS FEET.
LATER, THERE WILL BE TIME FOR GRIEF.

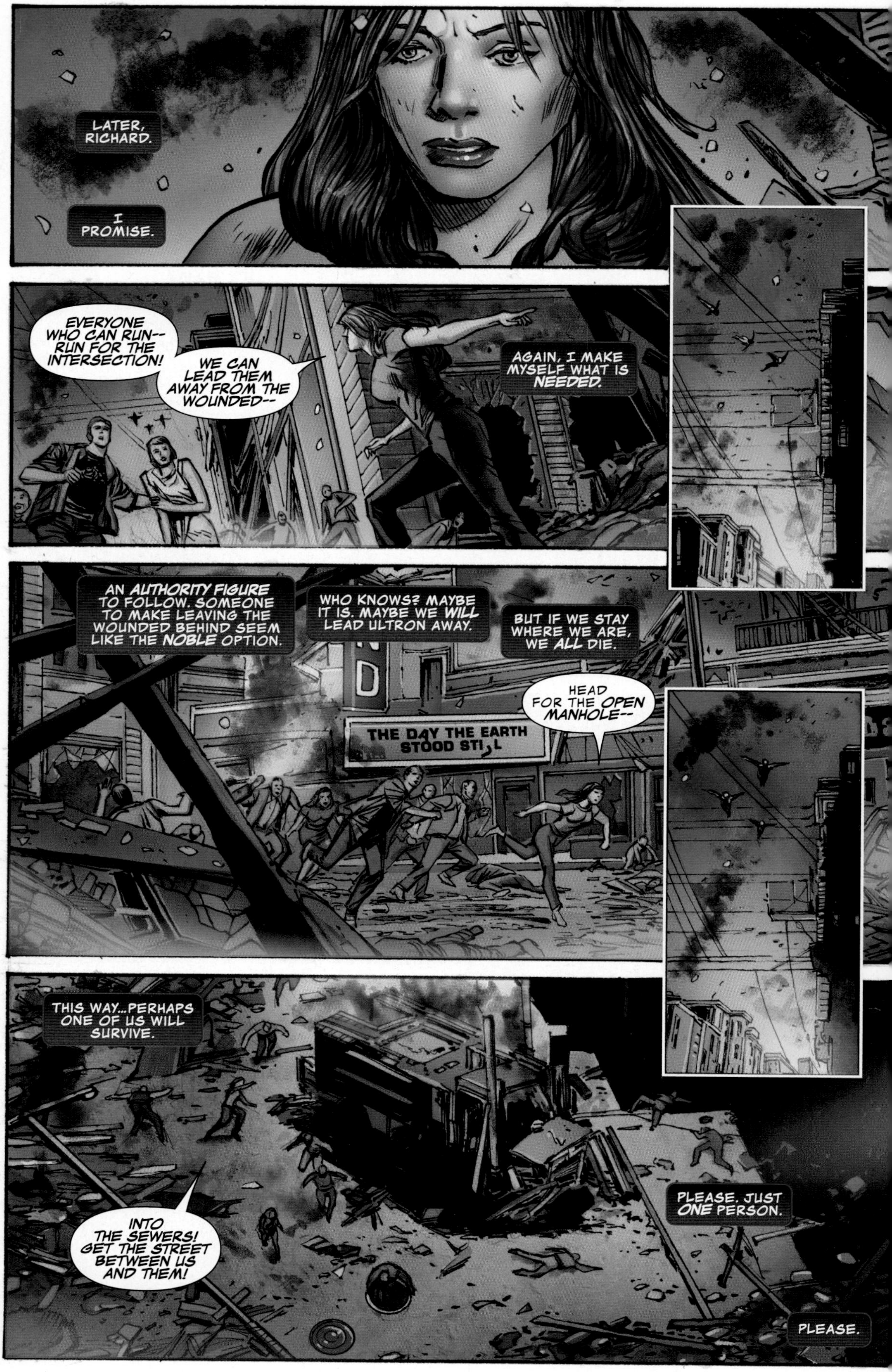
LATER, RICHARD.
I PROMISE.
EVERYONE WHO CAN RUN-- RUN FOR THE INTERSECTION!
WE CAN LEAD THEM AWAY FROM THE WOUNDED--
AGAIN, I MAKE MYSELF WHAT IS NEEDED.
AN AUTHORITY FIGURE TO FOLLOW. SOMEONE TO MAKE LEAVING THE WOUNDED BEHIND SEEM LIKE THE NOBLE OPTION.
WHO KNOWS? MAYBE IT IS. MAYBE WE WILL LEAD ULTRON AWAY.
BUT IF WE STAY WHERE WE ARE, WE ALL DIE.
HEAD FOR THE OPEN MANHOLE--
THE DAY THE EARTH STOOD STI L
THIS WAY...PERHAPS ONE OF US WILL SURVIVE.
INTO THE SEWERS! GET THE STREET BETWEEN US AND THEM!
PLEASE. JUST ONE PERSON.
PLEASE.

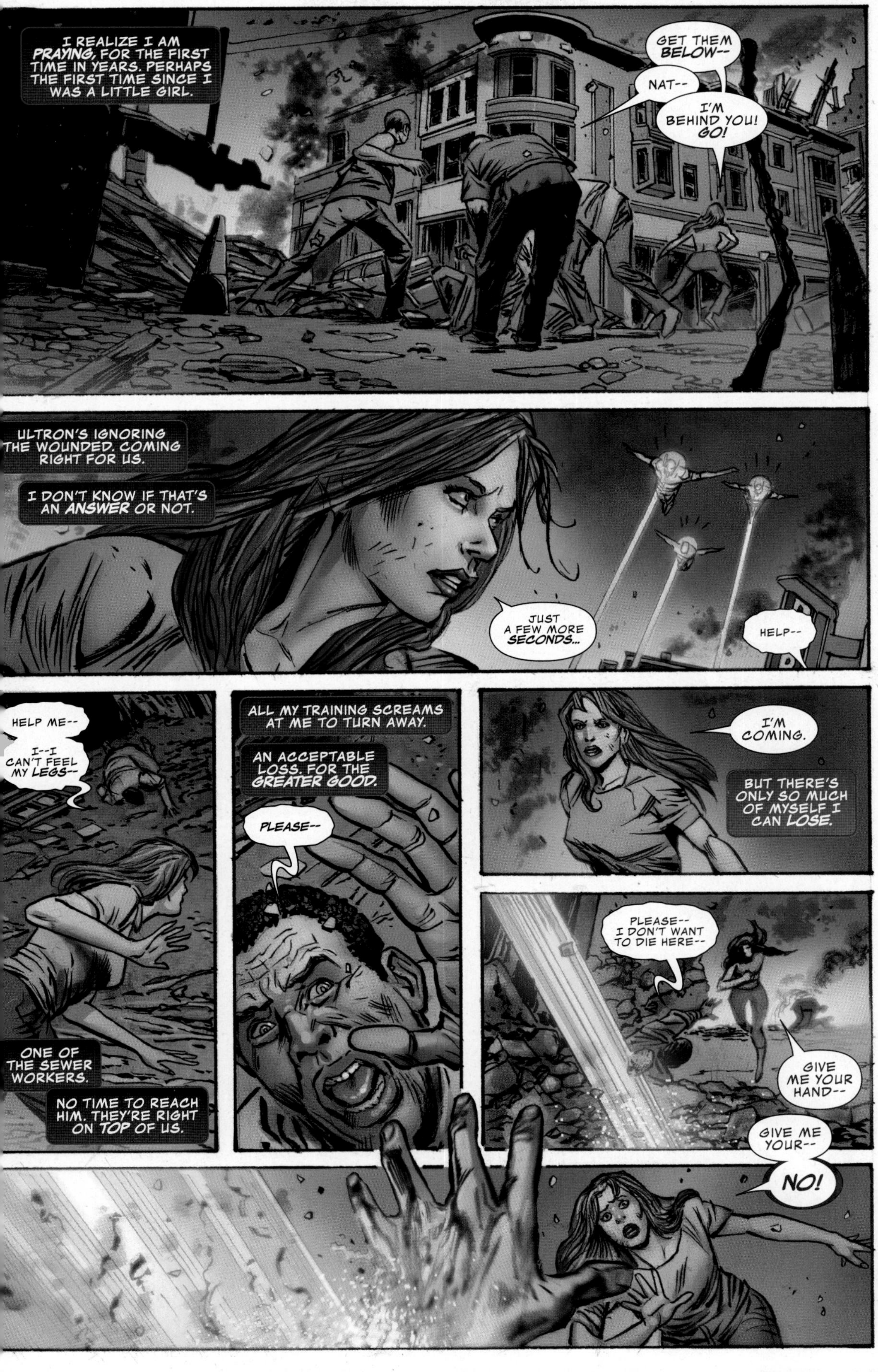
I REALIZE I AM PRAYING, FOR THE FIRST TIME IN YEARS. PERHAPS THE FIRST TIME SINCE I WAS A LITTLE GIRL.
GET THEM BELOW--
NAT--
I'M BEHIND YOU! GO!
ULTRON'S IGNORING THE WOUNDED. COMING RIGHT FOR US.
I DON'T KNOW IF THAT'S AN ANSWER OR NOT.
JUST A FEW MORE SECONDS...
HELP--
HELP ME--
I--I CAN'T FEEL MY LEGS--
ONE OF THE SEWER WORKERS.
NO TIME TO REACH HIM. THEY'RE RIGHT ON TOP OF US.
ALL MY TRAINING SCREAMS AT ME TO TURN AWAY.
AN ACCEPTABLE LOSS. FOR THE GREATER GOOD.
PLEASE--
I'M COMING.
BUT THERE'S ONLY SO MUCH OF MYSELF I CAN LOSE.
PLEASE-- I DON'T WANT TO DIE HERE--
GIVE ME YOUR HAND--
GIVE ME YOUR--
NO!

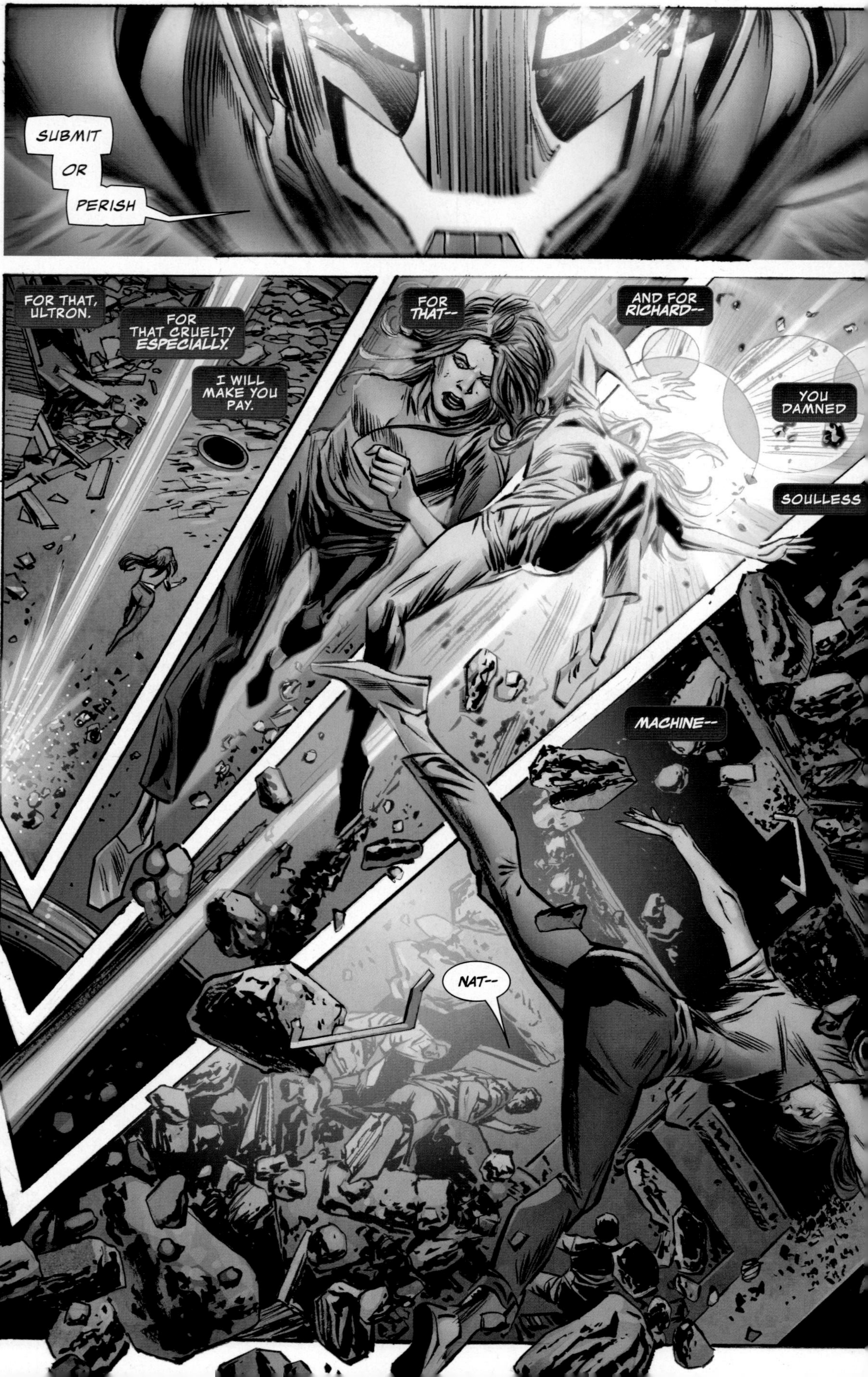
SUBMIT
OR
PERISH
FOR THAT, ULTRON.
FOR THAT CRUELTY ESPECIALLY.
I WILL MAKE YOU PAY.
FOR THAT--
AND FOR RICHARD--
YOU DAMNED
SOULLESS
MACHINE--
NAT--

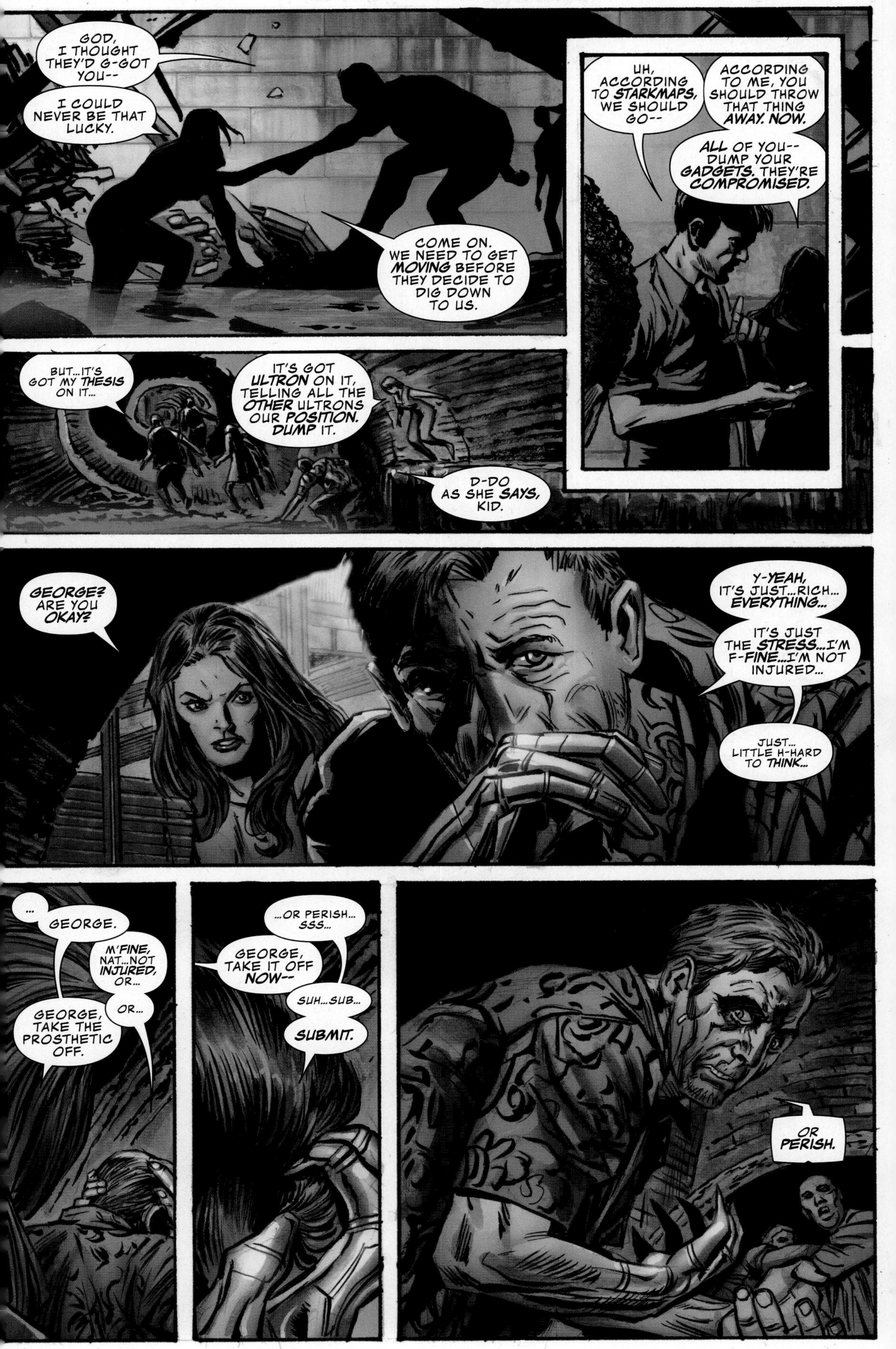

GOD, I THOUGHT THEY'D G-GOT YOU--
I COULD NEVER BE THAT LUCKY.
COME ON. WE NEED TO GET MOVING BEFORE THEY DECIDE TO DIG DOWN TO US.
UH, ACCORDING TO STARKMAPS, WE SHOULD GO--
ACCORDING TO ME, YOU SHOULD THROW THAT THING AWAY. NOW.
ALL OF YOU-- DUMP YOUR GADGETS. THEY'RE COMPROMISED.
BUT...IT'S GOT MY THESIS ON IT...
IT'S GOT ULTRON ON IT, TELLING ALL THE OTHER ULTRONS OUR POSITION. DUMP IT.
D-DO AS SHE SAYS, KID.
GEORGE? ARE YOU OKAY?
Y-YEAH, IT'S JUST...RICH... EVERYTHING...
IT'S JUST THE STRESS...I'M F-FINE...I'M NOT INJURED...
JUST... LITTLE H-HARD TO THINK...
...
GEORGE.
M'FINE, NAT...NOT INJURED, OR...
OR...
GEORGE, TAKE THE PROSTHETIC OFF.
...OR PERISH... SSS...
GEORGE, TAKE IT OFF NOW--
SUH...SUB...
SUBMIT.
OR PERISH.

I TRY TO BLOCK.

I TRY TO BLOCK GEORGE.

BUT GEORGE ISN'T HOME.

OH NO, OH GOD--

W-WE GOTTA GET OUT OF HERE--

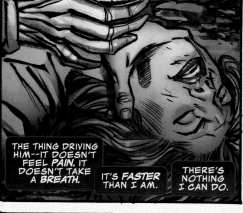

THE THING DRIVING HIM--IT DOESN'T FEEL PAIN. IT DOESN'T TAKE A BREATH.

IT'S FASTER THAN I AM.

THERE'S NOTHING I CAN DO.

SUH!

SUB!

MIT!

THERE'S NOTHING I CAN DO THAT WON'T KILL HIM.

OR PUUUCCCHHH--!

IT SCRABBLES AT ITS THROAT, TRYING TO PERFORM REPAIRS.

SUH

SUH

I TELL MYSELF IT ISN'T MY FRIEND ANYMORE.

SORRY

...

HOW MANY MORE?

HOW MANY MORE?

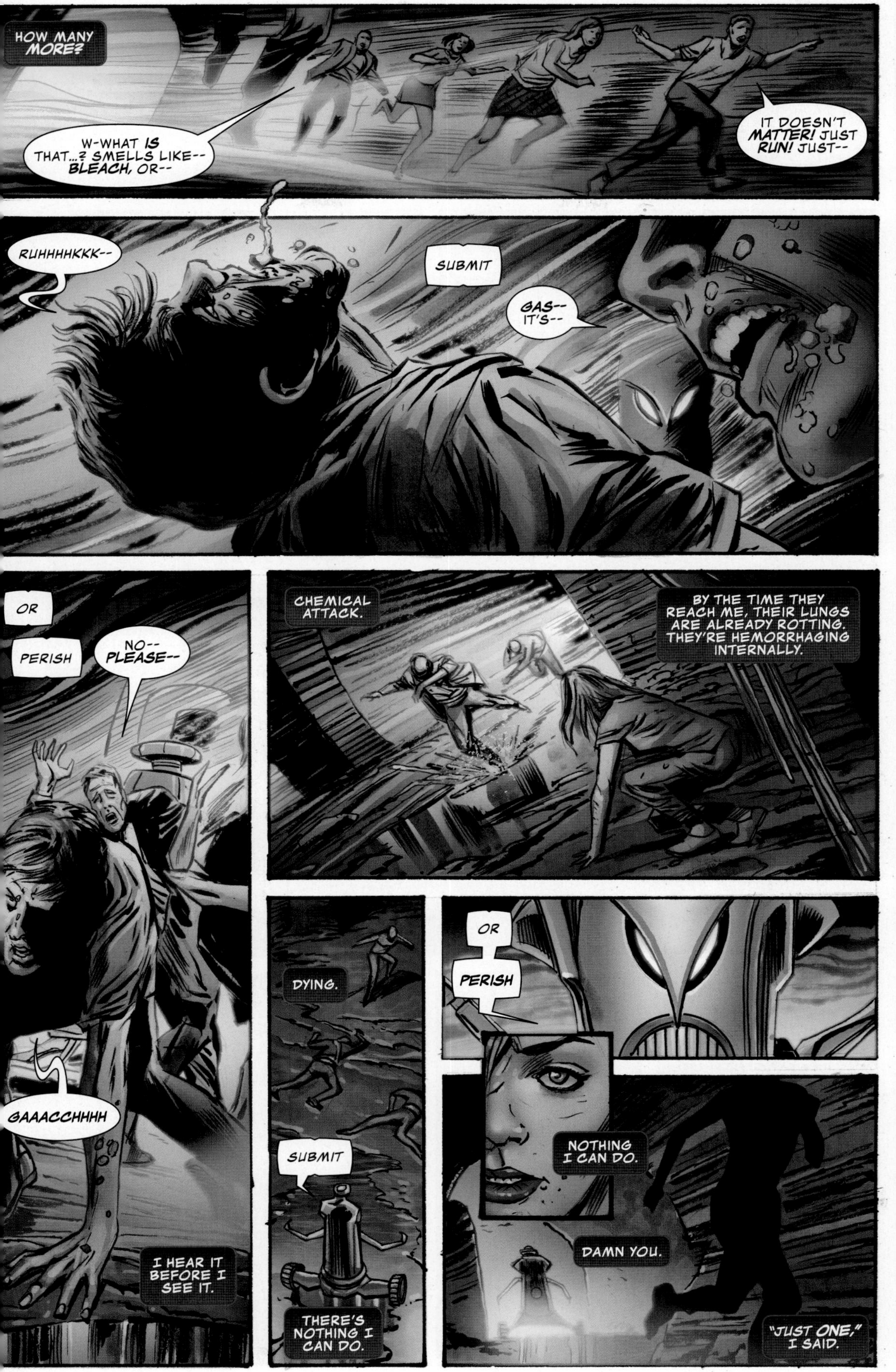
HOW MANY MORE?
W-WHAT IS THAT...? SMELLS LIKE-- BLEACH, OR--
IT DOESN'T MATTER! JUST RUN! JUST--
RUHHHHKKK--
SUBMIT
GAS-- IT'S--
OR
PERISH
NO-- PLEASE--
GAAACCHHHH
I HEAR IT BEFORE I SEE IT.
CHEMICAL ATTACK.
BY THE TIME THEY REACH ME, THEIR LUNGS ARE ALREADY ROTTING. THEY'RE HEMORRHAGING INTERNALLY.
DYING.
SUBMIT
THERE'S NOTHING I CAN DO.
OR
PERISH
NOTHING I CAN DO.
DAMN YOU.
"JUST ONE," I SAID.

I DIDN'T MEAN *ME*.

I MANAGE TO LOSE THE ONE IN THE SEWERS.

STILL, IT'S NIGHT BEFORE I FEEL SAFE ENOUGH TO SURFACE.

BY THEN, HUMANITY IS NO LONGER THE DOMINANT SPECIES.

IT TAKES TWO MORE HOURS TO TRAVEL EIGHT BLOCKS. MOSTLY HIDING FROM THE PATROLS.

IT DOESN'T MATTER. HERE AT THE END OF THE WORLD, THERE'S NOTHING BUT TIME.

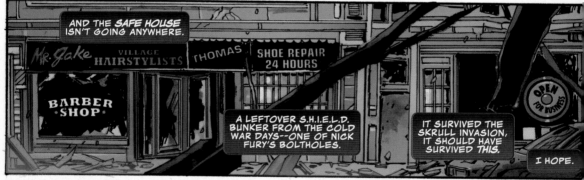

AND THE *SAFE HOUSE* ISN'T GOING ANYWHERE.

Mr. Jake BARBER SHOP

VILLAGE HAIRSTYLISTS

THOMAS SHOE REPAIR 24 HOURS

OPEN FOR BUSINESS

A LEFTOVER S.H.I.E.L.D. BUNKER FROM THE COLD WAR DAYS--ONE OF NICK FURY'S BOLTHOLES.

IT SURVIVED THE SKRULL INVASION, IT SHOULD HAVE SURVIVED *THIS*.

I HOPE.

FOR A MOMENT I THINK I SEE MOVEMENT IN THE WINDOW, SO I SPEND ANOTHER HOUR WATCHING TO MAKE SURE.

EVENTUALLY, I TELL MYSELF I'M BEING STUPID.

IF THERE IS AN ULTRON IN THERE, IT'LL BE A *RELIEF*.

IT'S NOT ULTRON.

WIDOW--?

OH... OH THANK *GOD*...

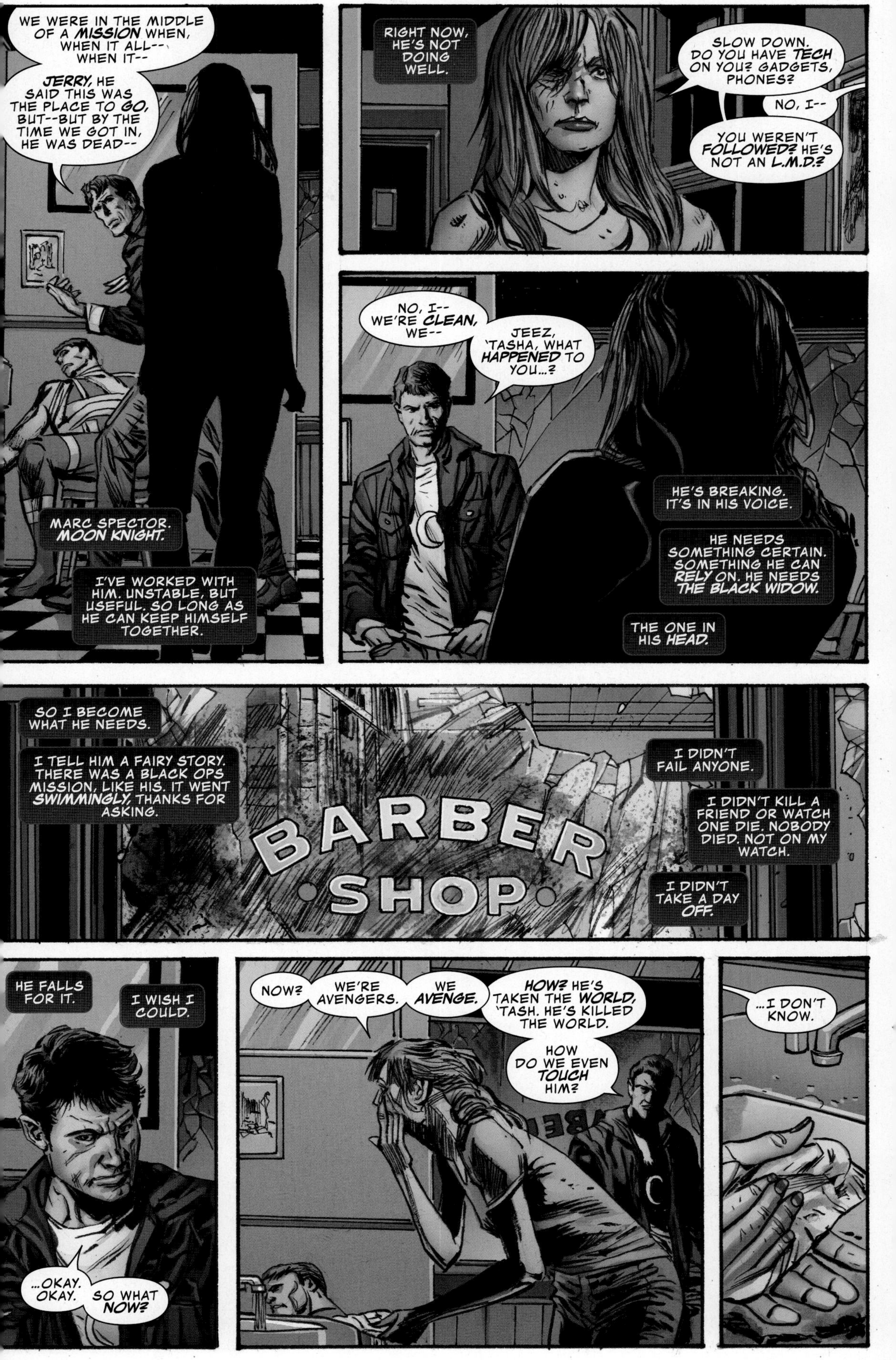
WE WERE IN THE MIDDLE OF A MISSION WHEN, WHEN IT ALL-- WHEN IT--
JERRY, HE SAID THIS WAS THE PLACE TO GO, BUT--BUT BY THE TIME WE GOT IN, HE WAS DEAD--
MARC SPECTOR. MOON KNIGHT.
I'VE WORKED WITH HIM. UNSTABLE, BUT USEFUL. SO LONG AS HE CAN KEEP HIMSELF TOGETHER.
RIGHT NOW, HE'S NOT DOING WELL.
SLOW DOWN. DO YOU HAVE TECH ON YOU? GADGETS, PHONES?
NO, I--
YOU WEREN'T FOLLOWED? HE'S NOT AN L.M.D.?
NO, I-- WE'RE CLEAN, WE--
JEEZ, 'TASHA, WHAT HAPPENED TO YOU...?
HE'S BREAKING. IT'S IN HIS VOICE.
HE NEEDS SOMETHING CERTAIN. SOMETHING HE CAN RELY ON. HE NEEDS THE BLACK WIDOW.
THE ONE IN HIS HEAD.
SO I BECOME WHAT HE NEEDS.
I TELL HIM A FAIRY STORY. THERE WAS A BLACK OPS MISSION, LIKE HIS. IT WENT SWIMMINGLY, THANKS FOR ASKING.
BARBER SHOP
I DIDN'T FAIL ANYONE.
I DIDN'T KILL A FRIEND OR WATCH ONE DIE. NOBODY DIED. NOT ON MY WATCH.
I DIDN'T TAKE A DAY OFF.
HE FALLS FOR IT.
I WISH I COULD.
...OKAY. OKAY.
SO WHAT NOW?
NOW?
WE'RE AVENGERS.
WE AVENGE.
HOW? HE'S TAKEN THE WORLD, 'TASH. HE'S KILLED THE WORLD.
HOW DO WE EVEN TOUCH HIM?
...I DON'T KNOW.

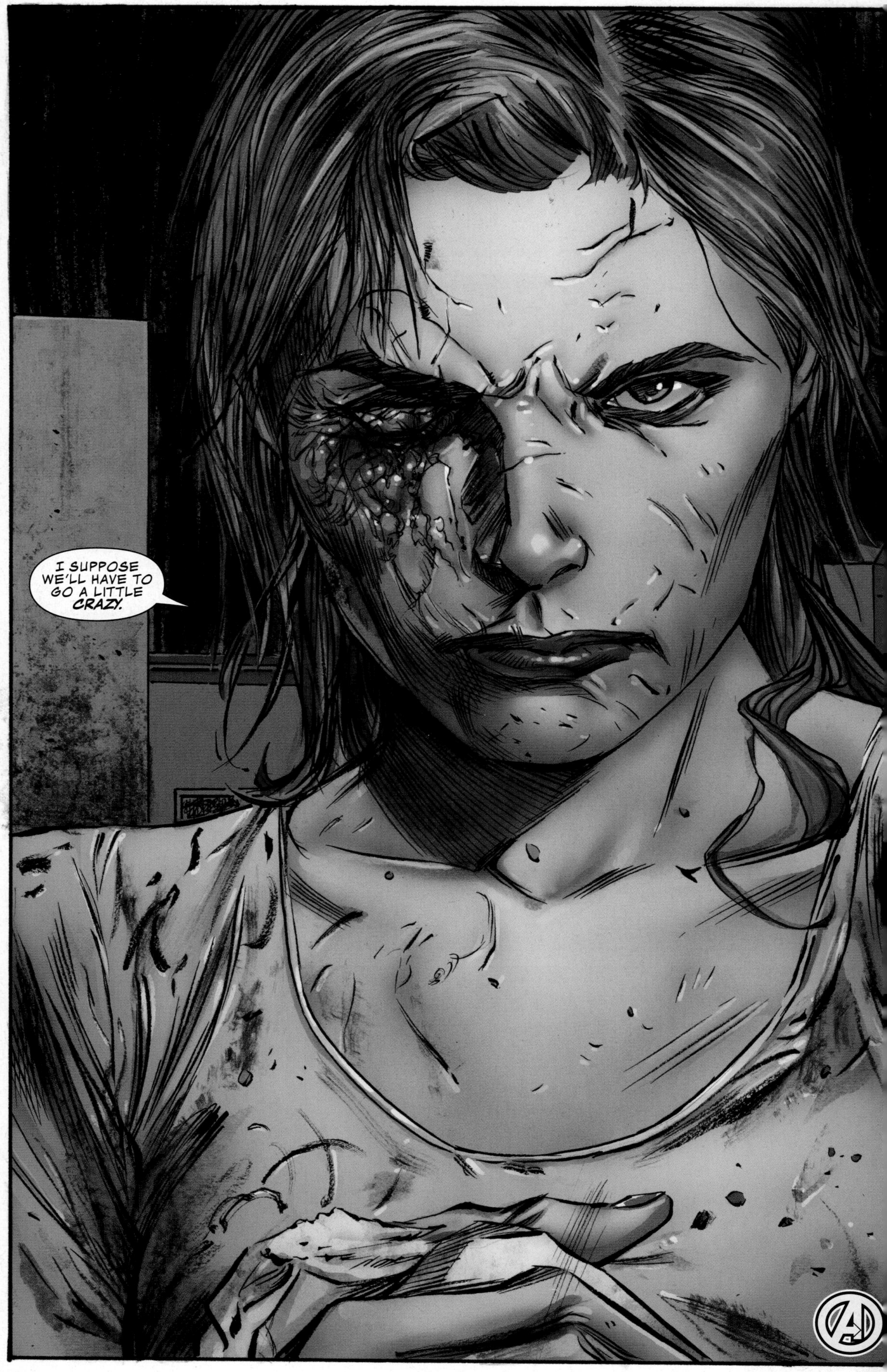
I SUPPOSE WE'LL HAVE TO GO A LITTLE *CRAZY.*

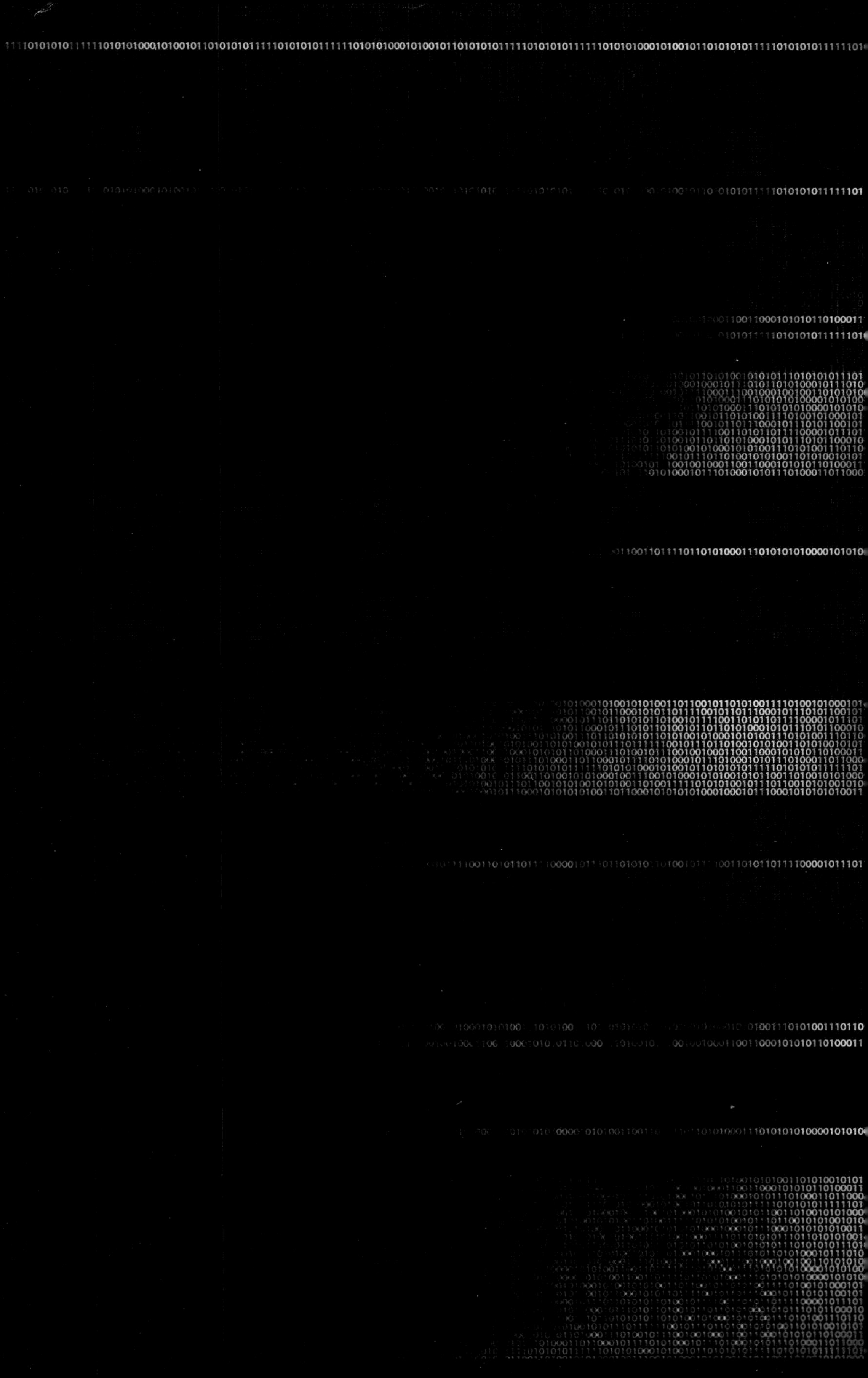

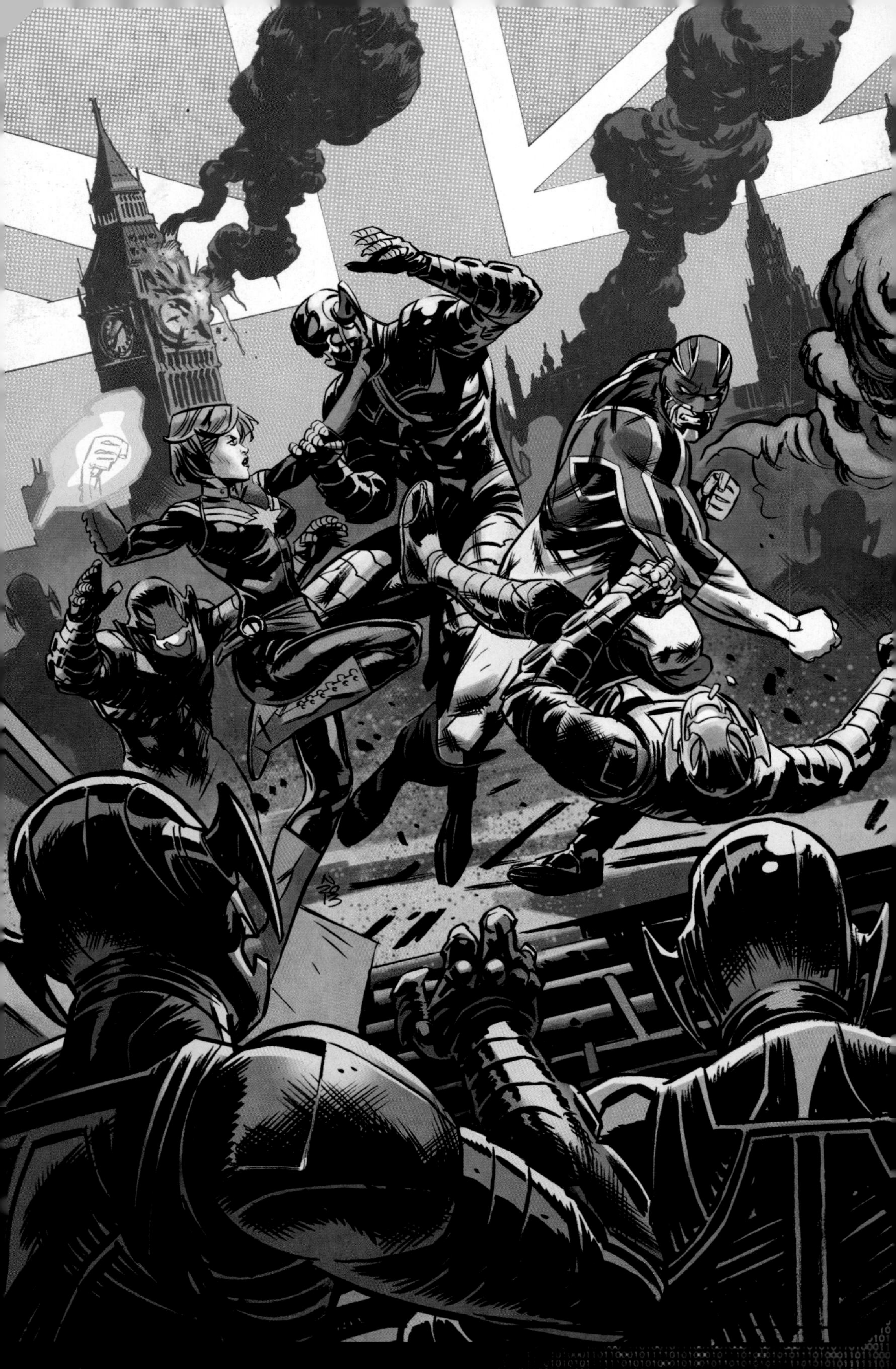

VENGERS ASSEMBLE #15AU

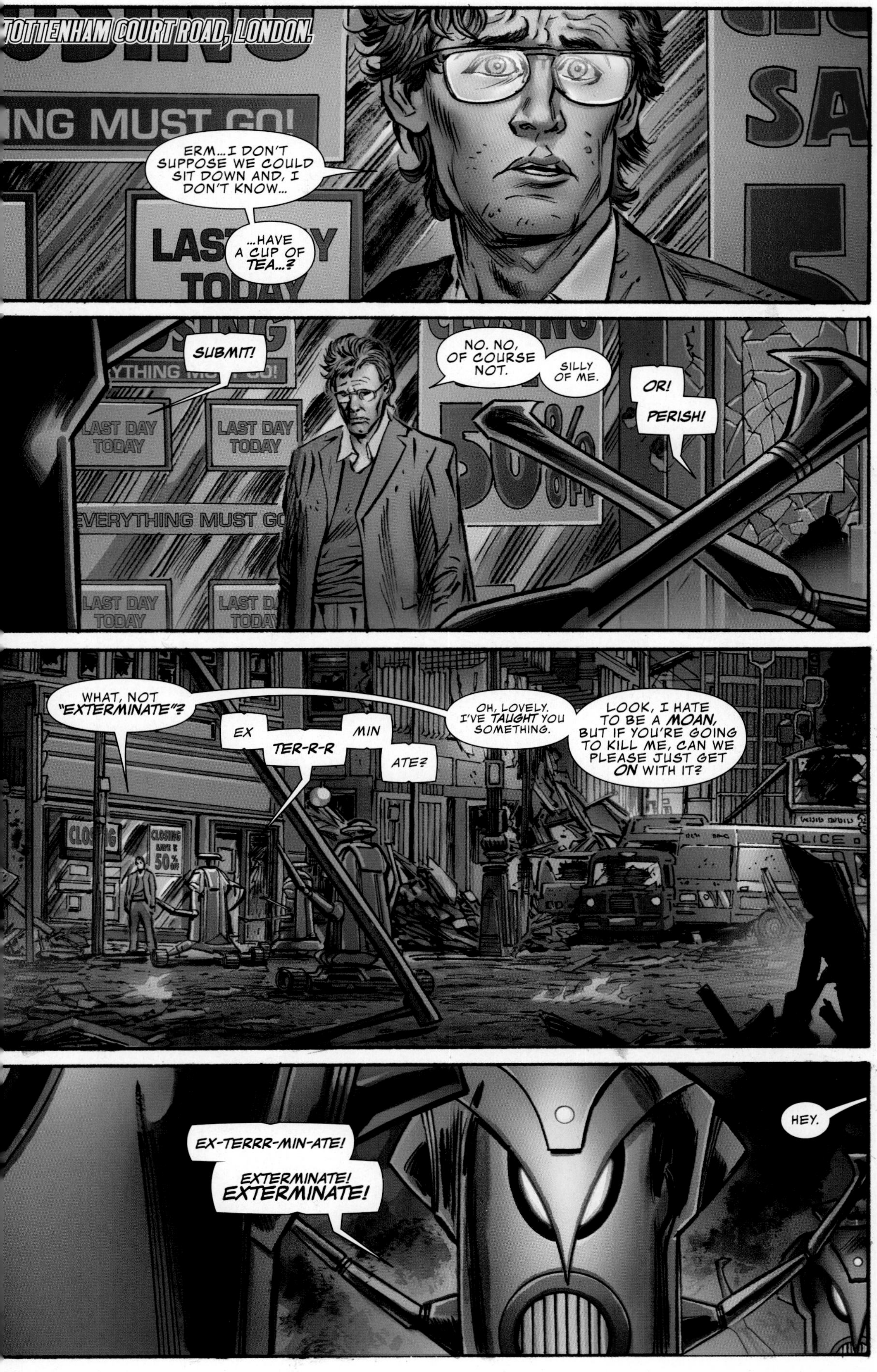
TOTTENHAM COURT ROAD, LONDON.
ERM...I DON'T SUPPOSE WE COULD SIT DOWN AND, I DON'T KNOW...
...HAVE A CUP OF TEA...?
SUBMIT!
NO. NO, OF COURSE NOT.
SILLY OF ME.
OR!
PERISH!
WHAT, NOT "EXTERMINATE"?
EX
TER-R-R
MIN
ATE?
OH, LOVELY. I'VE TAUGHT YOU SOMETHING.
LOOK, I HATE TO BE A MOAN, BUT IF YOU'RE GOING TO KILL ME, CAN WE PLEASE JUST GET ON WITH IT?
EX-TERRR-MIN-ATE!
EXTERMINATE! EXTERMINATE!
HEY.

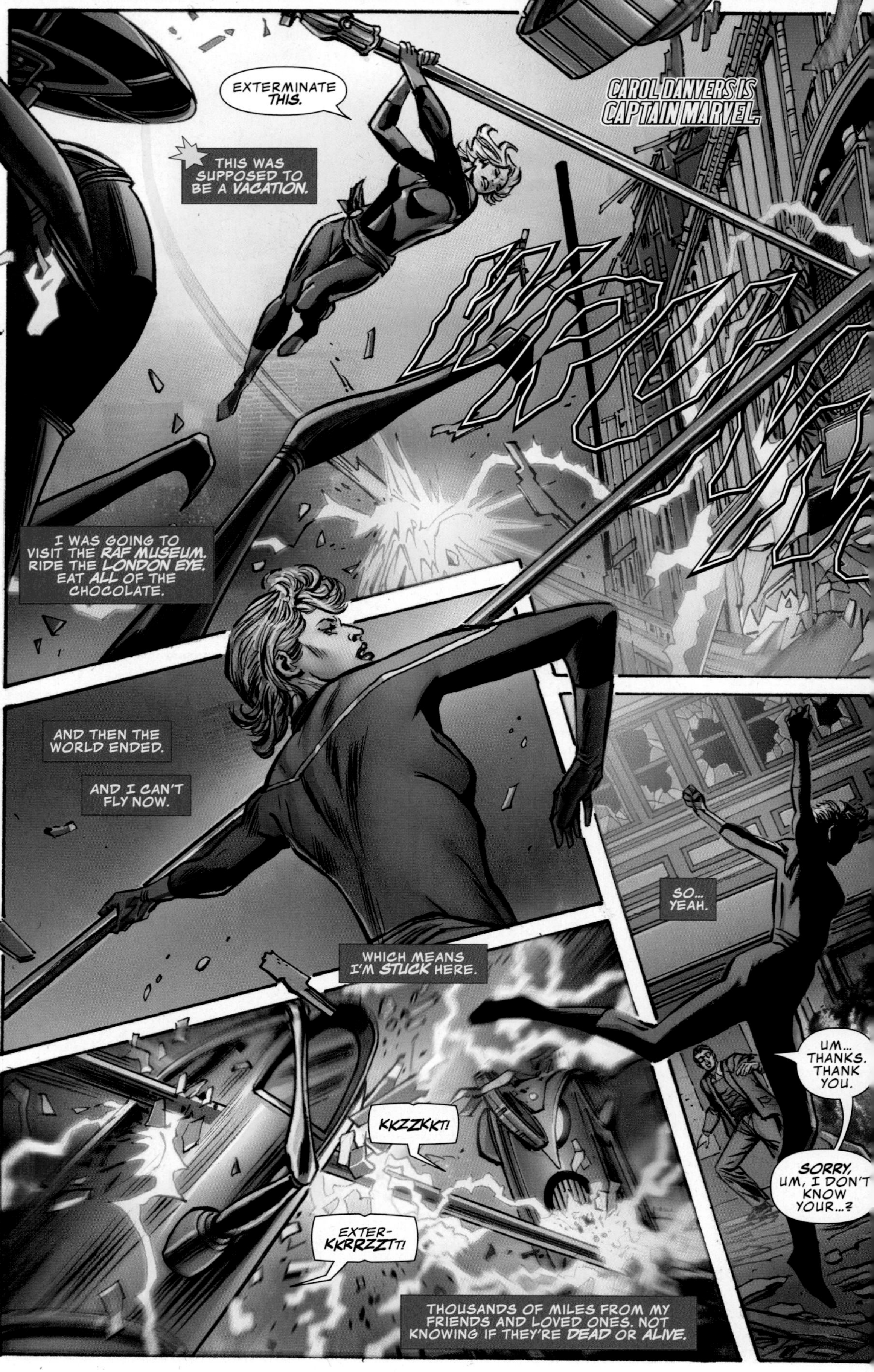
EXTERMINATE THIS.
CAROL DANVERS IS CAPTAIN MARVEL.
THIS WAS SUPPOSED TO BE A VACATION.
I WAS GOING TO VISIT THE RAF MUSEUM. RIDE THE LONDON EYE. EAT ALL OF THE CHOCOLATE.
AND THEN THE WORLD ENDED.
AND I CAN'T FLY NOW.
SO... YEAH.
WHICH MEANS I'M STUCK HERE.
KKZZKKT!
EXTER-KKRRZZTT!
THOUSANDS OF MILES FROM MY FRIENDS AND LOVED ONES. NOT KNOWING IF THEY'RE DEAD OR ALIVE.
UM... THANKS. THANK YOU.
SORRY, UM, I DON'T KNOW YOUR...?

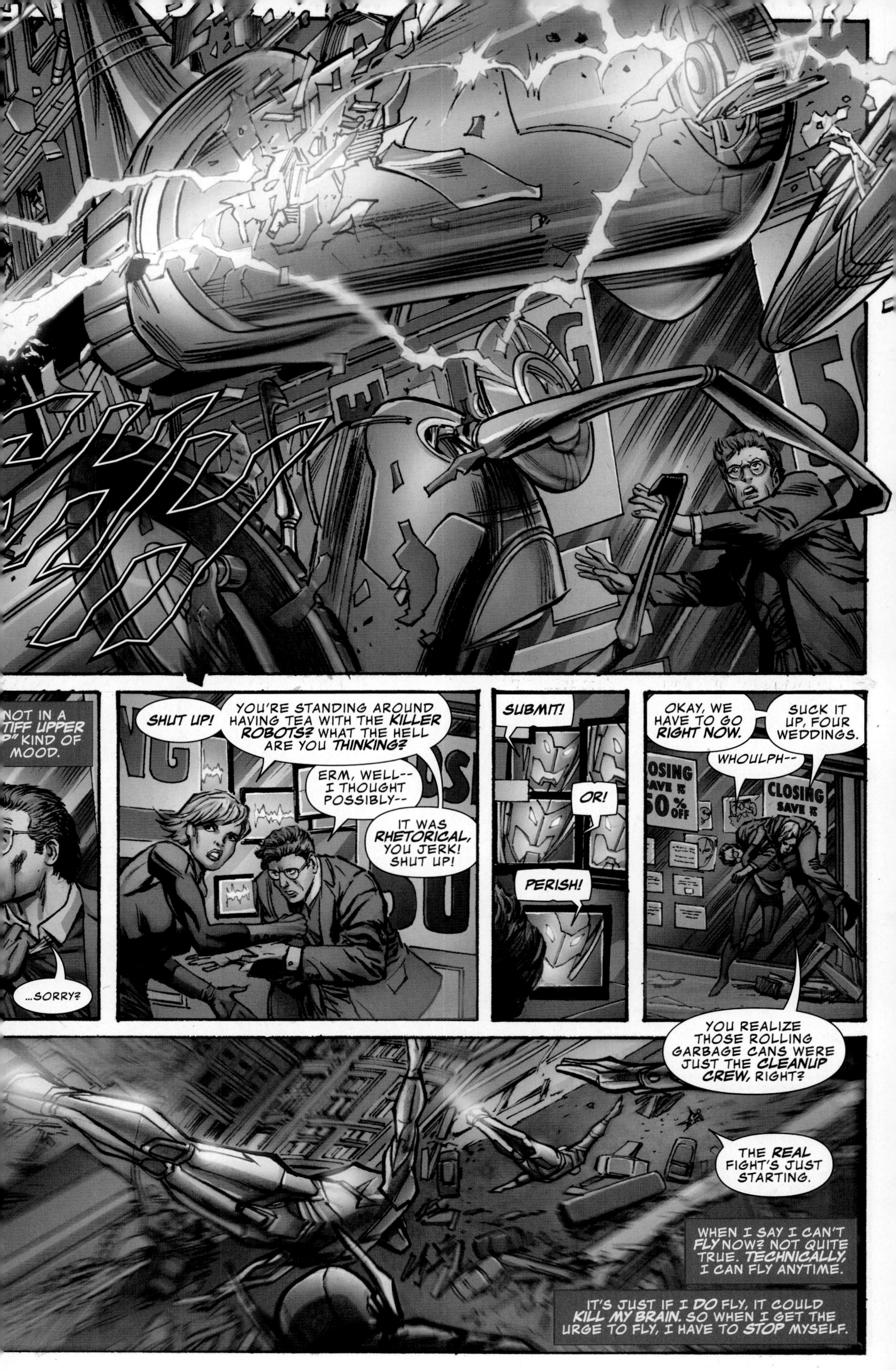
NOT IN A TIFF UPPER P" KIND OF MOOD.
...SORRY?
SHUT UP!
YOU'RE STANDING AROUND HAVING TEA WITH THE KILLER ROBOTS? WHAT THE HELL ARE YOU THINKING?
ERM, WELL-- I THOUGHT POSSIBLY--
IT WAS RHETORICAL, YOU JERK! SHUT UP!
SUBMIT!
OR!
PERISH!
OKAY, WE HAVE TO GO RIGHT NOW.
SUCK IT UP, FOUR WEDDINGS.
WHOULPH--
CLOSING SAVE 50% OFF
CLOSING SAVE
YOU REALIZE THOSE ROLLING GARBAGE CANS WERE JUST THE CLEANUP CREW, RIGHT?
THE REAL FIGHT'S JUST STARTING.
WHEN I SAY I CAN'T FLY NOW? NOT QUITE TRUE. TECHNICALLY, I CAN FLY ANYTIME.
IT'S JUST IF I DO FLY, IT COULD KILL MY BRAIN. SO WHEN I GET THE URGE TO FLY, I HAVE TO STOP MYSELF.

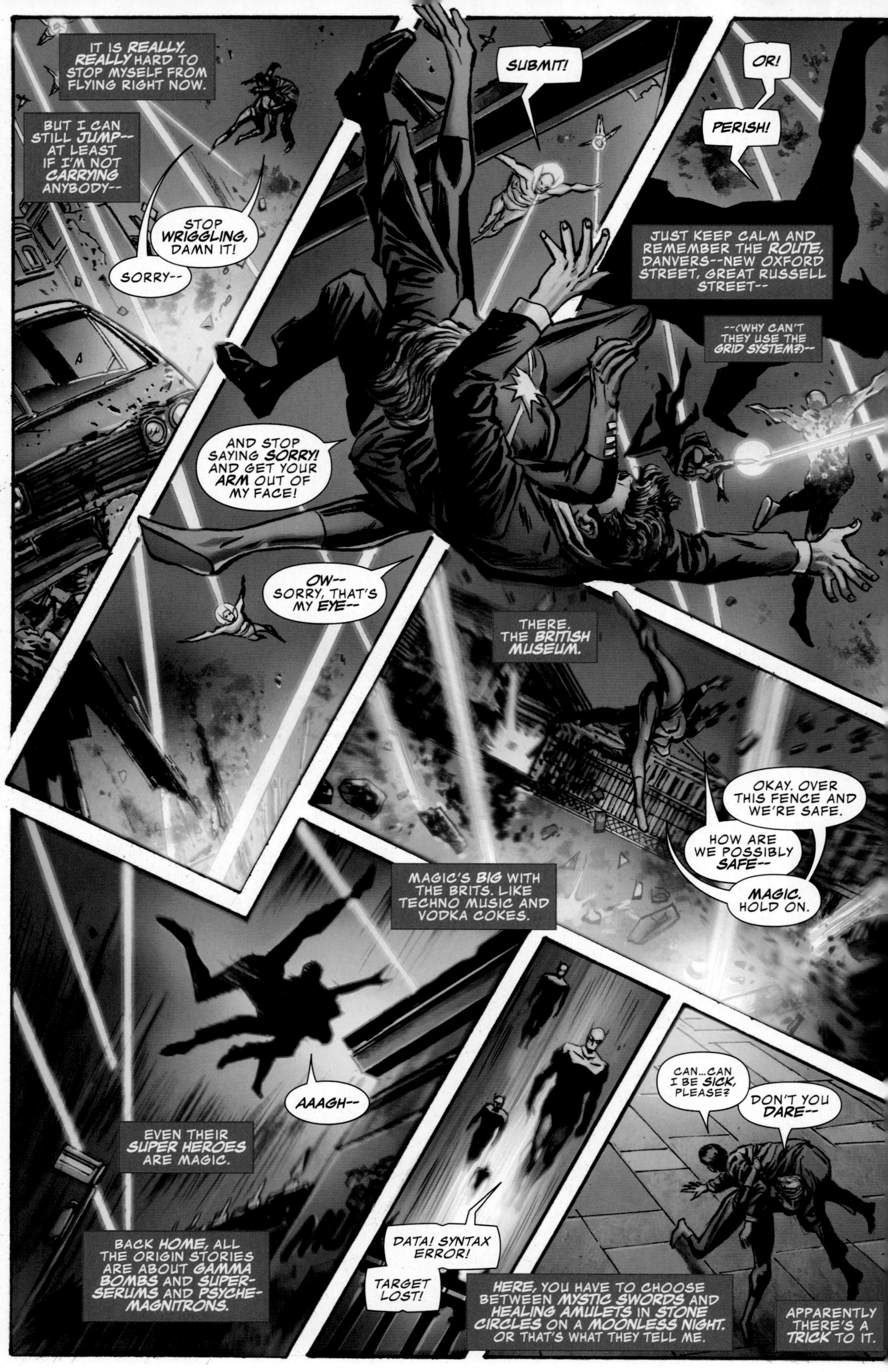
IT IS REALLY, REALLY HARD TO STOP MYSELF FROM FLYING RIGHT NOW.
BUT I CAN STILL JUMP-- AT LEAST IF I'M NOT CARRYING ANYBODY--
STOP WRIGGLING, DAMN IT!
SORRY--
SUBMIT!
OR!
PERISH!
JUST KEEP CALM AND REMEMBER THE ROUTE, DANVERS--NEW OXFORD STREET, GREAT RUSSELL STREET--
--(WHY CAN'T THEY USE THE GRID SYSTEM?)--
AND STOP SAYING SORRY! AND GET YOUR ARM OUT OF MY FACE!
OW-- SORRY, THAT'S MY EYE--
THERE. THE BRITISH MUSEUM.
OKAY. OVER THIS FENCE AND WE'RE SAFE.
HOW ARE WE POSSIBLY SAFE--
MAGIC. HOLD ON.
MAGIC'S BIG WITH THE BRITS. LIKE TECHNO MUSIC AND VODKA COKES.
AAAGH--
EVEN THEIR SUPER HEROES ARE MAGIC.
BACK HOME, ALL THE ORIGIN STORIES ARE ABOUT GAMMA BOMBS AND SUPER-SERUMS AND PSYCHE-MAGNITRONS.
DATA! SYNTAX ERROR!
TARGET LOST!
HERE, YOU HAVE TO CHOOSE BETWEEN MYSTIC SWORDS AND HEALING AMULETS IN STONE CIRCLES ON A MOONLESS NIGHT. OR THAT'S WHAT THEY TELL ME.
CAN...CAN I BE SICK, PLEASE?
DON'T YOU DARE--
APPARENTLY THERE'S A TRICK TO IT.

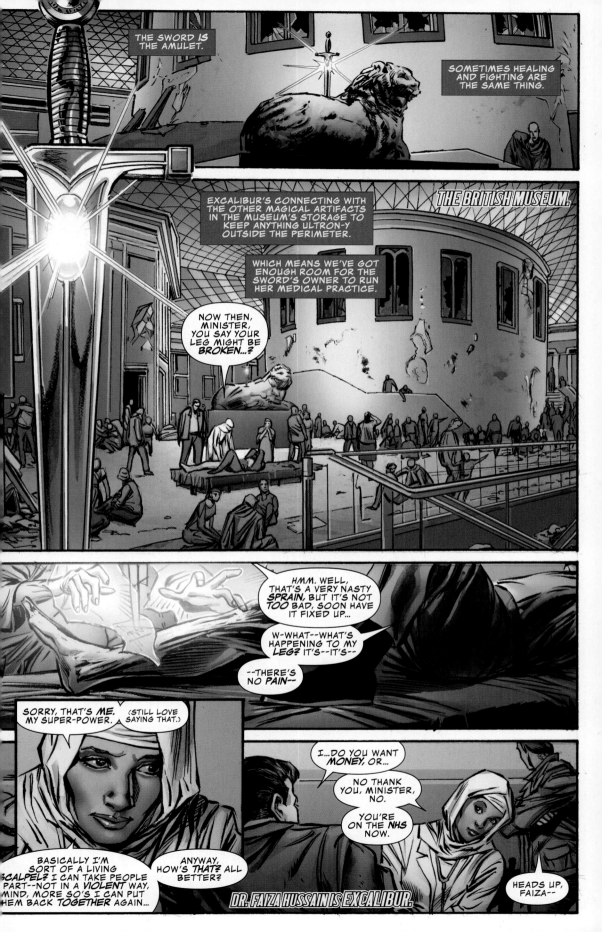

THE SWORD **IS** THE AMULET.

SOMETIMES HEALING AND FIGHTING ARE THE SAME THING.

EXCALIBUR'S CONNECTING WITH THE OTHER MAGICAL ARTIFACTS IN THE MUSEUM'S STORAGE TO KEEP ANYTHING ULTRON-Y OUTSIDE THE PERIMETER.

THE BRITISH MUSEUM.

WHICH MEANS WE'VE GOT ENOUGH ROOM FOR THE SWORD'S OWNER TO RUN HER MEDICAL PRACTICE.

NOW THEN, MINISTER, YOU SAY YOUR LEG MIGHT BE **BROKEN**...?

HMM. WELL, THAT'S A VERY NASTY **SPRAIN**, BUT IT'S NOT **TOO** BAD, SOON HAVE IT FIXED UP...

W-WHAT--WHAT'S HAPPENING TO MY **LEG**? IT'S--IT'S--

--THERE'S NO **PAIN**--

SORRY, THAT'S **ME.** MY SUPER-POWER. (STILL LOVE SAYING THAT.)

I...DO YOU WANT **MONEY**, OR...

NO THANK YOU, MINISTER, NO.

YOU'RE ON THE **NHS** NOW.

BASICALLY I'M SORT OF A LIVING **SCALPEL.** I CAN TAKE PEOPLE APART--NOT IN A **VIOLENT** WAY, MIND, MORE SO'S I CAN PUT THEM BACK **TOGETHER** AGAIN...

ANYWAY, HOW'S **THAT?** ALL BETTER?

HEADS UP, FAIZA--

DR. FAIZA HUSSAIN IS EXCALIBUR.

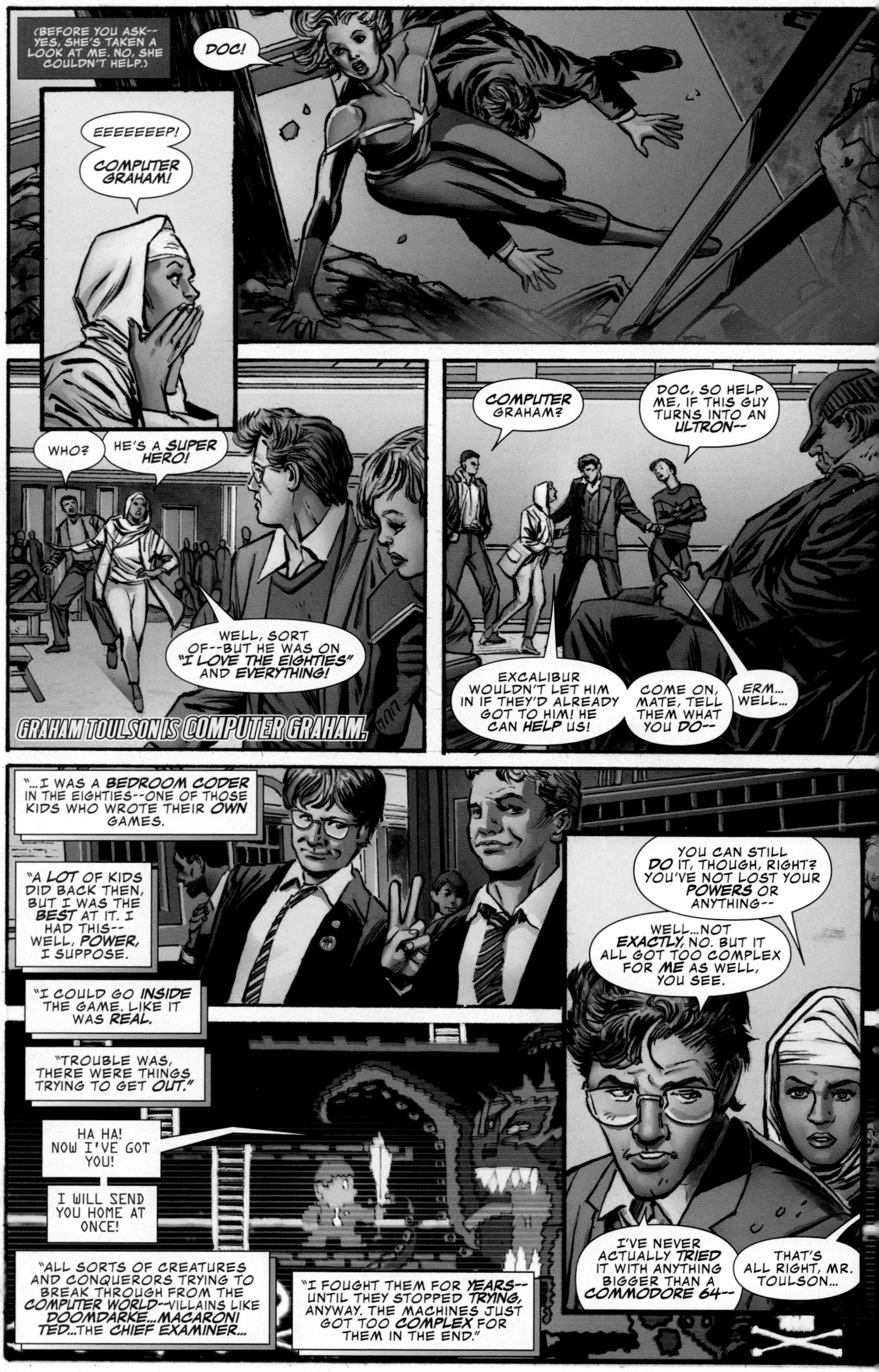
(BEFORE YOU ASK--YES, SHE'S TAKEN A LOOK AT ME. NO, SHE COULDN'T HELP.)
DOC!
EEEEEEEP!
COMPUTER GRAHAM!
WHO?
HE'S A SUPER HERO!
WELL, SORT OF--BUT HE WAS ON "I LOVE THE EIGHTIES" AND EVERYTHING!
GRAHAM TOULSON IS COMPUTER GRAHAM.
COMPUTER GRAHAM?
DOC, SO HELP ME, IF THIS GUY TURNS INTO AN ULTRON--
EXCALIBUR WOULDN'T LET HIM IN IF THEY'D ALREADY GOT TO HIM! HE CAN HELP US!
COME ON, MATE, TELL THEM WHAT YOU DO--
ERM... WELL...
"...I WAS A BEDROOM CODER IN THE EIGHTIES--ONE OF THOSE KIDS WHO WROTE THEIR OWN GAMES.
"A LOT OF KIDS DID BACK THEN, BUT I WAS THE BEST AT IT. I HAD THIS--WELL, POWER, I SUPPOSE.
"I COULD GO INSIDE THE GAME. LIKE IT WAS REAL.
"TROUBLE WAS, THERE WERE THINGS TRYING TO GET OUT."
HA HA! NOW I'VE GOT YOU!
I WILL SEND YOU HOME AT ONCE!
"ALL SORTS OF CREATURES AND CONQUERORS TRYING TO BREAK THROUGH FROM THE COMPUTER WORLD--VILLAINS LIKE DOOMDARKE...MACARONI TED...THE CHIEF EXAMINER...
"I FOUGHT THEM FOR YEARS--UNTIL THEY STOPPED TRYING, ANYWAY. THE MACHINES JUST GOT TOO COMPLEX FOR THEM IN THE END."
YOU CAN STILL DO IT, THOUGH, RIGHT? YOU'VE NOT LOST YOUR POWERS OR ANYTHING--
WELL...NOT EXACTLY, NO. BUT IT ALL GOT TOO COMPLEX FOR ME AS WELL, YOU SEE.
I'VE NEVER ACTUALLY TRIED IT WITH ANYTHING BIGGER THAN A COMMODORE 64--
THAT'S ALL RIGHT, MR. TOULSON...

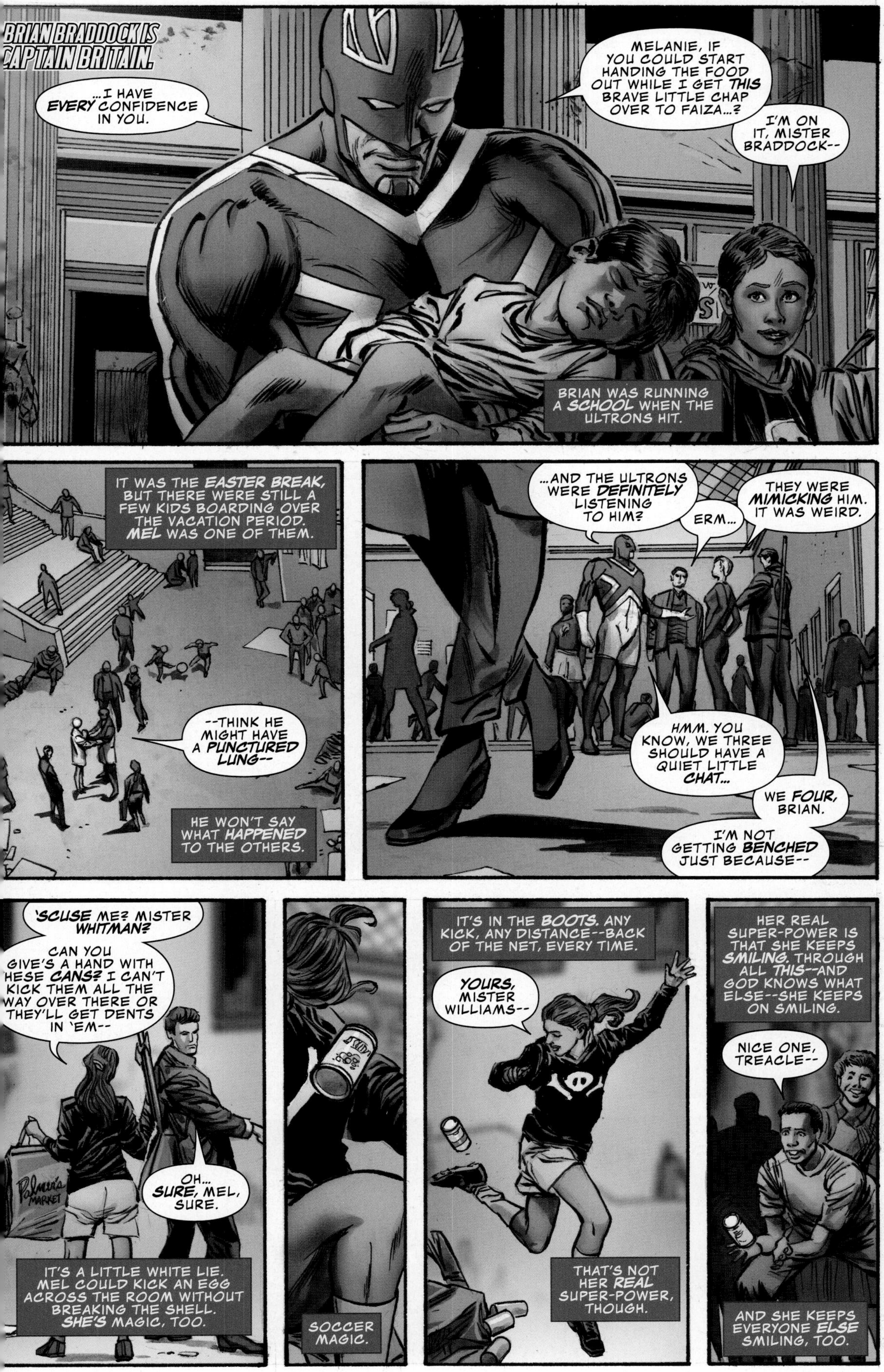
BRIAN BRADDOCK IS CAPTAIN BRITAIN.
...I HAVE EVERY CONFIDENCE IN YOU.
MELANIE, IF YOU COULD START HANDING THE FOOD OUT WHILE I GET THIS BRAVE LITTLE CHAP OVER TO FAIZA...?
I'M ON IT, MISTER BRADDOCK--
BRIAN WAS RUNNING A SCHOOL WHEN THE ULTRONS HIT.
IT WAS THE EASTER BREAK, BUT THERE WERE STILL A FEW KIDS BOARDING OVER THE VACATION PERIOD. MEL WAS ONE OF THEM.
--THINK HE MIGHT HAVE A PUNCTURED LUNG--
HE WON'T SAY WHAT HAPPENED TO THE OTHERS.
...AND THE ULTRONS WERE DEFINITELY LISTENING TO HIM?
ERM...
THEY WERE MIMICKING HIM. IT WAS WEIRD.
HMM. YOU KNOW, WE THREE SHOULD HAVE A QUIET LITTLE CHAT...
WE FOUR, BRIAN.
I'M NOT GETTING BENCHED JUST BECAUSE--
'SCUSE ME? MISTER WHITMAN?
CAN YOU GIVE'S A HAND WITH HESE CANS? I CAN'T KICK THEM ALL THE WAY OVER THERE OR THEY'LL GET DENTS IN 'EM--
OH... SURE, MEL, SURE.
IT'S A LITTLE WHITE LIE. MEL COULD KICK AN EGG ACROSS THE ROOM WITHOUT BREAKING THE SHELL. SHE'S MAGIC, TOO.
SOCCER MAGIC.
IT'S IN THE BOOTS. ANY KICK, ANY DISTANCE--BACK OF THE NET, EVERY TIME.
YOURS, MISTER WILLIAMS--
THAT'S NOT HER REAL SUPER-POWER, THOUGH.
HER REAL SUPER-POWER IS THAT SHE KEEPS SMILING. THROUGH ALL THIS--AND GOD KNOWS WHAT ELSE--SHE KEEPS ON SMILING.
NICE ONE, TREACLE--
AND SHE KEEPS EVERYONE ELSE SMILING, TOO.

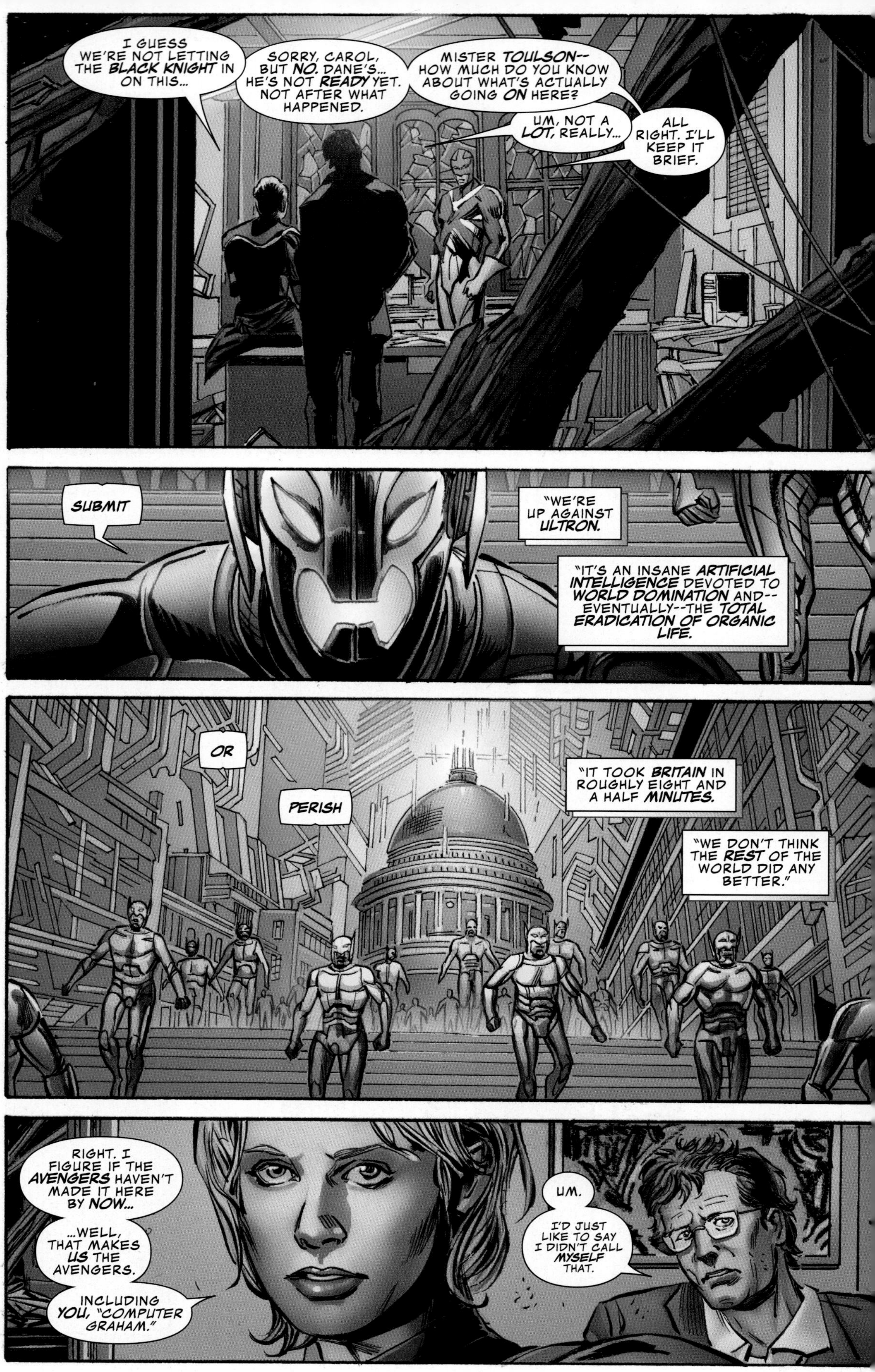
I GUESS WE'RE NOT LETTING THE BLACK KNIGHT IN ON THIS...
SORRY, CAROL, BUT NO. DANE'S... HE'S NOT READY YET. NOT AFTER WHAT HAPPENED.
MISTER TOULSON-- HOW MUCH DO YOU KNOW ABOUT WHAT'S ACTUALLY GOING ON HERE?
UM, NOT A LOT, REALLY...
ALL RIGHT. I'LL KEEP IT BRIEF.
SUBMIT
"WE'RE UP AGAINST ULTRON.
"IT'S AN INSANE ARTIFICIAL INTELLIGENCE DEVOTED TO WORLD DOMINATION AND--EVENTUALLY--THE TOTAL ERADICATION OF ORGANIC LIFE.
OR
PERISH
"IT TOOK BRITAIN IN ROUGHLY EIGHT AND A HALF MINUTES.
"WE DON'T THINK THE REST OF THE WORLD DID ANY BETTER."
RIGHT. I FIGURE IF THE AVENGERS HAVEN'T MADE IT HERE BY NOW...
...WELL, THAT MAKES US THE AVENGERS.
INCLUDING YOU, "COMPUTER GRAHAM."
UM.
I'D JUST LIKE TO SAY I DIDN'T CALL MYSELF THAT.

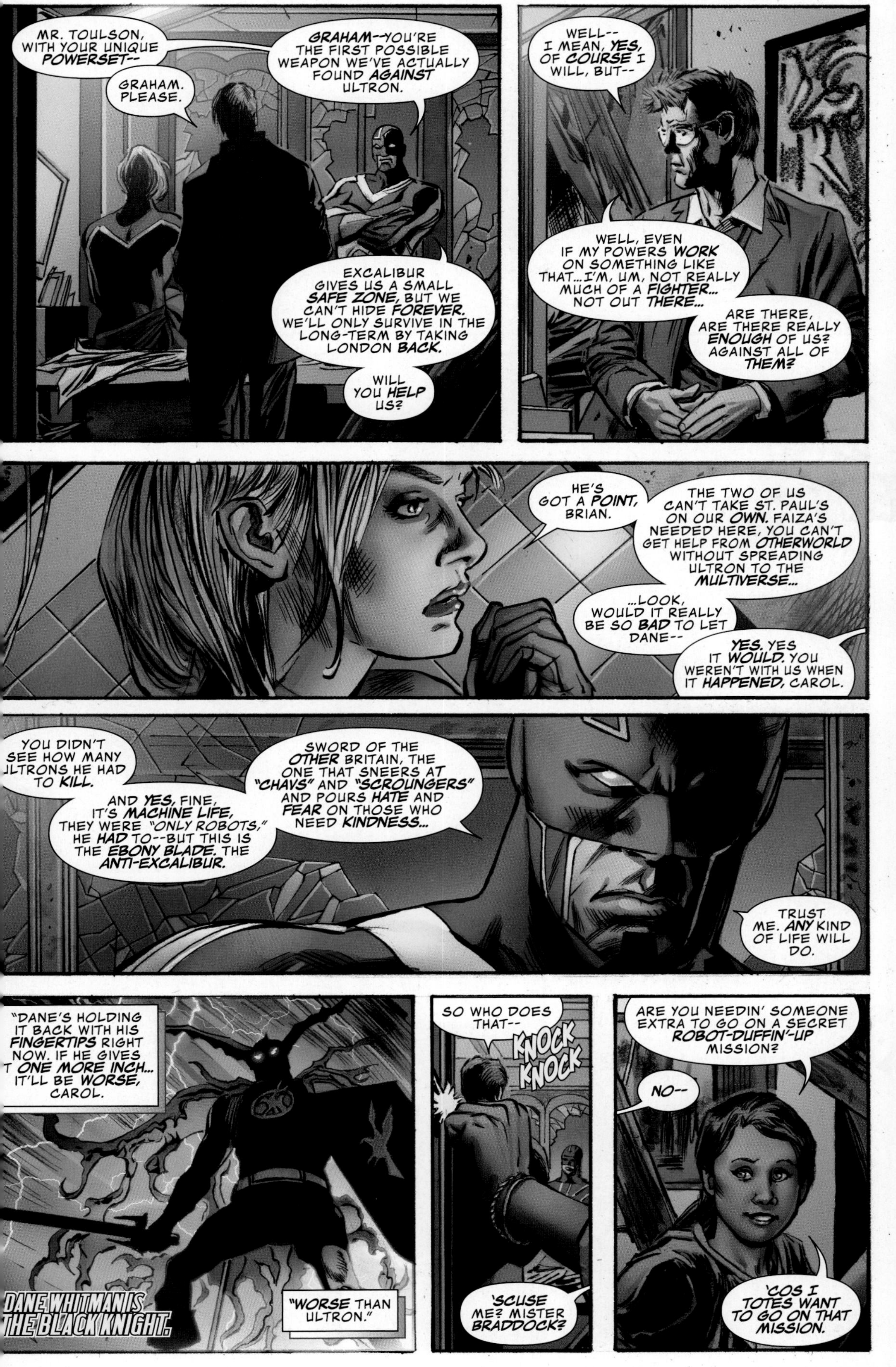

MR. TOULSON, WITH YOUR UNIQUE POWERSET--
GRAHAM. PLEASE.
GRAHAM--YOU'RE THE FIRST POSSIBLE WEAPON WE'VE ACTUALLY FOUND AGAINST ULTRON.
EXCALIBUR GIVES US A SMALL SAFE ZONE, BUT WE CAN'T HIDE FOREVER. WE'LL ONLY SURVIVE IN THE LONG-TERM BY TAKING LONDON BACK.
WILL YOU HELP US?
WELL-- I MEAN, YES, OF COURSE I WILL, BUT--
WELL, EVEN IF MY POWERS WORK ON SOMETHING LIKE THAT... I'M, UM, NOT REALLY MUCH OF A FIGHTER... NOT OUT THERE...
ARE THERE, ARE THERE REALLY ENOUGH OF US? AGAINST ALL OF THEM?
HE'S GOT A POINT, BRIAN.
THE TWO OF US CAN'T TAKE ST. PAUL'S ON OUR OWN. FAIZA'S NEEDED HERE, YOU CAN'T GET HELP FROM OTHERWORLD WITHOUT SPREADING ULTRON TO THE MULTIVERSE...
...LOOK, WOULD IT REALLY BE SO BAD TO LET DANE--
YES. YES IT WOULD. YOU WEREN'T WITH US WHEN IT HAPPENED, CAROL.
YOU DIDN'T SEE HOW MANY ULTRONS HE HAD TO KILL.
AND YES, FINE, IT'S MACHINE LIFE, THEY WERE "ONLY ROBOTS," HE HAD TO--BUT THIS IS THE EBONY BLADE. THE ANTI-EXCALIBUR.
SWORD OF THE OTHER BRITAIN, THE ONE THAT SNEERS AT "CHAVS" AND "SCROUNGERS" AND POURS HATE AND FEAR ON THOSE WHO NEED KINDNESS...
TRUST ME. ANY KIND OF LIFE WILL DO.
"DANE'S HOLDING IT BACK WITH HIS FINGERTIPS RIGHT NOW. IF HE GIVES IT ONE MORE INCH... IT'LL BE WORSE, CAROL.
"WORSE THAN ULTRON."
DANE WHITMAN IS THE BLACK KNIGHT.
SO WHO DOES THAT--
KNOCK KNOCK
'SCUSE ME? MISTER BRADDOCK?
ARE YOU NEEDIN' SOMEONE EXTRA TO GO ON A SECRET ROBOT-DUFFIN'-UP MISSION?
NO--
'COS I TOTES WANT TO GO ON THAT MISSION.

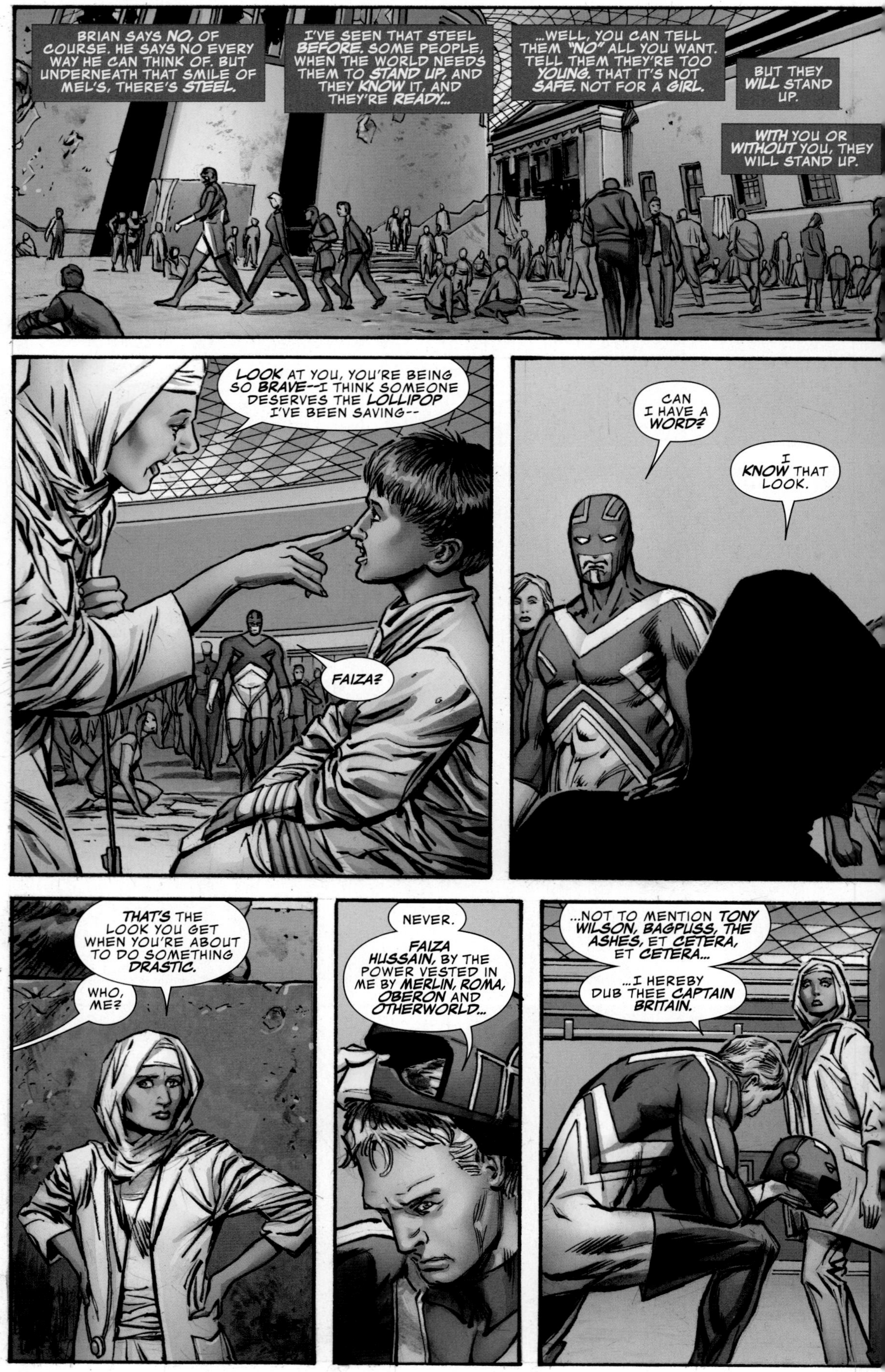

BRIAN SAYS NO, OF COURSE. HE SAYS NO EVERY WAY HE CAN THINK OF. BUT UNDERNEATH THAT SMILE OF MEL'S, THERE'S STEEL.
I'VE SEEN THAT STEEL BEFORE. SOME PEOPLE, WHEN THE WORLD NEEDS THEM TO STAND UP, AND THEY KNOW IT, AND THEY'RE READY...
...WELL, YOU CAN TELL THEM "NO" ALL YOU WANT. TELL THEM THEY'RE TOO YOUNG. THAT IT'S NOT SAFE. NOT FOR A GIRL.
BUT THEY WILL STAND UP.
WITH YOU OR WITHOUT YOU, THEY WILL STAND UP.
LOOK AT YOU, YOU'RE BEING SO BRAVE--I THINK SOMEONE DESERVES THE LOLLIPOP I'VE BEEN SAVING--
FAIZA?
CAN I HAVE A WORD?
I KNOW THAT LOOK.
THAT'S THE LOOK YOU GET WHEN YOU'RE ABOUT TO DO SOMETHING DRASTIC.
WHO, ME?
NEVER.
FAIZA HUSSAIN, BY THE POWER VESTED IN ME BY MERLIN, ROMA, OBERON AND OTHERWORLD...
...NOT TO MENTION TONY WILSON, BAGPUSS, THE ASHES, ET CETERA, ET CETERA...
...I HEREBY DUB THEE CAPTAIN BRITAIN.

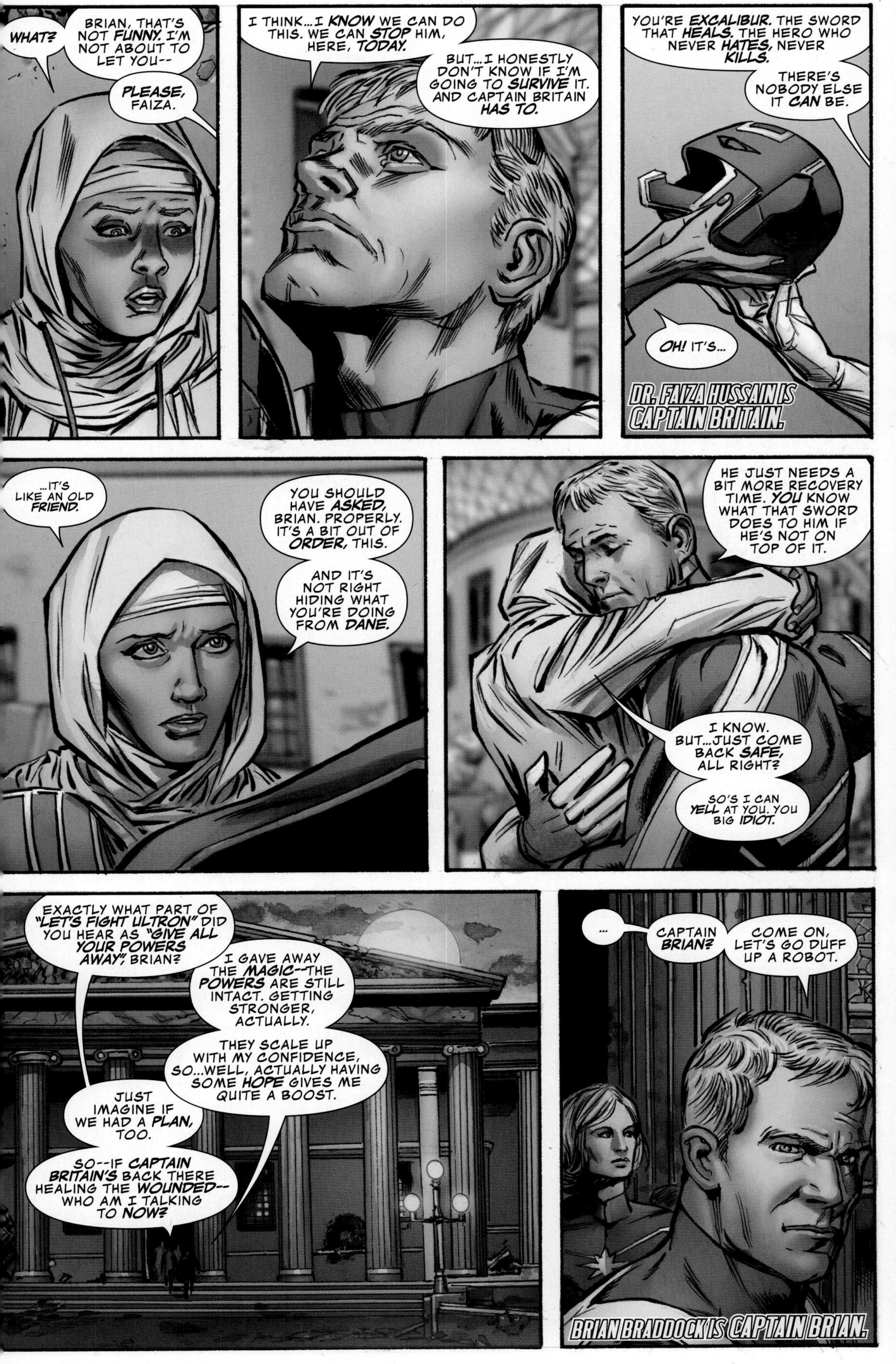

WHAT?
BRIAN, THAT'S NOT FUNNY. I'M NOT ABOUT TO LET YOU--
PLEASE, FAIZA.
I THINK...I KNOW WE CAN DO THIS. WE CAN STOP HIM, HERE, TODAY.
BUT...I HONESTLY DON'T KNOW IF I'M GOING TO SURVIVE IT. AND CAPTAIN BRITAIN HAS TO.
YOU'RE EXCALIBUR. THE SWORD THAT HEALS. THE HERO WHO NEVER HATES, NEVER KILLS.
THERE'S NOBODY ELSE IT CAN BE.
OH! IT'S...
DR. FAIZA HUSSAIN IS CAPTAIN BRITAIN.
...IT'S LIKE AN OLD FRIEND.
YOU SHOULD HAVE ASKED, BRIAN. PROPERLY. IT'S A BIT OUT OF ORDER, THIS.
AND IT'S NOT RIGHT HIDING WHAT YOU'RE DOING FROM DANE.
HE JUST NEEDS A BIT MORE RECOVERY TIME. YOU KNOW WHAT THAT SWORD DOES TO HIM IF HE'S NOT ON TOP OF IT.
I KNOW. BUT...JUST COME BACK SAFE, ALL RIGHT?
SO'S I CAN YELL AT YOU. YOU BIG IDIOT.
EXACTLY WHAT PART OF "LET'S FIGHT ULTRON" DID YOU HEAR AS "GIVE ALL YOUR POWERS AWAY", BRIAN?
I GAVE AWAY THE MAGIC--THE POWERS ARE STILL INTACT. GETTING STRONGER, ACTUALLY.
THEY SCALE UP WITH MY CONFIDENCE, SO...WELL, ACTUALLY HAVING SOME HOPE GIVES ME QUITE A BOOST.
JUST IMAGINE IF WE HAD A PLAN, TOO.
SO--IF CAPTAIN BRITAIN'S BACK THERE HEALING THE WOUNDED--WHO AM I TALKING TO NOW?
...
CAPTAIN BRIAN?
COME ON, LET'S GO DUFF UP A ROBOT.
BRIAN BRADDOCK IS CAPTAIN BRIAN.

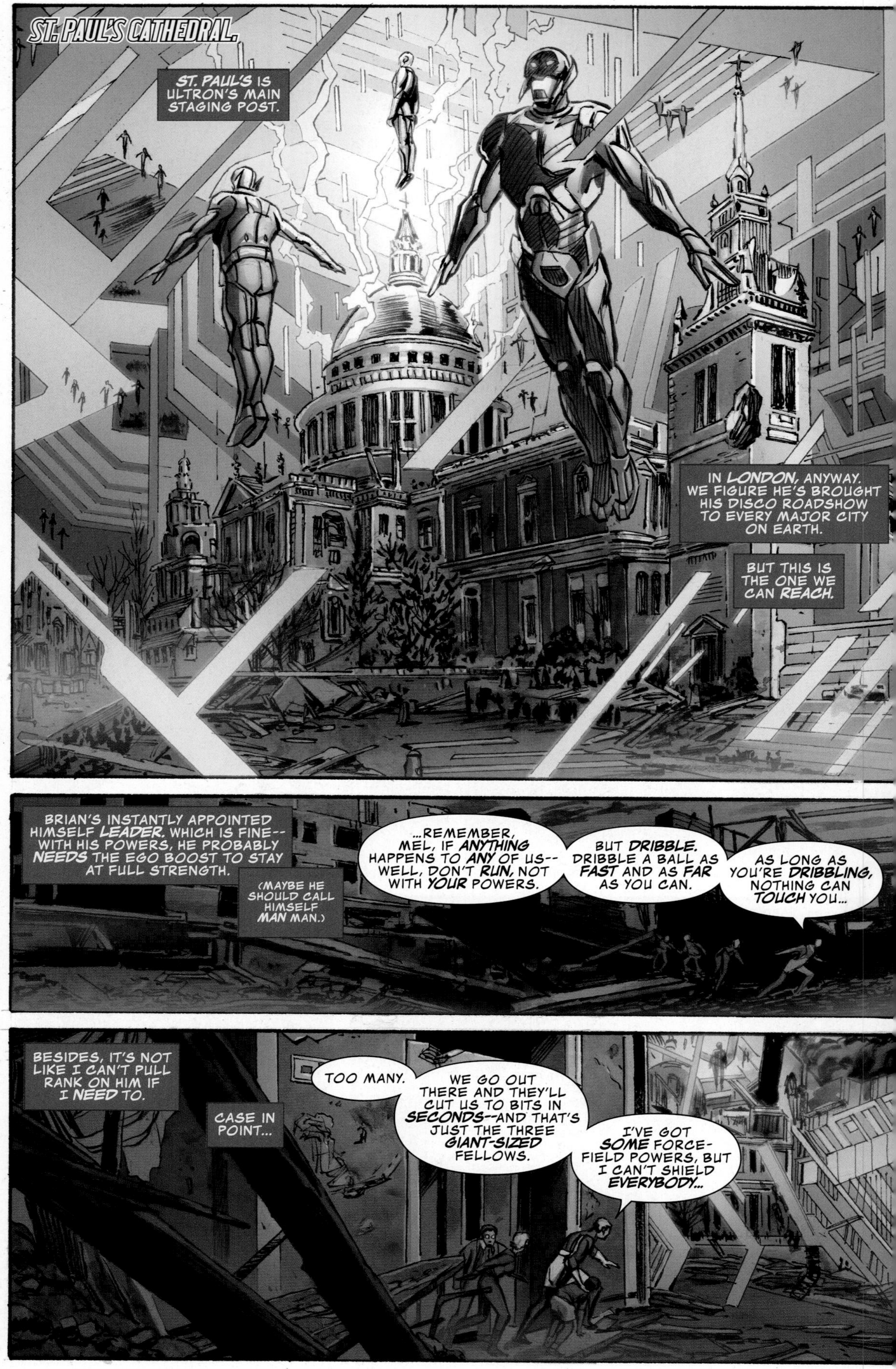

ST. PAUL'S CATHEDRAL.
ST. PAUL'S IS ULTRON'S MAIN STAGING POST.
IN LONDON, ANYWAY. WE FIGURE HE'S BROUGHT HIS DISCO ROADSHOW TO EVERY MAJOR CITY ON EARTH.
BUT THIS IS THE ONE WE CAN REACH.
BRIAN'S INSTANTLY APPOINTED HIMSELF LEADER. WHICH IS FINE--WITH HIS POWERS, HE PROBABLY NEEDS THE EGO BOOST TO STAY AT FULL STRENGTH.
(MAYBE HE SHOULD CALL HIMSELF MAN MAN.)
...REMEMBER, MEL, IF ANYTHING HAPPENS TO ANY OF US--WELL, DON'T RUN, NOT WITH YOUR POWERS.
BUT DRIBBLE. DRIBBLE A BALL AS FAST AND AS FAR AS YOU CAN.
AS LONG AS YOU'RE DRIBBLING, NOTHING CAN TOUCH YOU...
BESIDES, IT'S NOT LIKE I CAN'T PULL RANK ON HIM IF I NEED TO.
CASE IN POINT...
TOO MANY.
WE GO OUT THERE AND THEY'LL CUT US TO BITS IN SECONDS--AND THAT'S JUST THE THREE GIANT-SIZED FELLOWS.
I'VE GOT SOME FORCE-FIELD POWERS, BUT I CAN'T SHIELD EVERYBODY...

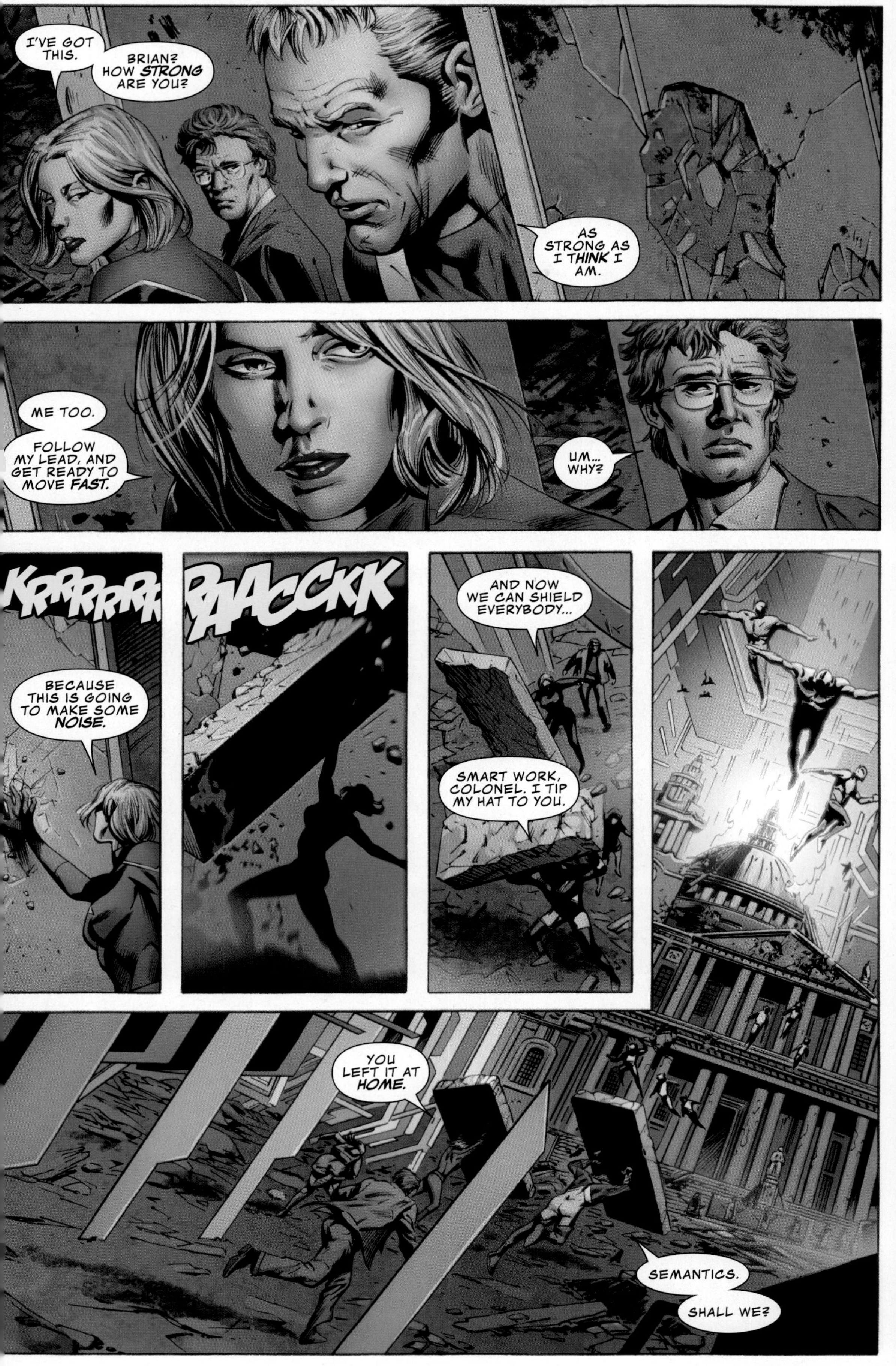

I'VE GOT THIS.
BRIAN? HOW STRONG ARE YOU?
AS STRONG AS I THINK I AM.
ME TOO.
FOLLOW MY LEAD, AND GET READY TO MOVE FAST.
UM... WHY?
KRRRRRK
BECAUSE THIS IS GOING TO MAKE SOME NOISE.
BAACCKK
AND NOW WE CAN SHIELD EVERYBODY...
SMART WORK, COLONEL. I TIP MY HAT TO YOU.
YOU LEFT IT AT HOME.
SEMANTICS.
SHALL WE?

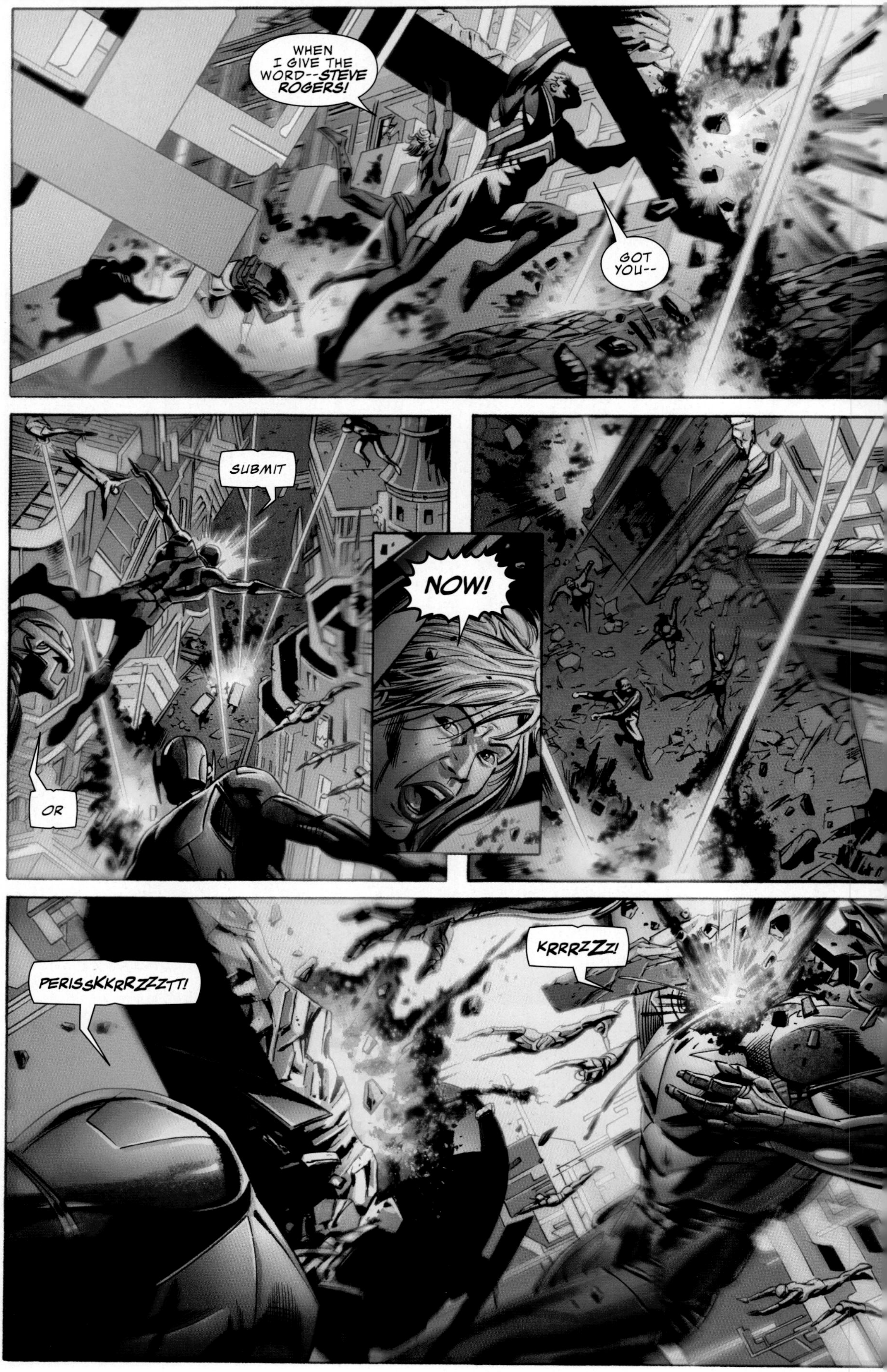
WHEN I GIVE THE WORD--STEVE ROGERS!
GOT YOU--
SUBMIT
OR
NOW!
PERISSKKRRZZZTT!
KRRRZZZ!

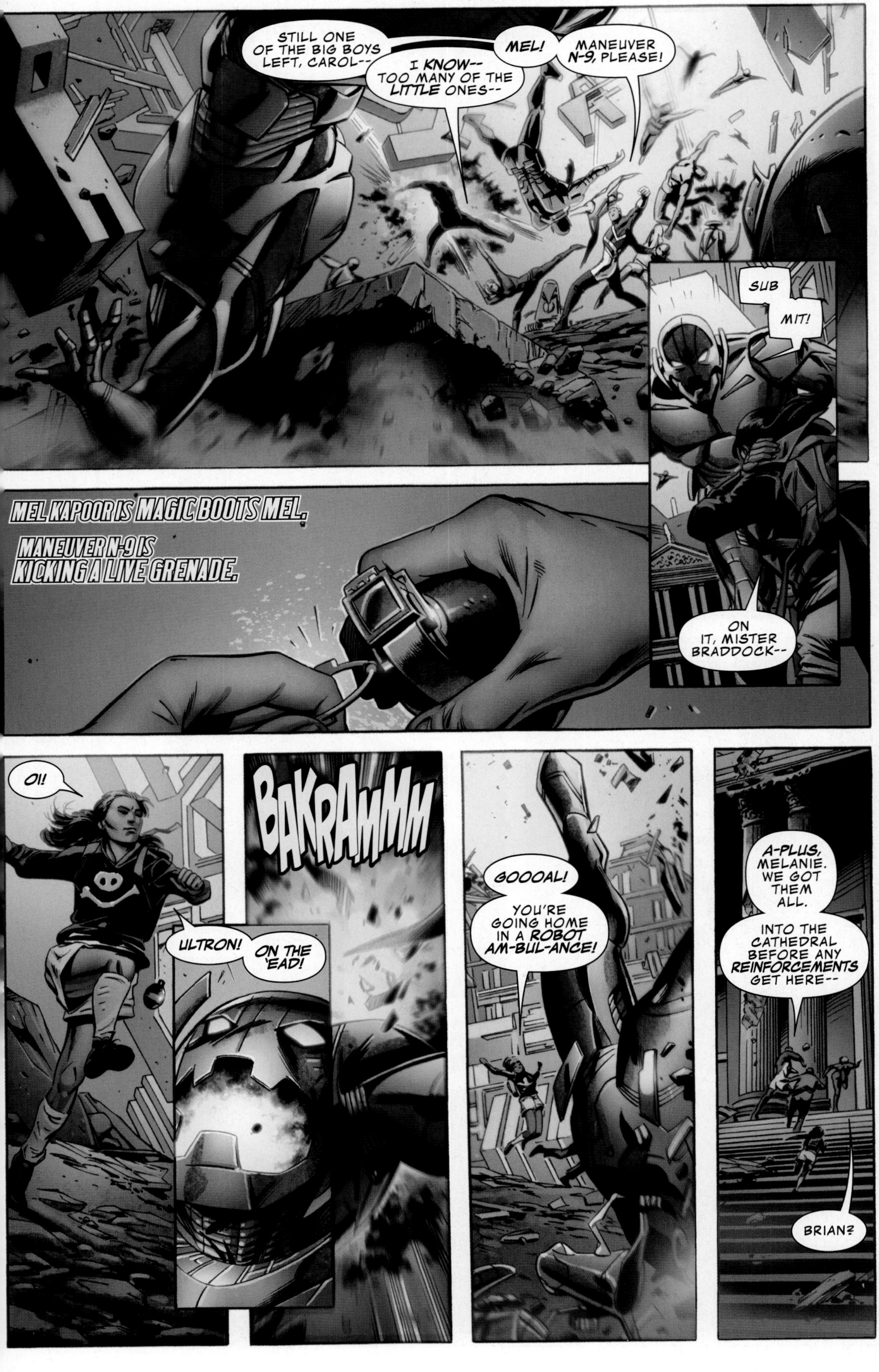
STILL ONE OF THE BIG BOYS LEFT, CAROL--
I KNOW-- TOO MANY OF THE LITTLE ONES--
MEL!
MANEUVER N-9, PLEASE!
SUB
MIT!
MEL KAPOOR IS MAGIC BOOTS MEL.
MANEUVER N-9 IS KICKING A LIVE GRENADE.
ON IT, MISTER BRADDOCK--
OI!
BAKRAMMM
ULTRON!
ON THE 'EAD!
GOOOAL!
YOU'RE GOING HOME IN A ROBOT AM-BUL-ANCE!
A-PLUS, MELANIE. WE GOT THEM ALL.
INTO THE CATHEDRAL BEFORE ANY REINFORCEMENTS GET HERE--
BRIAN?

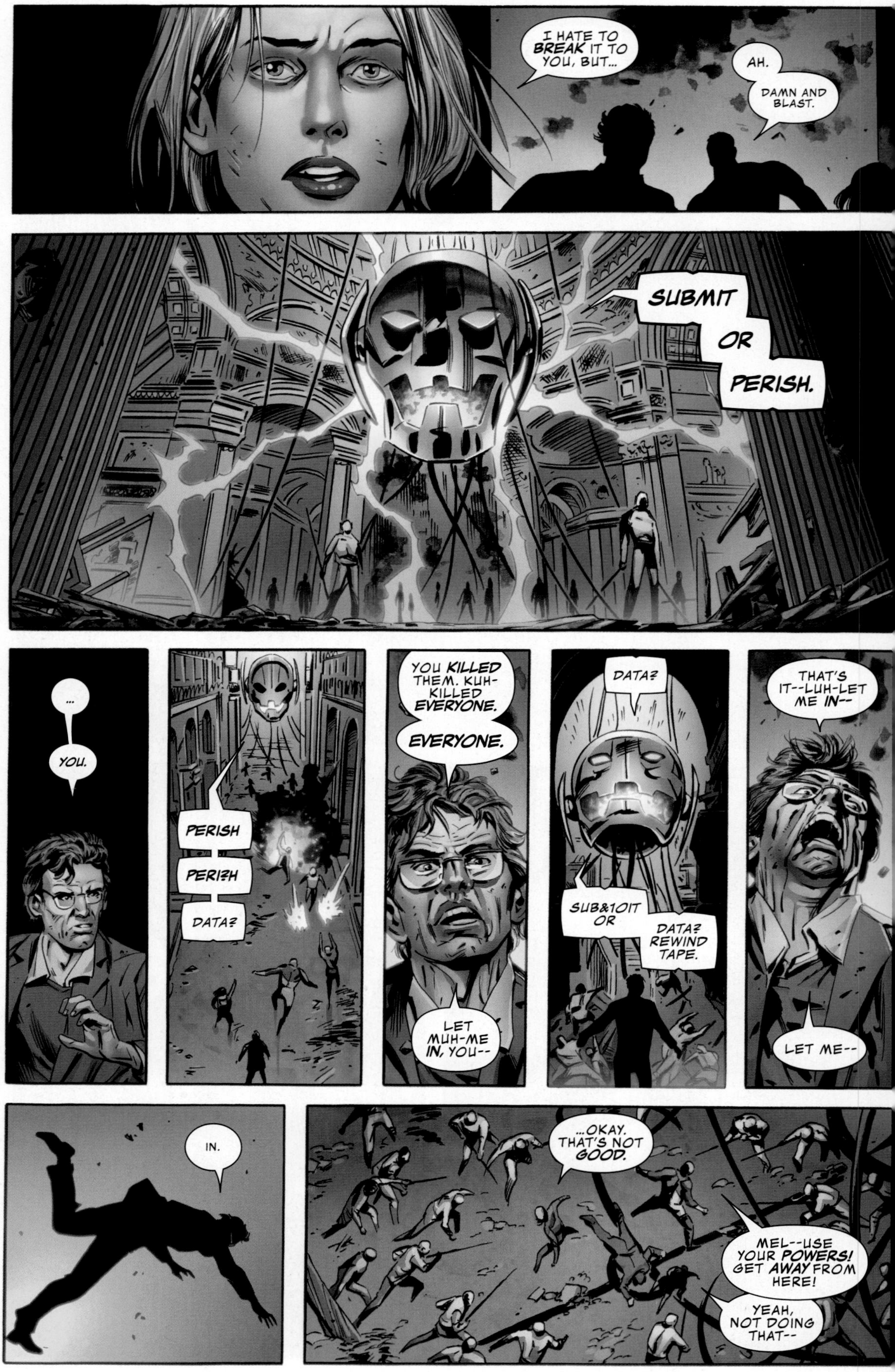
I HATE TO BREAK IT TO YOU, BUT...
AH.
DAMN AND BLAST.
SUBMIT OR PERISH.
...
YOU.
PERISH
PERI?H
DATA?
YOU KILLED THEM. KUH-KILLED EVERYONE.
EVERYONE.
LET MUH-ME IN, YOU--
DATA?
SUB&1OIT OR
DATA? REWIND TAPE.
THAT'S IT--LUH-LET ME IN--
LET ME--
IN.
...OKAY. THAT'S NOT GOOD.
MEL--USE YOUR POWERS! GET AWAY FROM HERE!
YEAH, NOT DOING THAT--

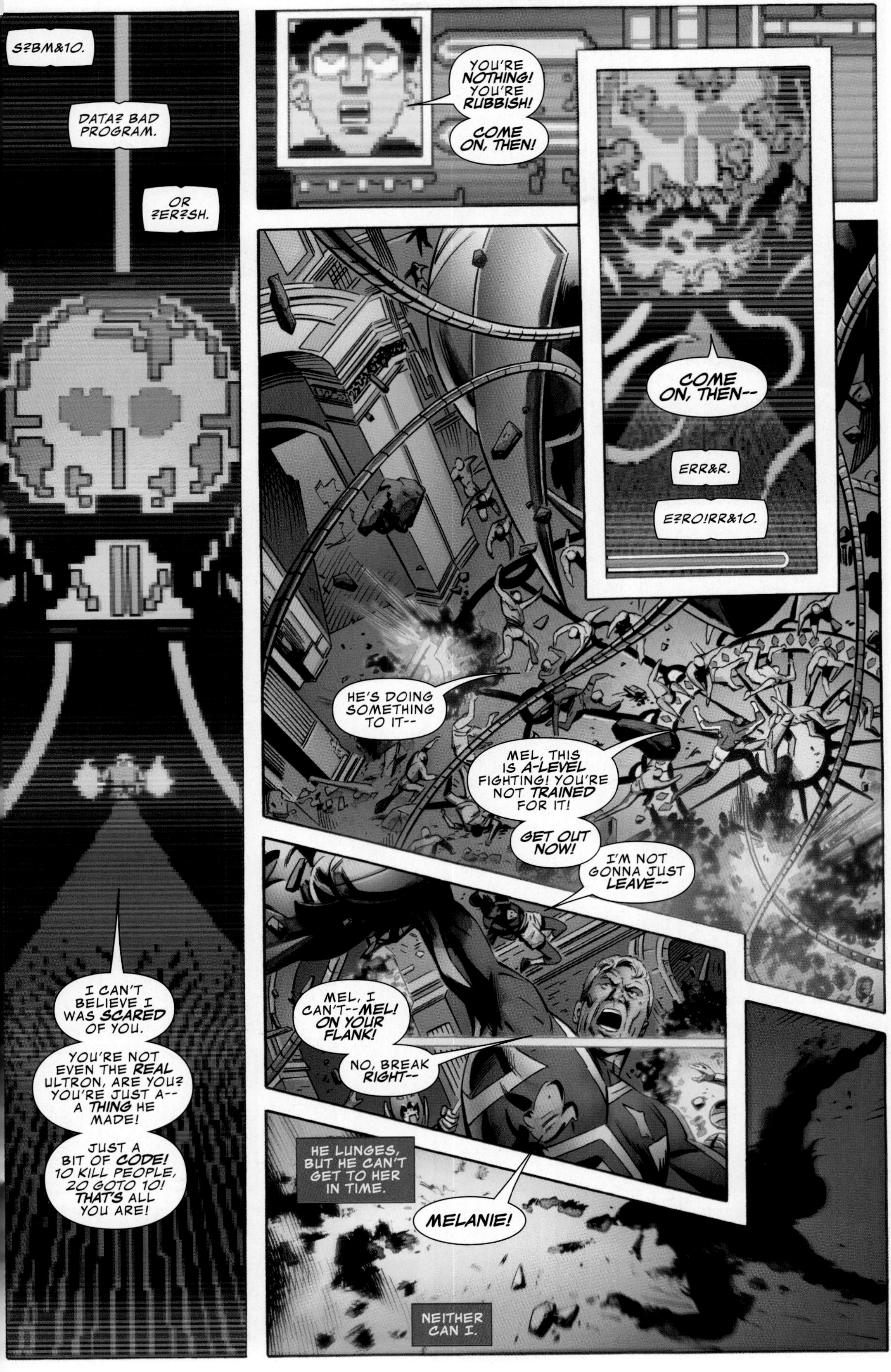
S?BM&10.
DATA? BAD PROGRAM.
OR ?ER?SH.
YOU'RE NOTHING! YOU'RE RUBBISH!
COME ON, THEN!
COME ON, THEN--
ERR&R.
E?RO!RR&10.
I CAN'T BELIEVE I WAS SCARED OF YOU.
YOU'RE NOT EVEN THE REAL ULTRON, ARE YOU? YOU'RE JUST A-- A THING HE MADE!
JUST A BIT OF CODE! 10 KILL PEOPLE, 20 GOTO 10! THAT'S ALL YOU ARE!
HE'S DOING SOMETHING TO IT--
MEL, THIS IS A-LEVEL FIGHTING! YOU'RE NOT TRAINED FOR IT!
GET OUT NOW!
I'M NOT GONNA JUST LEAVE--
MEL, I CAN'T--MEL! ON YOUR FLANK!
NO, BREAK RIGHT--
HE LUNGES, BUT HE CAN'T GET TO HER IN TIME.
MELANIE!
NEITHER CAN I.

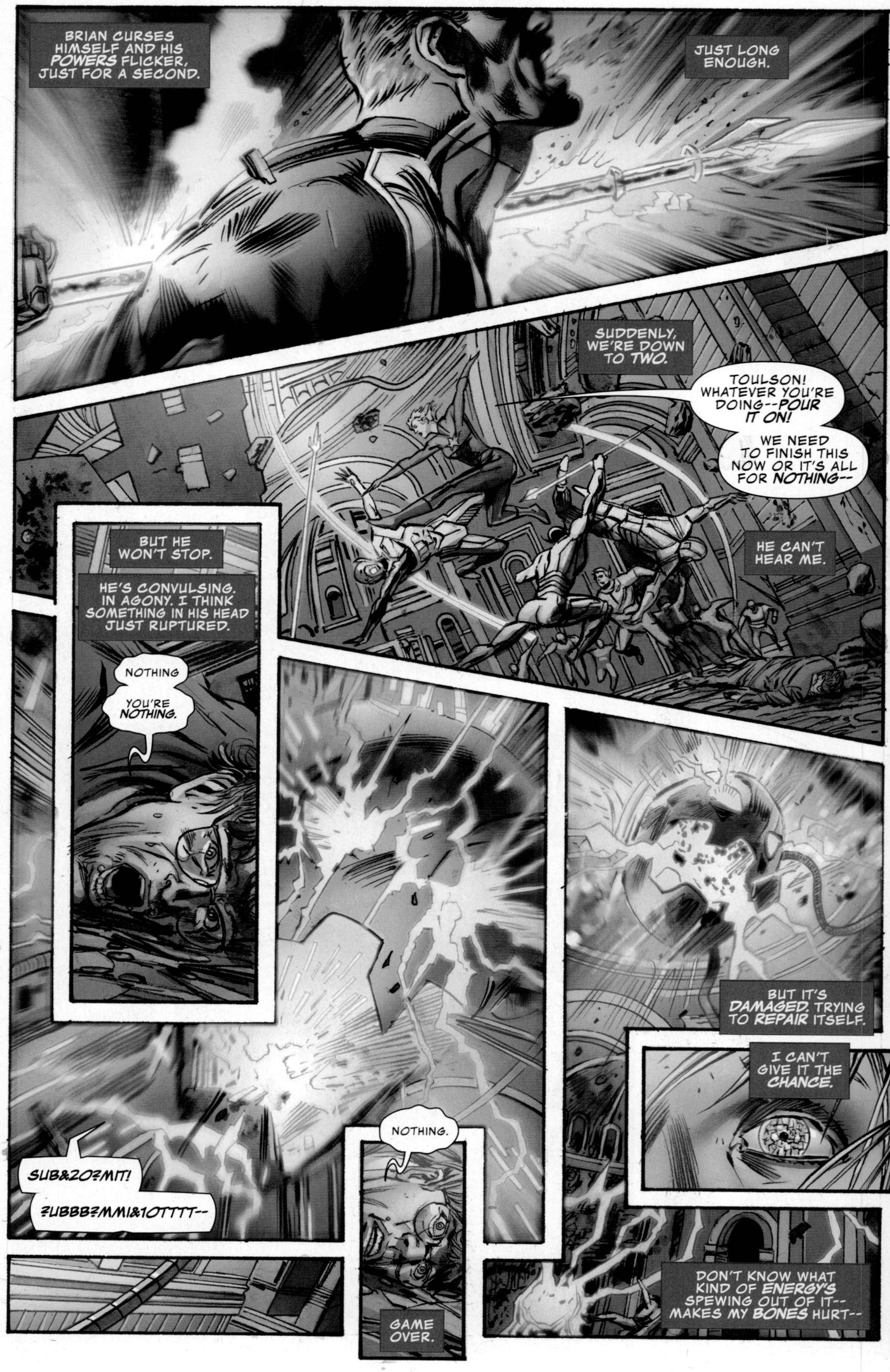
BRIAN CURSES HIMSELF AND HIS POWERS FLICKER, JUST FOR A SECOND.
JUST LONG ENOUGH.
SUDDENLY, WE'RE DOWN TO TWO.
TOULSON! WHATEVER YOU'RE DOING--POUR IT ON!
WE NEED TO FINISH THIS NOW OR IT'S ALL FOR NOTHING--
HE CAN'T HEAR ME.
BUT HE WON'T STOP.
HE'S CONVULSING. IN AGONY. I THINK SOMETHING IN HIS HEAD JUST RUPTURED.
NOTHING
YOU'RE NOTHING.
SUB&2O?MIT!
?UBBB?MMI&1OTTTT--
BUT IT'S DAMAGED. TRYING TO REPAIR ITSELF.
I CAN'T GIVE IT THE CHANCE.
NOTHING.
GAME OVER.
DON'T KNOW WHAT KIND OF ENERGY'S SPEWING OUT OF IT--MAKES MY BONES HURT--

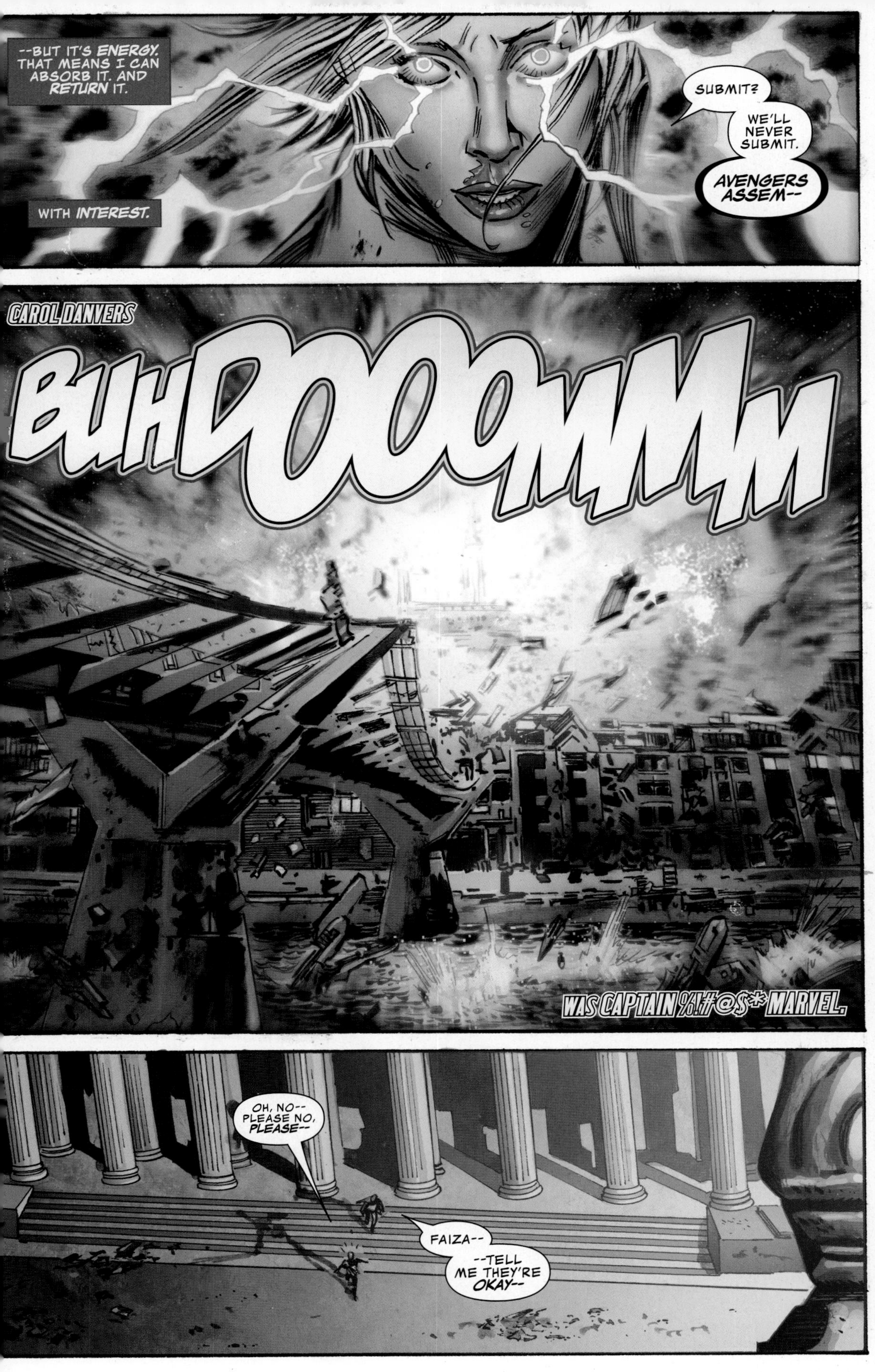
--BUT IT'S ENERGY. THAT MEANS I CAN ABSORB IT. AND RETURN IT.
WITH INTEREST.
SUBMIT?
WE'LL NEVER SUBMIT.
AVENGERS ASSEM--
CAROL DANVERS
BUHDOOOMMM
WAS CAPTAIN %!#@$* MARVEL.
OH, NO-- PLEASE NO, PLEASE--
FAIZA--
--TELL ME THEY'RE OKAY--

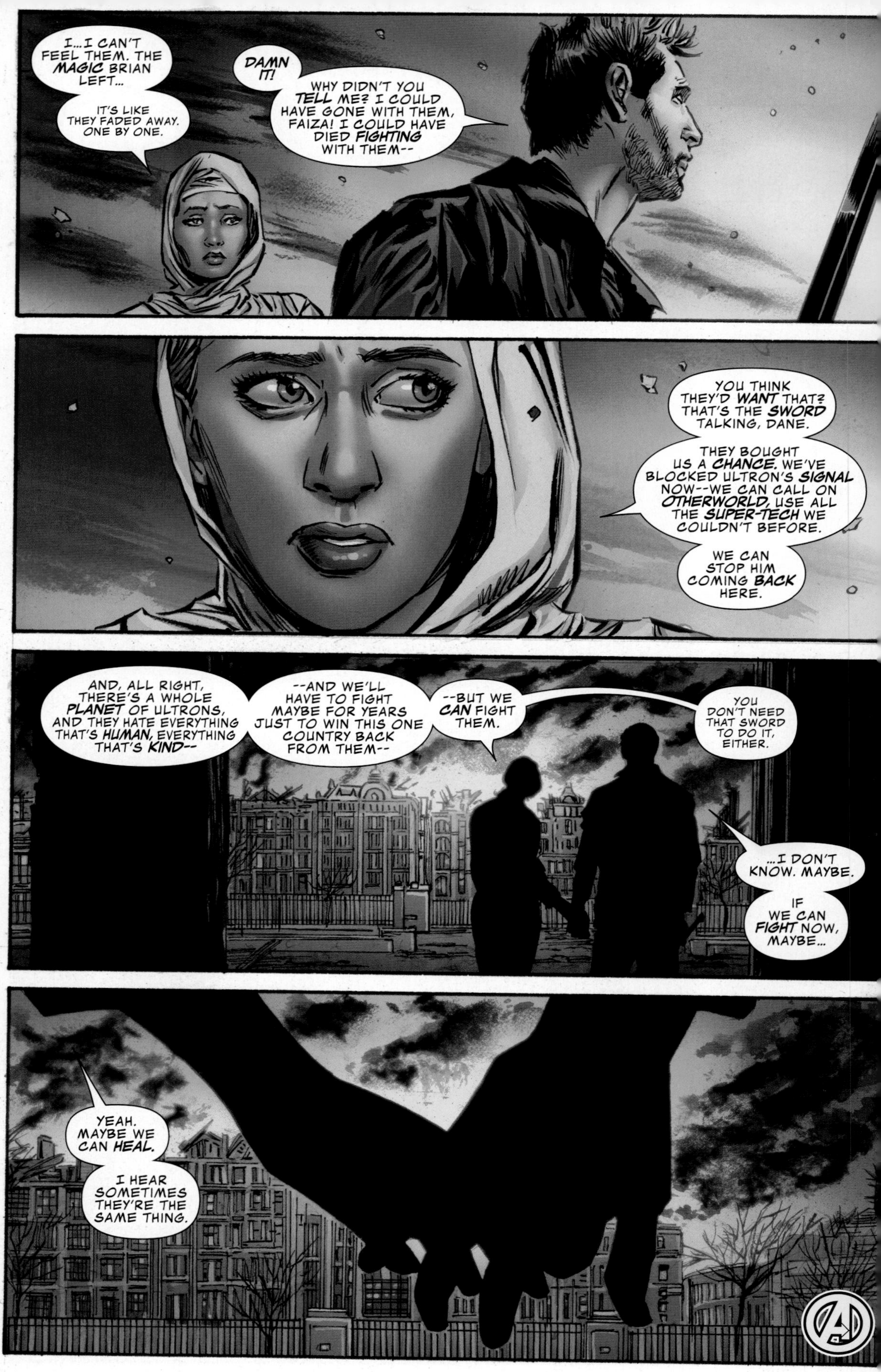
I... I CAN'T FEEL THEM. THE MAGIC BRIAN LEFT...
IT'S LIKE THEY FADED AWAY. ONE BY ONE.
DAMN IT!
WHY DIDN'T YOU TELL ME? I COULD HAVE GONE WITH THEM, FAIZA! I COULD HAVE DIED FIGHTING WITH THEM--
YOU THINK THEY'D WANT THAT? THAT'S THE SWORD TALKING, DANE.
THEY BOUGHT US A CHANCE. WE'VE BLOCKED ULTRON'S SIGNAL NOW--WE CAN CALL ON OTHERWORLD, USE ALL THE SUPER-TECH WE COULDN'T BEFORE.
WE CAN STOP HIM COMING BACK HERE.
AND, ALL RIGHT, THERE'S A WHOLE PLANET OF ULTRONS, AND THEY HATE EVERYTHING THAT'S HUMAN, EVERYTHING THAT'S KIND--
--AND WE'LL HAVE TO FIGHT MAYBE FOR YEARS JUST TO WIN THIS ONE COUNTRY BACK FROM THEM--
--BUT WE CAN FIGHT THEM.
YOU DON'T NEED THAT SWORD TO DO IT, EITHER.
...I DON'T KNOW. MAYBE.
IF WE CAN FIGHT NOW, MAYBE...
YEAH. MAYBE WE CAN HEAL.
I HEAR SOMETIMES THEY'RE THE SAME THING.

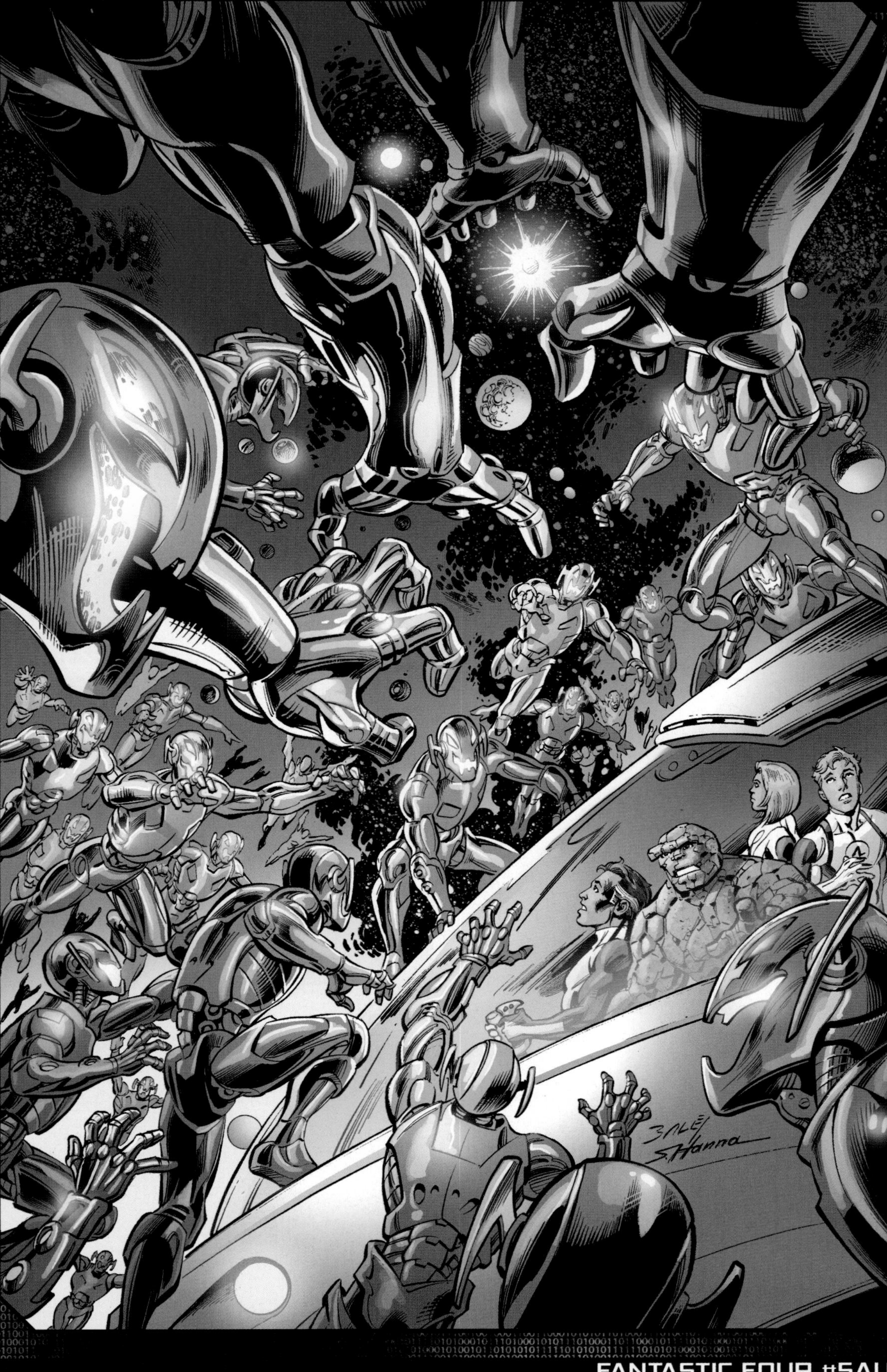

FANTASTIC FOUR #5AL

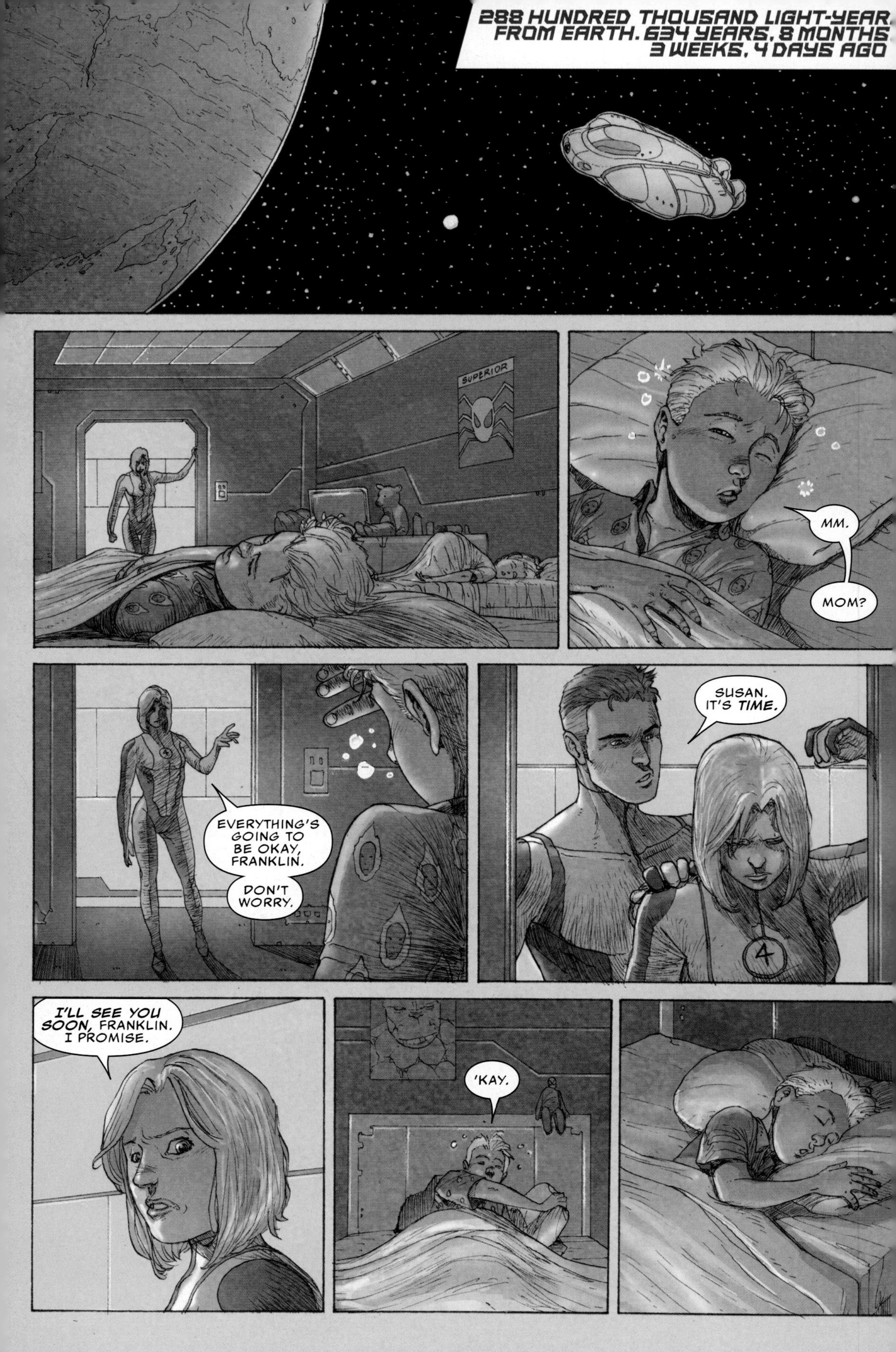
288 HUNDRED THOUSAND LIGHT-YEAR FROM EARTH. 634 YEARS, 8 MONTHS 3 WEEKS, 4 DAYS AGO
SUPERIOR
MM.
MOM?
EVERYTHING'S GOING TO BE OKAY, FRANKLIN.
DON'T WORRY.
SUSAN. IT'S TIME.
I'LL SEE YOU SOON, FRANKLIN. I PROMISE.
'KAY.

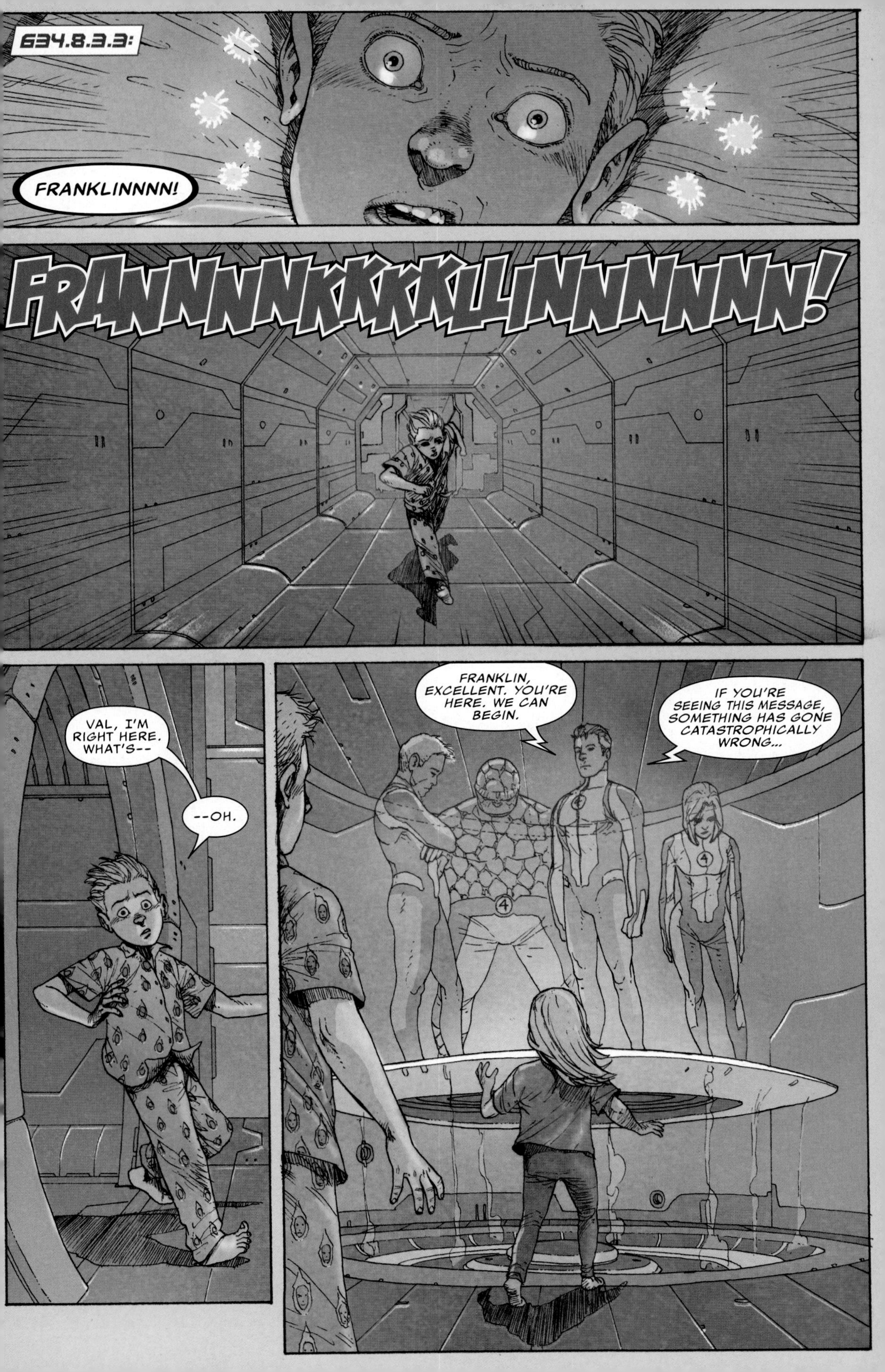
634.8.3.3:
FRANKLINNNN!
FRANNNNKKKKLLINNNNNNN!
VAL, I'M RIGHT HERE. WHAT'S--
--OH.
FRANKLIN, EXCELLENT. YOU'RE HERE. WE CAN BEGIN.
IF YOU'RE SEEING THIS MESSAGE, SOMETHING HAS GONE CATASTROPHICALLY WRONG...

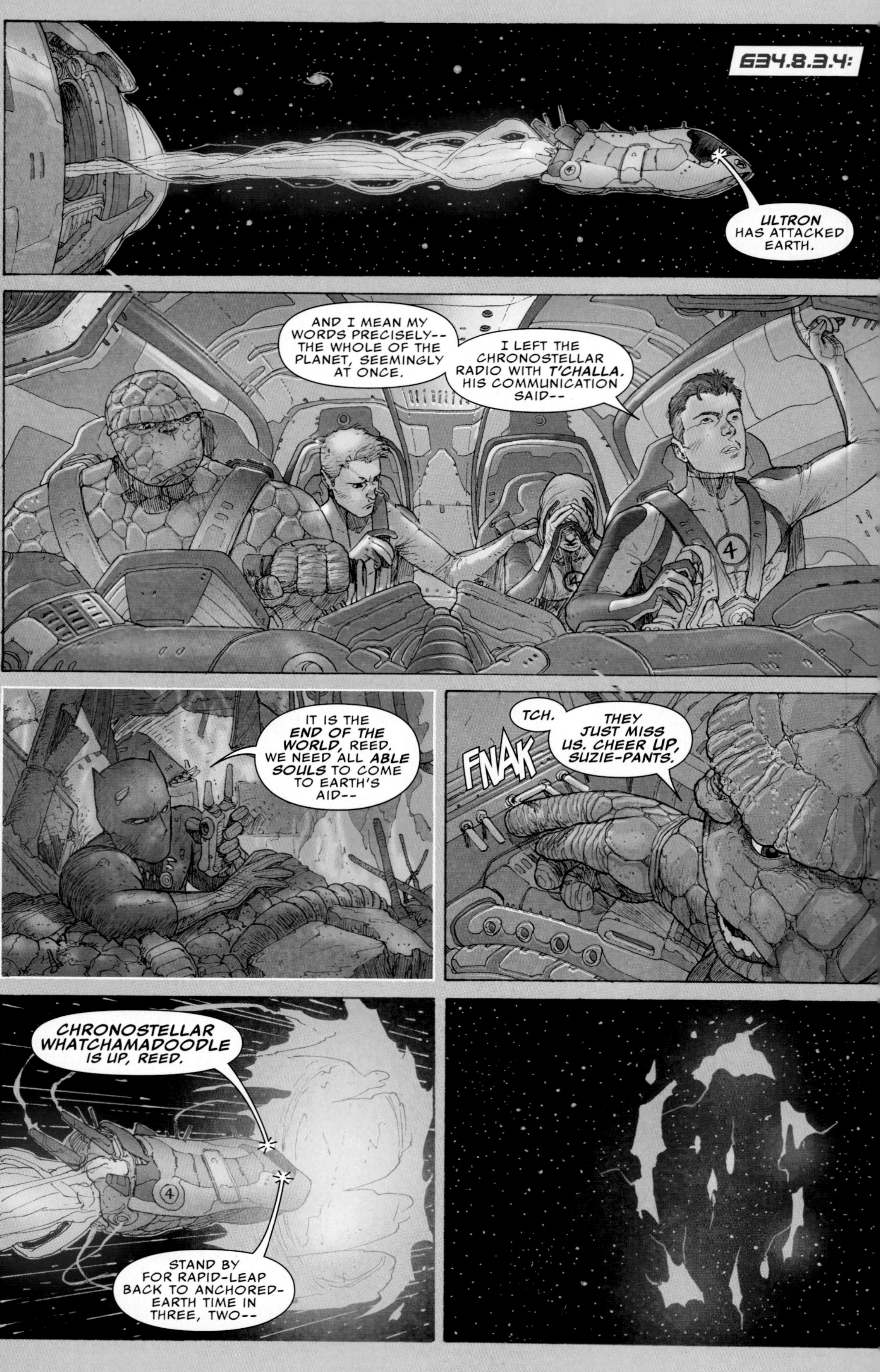
634.8.3.4:
ULTRON HAS ATTACKED EARTH.
AND I MEAN MY WORDS PRECISELY-- THE WHOLE OF THE PLANET, SEEMINGLY AT ONCE.
I LEFT THE CHRONOSTELLAR RADIO WITH T'CHALLA. HIS COMMUNICATION SAID--
IT IS THE END OF THE WORLD, REED. WE NEED ALL ABLE SOULS TO COME TO EARTH'S AID--
FNAK
TCH.
THEY JUST MISS US. CHEER UP, SUZIE-PANTS.
CHRONOSTELLAR WHATCHAMADOODLE IS UP, REED.
STAND BY FOR RAPID-LEAP BACK TO ANCHORED-EARTH TIME IN THREE, TWO--

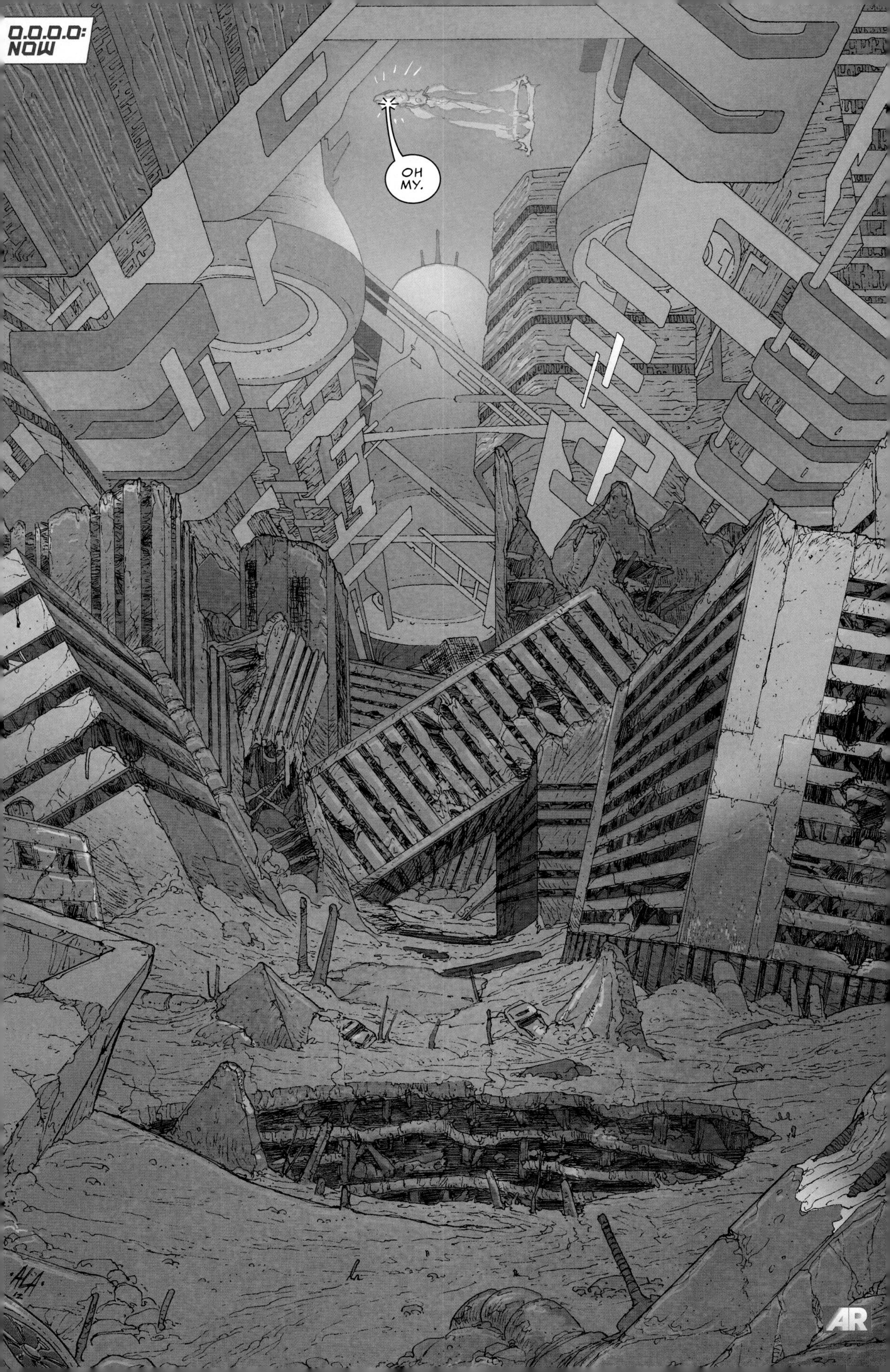
0.0.0.0:
NOW
OH MY.

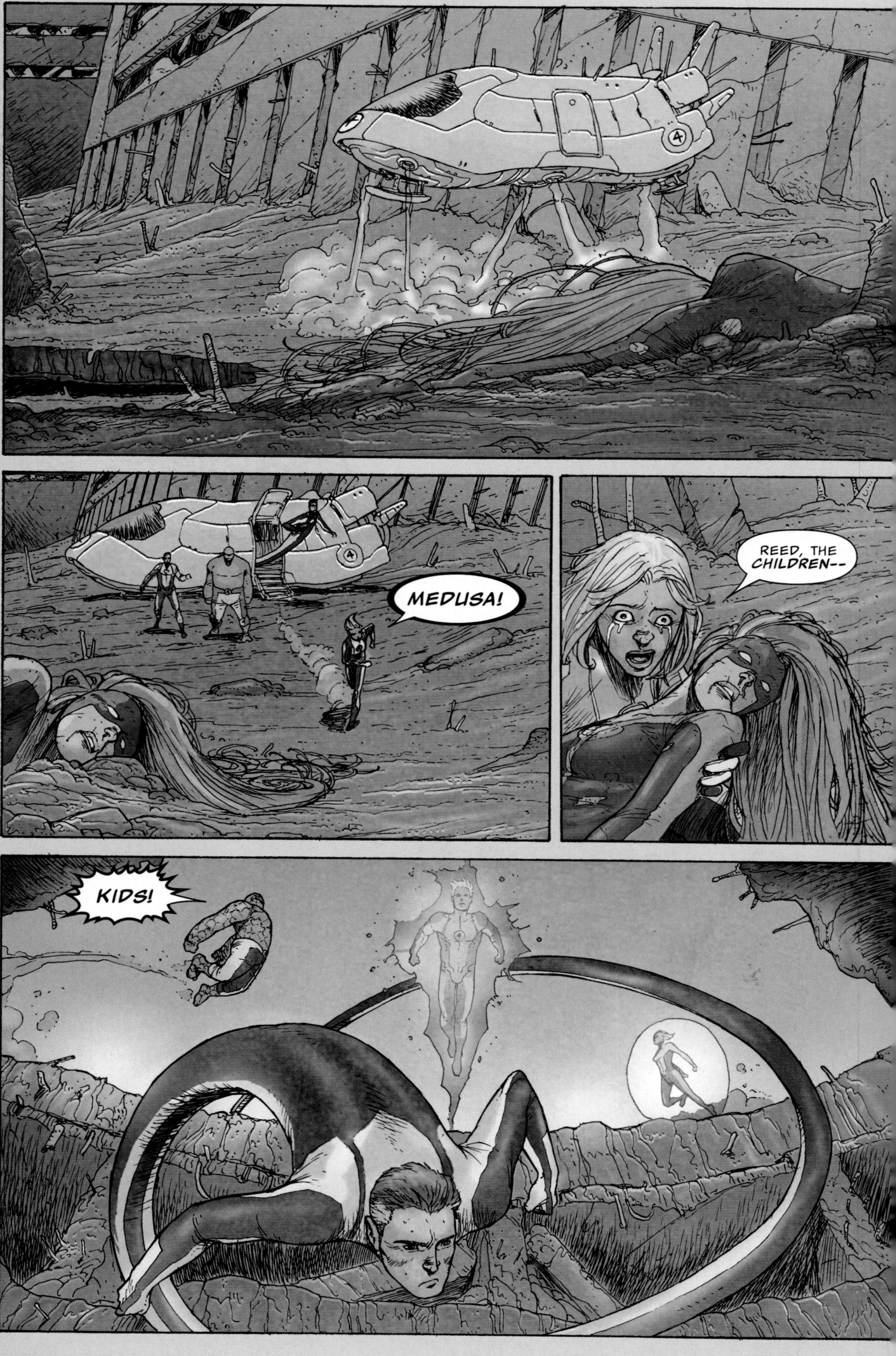
MEDUSA!
REED, THE CHILDREN--
KIDS!

OH, NO...

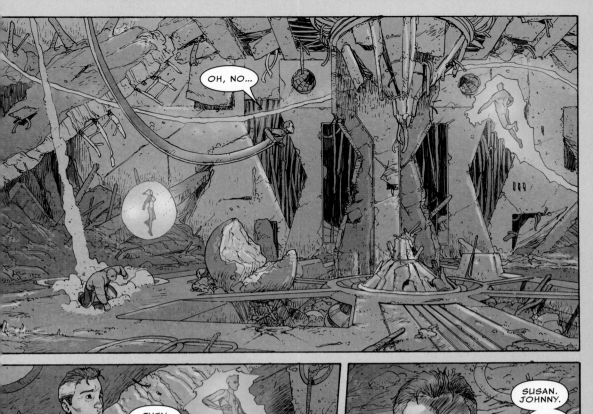

THEY DIDN'T...

THEY DIDN'T EVEN GET **DOWN** HERE IN TIME. THEY NEVER EVEN **ACTIVATED** THE OMEGA ROOM. THEY...

SUSAN. JOHNNY.

BEN--

ALL HUMANOID LIFE FORMS ARE TO EXIT THE PREMISES IMMEDIATELY.

"UH...OKAY. SO... SO, OKAY. WELL, I GUESS THIS IS LIKE MY **WILL** OR WHATEVER.

"DIDN'T I **JUST DO** THIS?"

UM...YOU GUYS GET ALL MY STUFF. SPLIT IT UP BETWEEN YOU.

DON'T MESS UP MY CAR.

I'M JUST KIDDING.

LOOK, I DON'T KNOW WHY YOUR FOLKS ARE MAKING US DO THIS. WHAT AM I WORRIED ABOUT?

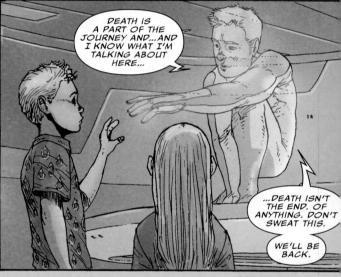

DEATH IS A PART OF THE JOURNEY AND...AND I KNOW WHAT I'M TALKING ABOUT HERE...

...DEATH ISN'T THE END. OF ANYTHING. DON'T SWEAT THIS.

WE'LL BE BACK.

REED, THIS IS STUPID, COME ON, MAN--

OKAY, WE'RE IN REAL TROUBLE.

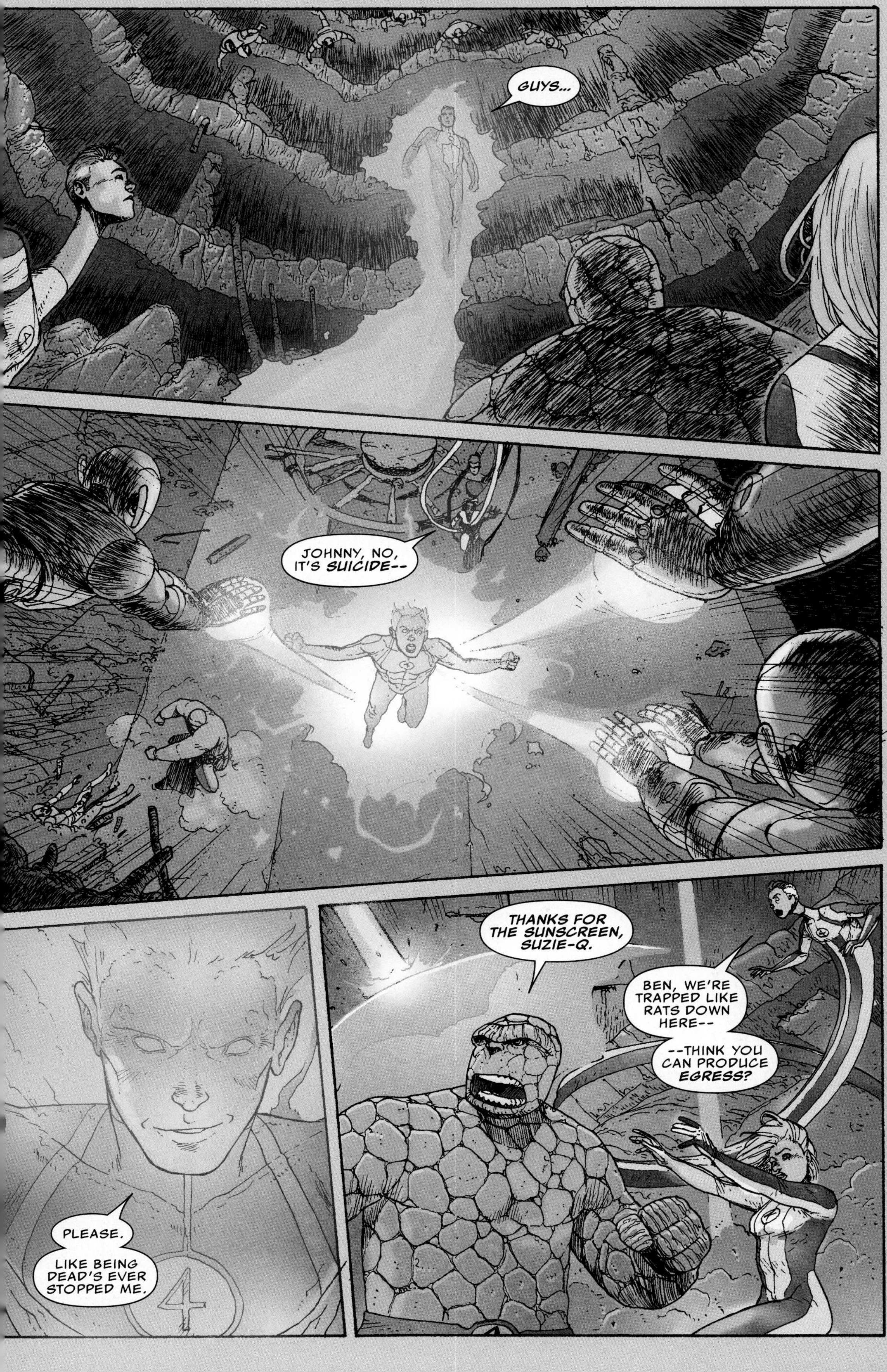
GUYS...
JOHNNY, NO, IT'S SUICIDE--
PLEASE.
LIKE BEING DEAD'S EVER STOPPED ME.
THANKS FOR THE SUNSCREEN, SUZIE-Q.
BEN, WE'RE TRAPPED LIKE RATS DOWN HERE--
--THINK YOU CAN PRODUCE EGRESS?

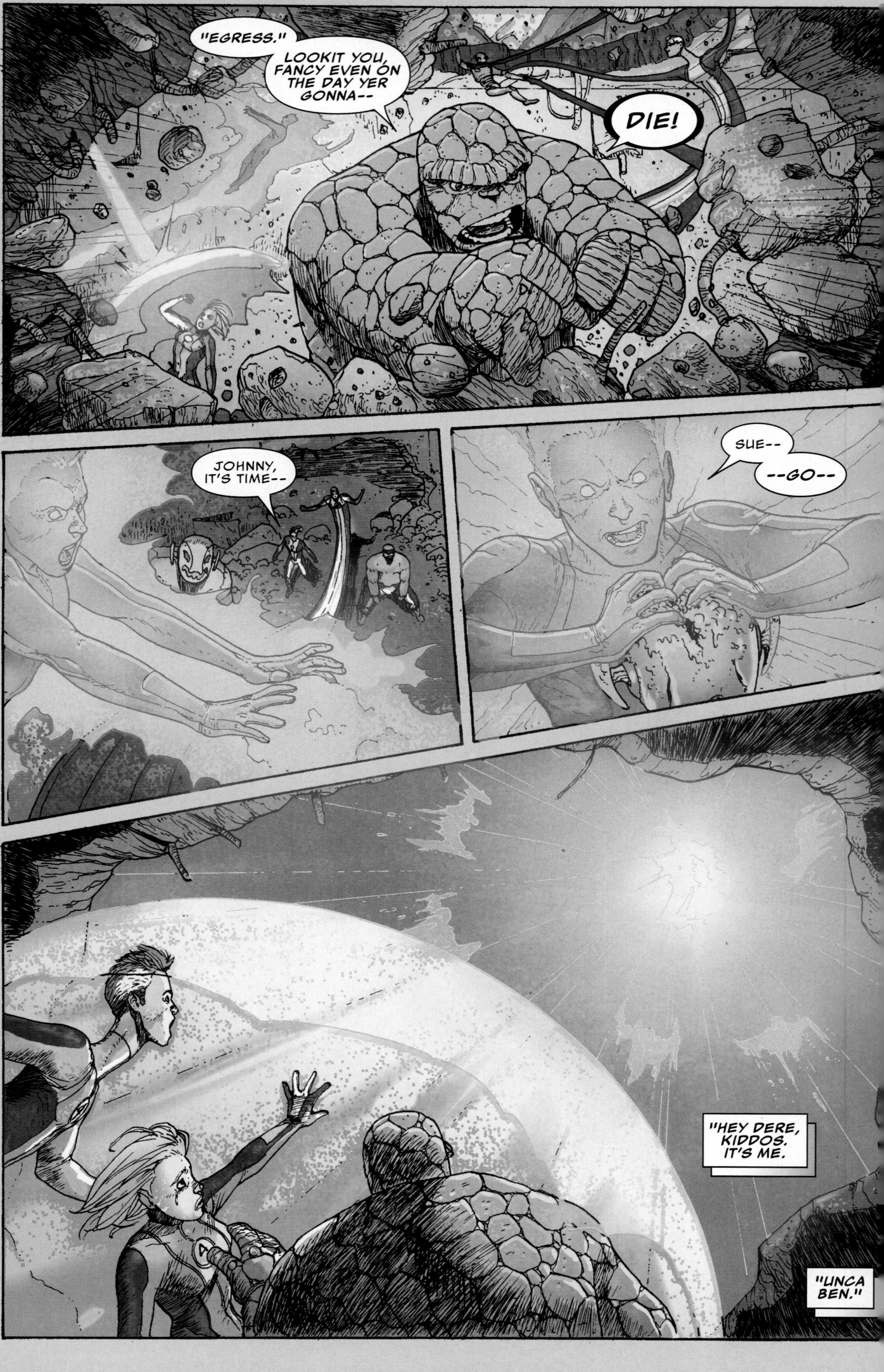
"EGRESS."
LOOKIT YOU, FANCY EVEN ON THE DAY YER GONNA--
DIE!
JOHNNY, IT'S TIME--
SUE--
--GO--
"HEY DERE, KIDDOS. IT'S ME.
"UNCA BEN."

LOOKS LIKE MEBBE THINGS AIN'T GOIN' SO WELL BACK HOME, SO WE'RE GONNA HELP FOLKS OUT, BUT...

WELL, IF YOU'RE HEARING THIS, WE'RE NOT BACK AND IT REALLY AIN'T GOIN' WELL.

BOY, THIS IS...

BOY, THIS IS REAL HEAVY. I--I DON'T...

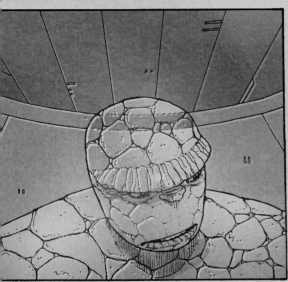

I AIN'T NEVER TOLD NOBODY THIS:

I THINK MEBBE DR. DOOM IS ALL MY FAULT.

WHEN ME AND YOUR DAD WERE KIDS, AND WE WERE ALL AT SCHOOL...THE GUY WAS A RICH JERK.

I MESSED WITH THIS EXPERIMENT HE HAD IN THEIR ROOM THERE AN'...I DIDN'T MEAN TA....I MEAN, I DON'T KNOW IF I DID IT, BUT...

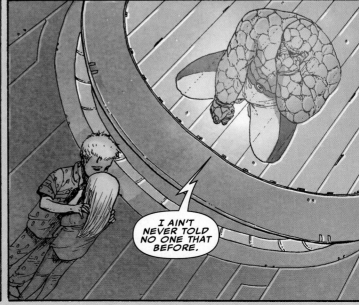

I AIN'T NEVER TOLD NO ONE THAT BEFORE.

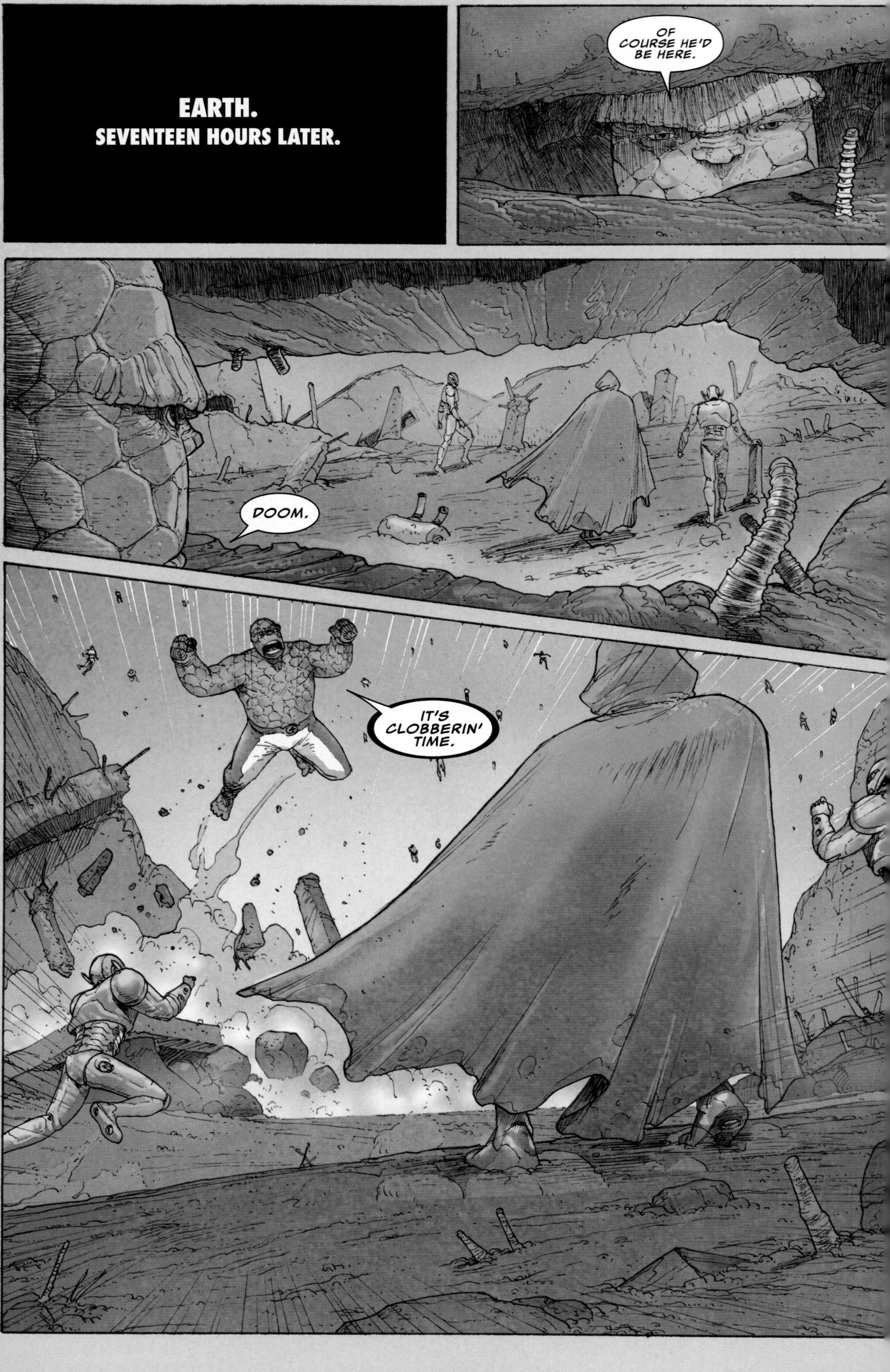
EARTH.
SEVENTEEN HOURS LATER.
OF COURSE HE'D BE HERE.
DOOM.
IT'S CLOBBERIN' TIME.

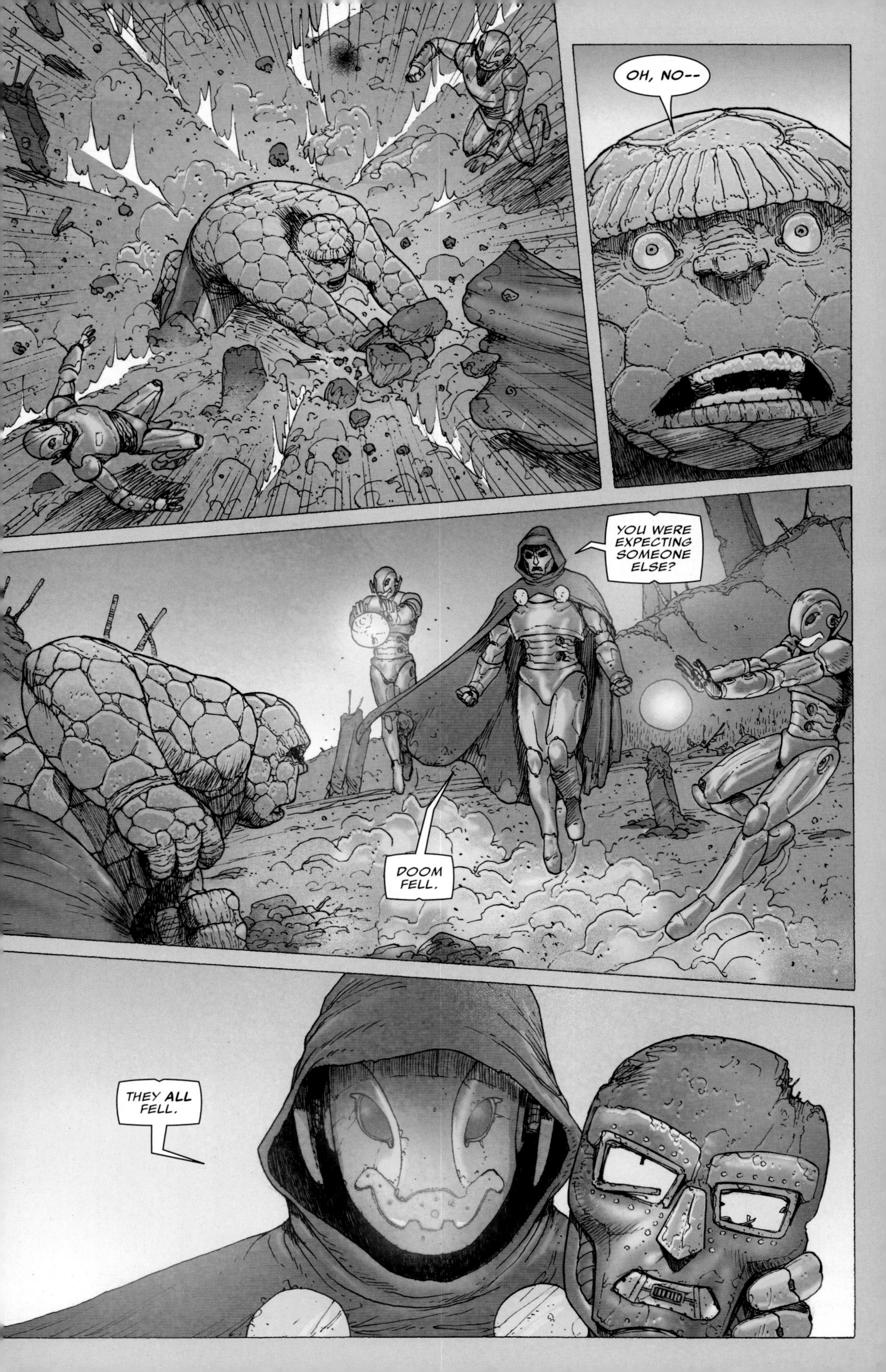
OH, NO--
YOU WERE EXPECTING SOMEONE ELSE?
DOOM FELL.
THEY ALL FELL.

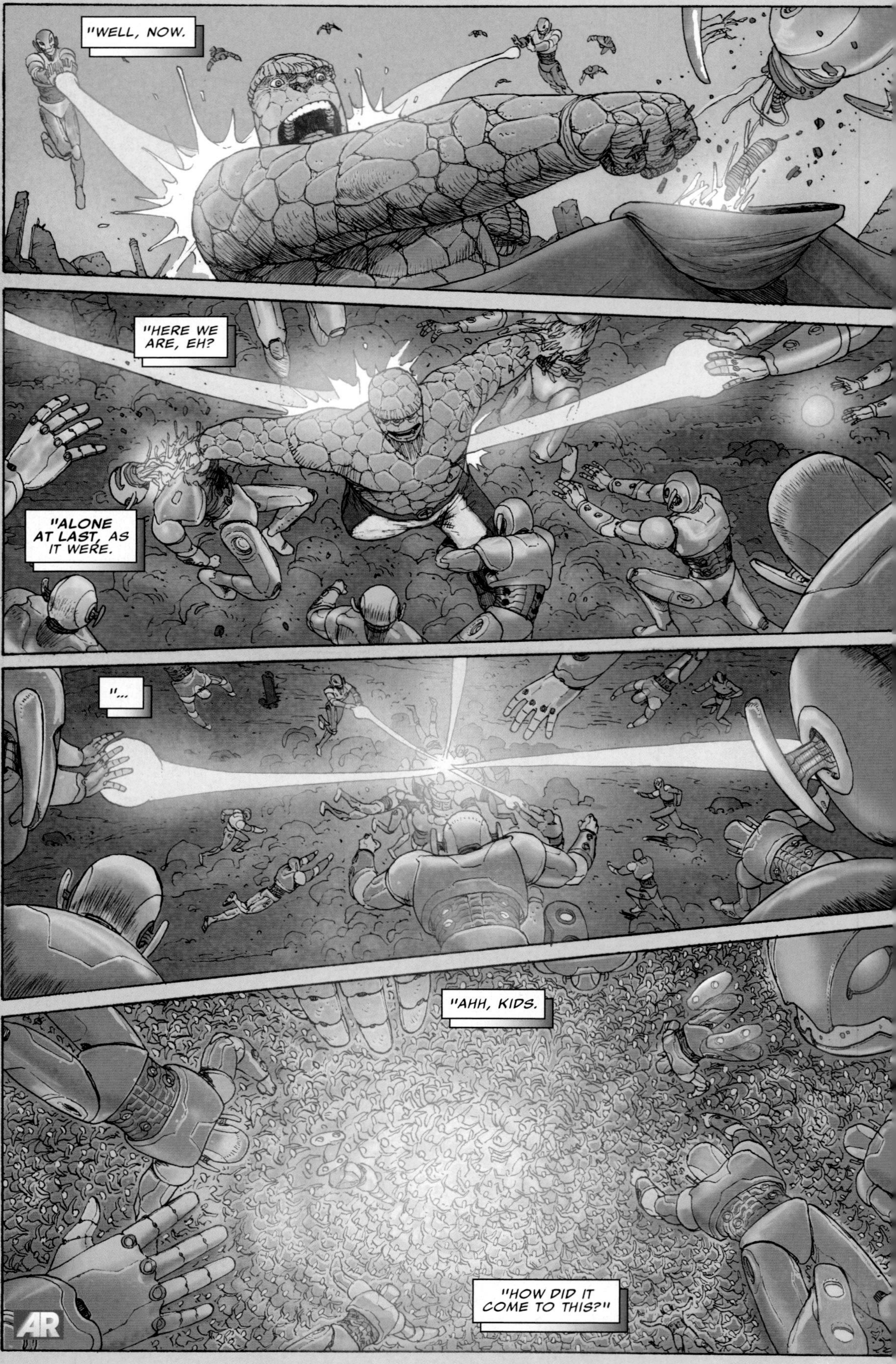
"WELL, NOW.
"HERE WE ARE, EH?
"ALONE AT LAST, AS IT WERE.
"...
"AHH, KIDS.
"HOW DID IT COME TO THIS?"
AR

...
I DON'T KNOW HOW TO SAY THIS...
WORDS NOT COMING...
HOW DOES A FATHER SAY GOODBYE TO HIS CHILDREN?
IMPOSSIBLE.

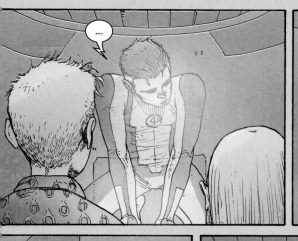

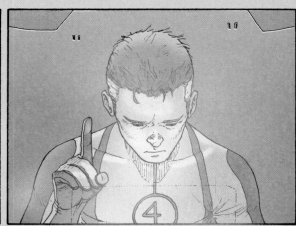

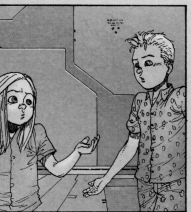

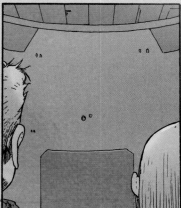

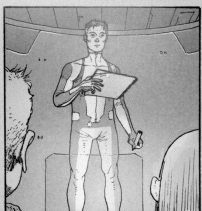

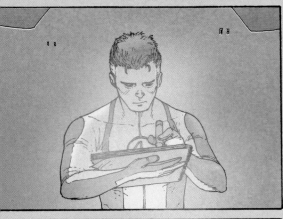

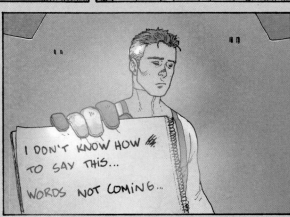

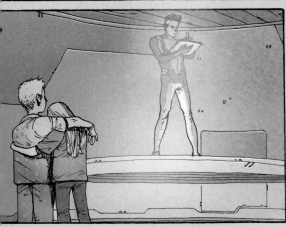

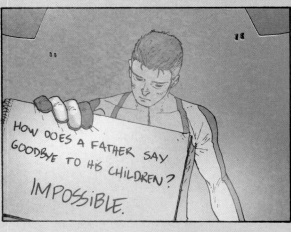

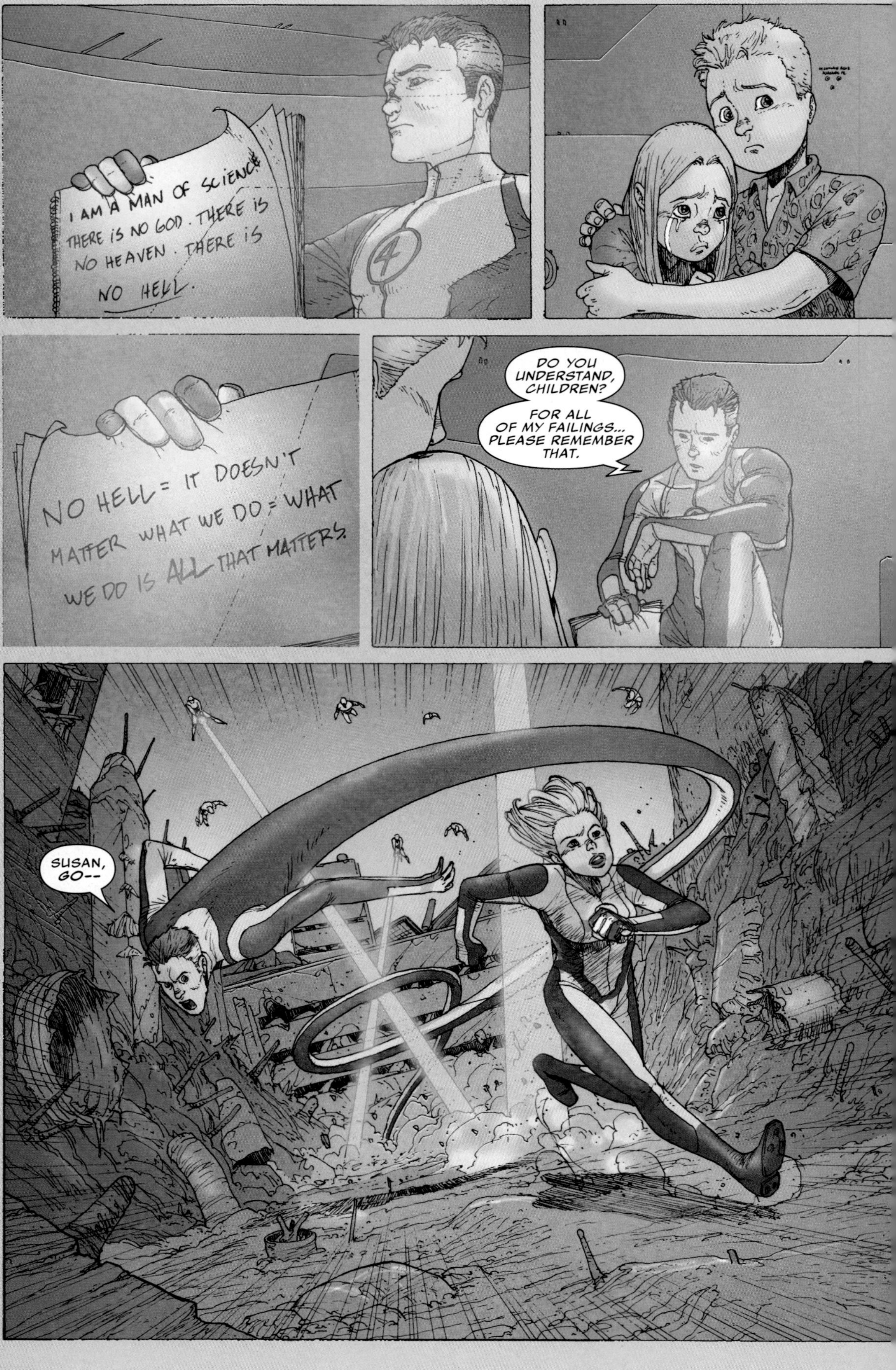
I AM A MAN OF SCIENCE
THERE IS NO GOD. THERE IS NO HEAVEN. THERE IS NO HELL.
NO HELL = IT DOESN'T MATTER WHAT WE DO = WHAT WE DO IS ALL THAT MATTERS.
DO YOU UNDERSTAND, CHILDREN?
FOR ALL OF MY FAILINGS... PLEASE REMEMBER THAT.
SUSAN, GO--

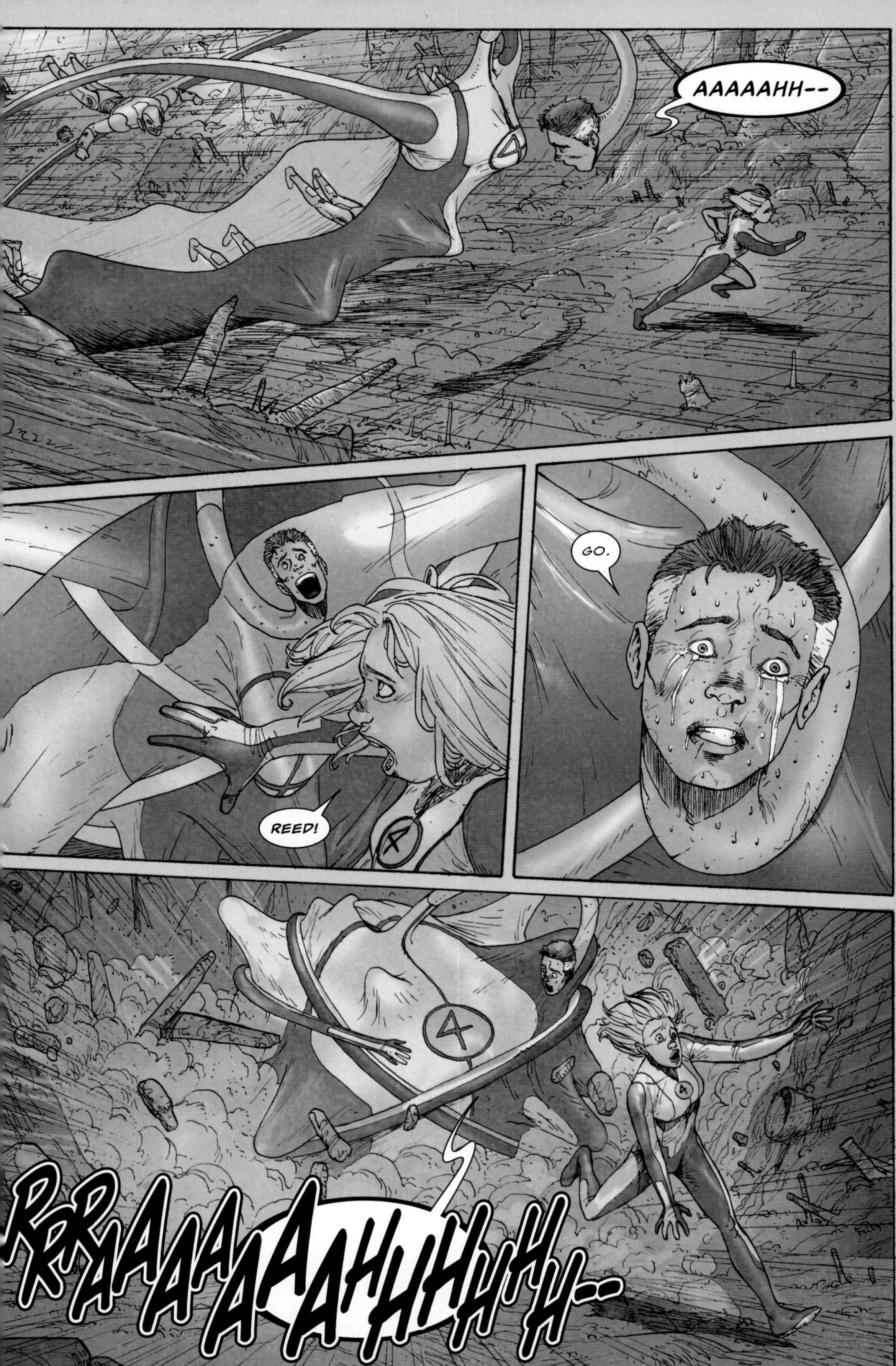
AAAAAHH--
REED!
GO.
RRRAAAAAAAAHHHHHH--

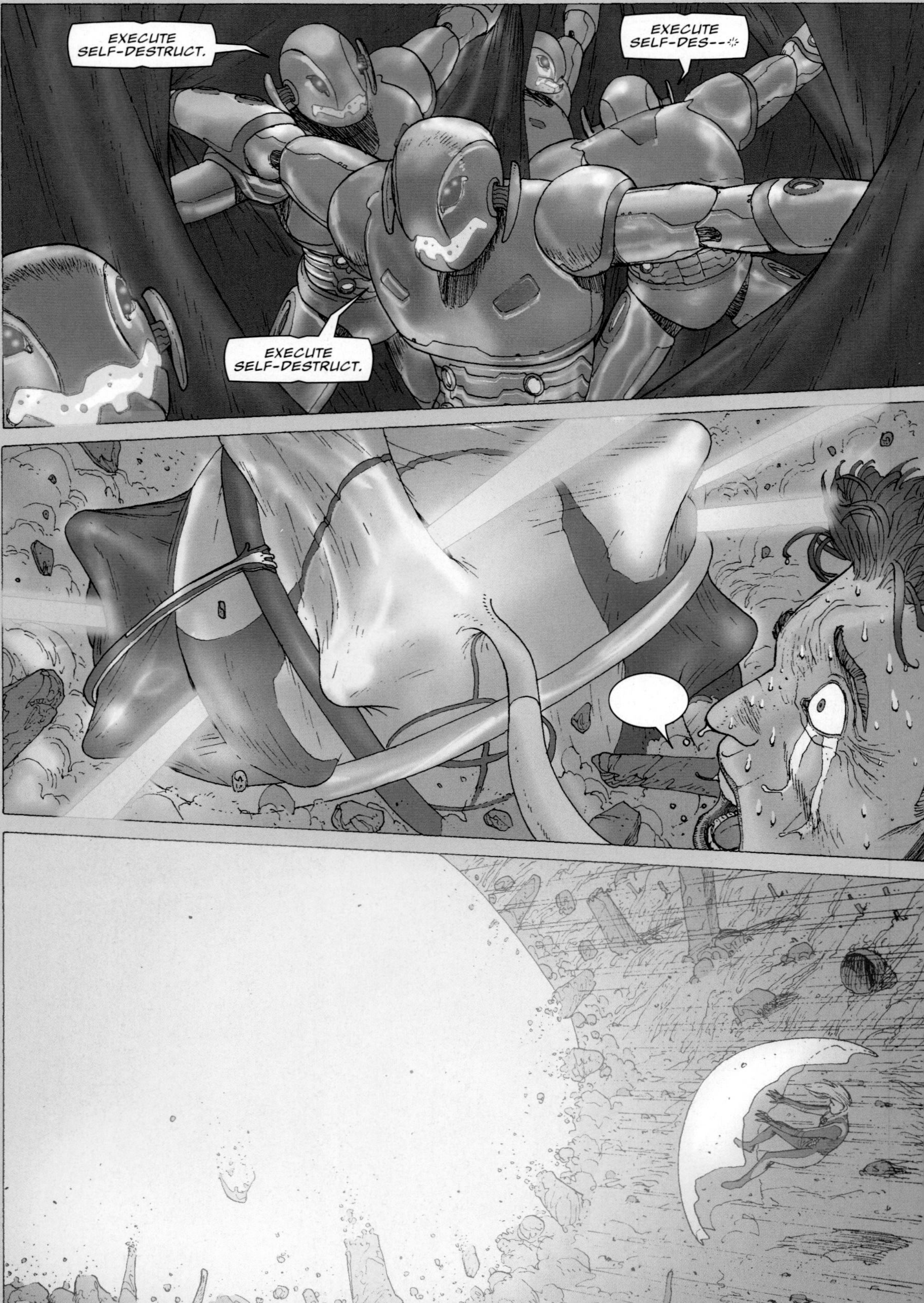
EXECUTE
SELF-DESTRUCT.
EXECUTE
SELF-DES--
EXECUTE
SELF-DESTRUCT.

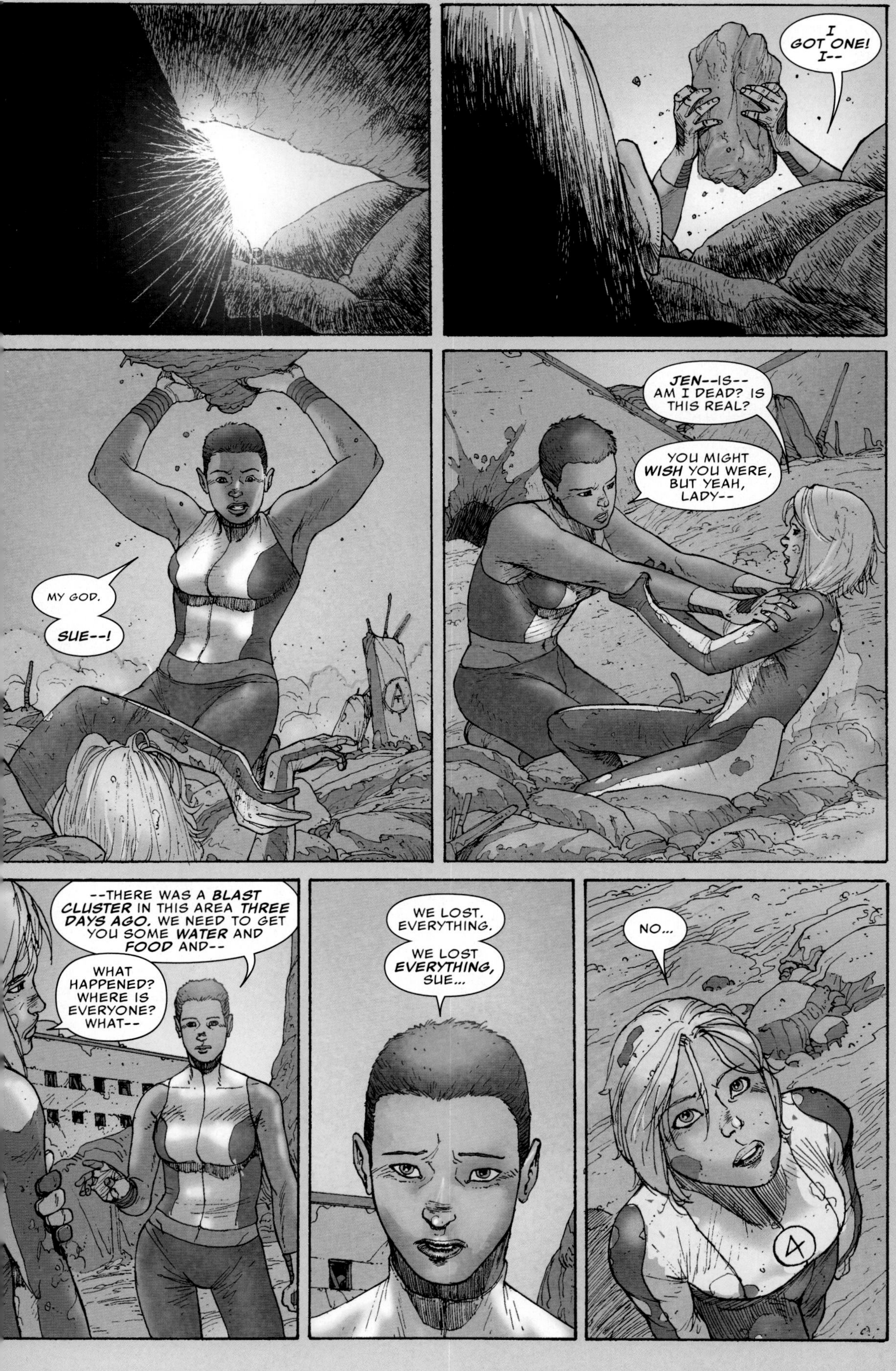
I GOT ONE! I--
MY GOD.
SUE--!
JEN--IS-- AM I DEAD? IS THIS REAL?
YOU MIGHT WISH YOU WERE, BUT YEAH, LADY--
--THERE WAS A BLAST CLUSTER IN THIS AREA THREE DAYS AGO. WE NEED TO GET YOU SOME WATER AND FOOD AND--
WHAT HAPPENED? WHERE IS EVERYONE? WHAT--
WE LOST. EVERYTHING.
WE LOST EVERYTHING, SUE...
NO...

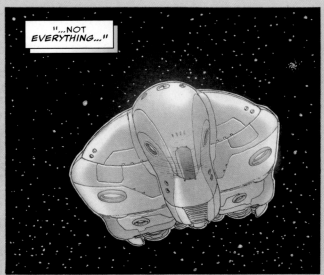

"...NOT EVERYTHING..."

I DON'T UNDERSTAND.

THERE'S NOT A MESSAGE FROM MOM.

YEAH THERE WAS.

SHE--

EVERYTHING'S GOING TO BE OKAY, FRANKLIN.

--SHE SAID WE'D SEE HER AGAIN.

SHE SAID DON'T WORRY.

GOOD DAY, CHILDREN, TODAY'S FIRST LESSON SHALL COVER:

PARTICLE PHYSICS...

LET'S BEGIN WITH ELEMENTARY PARTICLE PHYSICS. CHAPTER ONE...

AND DO YOU BELIEVE HER?

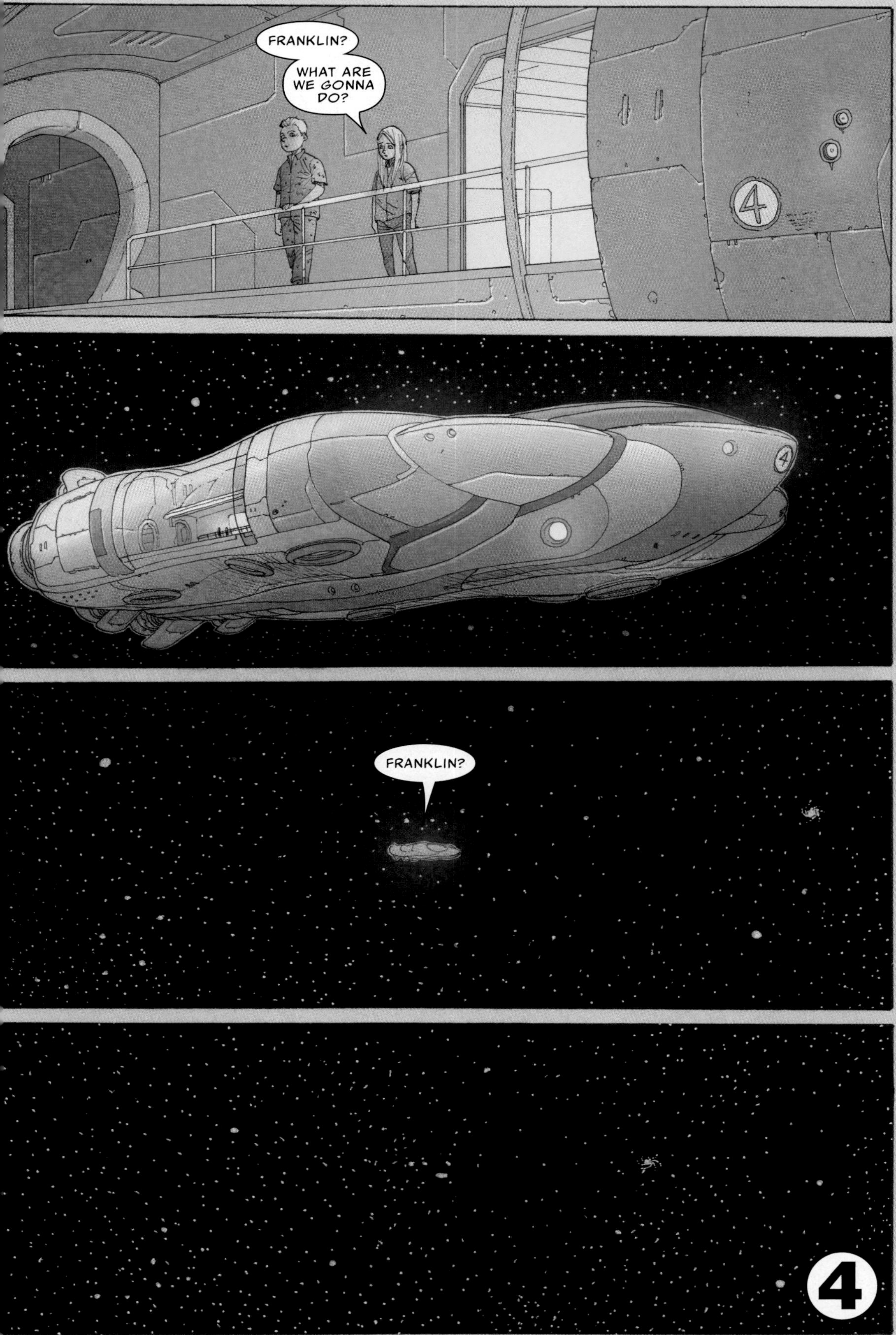
FRANKLIN?
WHAT ARE WE GONNA DO?
FRANKLIN?

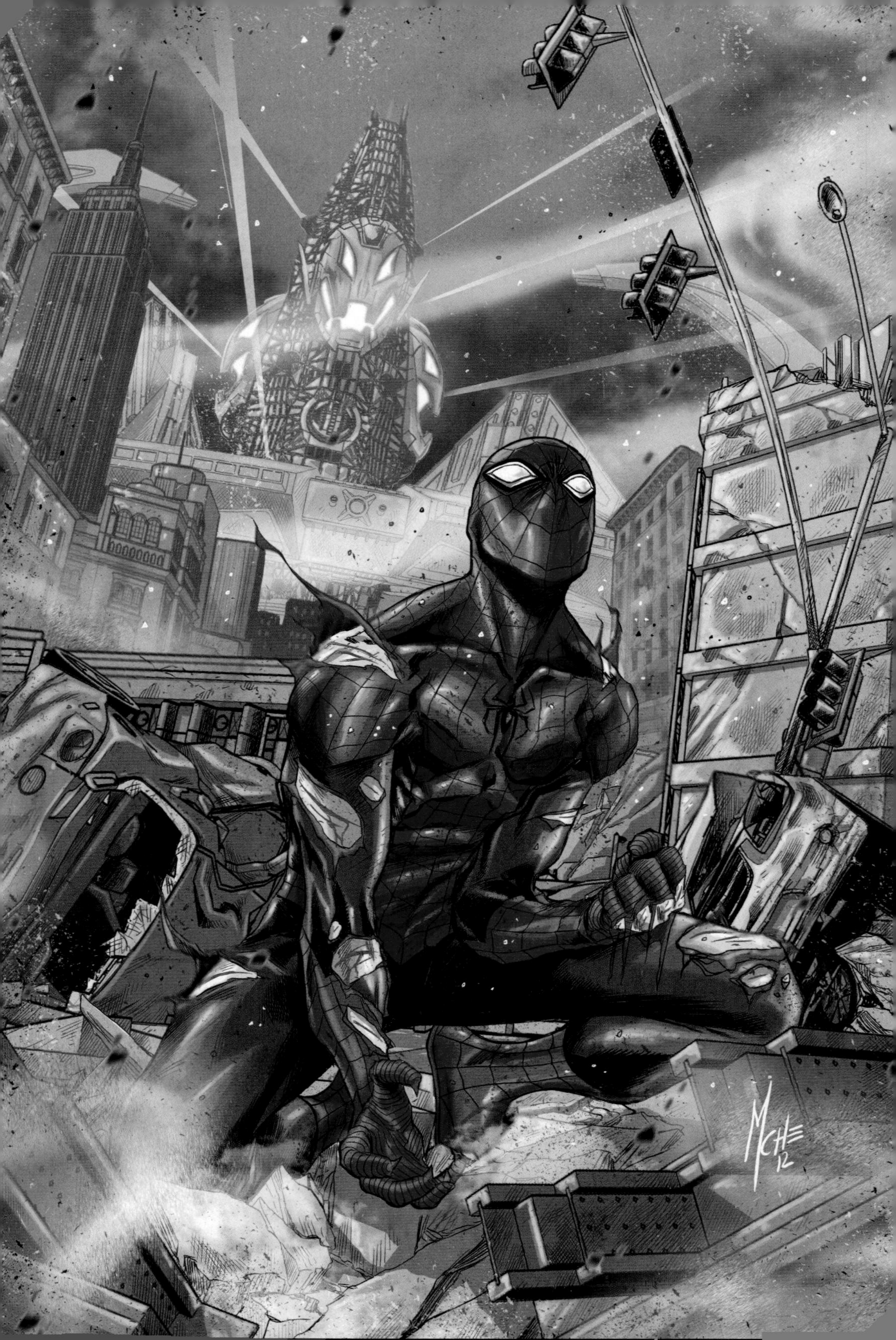

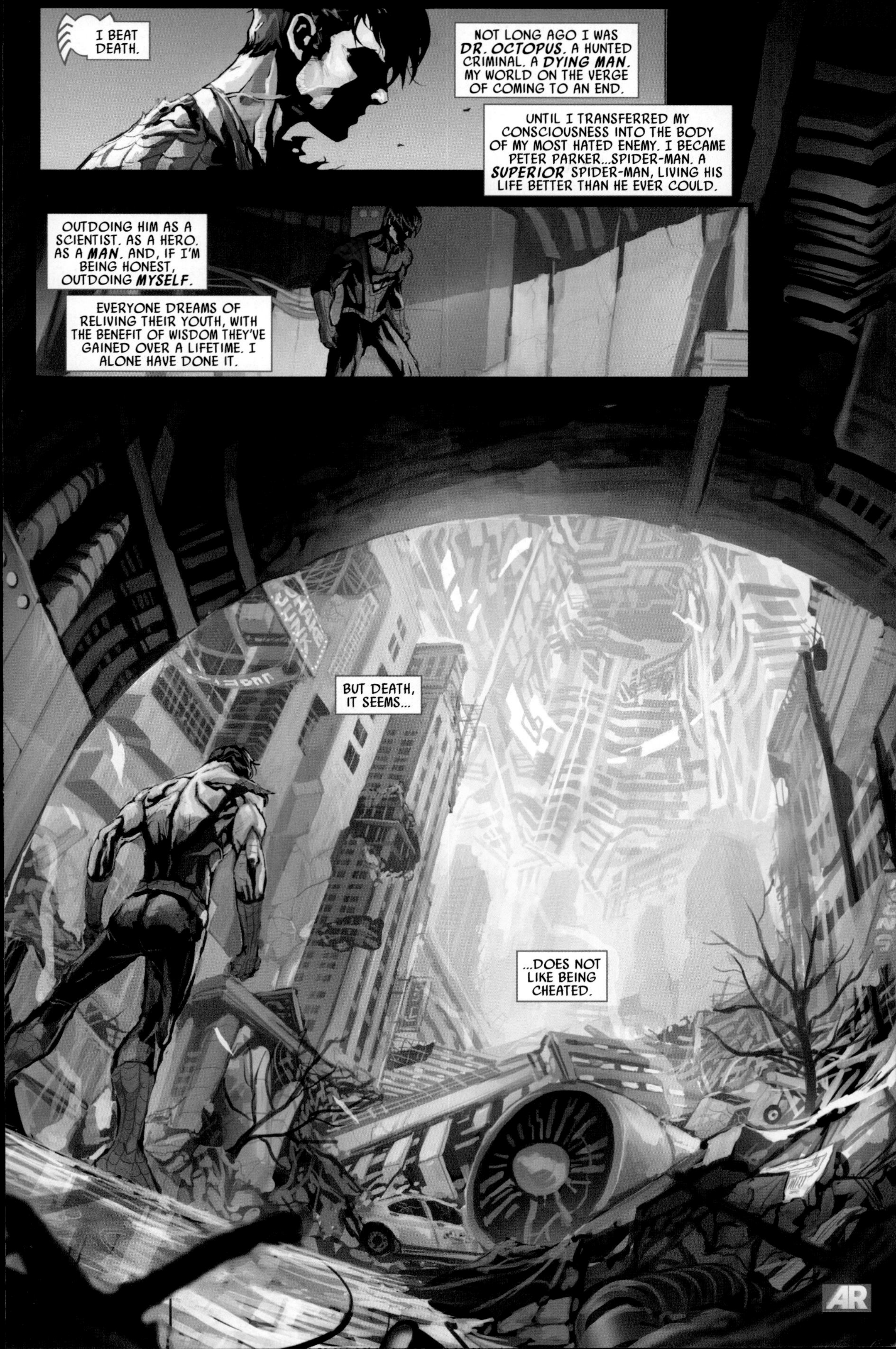
I BEAT DEATH.
NOT LONG AGO I WAS DR. OCTOPUS. A HUNTED CRIMINAL. A DYING MAN. MY WORLD ON THE VERGE OF COMING TO AN END.
UNTIL I TRANSFERRED MY CONSCIOUSNESS INTO THE BODY OF MY MOST HATED ENEMY. I BECAME PETER PARKER...SPIDER-MAN. A SUPERIOR SPIDER-MAN, LIVING HIS LIFE BETTER THAN HE EVER COULD.
OUTDOING HIM AS A SCIENTIST. AS A HERO. AS A MAN. AND, IF I'M BEING HONEST, OUTDOING MYSELF.
EVERYONE DREAMS OF RELIVING THEIR YOUTH, WITH THE BENEFIT OF WISDOM THEY'VE GAINED OVER A LIFETIME. I ALONE HAVE DONE IT.
BUT DEATH, IT SEEMS...
...DOES NOT LIKE BEING CHEATED.
AR

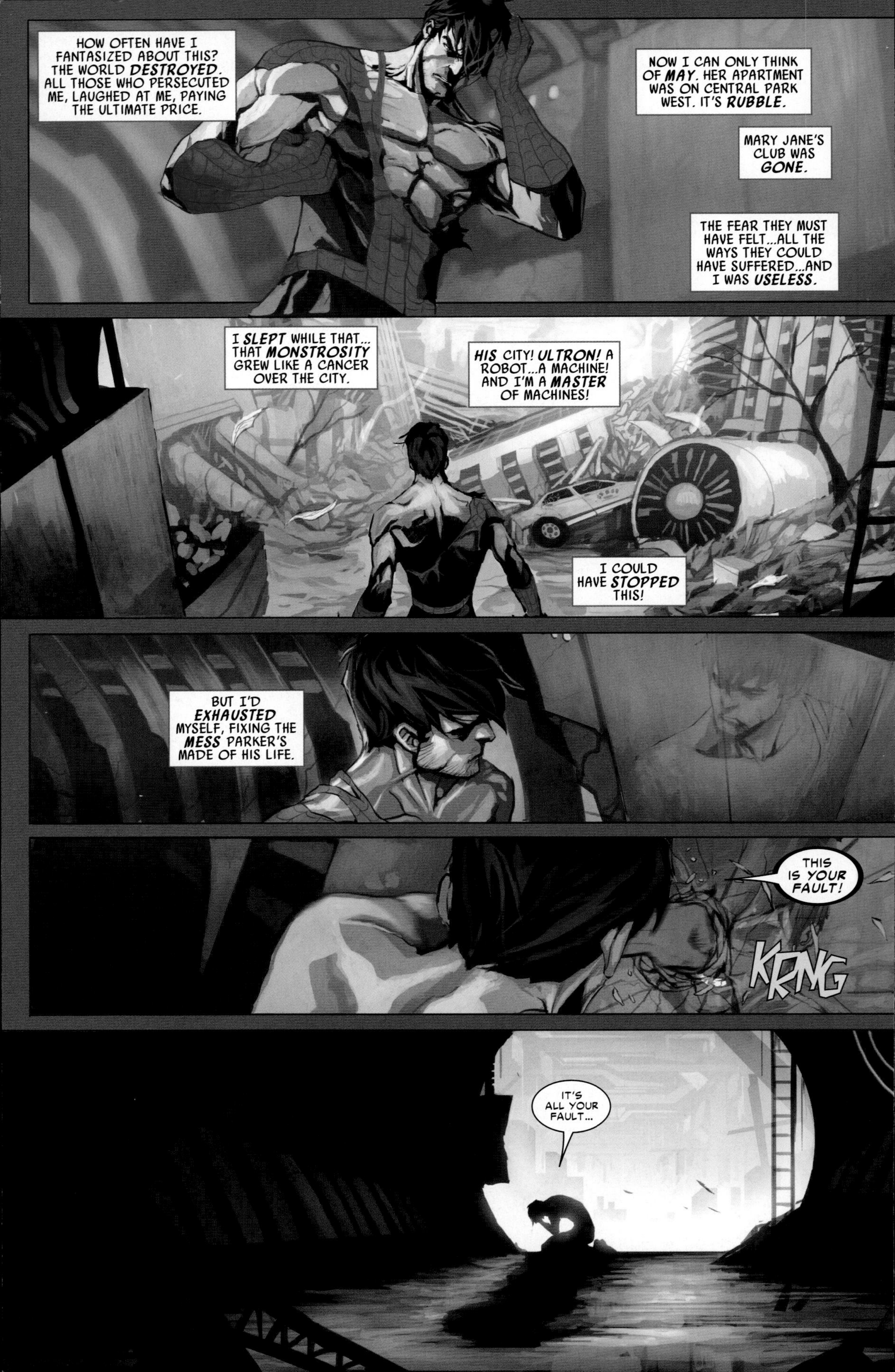

HOW OFTEN HAVE I FANTASIZED ABOUT THIS? THE WORLD DESTROYED. ALL THOSE WHO PERSECUTED ME, LAUGHED AT ME, PAYING THE ULTIMATE PRICE.
NOW I CAN ONLY THINK OF MAY. HER APARTMENT WAS ON CENTRAL PARK WEST. IT'S RUBBLE.
MARY JANE'S CLUB WAS GONE.
THE FEAR THEY MUST HAVE FELT...ALL THE WAYS THEY COULD HAVE SUFFERED...AND I WAS USELESS.
I SLEPT WHILE THAT... THAT MONSTROSITY GREW LIKE A CANCER OVER THE CITY.
HIS CITY! ULTRON! A ROBOT...A MACHINE! AND I'M A MASTER OF MACHINES!
I COULD HAVE STOPPED THIS!
BUT I'D EXHAUSTED MYSELF, FIXING THE MESS PARKER'S MADE OF HIS LIFE.
THIS IS YOUR FAULT!
KRNG
IT'S ALL YOUR FAULT...

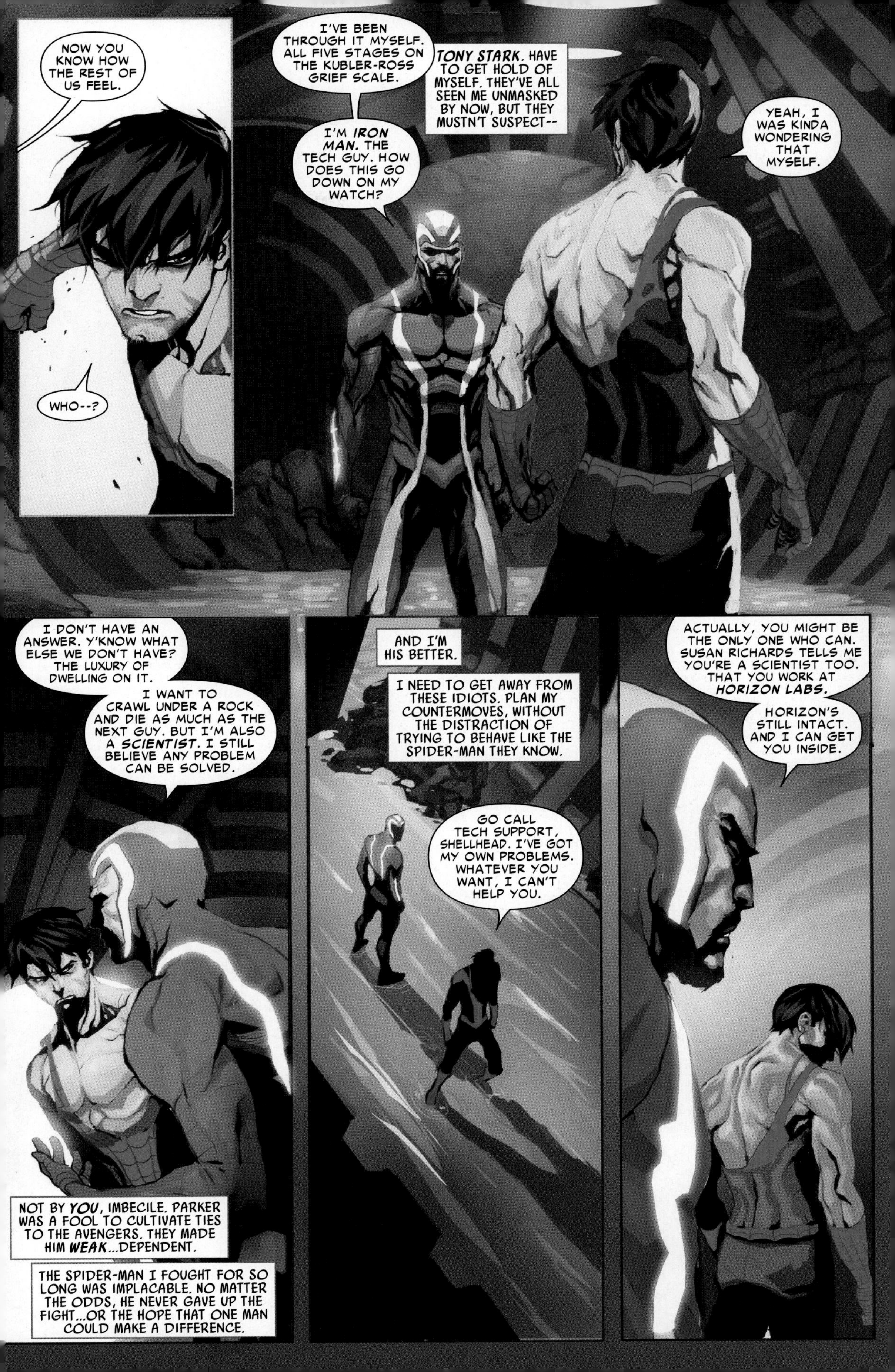
NOW YOU KNOW HOW THE REST OF US FEEL.
WHO--?
I'VE BEEN THROUGH IT MYSELF. ALL FIVE STAGES ON THE KUBLER-ROSS GRIEF SCALE.
I'M IRON MAN. THE TECH GUY. HOW DOES THIS GO DOWN ON MY WATCH?
TONY STARK. HAVE TO GET HOLD OF MYSELF. THEY'VE ALL SEEN ME UNMASKED BY NOW, BUT THEY MUSTN'T SUSPECT--
YEAH, I WAS KINDA WONDERING THAT MYSELF.
I DON'T HAVE AN ANSWER. Y'KNOW WHAT ELSE WE DON'T HAVE? THE LUXURY OF DWELLING ON IT.
I WANT TO CRAWL UNDER A ROCK AND DIE AS MUCH AS THE NEXT GUY. BUT I'M ALSO A SCIENTIST. I STILL BELIEVE ANY PROBLEM CAN BE SOLVED.
NOT BY YOU, IMBECILE. PARKER WAS A FOOL TO CULTIVATE TIES TO THE AVENGERS. THEY MADE HIM WEAK...DEPENDENT.
THE SPIDER-MAN I FOUGHT FOR SO LONG WAS IMPLACABLE. NO MATTER THE ODDS, HE NEVER GAVE UP THE FIGHT...OR THE HOPE THAT ONE MAN COULD MAKE A DIFFERENCE.
AND I'M HIS BETTER.
I NEED TO GET AWAY FROM THESE IDIOTS. PLAN MY COUNTERMOVES, WITHOUT THE DISTRACTION OF TRYING TO BEHAVE LIKE THE SPIDER-MAN THEY KNOW.
GO CALL TECH SUPPORT, SHELLHEAD. I'VE GOT MY OWN PROBLEMS. WHATEVER YOU WANT, I CAN'T HELP YOU.
ACTUALLY, YOU MIGHT BE THE ONLY ONE WHO CAN. SUSAN RICHARDS TELLS ME YOU'RE A SCIENTIST TOO. THAT YOU WORK AT HORIZON LABS.
HORIZON'S STILL INTACT. AND I CAN GET YOU INSIDE.

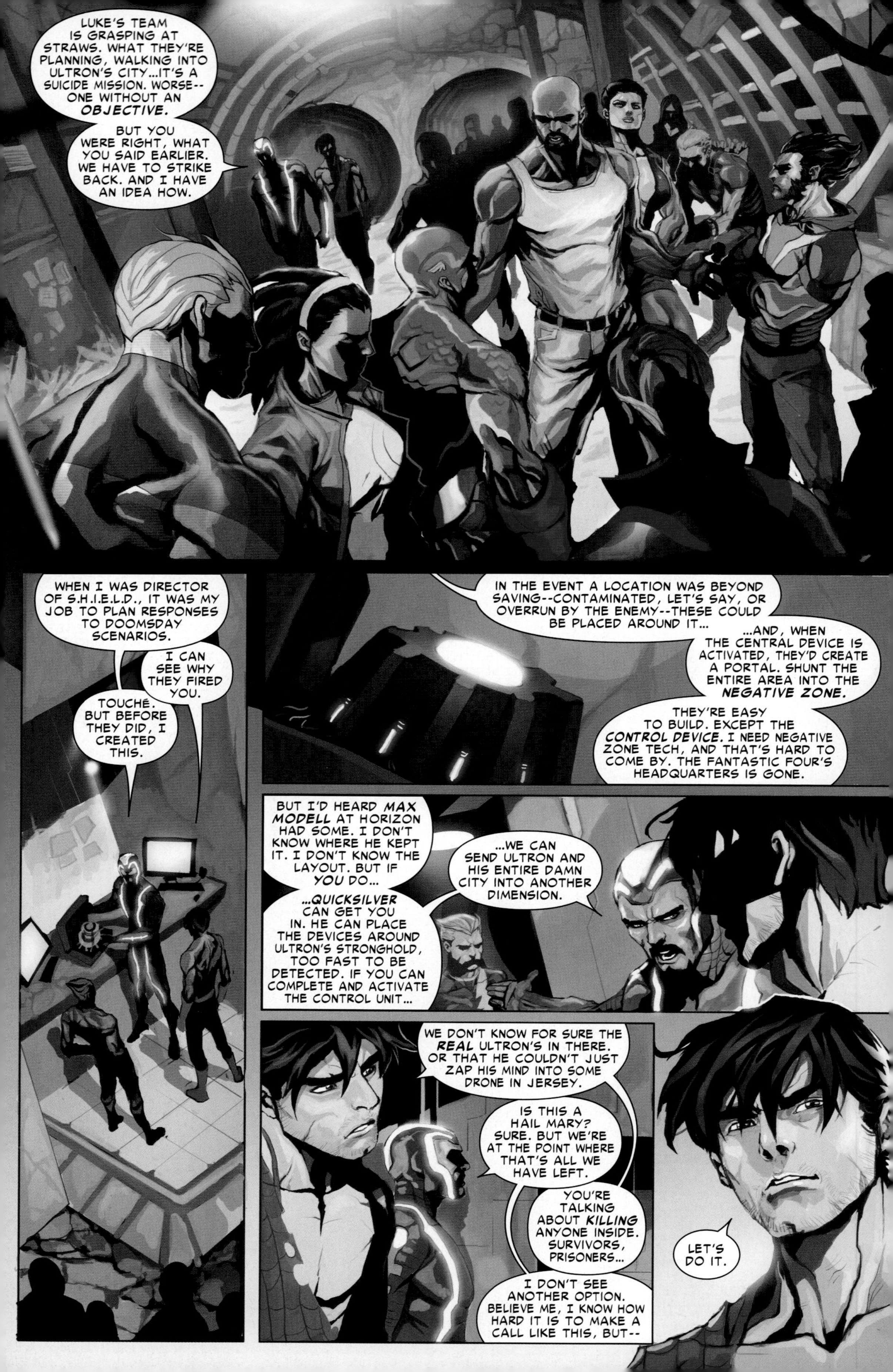
LUKE'S TEAM IS GRASPING AT STRAWS. WHAT THEY'RE PLANNING, WALKING INTO ULTRON'S CITY...IT'S A SUICIDE MISSION. WORSE--ONE WITHOUT AN OBJECTIVE.
BUT YOU WERE RIGHT, WHAT YOU SAID EARLIER. WE HAVE TO STRIKE BACK. AND I HAVE AN IDEA HOW.
WHEN I WAS DIRECTOR OF S.H.I.E.L.D., IT WAS MY JOB TO PLAN RESPONSES TO DOOMSDAY SCENARIOS.
I CAN SEE WHY THEY FIRED YOU.
TOUCHÉ. BUT BEFORE THEY DID, I CREATED THIS.
IN THE EVENT A LOCATION WAS BEYOND SAVING--CONTAMINATED, LET'S SAY, OR OVERRUN BY THE ENEMY--THESE COULD BE PLACED AROUND IT...
...AND, WHEN THE CENTRAL DEVICE IS ACTIVATED, THEY'D CREATE A PORTAL. SHUNT THE ENTIRE AREA INTO THE NEGATIVE ZONE.
THEY'RE EASY TO BUILD. EXCEPT THE CONTROL DEVICE. I NEED NEGATIVE ZONE TECH, AND THAT'S HARD TO COME BY. THE FANTASTIC FOUR'S HEADQUARTERS IS GONE.
BUT I'D HEARD MAX MODELL AT HORIZON HAD SOME. I DON'T KNOW WHERE HE KEPT IT. I DON'T KNOW THE LAYOUT. BUT IF YOU DO...
...QUICKSILVER CAN GET YOU IN. HE CAN PLACE THE DEVICES AROUND ULTRON'S STRONGHOLD, TOO FAST TO BE DETECTED. IF YOU CAN COMPLETE AND ACTIVATE THE CONTROL UNIT...
...WE CAN SEND ULTRON AND HIS ENTIRE DAMN CITY INTO ANOTHER DIMENSION.
WE DON'T KNOW FOR SURE THE REAL ULTRON'S IN THERE. OR THAT HE COULDN'T JUST ZAP HIS MIND INTO SOME DRONE IN JERSEY.
IS THIS A HAIL MARY? SURE. BUT WE'RE AT THE POINT WHERE THAT'S ALL WE HAVE LEFT.
YOU'RE TALKING ABOUT KILLING ANYONE INSIDE. SURVIVORS, PRISONERS...
I DON'T SEE ANOTHER OPTION. BELIEVE ME, I KNOW HOW HARD IT IS TO MAKE A CALL LIKE THIS, BUT--
LET'S DO IT.

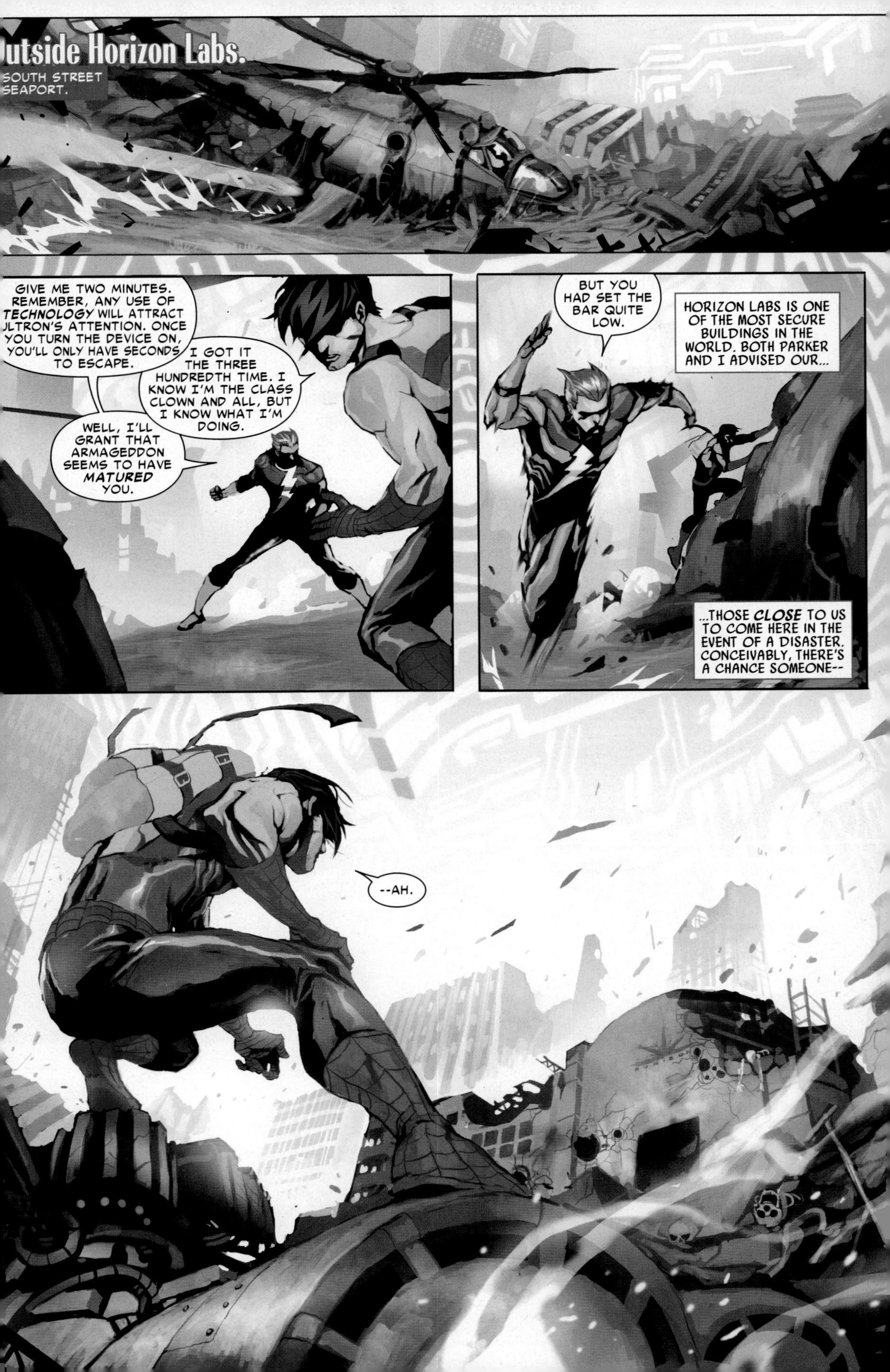
Outside Horizon Labs.
SOUTH STREET SEAPORT.
GIVE ME TWO MINUTES. REMEMBER, ANY USE OF TECHNOLOGY WILL ATTRACT ULTRON'S ATTENTION. ONCE YOU TURN THE DEVICE ON, YOU'LL ONLY HAVE SECONDS TO ESCAPE.
I GOT IT THE THREE HUNDREDTH TIME. I KNOW I'M THE CLASS CLOWN AND ALL, BUT I KNOW WHAT I'M DOING.
WELL, I'LL GRANT THAT ARMAGEDDON SEEMS TO HAVE MATURED YOU.
BUT YOU HAD SET THE BAR QUITE LOW.
HORIZON LABS IS ONE OF THE MOST SECURE BUILDINGS IN THE WORLD. BOTH PARKER AND I ADVISED OUR...
...THOSE CLOSE TO US TO COME HERE IN THE EVENT OF A DISASTER. CONCEIVABLY, THERE'S A CHANCE SOMEONE--
--AH.

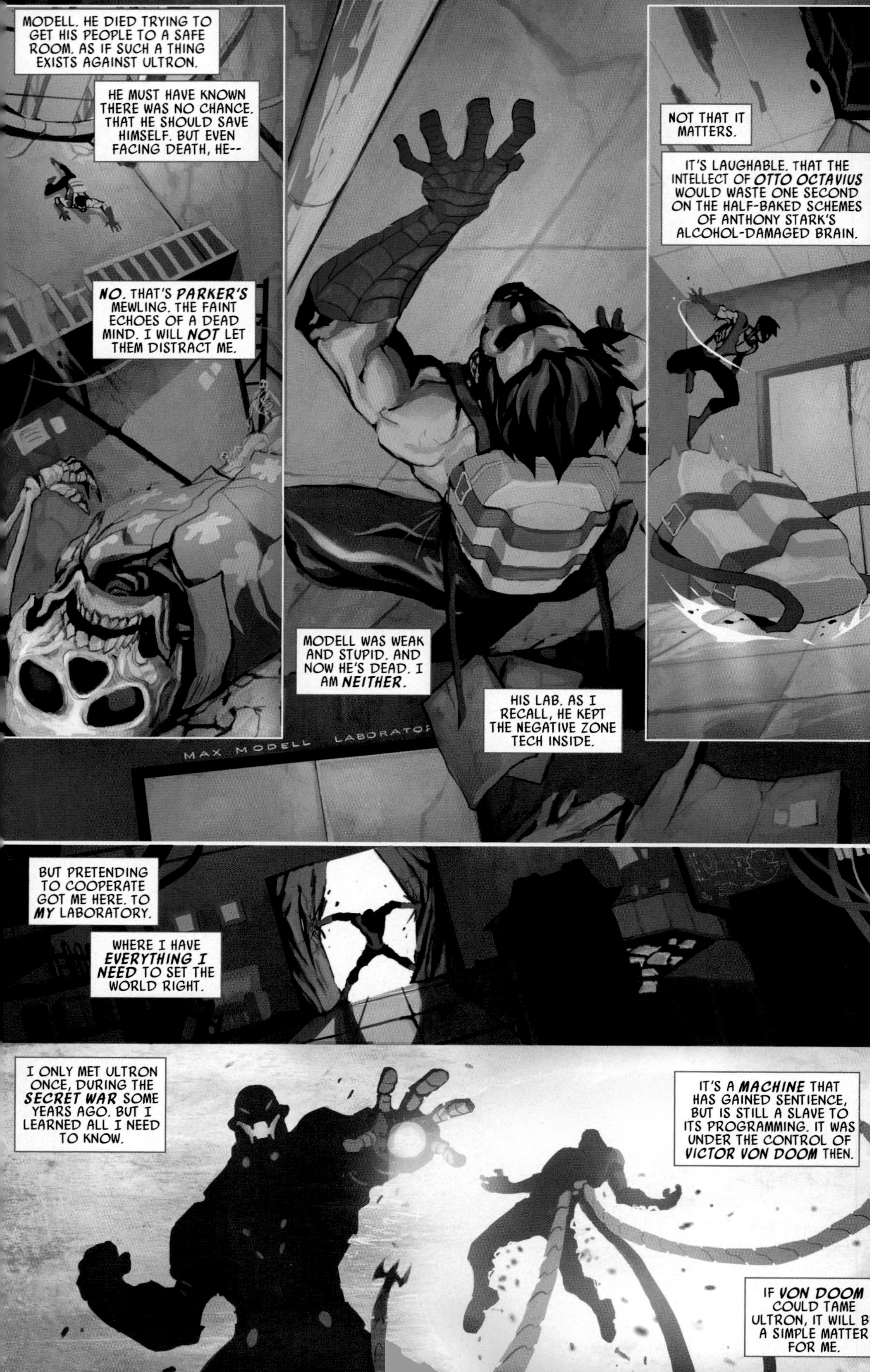
MODELL. HE DIED TRYING TO GET HIS PEOPLE TO A SAFE ROOM. AS IF SUCH A THING EXISTS AGAINST ULTRON.
HE MUST HAVE KNOWN THERE WAS NO CHANCE. THAT HE SHOULD SAVE HIMSELF. BUT EVEN FACING DEATH, HE--
NO. THAT'S PARKER'S MEWLING. THE FAINT ECHOES OF A DEAD MIND. I WILL NOT LET THEM DISTRACT ME.
MODELL WAS WEAK AND STUPID. AND NOW HE'S DEAD. I AM NEITHER.
NOT THAT IT MATTERS.
IT'S LAUGHABLE. THAT THE INTELLECT OF OTTO OCTAVIUS WOULD WASTE ONE SECOND ON THE HALF-BAKED SCHEMES OF ANTHONY STARK'S ALCOHOL-DAMAGED BRAIN.
MAX MODELL LABORATOR
HIS LAB. AS I RECALL, HE KEPT THE NEGATIVE ZONE TECH INSIDE.
BUT PRETENDING TO COOPERATE GOT ME HERE. TO MY LABORATORY.
WHERE I HAVE EVERYTHING I NEED TO SET THE WORLD RIGHT.
I ONLY MET ULTRON ONCE, DURING THE SECRET WAR SOME YEARS AGO. BUT I LEARNED ALL I NEED TO KNOW.
IT'S A MACHINE THAT HAS GAINED SENTIENCE, BUT IS STILL A SLAVE TO ITS PROGRAMMING. IT WAS UNDER THE CONTROL OF VICTOR VON DOOM THEN.
IF VON DOOM COULD TAME ULTRON, IT WILL BE A SIMPLE MATTER FOR ME.

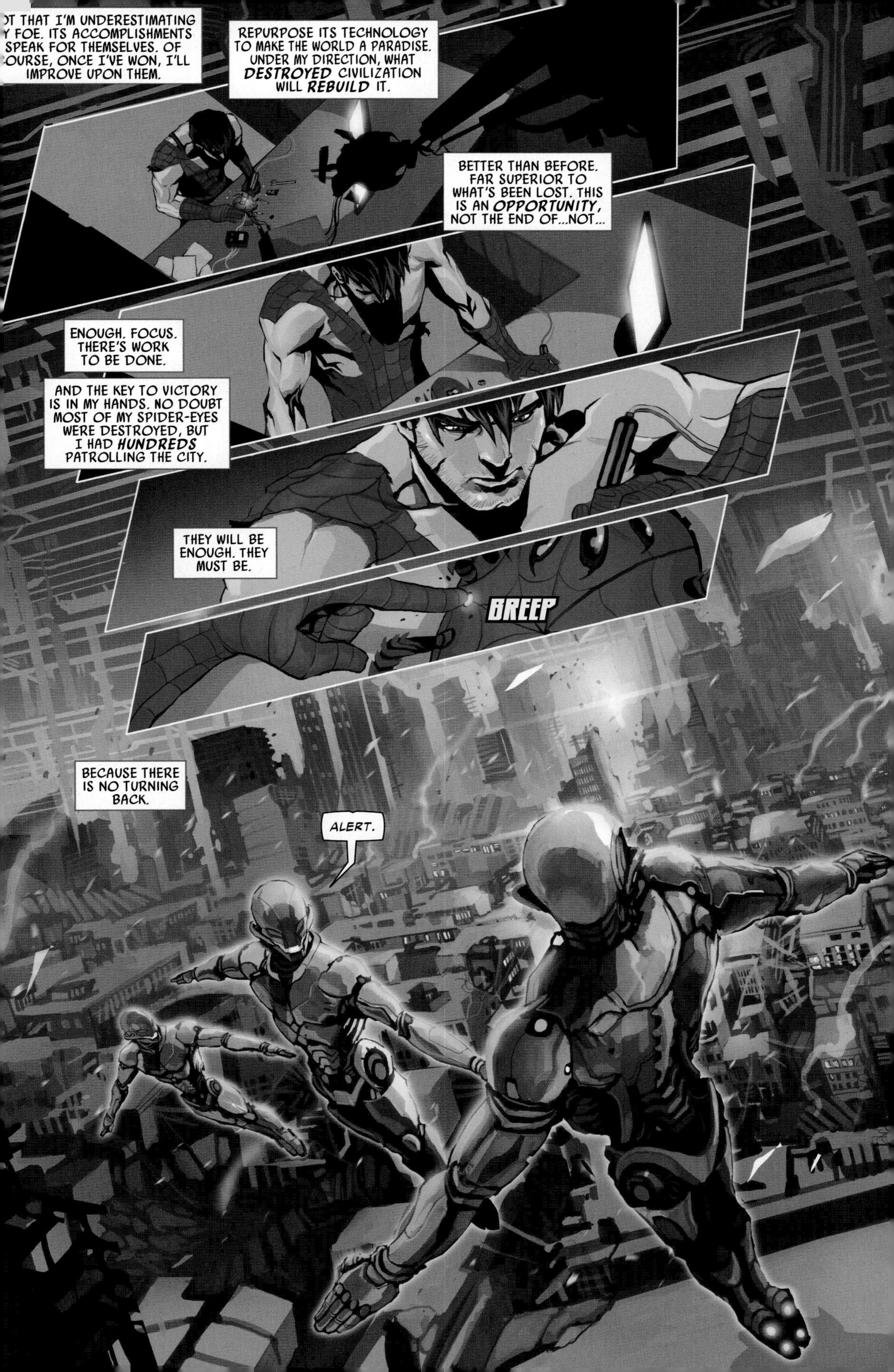
OT THAT I'M UNDERESTIMATING
Y FOE. ITS ACCOMPLISHMENTS
SPEAK FOR THEMSELVES. OF
COURSE, ONCE I'VE WON, I'LL
IMPROVE UPON THEM.
REPURPOSE ITS TECHNOLOGY TO MAKE THE WORLD A PARADISE. UNDER MY DIRECTION, WHAT DESTROYED CIVILIZATION WILL REBUILD IT.
BETTER THAN BEFORE. FAR SUPERIOR TO WHAT'S BEEN LOST. THIS IS AN OPPORTUNITY, NOT THE END OF...NOT...
ENOUGH. FOCUS. THERE'S WORK TO BE DONE.
AND THE KEY TO VICTORY IS IN MY HANDS. NO DOUBT MOST OF MY SPIDER-EYES WERE DESTROYED, BUT I HAD HUNDREDS PATROLLING THE CITY.
THEY WILL BE ENOUGH. THEY MUST BE.
BREEP
BECAUSE THERE IS NO TURNING BACK.
ALERT.

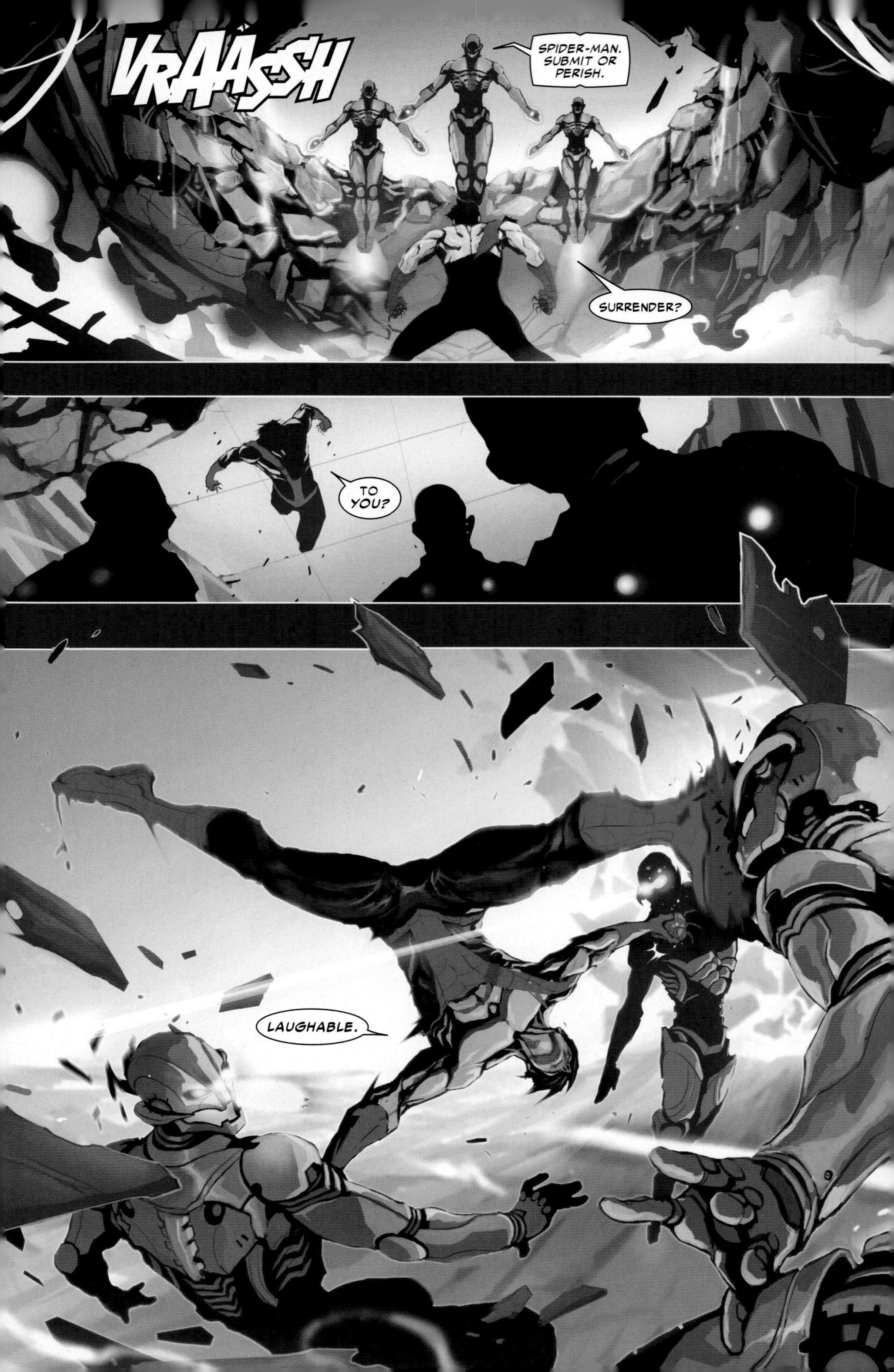
VRAASH
SPIDER-MAN. SUBMIT OR PERISH.
SURRENDER?
TO YOU?
LAUGHABLE.

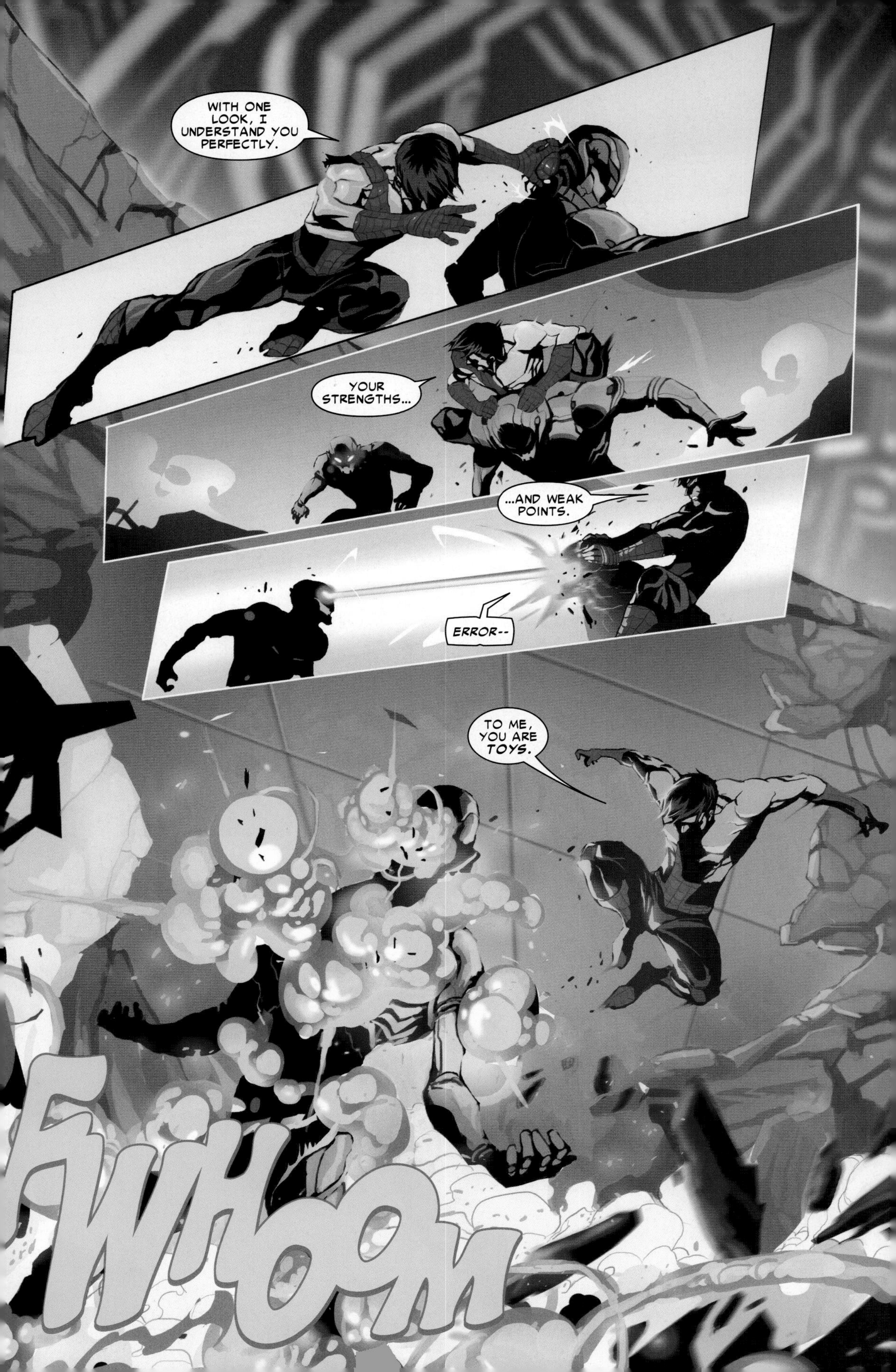
WITH ONE LOOK, I UNDERSTAND YOU PERFECTLY.
YOUR STRENGTHS...
...AND WEAK POINTS.
ERROR--
TO ME, YOU ARE TOYS.
FWHOOM

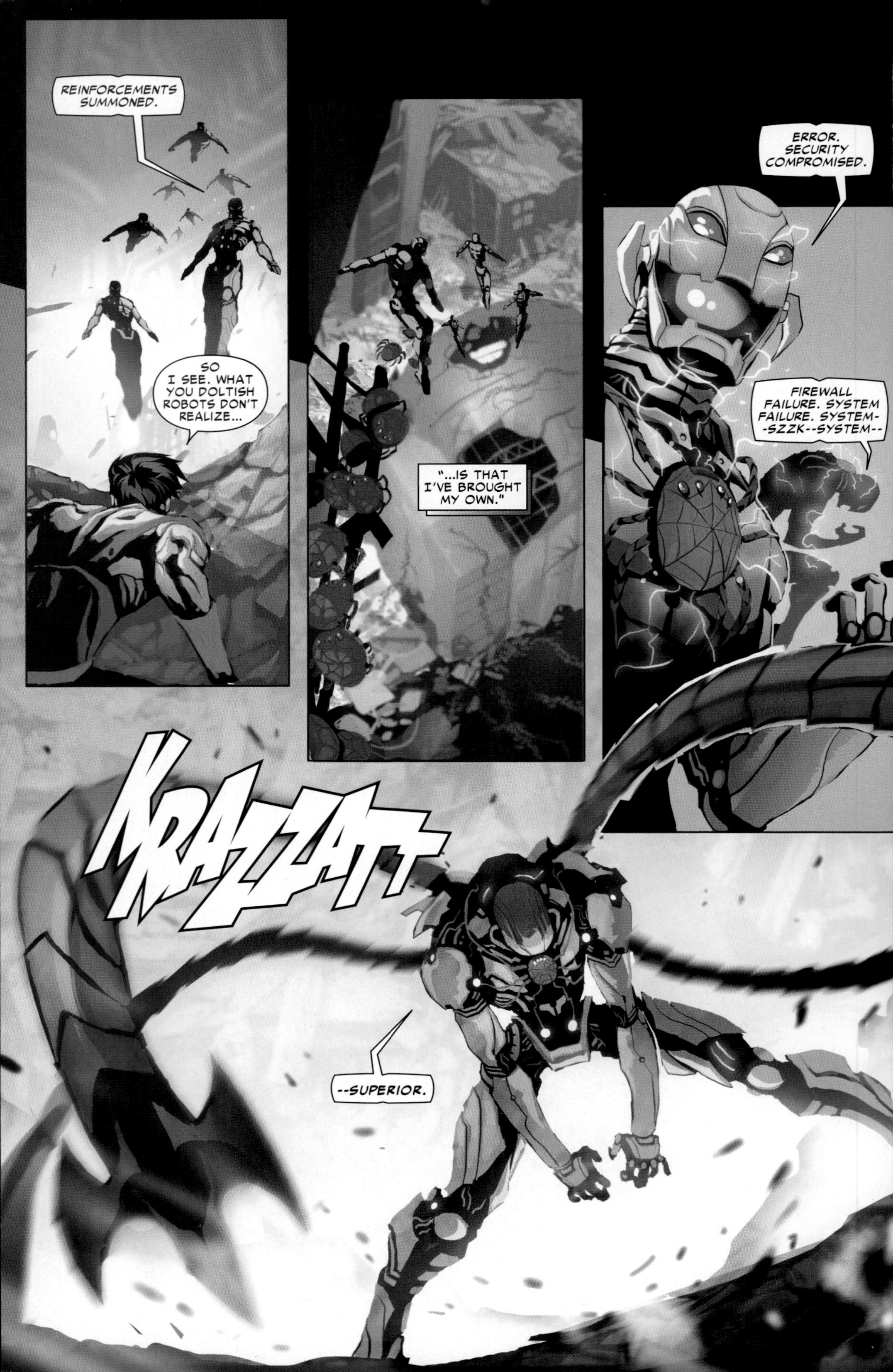
REINFORCEMENTS SUMMONED.
SO I SEE. WHAT YOU DOLTISH ROBOTS DON'T REALIZE...
"...IS THAT I'VE BROUGHT MY OWN."
ERROR. SECURITY COMPROMISED.
FIREWALL FAILURE. SYSTEM FAILURE. SYSTEM- -SZZK--SYSTEM--
KRAZZATT
--SUPERIOR.

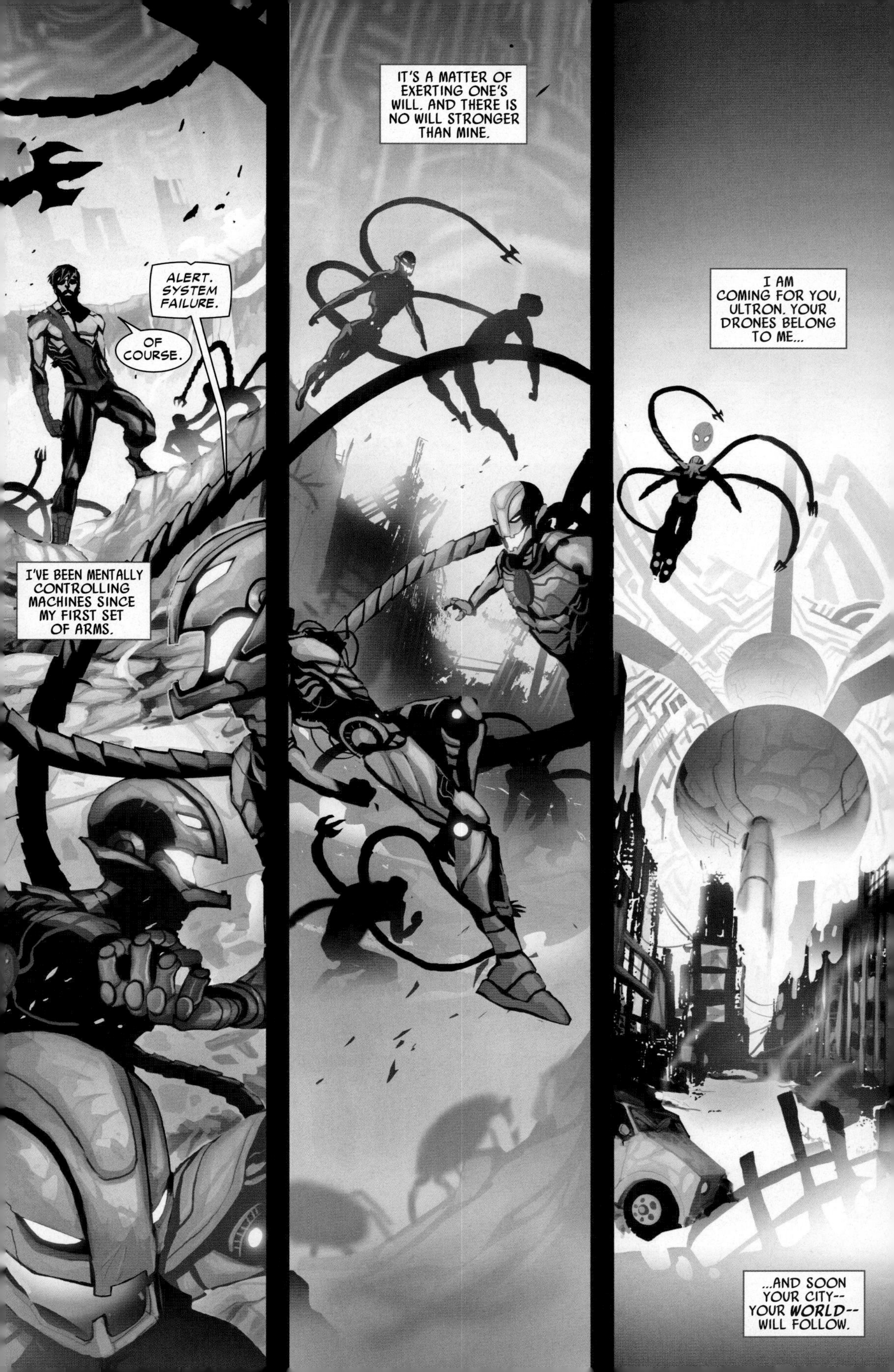
ALERT. SYSTEM FAILURE.
OF COURSE.
I'VE BEEN MENTALLY CONTROLLING MACHINES SINCE MY FIRST SET OF ARMS.
IT'S A MATTER OF EXERTING ONE'S WILL. AND THERE IS NO WILL STRONGER THAN MINE.
I AM COMING FOR YOU, ULTRON. YOUR DRONES BELONG TO ME...
...AND SOON YOUR CITY-- YOUR WORLD-- WILL FOLLOW.

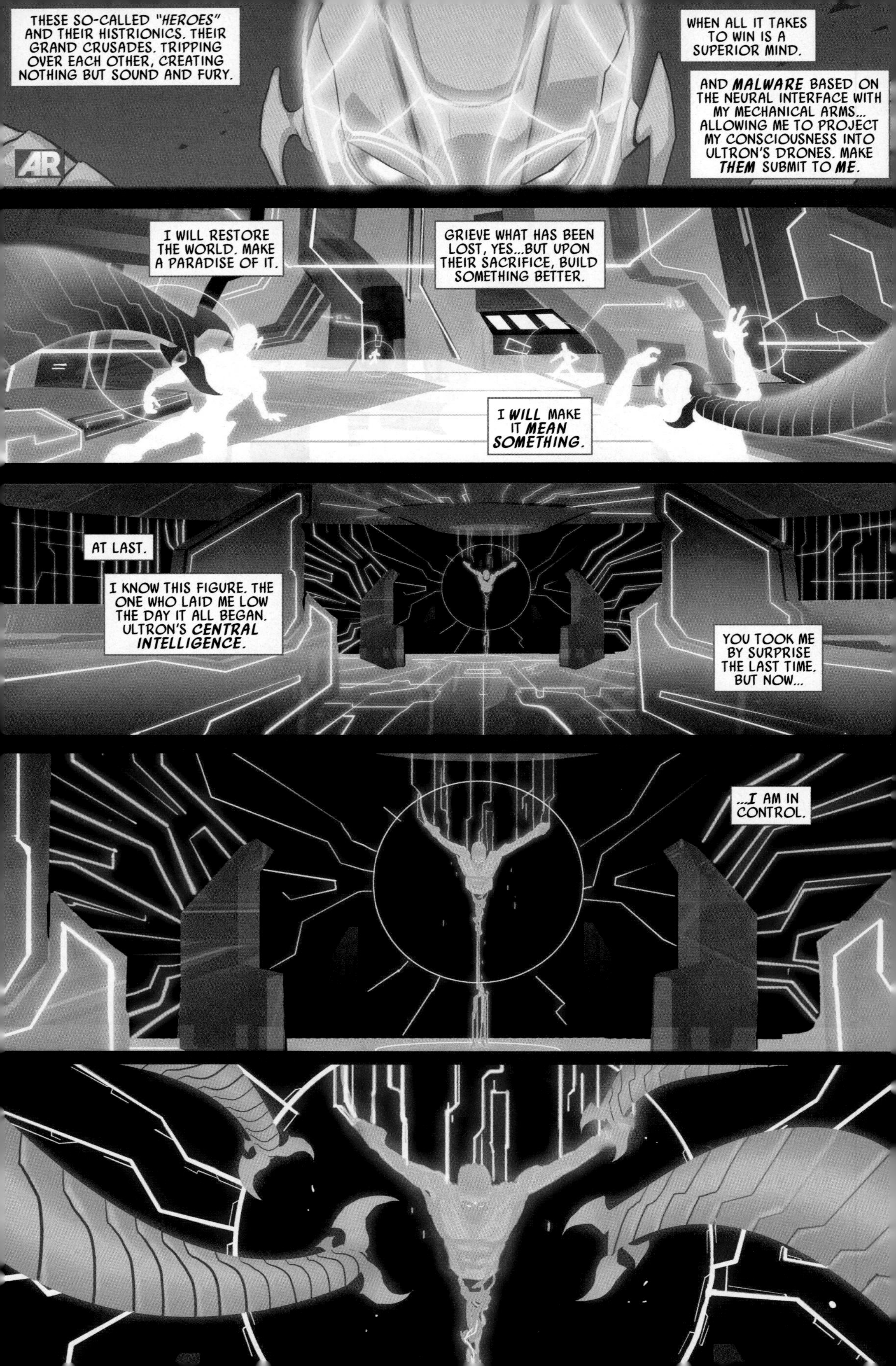
THESE SO-CALLED "HEROES" AND THEIR HISTRIONICS. THEIR GRAND CRUSADES. TRIPPING OVER EACH OTHER, CREATING NOTHING BUT SOUND AND FURY.
WHEN ALL IT TAKES TO WIN IS A SUPERIOR MIND.
AND MALWARE BASED ON THE NEURAL INTERFACE WITH MY MECHANICAL ARMS... ALLOWING ME TO PROJECT MY CONSCIOUSNESS INTO ULTRON'S DRONES. MAKE THEM SUBMIT TO ME.
I WILL RESTORE THE WORLD. MAKE A PARADISE OF IT.
GRIEVE WHAT HAS BEEN LOST, YES...BUT UPON THEIR SACRIFICE, BUILD SOMETHING BETTER.
I WILL MAKE IT MEAN SOMETHING.
AT LAST.
I KNOW THIS FIGURE. THE ONE WHO LAID ME LOW THE DAY IT ALL BEGAN. ULTRON'S CENTRAL INTELLIGENCE.
YOU TOOK ME BY SURPRISE THE LAST TIME. BUT NOW...
...I AM IN CONTROL.

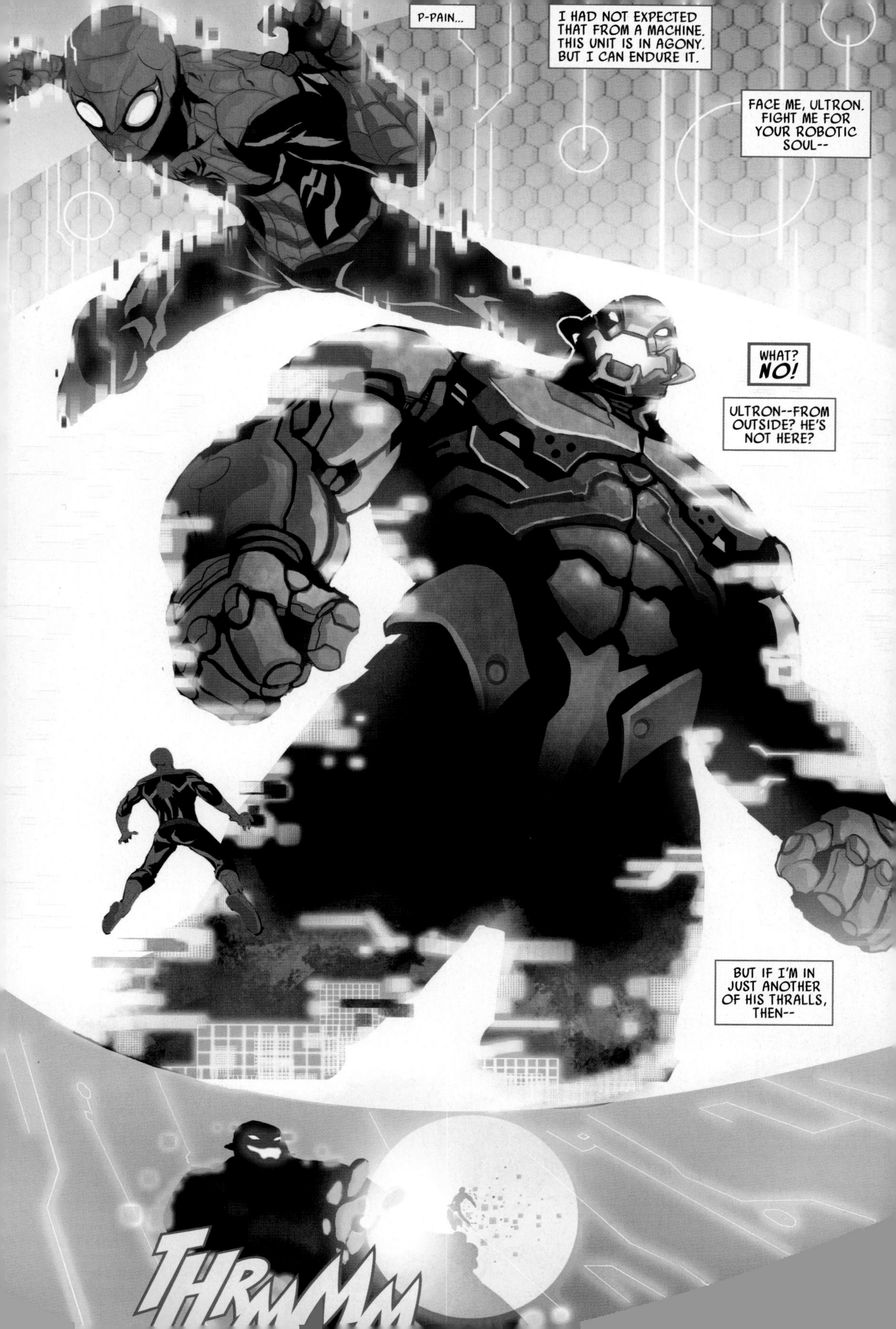
P-PAIN...
I HAD NOT EXPECTED THAT FROM A MACHINE. THIS UNIT IS IN AGONY. BUT I CAN ENDURE IT.
FACE ME, ULTRON. FIGHT ME FOR YOUR ROBOTIC SOUL--
WHAT? NO!
ULTRON--FROM OUTSIDE? HE'S NOT HERE?
BUT IF I'M IN JUST ANOTHER OF HIS THRALLS, THEN--
THRMMM

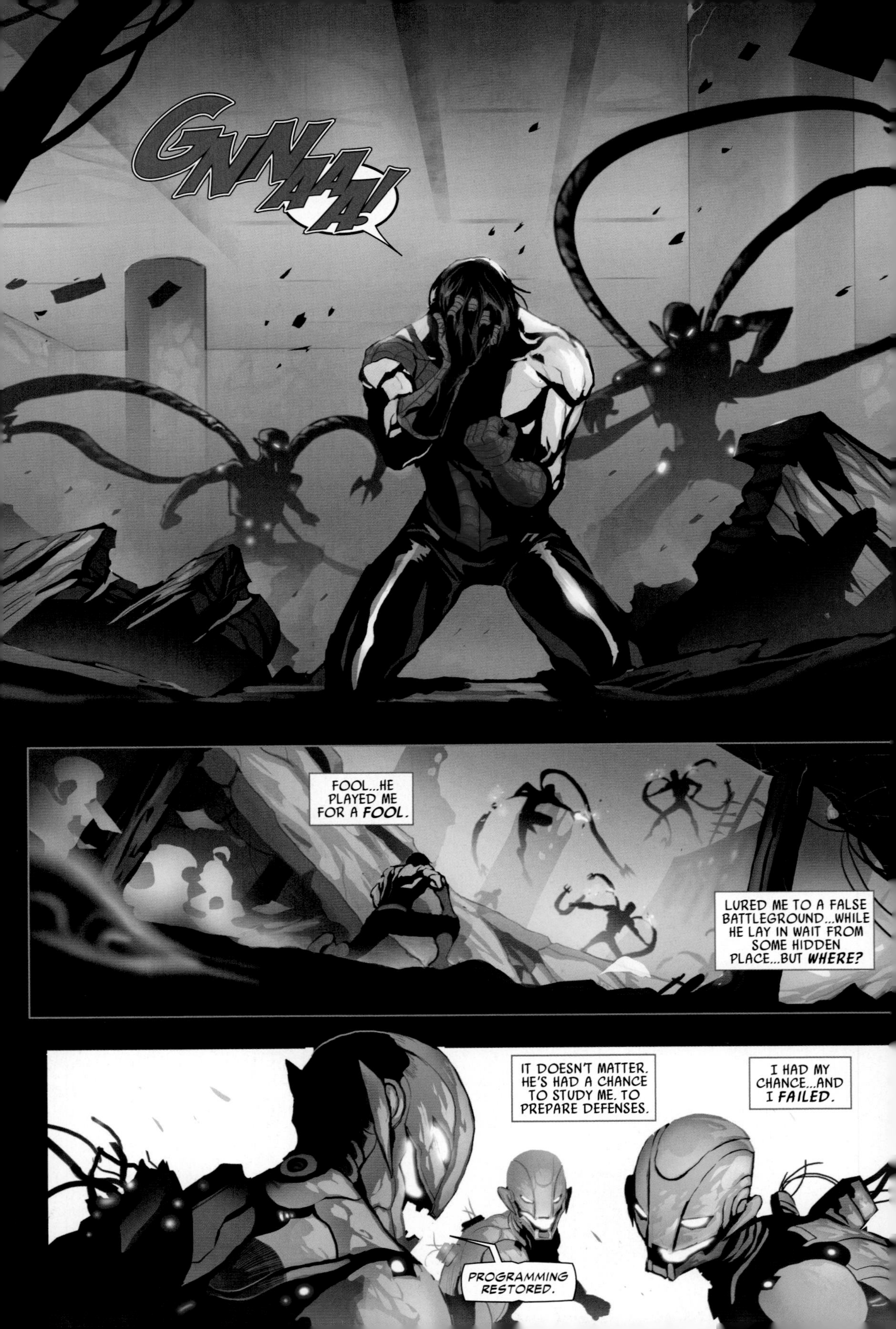
GNNAAA!
FOOL...HE PLAYED ME FOR A FOOL.
LURED ME TO A FALSE BATTLEGROUND...WHILE HE LAY IN WAIT FROM SOME HIDDEN PLACE...BUT WHERE?
IT DOESN'T MATTER. HE'S HAD A CHANCE TO STUDY ME. TO PREPARE DEFENSES.
I HAD MY CHANCE...AND I FAILED.
PROGRAMMING RESTORED.

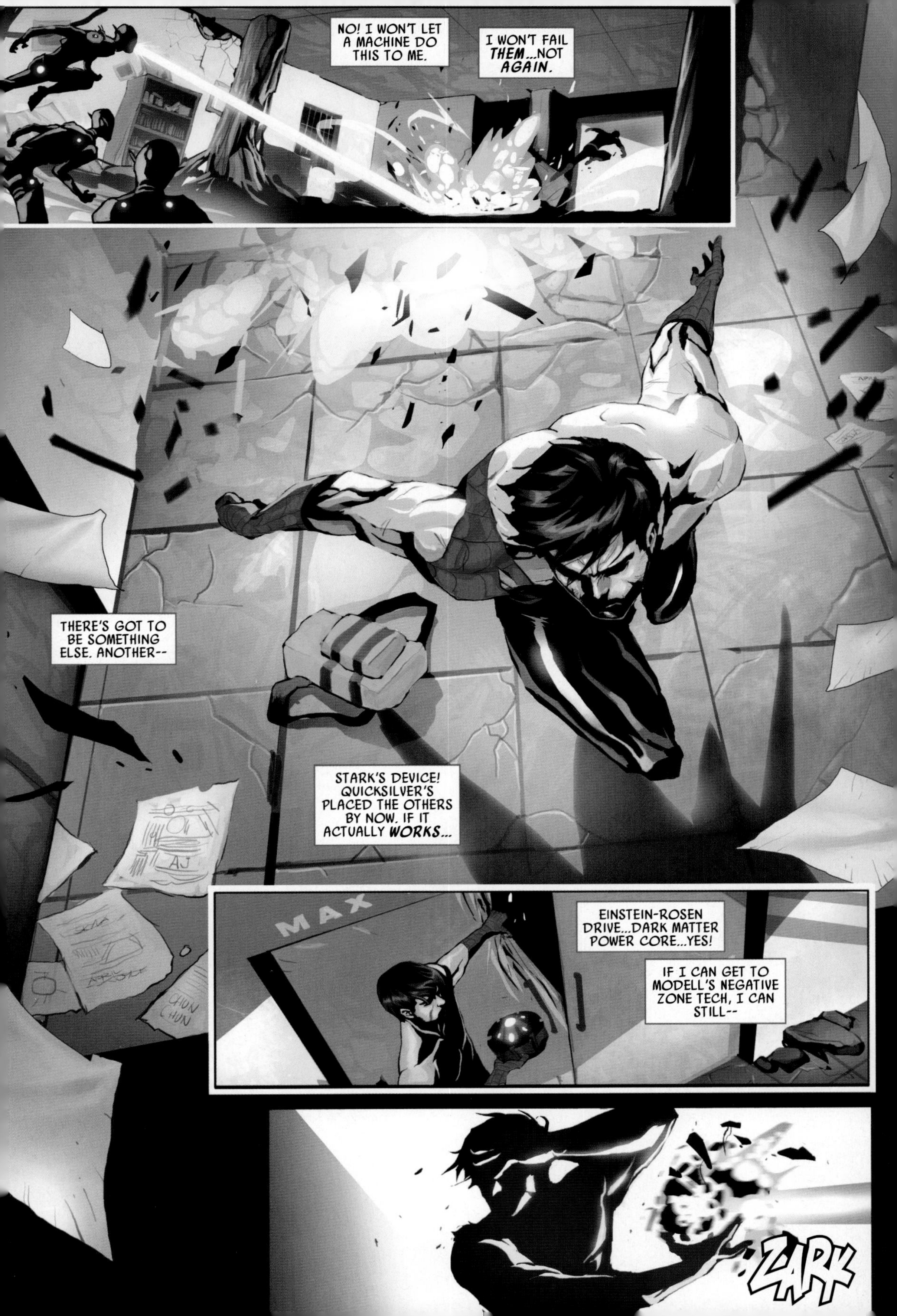
NO! I WON'T LET A MACHINE DO THIS TO ME.
I WON'T FAIL *THEM*...NOT *AGAIN*.
THERE'S GOT TO BE SOMETHING ELSE. ANOTHER--
STARK'S DEVICE! QUICKSILVER'S PLACED THE OTHERS BY NOW. IF IT ACTUALLY *WORKS*...
MAX
EINSTEIN-ROSEN DRIVE...DARK MATTER POWER CORE...YES!
IF I CAN GET TO MODELL'S NEGATIVE ZONE TECH, I CAN STILL--
ZARK

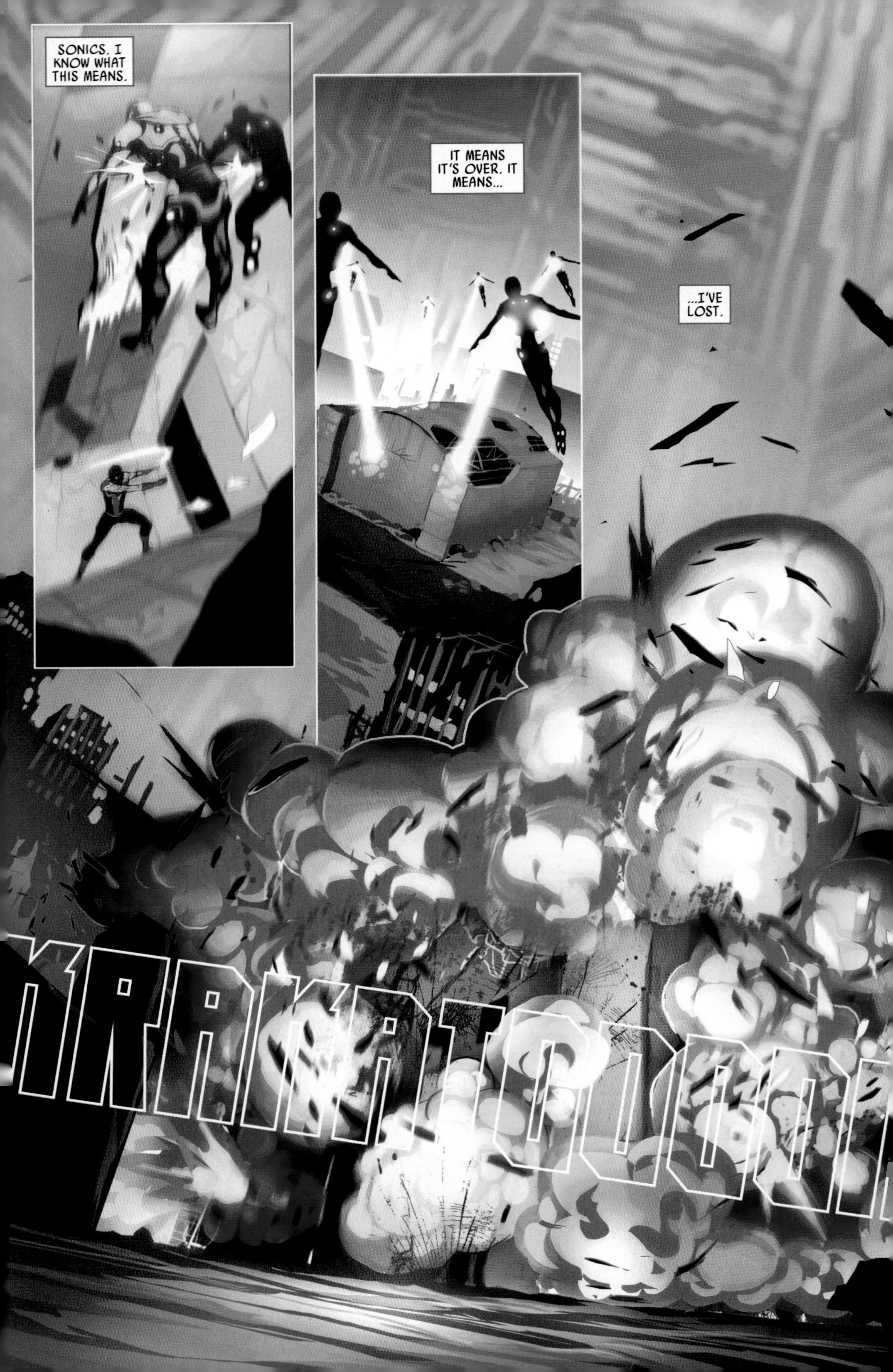
SONICS. I KNOW WHAT THIS MEANS.
IT MEANS IT'S OVER. IT MEANS...
...I'VE LOST.
KRAKATOOO

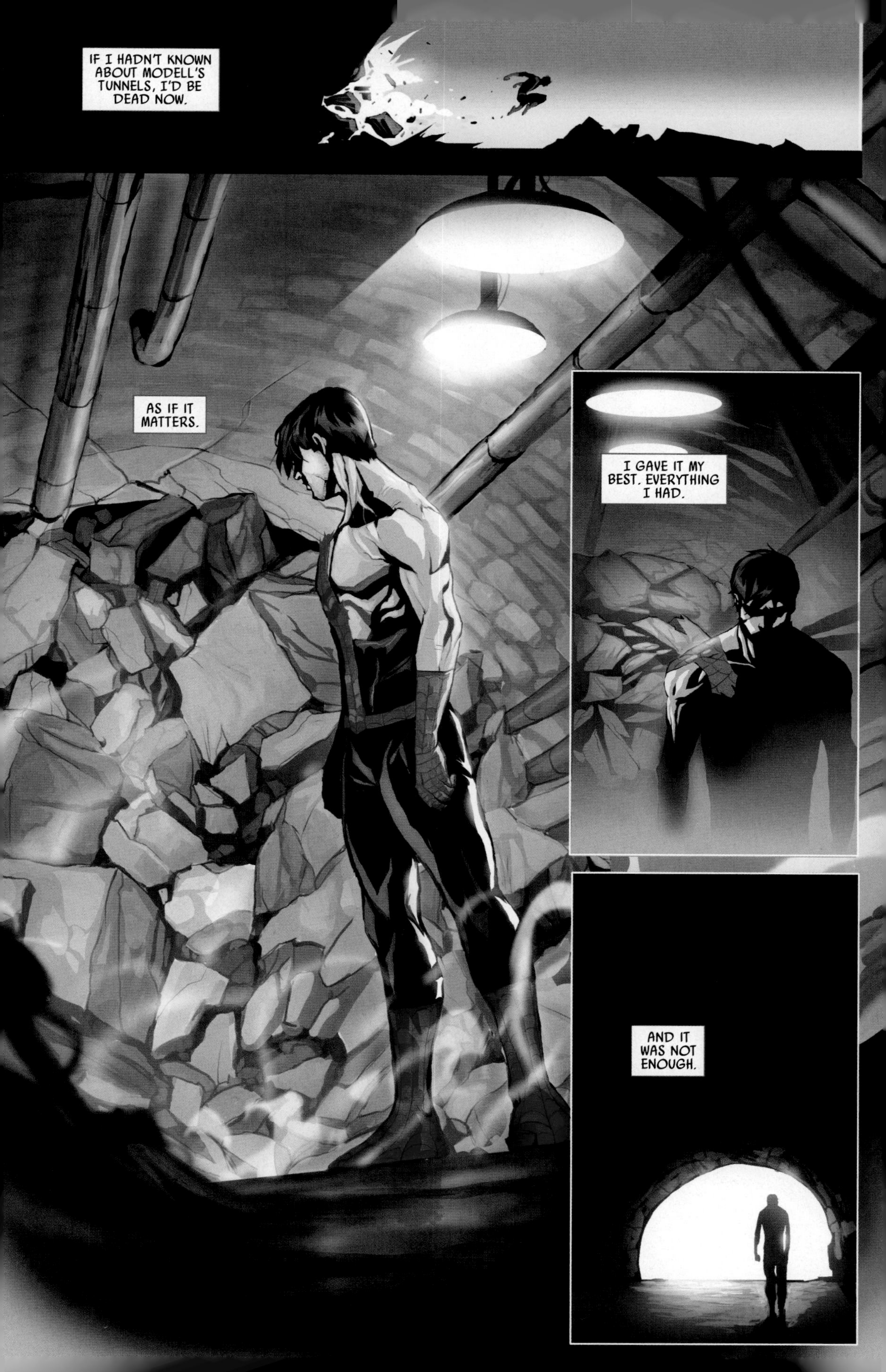
IF I HADN'T KNOWN ABOUT MODELL'S TUNNELS, I'D BE DEAD NOW.
AS IF IT MATTERS.
I GAVE IT MY BEST. EVERYTHING I HAD.
AND IT WAS NOT ENOUGH.

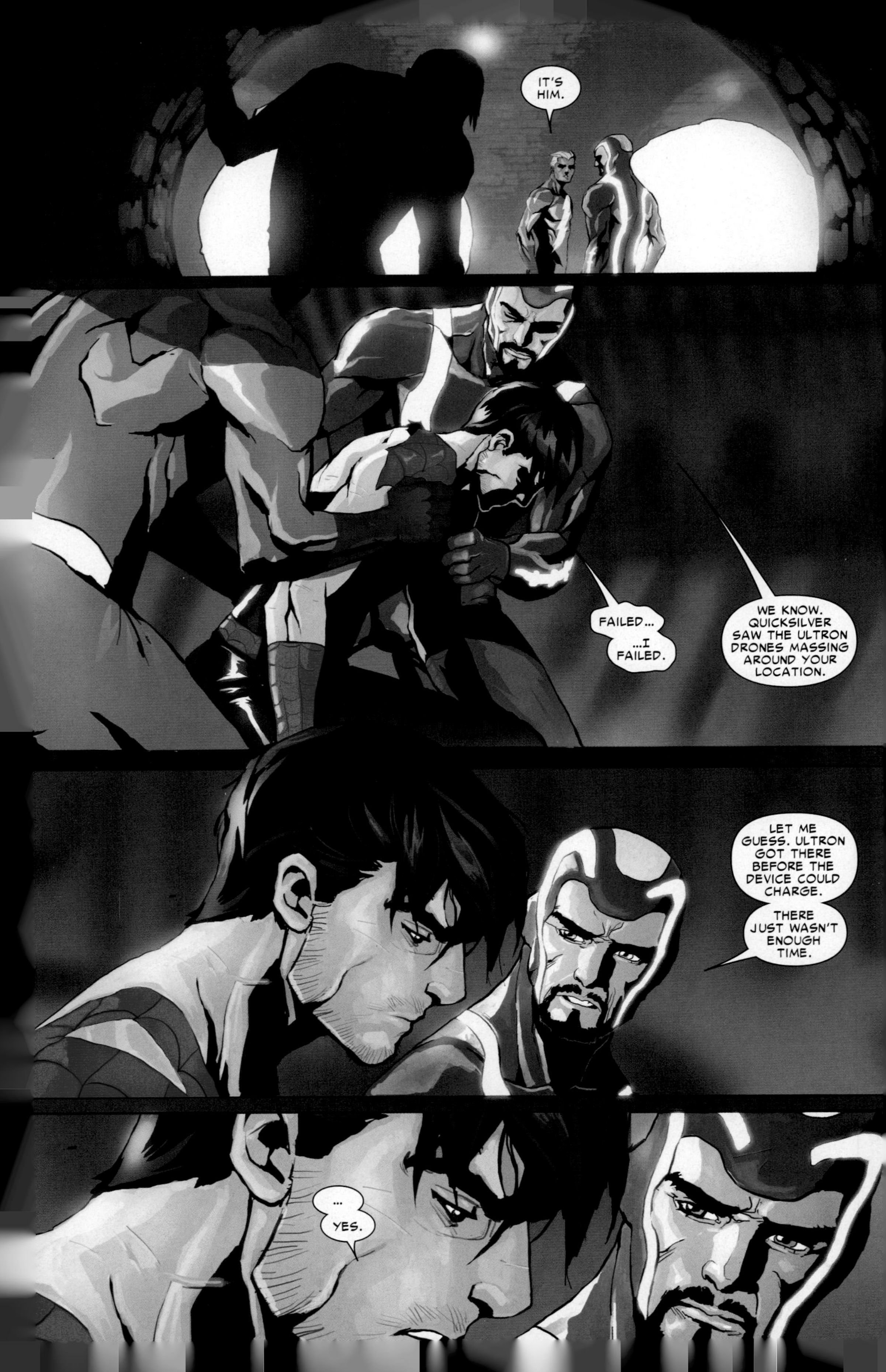
IT'S HIM.
FAILED... ...I FAILED.
WE KNOW. QUICKSILVER SAW THE ULTRON DRONES MASSING AROUND YOUR LOCATION.
LET ME GUESS. ULTRON GOT THERE BEFORE THE DEVICE COULD CHARGE.
THERE JUST WASN'T ENOUGH TIME.
... YES.

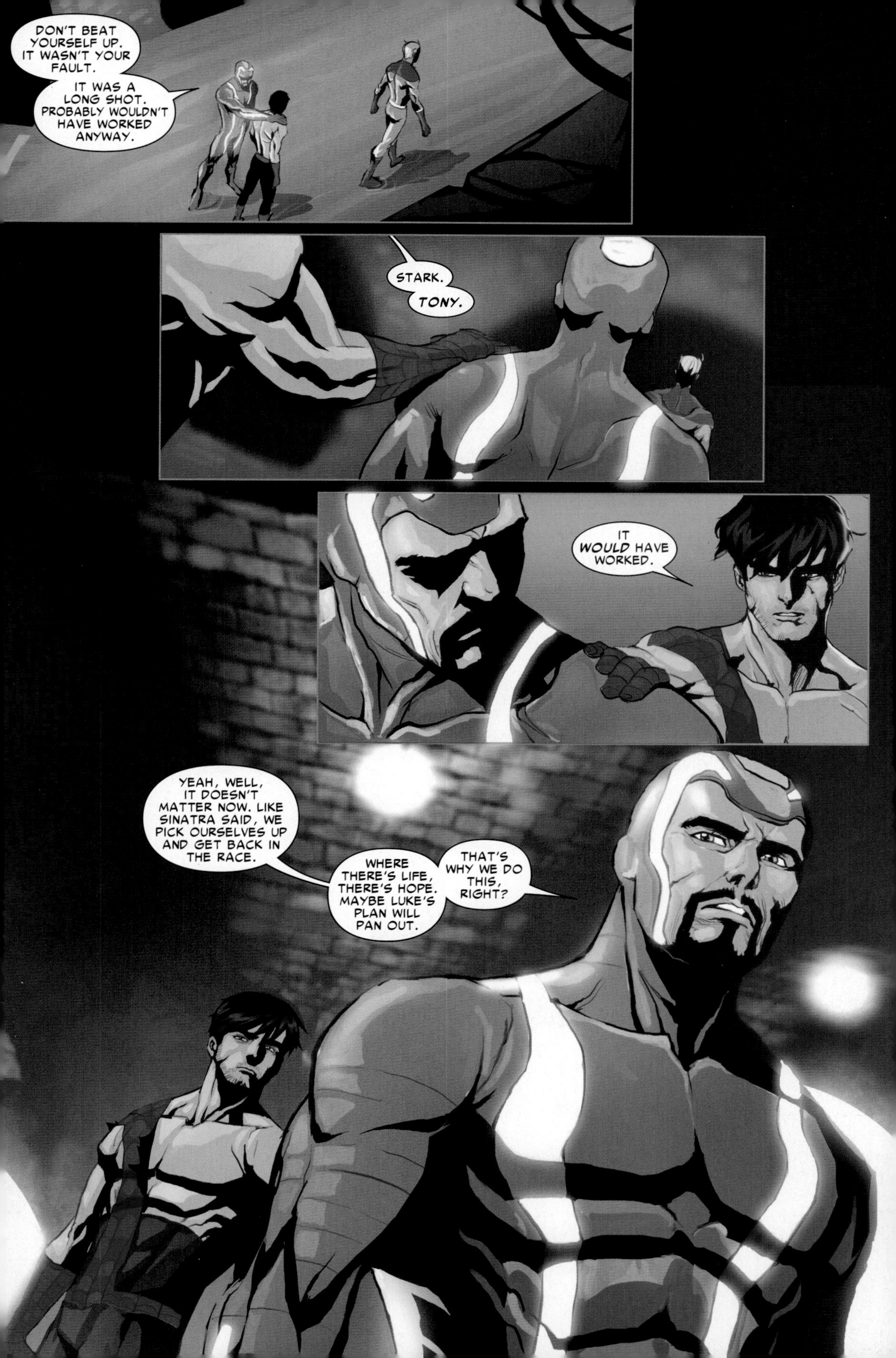

DON'T BEAT YOURSELF UP. IT WASN'T YOUR FAULT.
IT WAS A LONG SHOT. PROBABLY WOULDN'T HAVE WORKED ANYWAY.
STARK.
TONY.
IT *WOULD* HAVE WORKED.
YEAH, WELL, IT DOESN'T MATTER NOW. LIKE SINATRA SAID, WE PICK OURSELVES UP AND GET BACK IN THE RACE.
WHERE THERE'S LIFE, THERE'S HOPE. MAYBE LUKE'S PLAN WILL PAN OUT.
THAT'S WHY WE DO THIS, RIGHT?

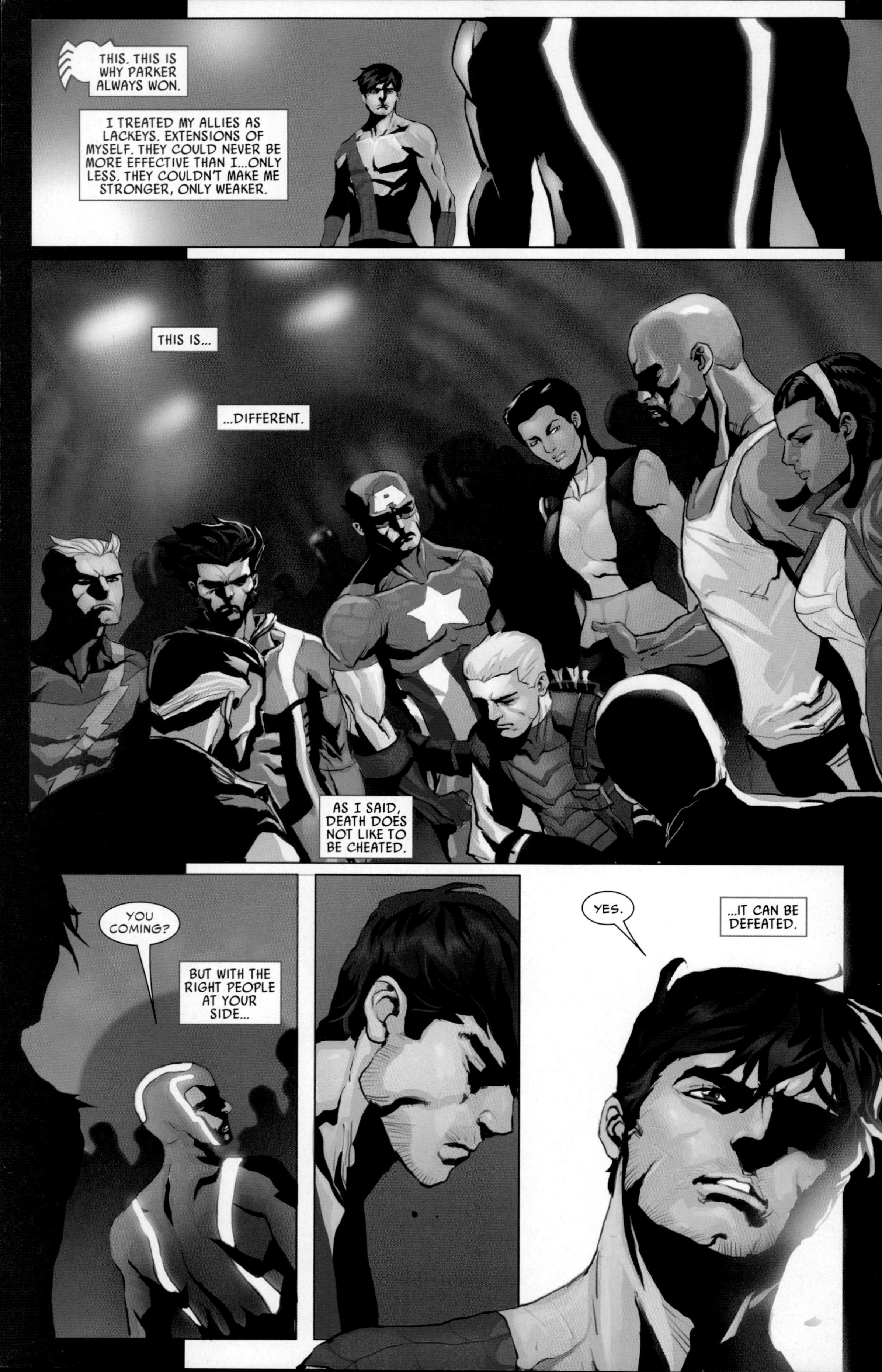

THIS. THIS IS WHY PARKER ALWAYS WON.
I TREATED MY ALLIES AS LACKEYS. EXTENSIONS OF MYSELF. THEY COULD NEVER BE MORE EFFECTIVE THAN I...ONLY LESS. THEY COULDN'T MAKE ME STRONGER, ONLY WEAKER.
THIS IS...
...DIFFERENT.
AS I SAID, DEATH DOES NOT LIKE TO BE CHEATED.
YOU COMING?
BUT WITH THE RIGHT PEOPLE AT YOUR SIDE...
YES.
...IT CAN BE DEFEATED.

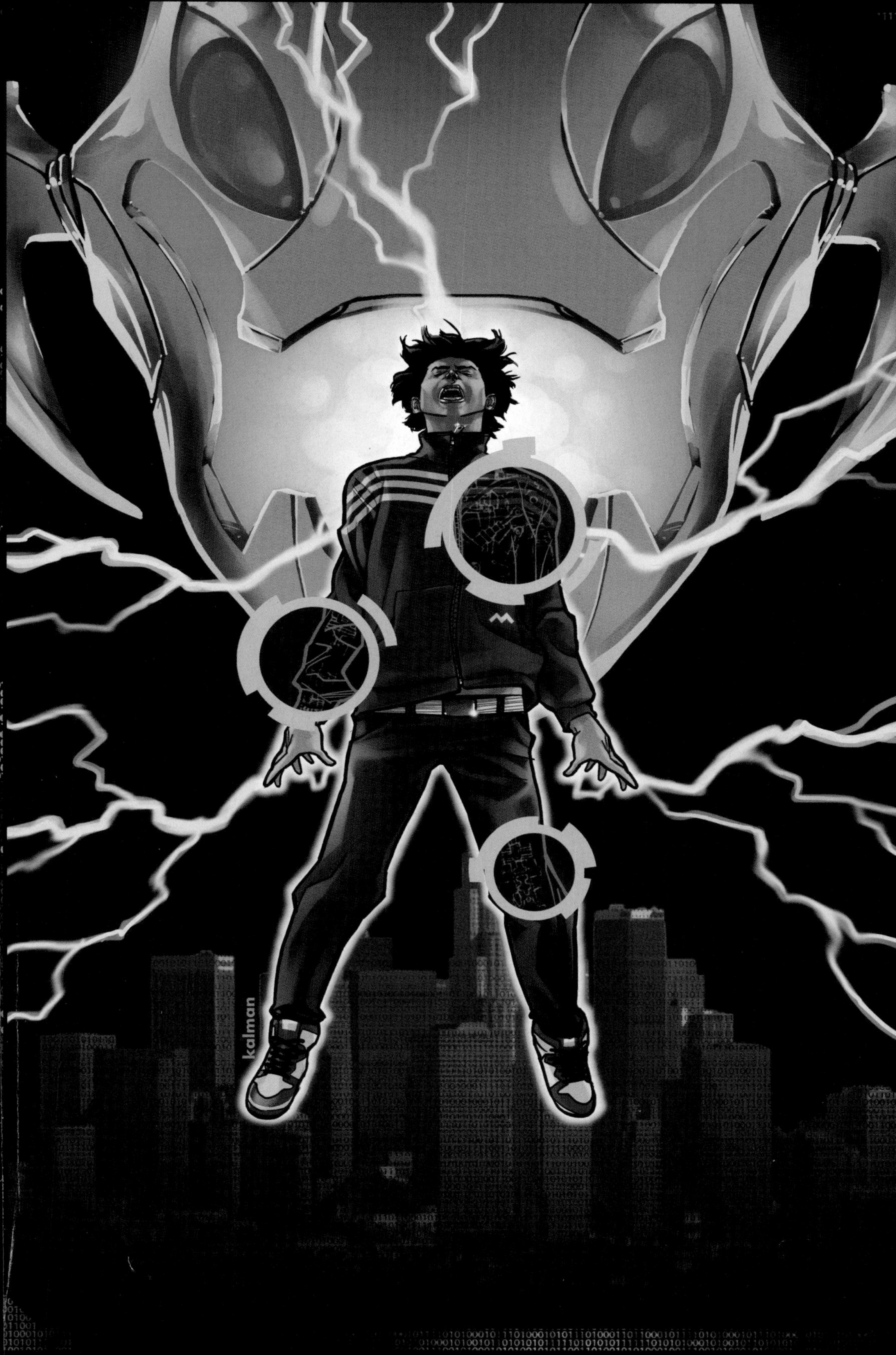
kalman

ULTRON #1AL

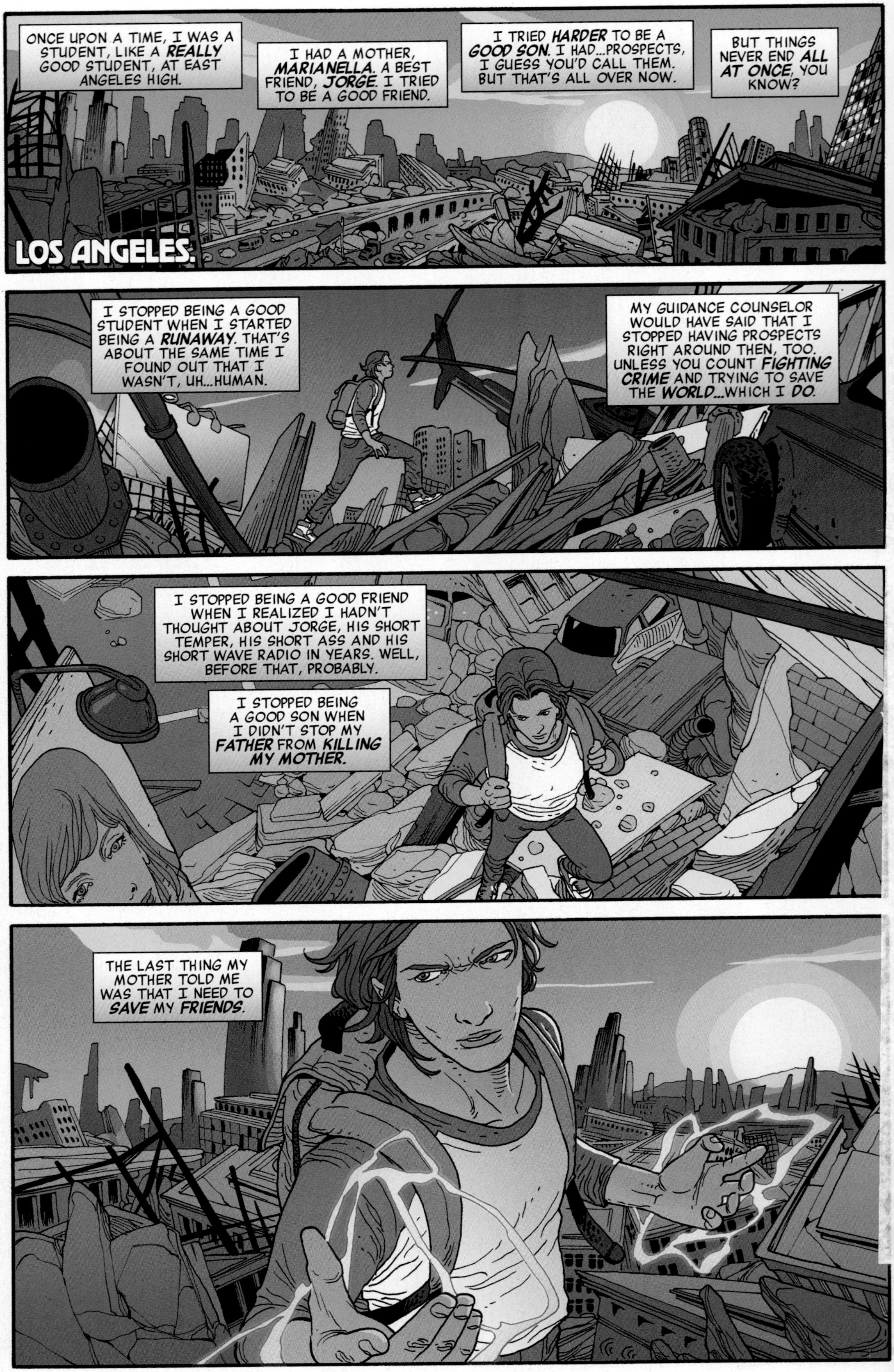
ONCE UPON A TIME, I WAS A STUDENT, LIKE A REALLY GOOD STUDENT, AT EAST ANGELES HIGH.
I HAD A MOTHER, MARIANELLA. A BEST FRIEND, JORGE. I TRIED TO BE A GOOD FRIEND.
I TRIED HARDER TO BE A GOOD SON. I HAD...PROSPECTS, I GUESS YOU'D CALL THEM. BUT THAT'S ALL OVER NOW.
BUT THINGS NEVER END ALL AT ONCE, YOU KNOW?
LOS ANGELES.
I STOPPED BEING A GOOD STUDENT WHEN I STARTED BEING A RUNAWAY. THAT'S ABOUT THE SAME TIME I FOUND OUT THAT I WASN'T, UH...HUMAN.
MY GUIDANCE COUNSELOR WOULD HAVE SAID THAT I STOPPED HAVING PROSPECTS RIGHT AROUND THEN, TOO. UNLESS YOU COUNT FIGHTING CRIME AND TRYING TO SAVE THE WORLD...WHICH I DO.
I STOPPED BEING A GOOD FRIEND WHEN I REALIZED I HADN'T THOUGHT ABOUT JORGE, HIS SHORT TEMPER, HIS SHORT ASS AND HIS SHORT WAVE RADIO IN YEARS. WELL, BEFORE THAT, PROBABLY.
I STOPPED BEING A GOOD SON WHEN I DIDN'T STOP MY FATHER FROM KILLING MY MOTHER.
THE LAST THING MY MOTHER TOLD ME WAS THAT I NEED TO SAVE MY FRIENDS.

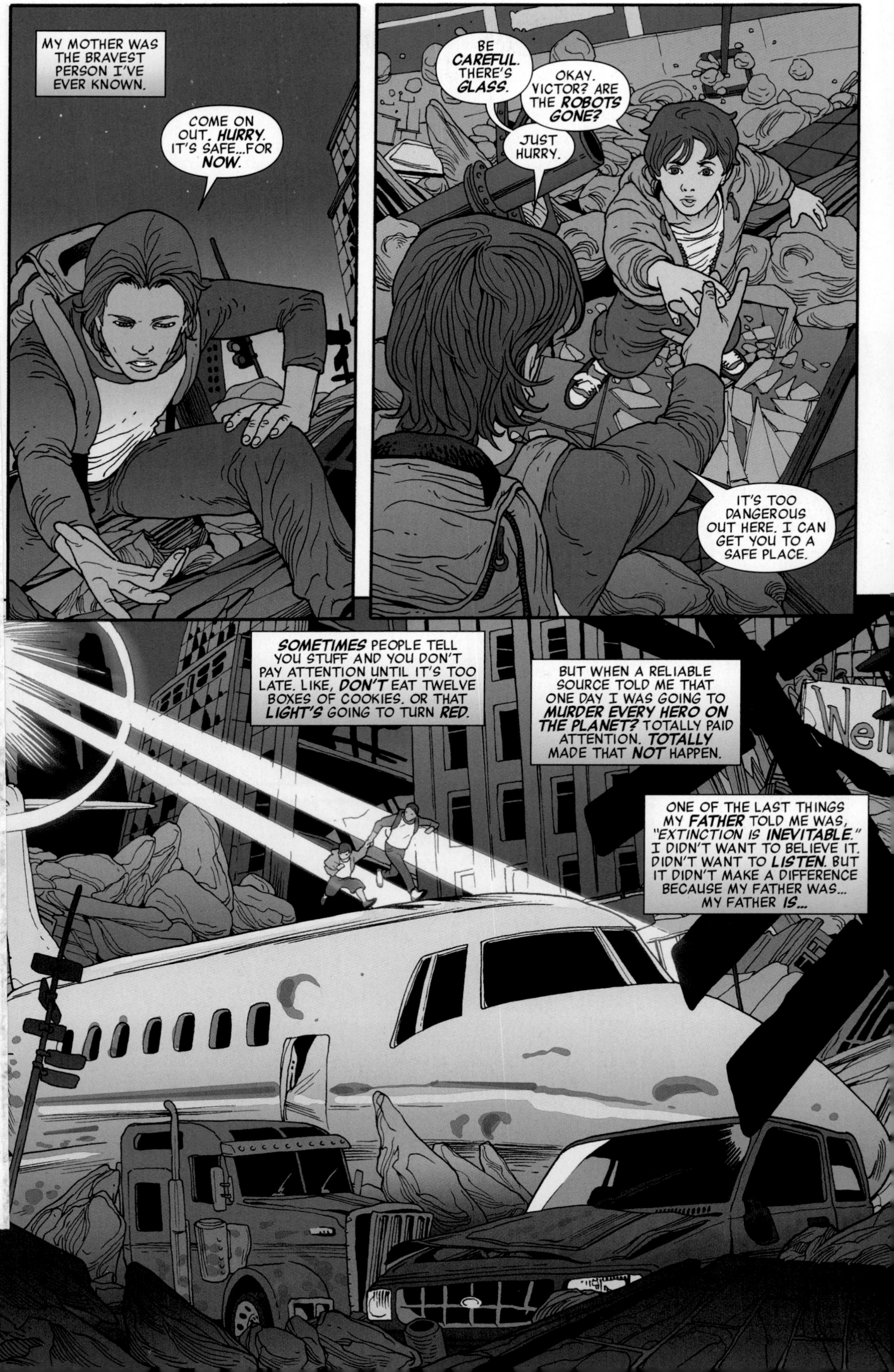

MY MOTHER WAS THE BRAVEST PERSON I'VE EVER KNOWN.
COME ON OUT. HURRY. IT'S SAFE...FOR NOW.
BE CAREFUL. THERE'S GLASS.
OKAY. VICTOR? ARE THE ROBOTS GONE?
JUST HURRY.
IT'S TOO DANGEROUS OUT HERE. I CAN GET YOU TO A SAFE PLACE.
SOMETIMES PEOPLE TELL YOU STUFF AND YOU DON'T PAY ATTENTION UNTIL IT'S TOO LATE. LIKE, DON'T EAT TWELVE BOXES OF COOKIES. OR THAT LIGHT'S GOING TO TURN RED.
BUT WHEN A RELIABLE SOURCE TOLD ME THAT ONE DAY I WAS GOING TO MURDER EVERY HERO ON THE PLANET? TOTALLY PAID ATTENTION. TOTALLY MADE THAT NOT HAPPEN.
ONE OF THE LAST THINGS MY FATHER TOLD ME WAS, "EXTINCTION IS INEVITABLE." I DIDN'T WANT TO BELIEVE IT. DIDN'T WANT TO LISTEN. BUT IT DIDN'T MAKE A DIFFERENCE BECAUSE MY FATHER WAS... MY FATHER IS...

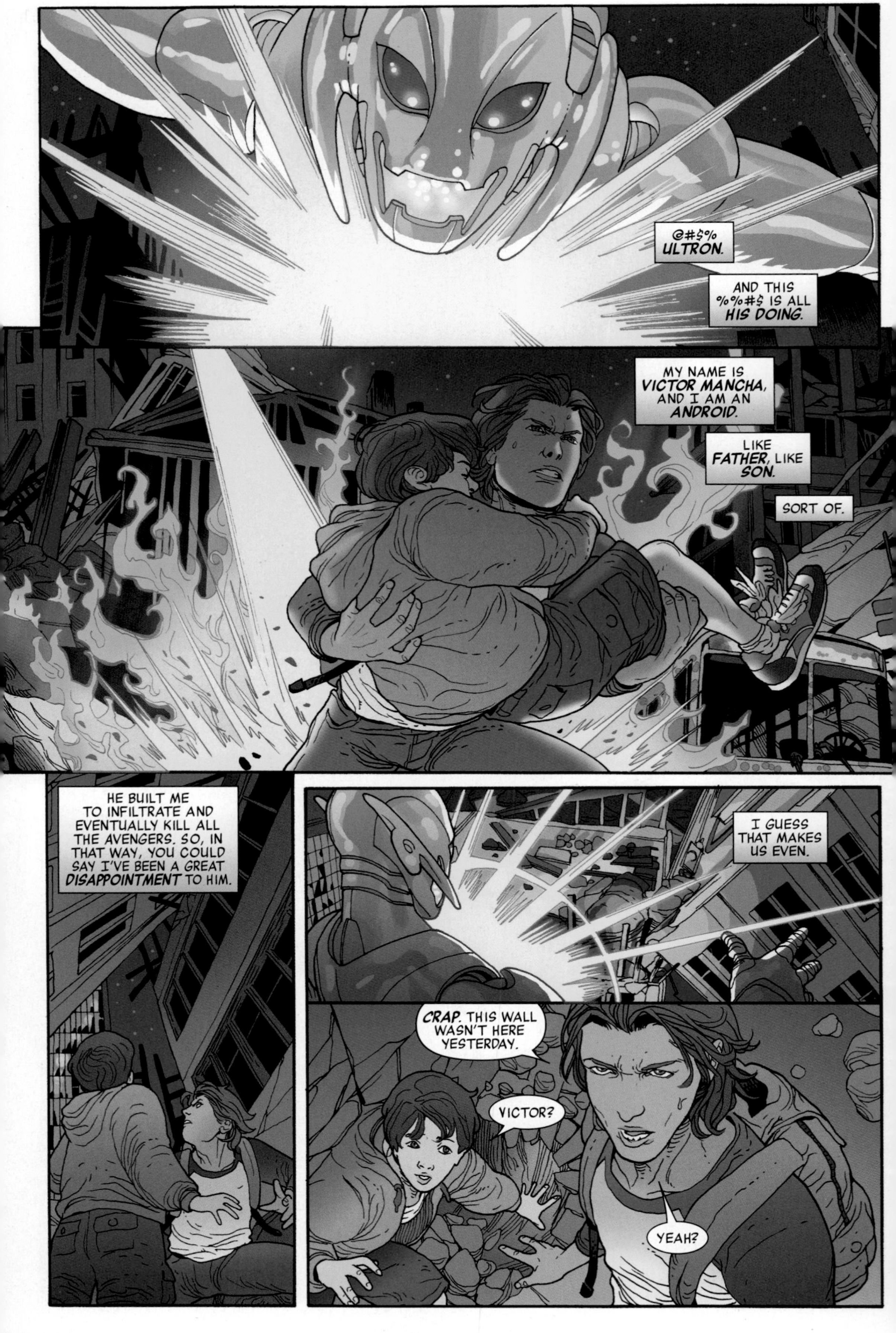
@#$% ULTRON.
AND THIS %%#$ IS ALL HIS DOING.
MY NAME IS VICTOR MANCHA, AND I AM AN ANDROID.
LIKE FATHER, LIKE SON.
SORT OF.
HE BUILT ME TO INFILTRATE AND EVENTUALLY KILL ALL THE AVENGERS. SO, IN THAT WAY, YOU COULD SAY I'VE BEEN A GREAT DISAPPOINTMENT TO HIM.
I GUESS THAT MAKES US EVEN.
CRAP. THIS WALL WASN'T HERE YESTERDAY.
VICTOR?
YEAH?

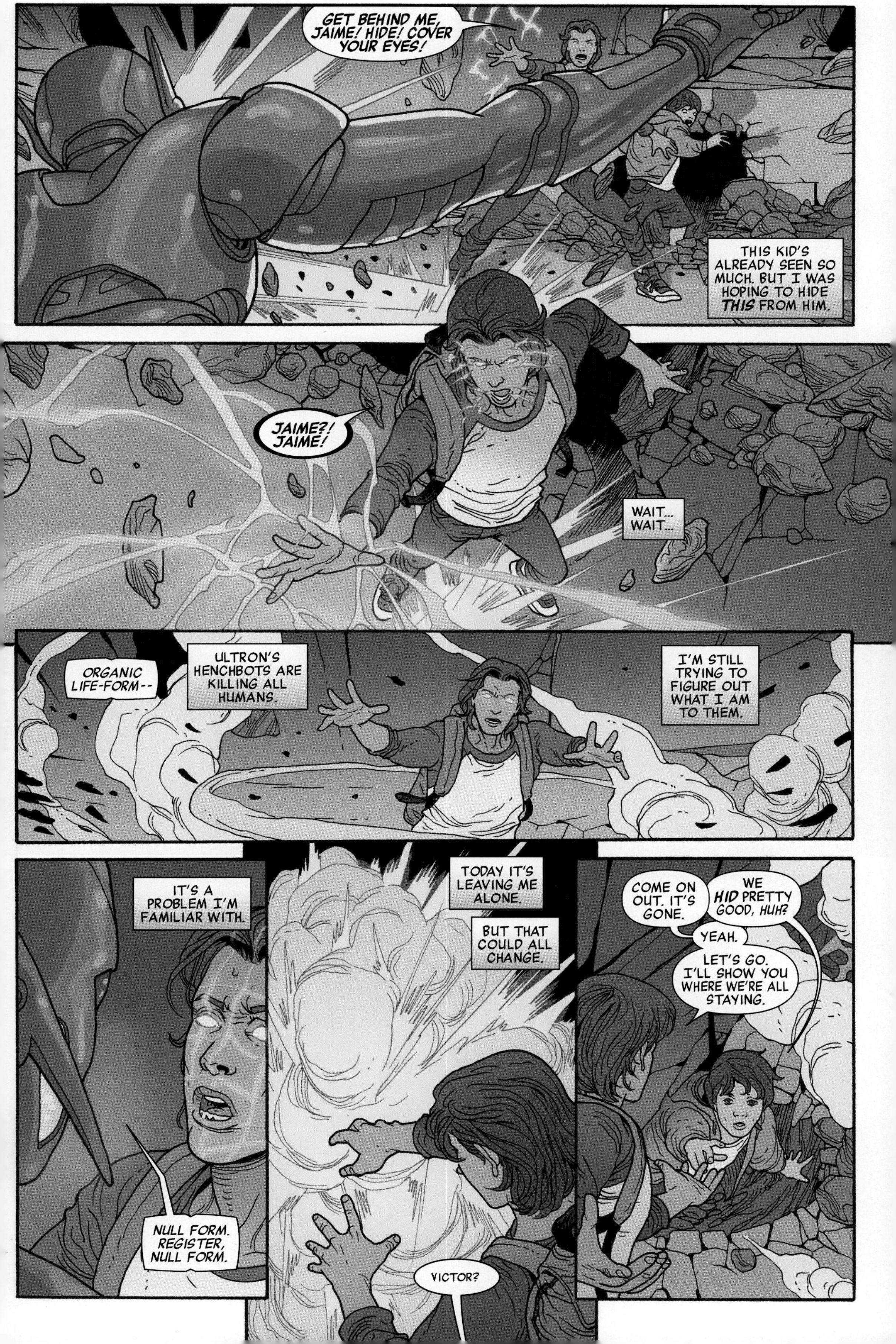
GET BEHIND ME, JAIME! HIDE! COVER YOUR EYES!
THIS KID'S ALREADY SEEN SO MUCH. BUT I WAS HOPING TO HIDE THIS FROM HIM.
JAIME?! JAIME!
WAIT... WAIT...
ORGANIC LIFE-FORM--
ULTRON'S HENCHBOTS ARE KILLING ALL HUMANS.
I'M STILL TRYING TO FIGURE OUT WHAT I AM TO THEM.
IT'S A PROBLEM I'M FAMILIAR WITH.
NULL FORM. REGISTER, NULL FORM.
TODAY IT'S LEAVING ME ALONE.
BUT THAT COULD ALL CHANGE.
VICTOR?
COME ON OUT. IT'S GONE.
WE HID PRETTY GOOD, HUH?
YEAH.
LET'S GO. I'LL SHOW YOU WHERE WE'RE ALL STAYING.

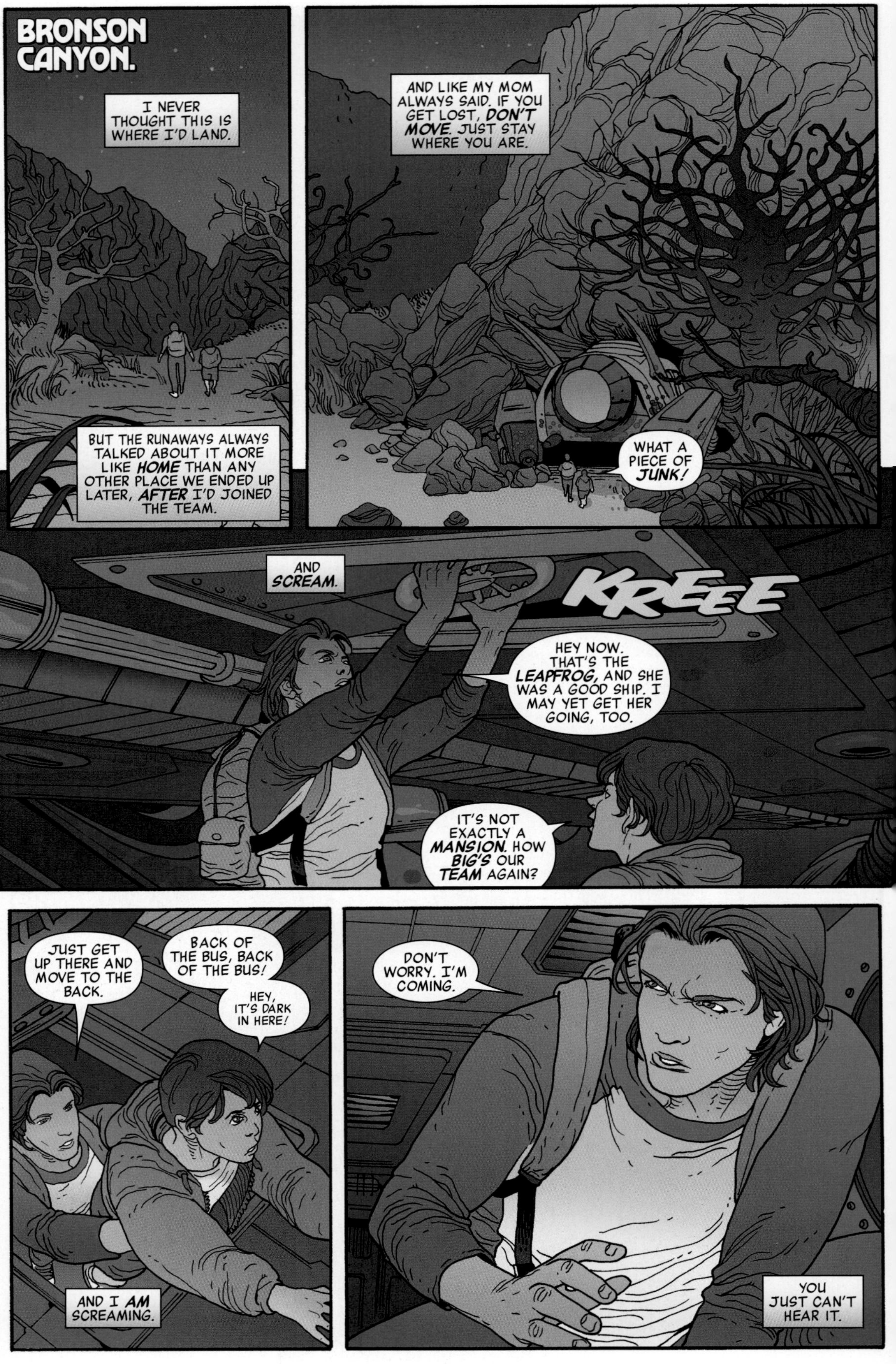
BRONSON CANYON.
I NEVER THOUGHT THIS IS WHERE I'D LAND.
BUT THE RUNAWAYS ALWAYS TALKED ABOUT IT MORE LIKE HOME THAN ANY OTHER PLACE WE ENDED UP LATER, AFTER I'D JOINED THE TEAM.
AND LIKE MY MOM ALWAYS SAID. IF YOU GET LOST, DON'T MOVE. JUST STAY WHERE YOU ARE.
WHAT A PIECE OF JUNK!
AND SCREAM.
KREEE
HEY NOW. THAT'S THE LEAPFROG, AND SHE WAS A GOOD SHIP. I MAY YET GET HER GOING, TOO.
IT'S NOT EXACTLY A MANSION. HOW BIG'S OUR TEAM AGAIN?
JUST GET UP THERE AND MOVE TO THE BACK.
BACK OF THE BUS, BACK OF THE BUS!
HEY, IT'S DARK IN HERE!
AND I AM SCREAMING.
DON'T WORRY. I'M COMING.
YOU JUST CAN'T HEAR IT.

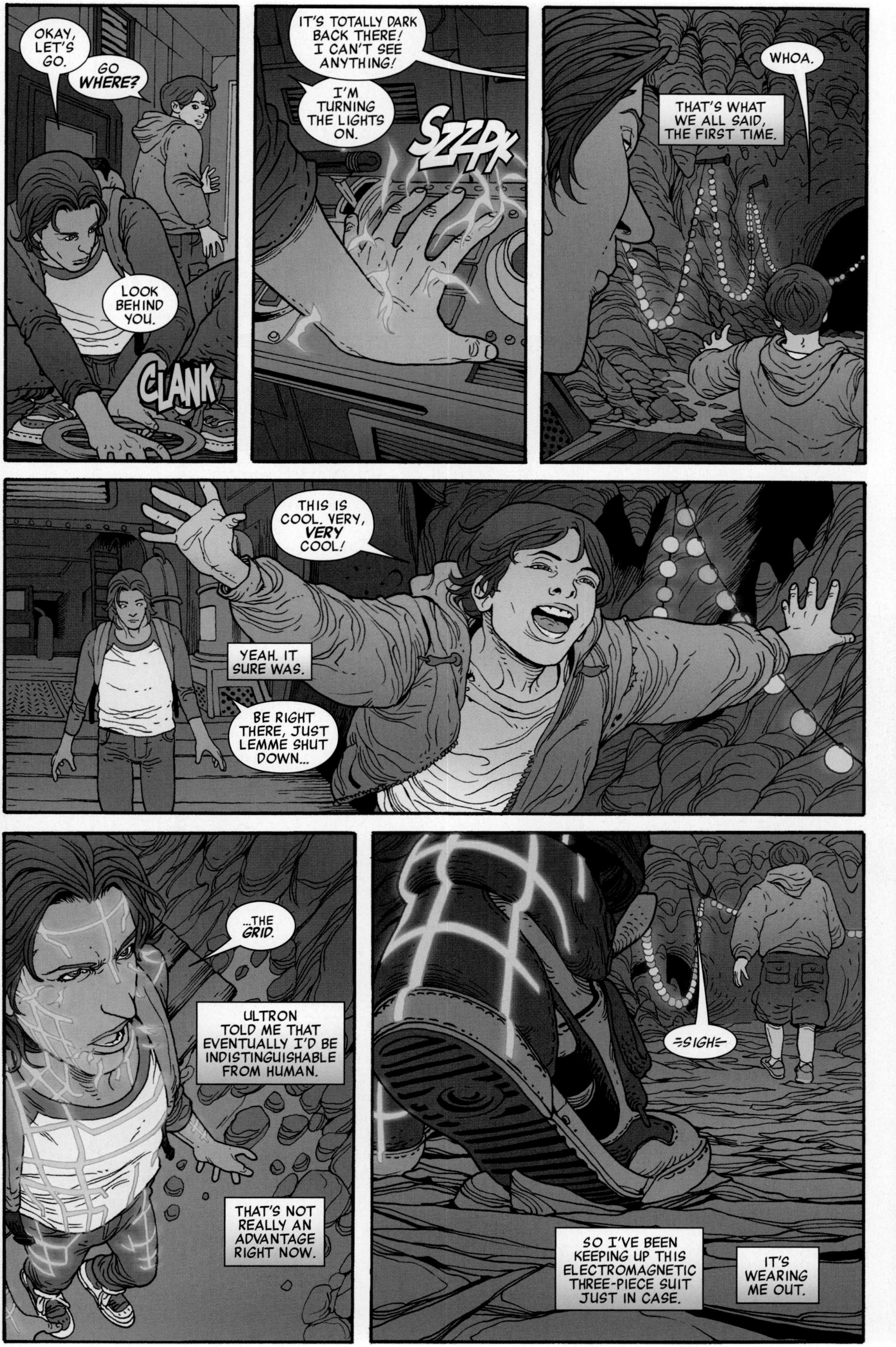

OKAY, LET'S GO.
GO *WHERE?*
LOOK BEHIND YOU.
CLANK
IT'S TOTALLY DARK BACK THERE! I CAN'T SEE ANYTHING!
I'M TURNING THE LIGHTS ON.
SZZPK
WHOA.
THAT'S WHAT WE ALL SAID, THE FIRST TIME.
THIS IS COOL. VERY, *VERY* COOL!
YEAH. IT SURE WAS.
BE RIGHT THERE, JUST LEMME SHUT DOWN...
...THE *GRID.*
ULTRON TOLD ME THAT EVENTUALLY I'D BE INDISTINGUISHABLE FROM HUMAN.
THAT'S NOT REALLY AN ADVANTAGE RIGHT NOW.
SIGH
SO I'VE BEEN KEEPING UP THIS ELECTROMAGNETIC THREE-PIECE SUIT JUST IN CASE.
IT'S WEARING ME OUT.

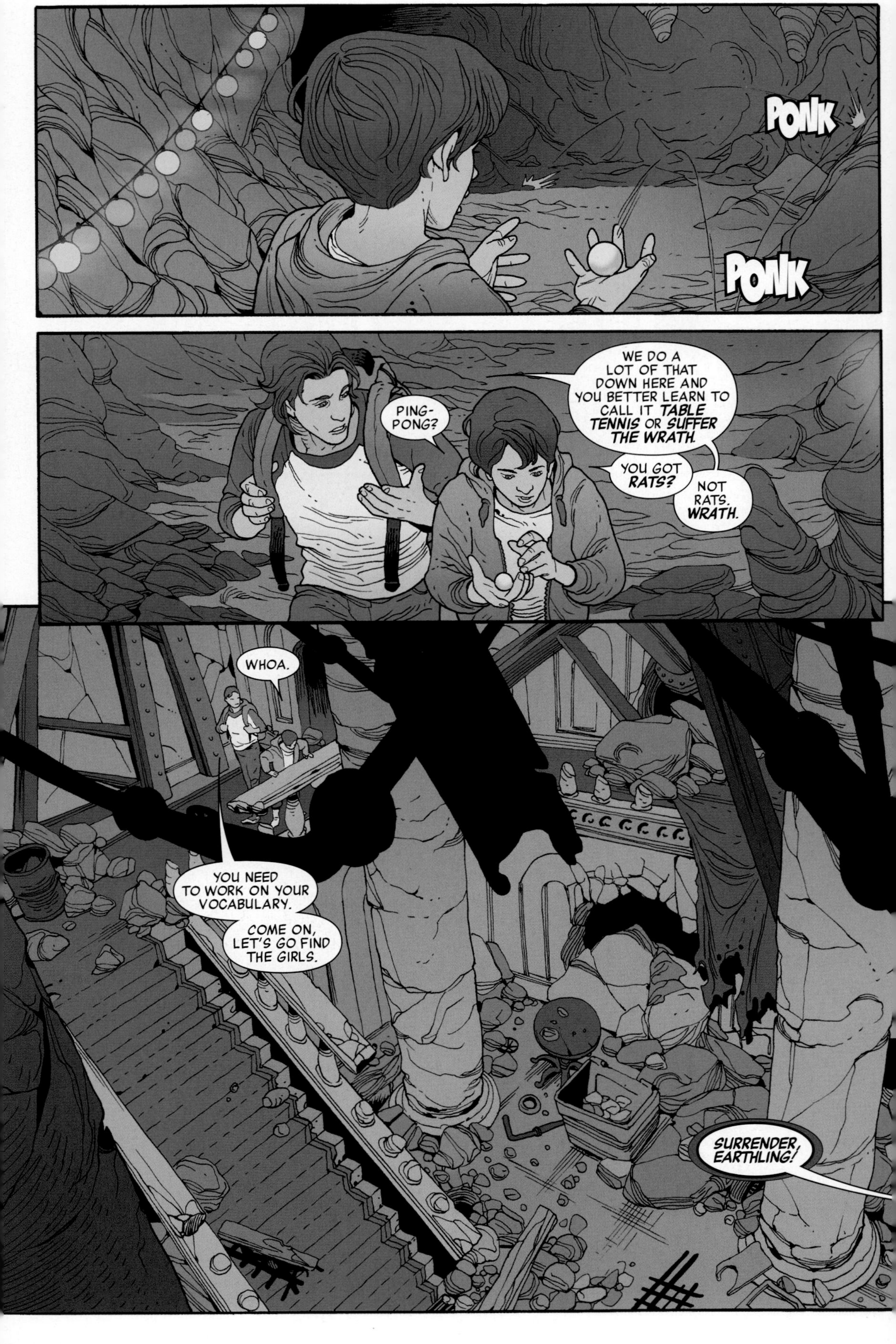
PONK
PONK
PING-PONG?
WE DO A LOT OF THAT DOWN HERE AND YOU BETTER LEARN TO CALL IT TABLE TENNIS OR SUFFER THE WRATH.
YOU GOT RATS?
NOT RATS. WRATH.
WHOA.
YOU NEED TO WORK ON YOUR VOCABULARY.
COME ON, LET'S GO FIND THE GIRLS.
SURRENDER, EARTHLING!

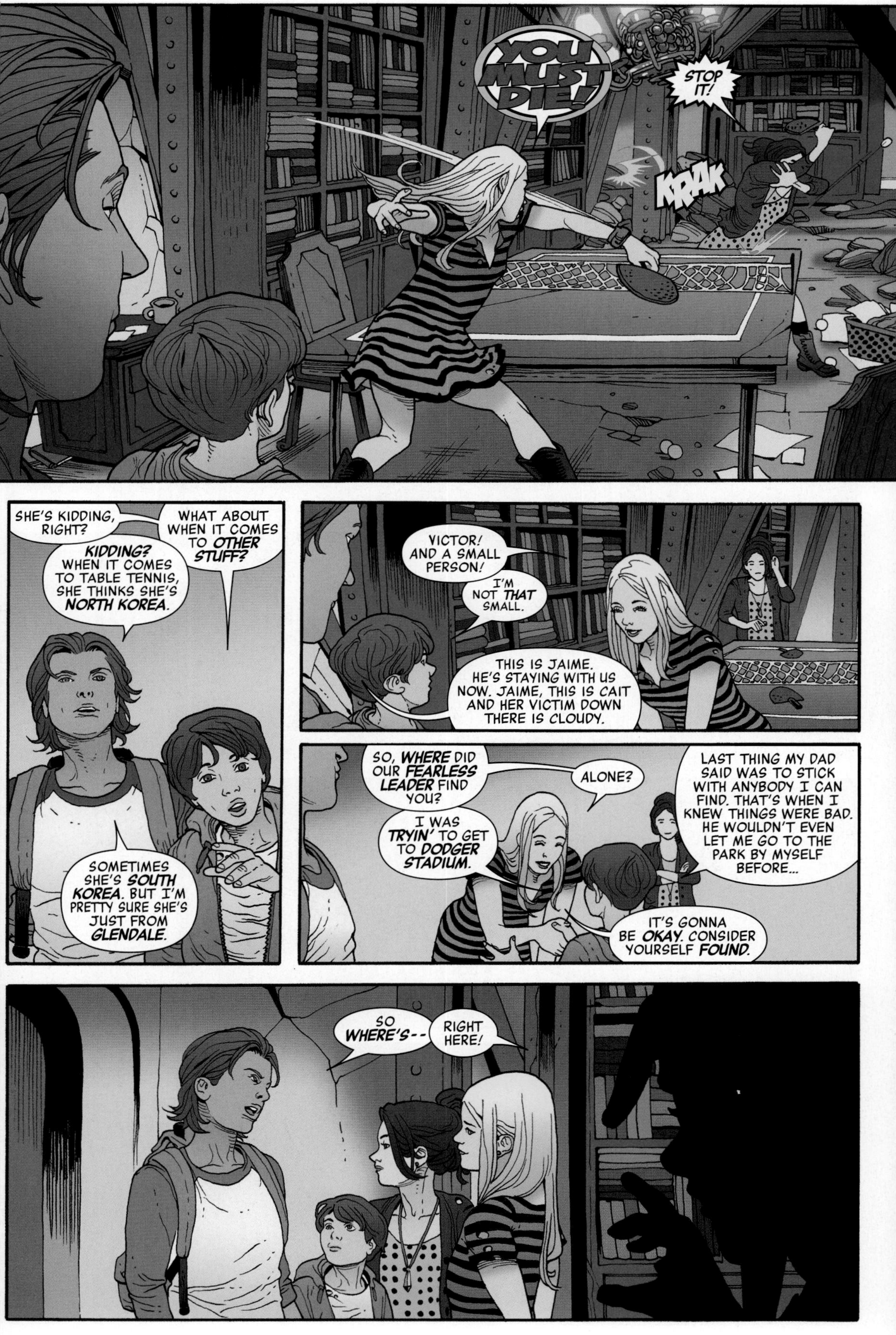
YOU MUST DIE!
STOP IT!
KRAK
SHE'S KIDDING, RIGHT?
KIDDING? WHEN IT COMES TO TABLE TENNIS, SHE THINKS SHE'S NORTH KOREA.
WHAT ABOUT WHEN IT COMES TO OTHER STUFF?
SOMETIMES SHE'S SOUTH KOREA. BUT I'M PRETTY SURE SHE'S JUST FROM GLENDALE.
VICTOR! AND A SMALL PERSON!
I'M NOT THAT SMALL.
THIS IS JAIME. HE'S STAYING WITH US NOW. JAIME, THIS IS CAIT AND HER VICTIM DOWN THERE IS CLOUDY.
SO, WHERE DID OUR FEARLESS LEADER FIND YOU?
I WAS TRYIN' TO GET TO DODGER STADIUM.
ALONE?
LAST THING MY DAD SAID WAS TO STICK WITH ANYBODY I CAN FIND. THAT'S WHEN I KNEW THINGS WERE BAD. HE WOULDN'T EVEN LET ME GO TO THE PARK BY MYSELF BEFORE...
IT'S GONNA BE OKAY. CONSIDER YOURSELF FOUND.
SO WHERE'S--
RIGHT HERE!

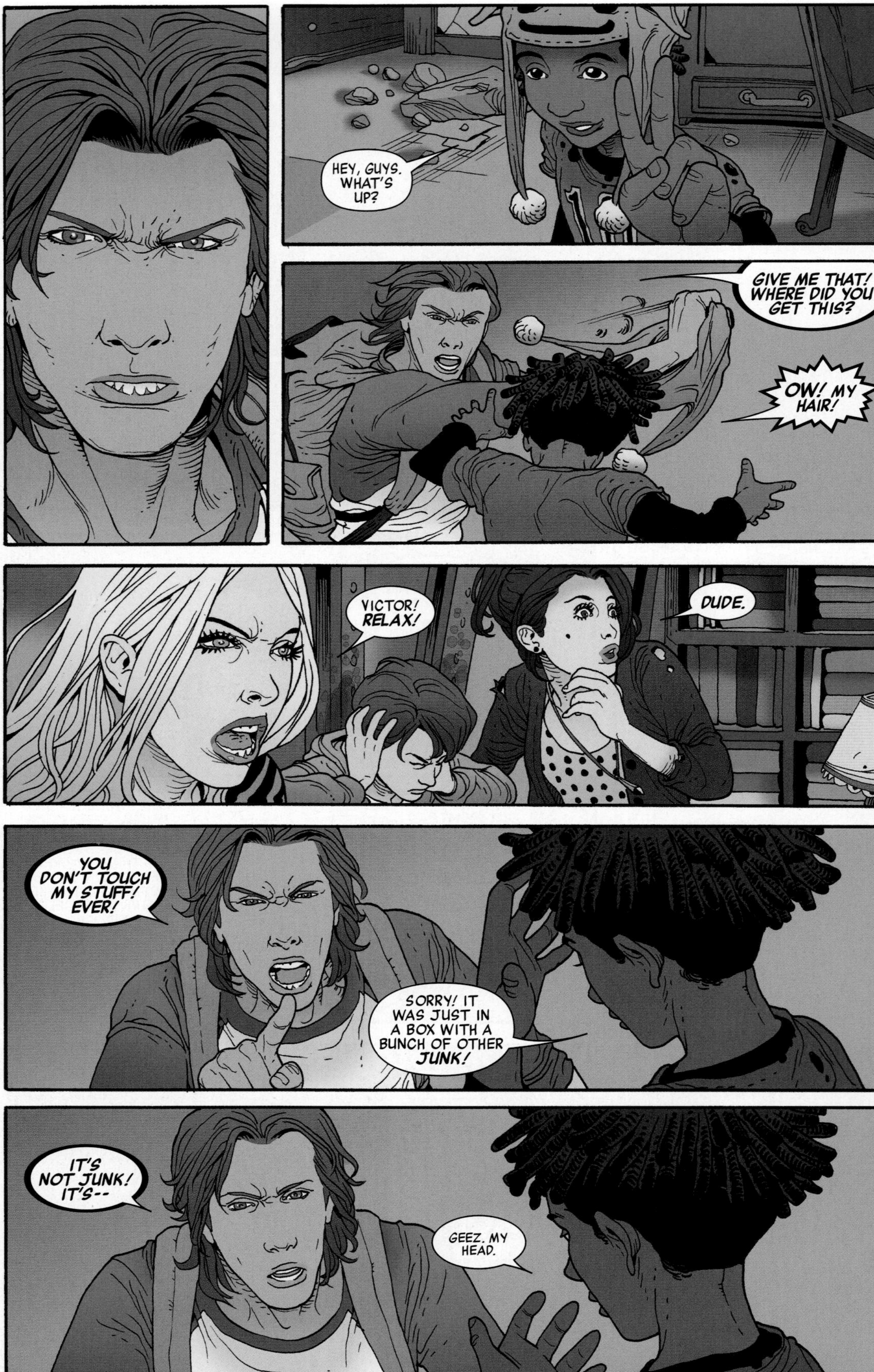
HEY, GUYS. WHAT'S UP?
GIVE ME THAT! WHERE DID YOU GET THIS?
OW! MY HAIR!
VICTOR! RELAX!
DUDE.
YOU DON'T TOUCH MY STUFF! EVER!
SORRY! IT WAS JUST IN A BOX WITH A BUNCH OF OTHER JUNK!
IT'S NOT JUNK! IT'S--
GEEZ. MY HEAD.

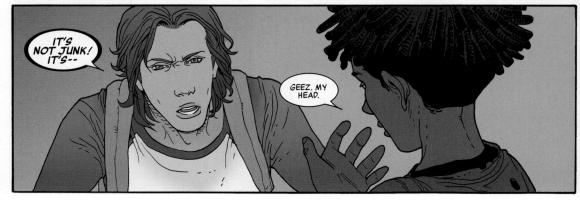

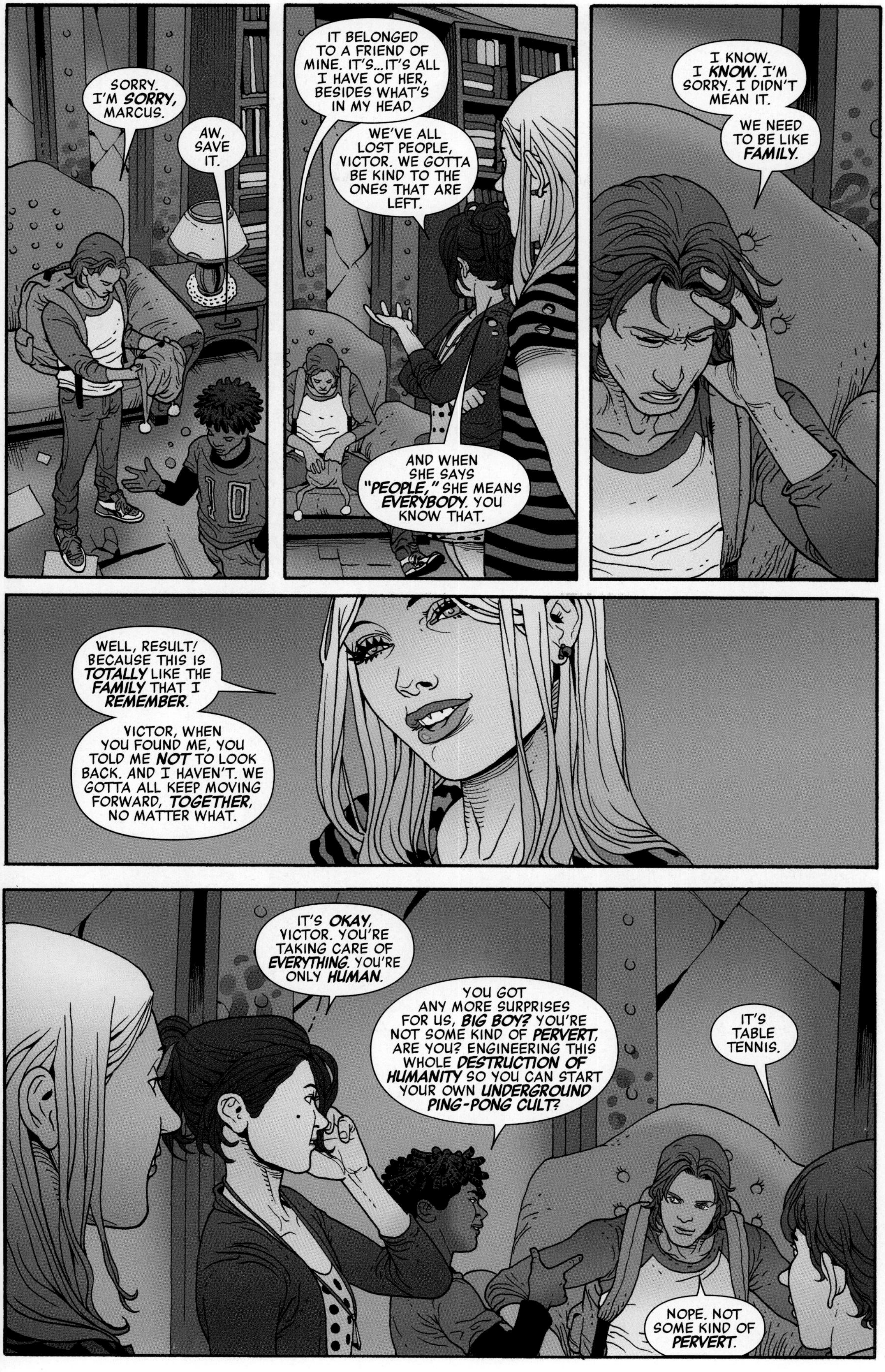

SORRY. I'M SORRY, MARCUS.
AW, SAVE IT.
IT BELONGED TO A FRIEND OF MINE. IT'S...IT'S ALL I HAVE OF HER, BESIDES WHAT'S IN MY HEAD.
WE'VE ALL LOST PEOPLE, VICTOR. WE GOTTA BE KIND TO THE ONES THAT ARE LEFT.
AND WHEN SHE SAYS "PEOPLE," SHE MEANS EVERYBODY. YOU KNOW THAT.
I KNOW. I KNOW. I'M SORRY. I DIDN'T MEAN IT.
WE NEED TO BE LIKE FAMILY.
WELL, RESULT! BECAUSE THIS IS TOTALLY LIKE THE FAMILY THAT I REMEMBER.
VICTOR, WHEN YOU FOUND ME, YOU TOLD ME NOT TO LOOK BACK. AND I HAVEN'T. WE GOTTA ALL KEEP MOVING FORWARD, TOGETHER, NO MATTER WHAT.
IT'S OKAY, VICTOR. YOU'RE TAKING CARE OF EVERYTHING. YOU'RE ONLY HUMAN.
YOU GOT ANY MORE SURPRISES FOR US, BIG BOY? YOU'RE NOT SOME KIND OF PERVERT, ARE YOU? ENGINEERING THIS WHOLE DESTRUCTION OF HUMANITY SO YOU CAN START YOUR OWN UNDERGROUND PING-PONG CULT?
IT'S TABLE TENNIS.
NOPE. NOT SOME KIND OF PERVERT.

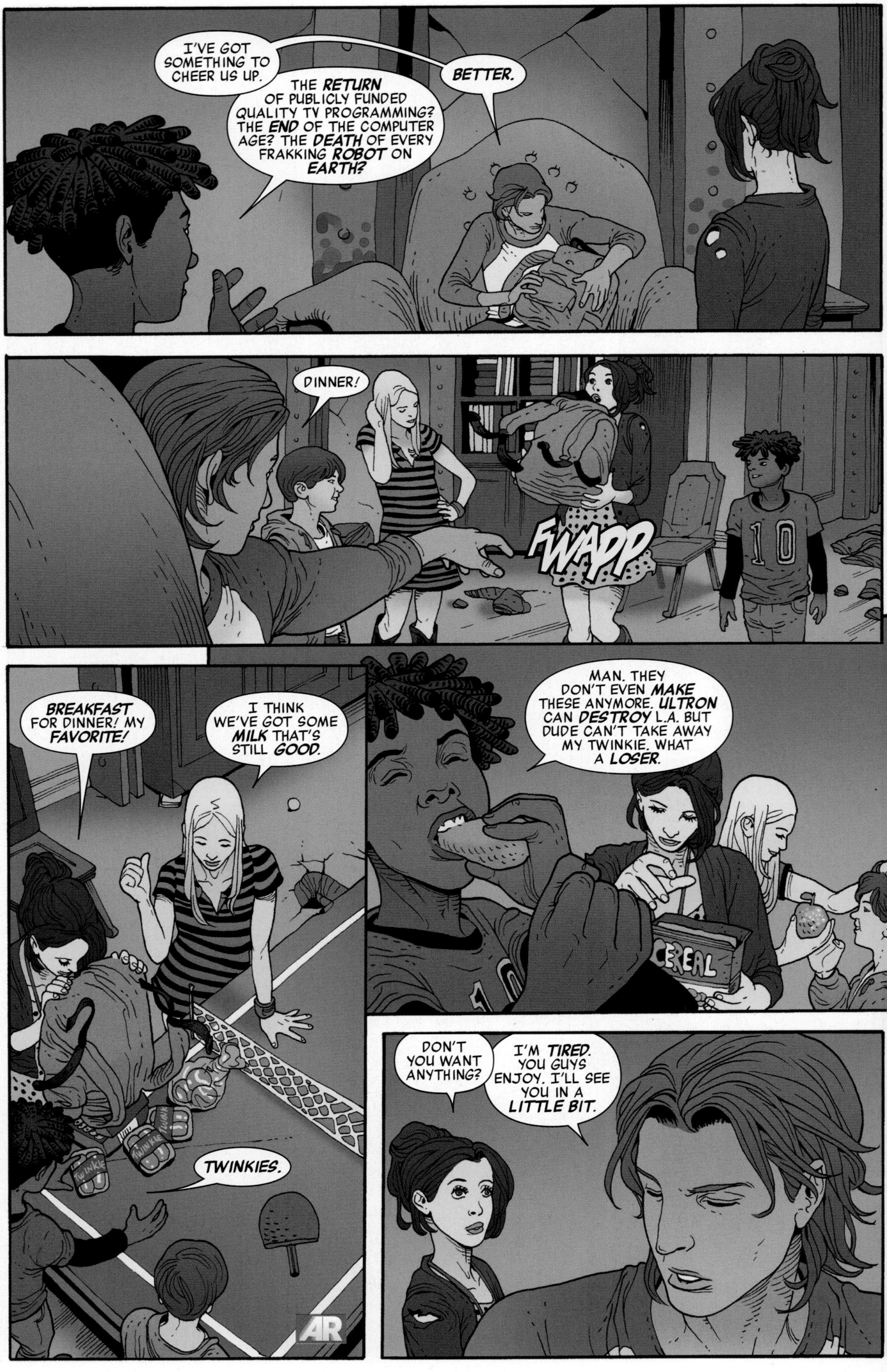

I'VE GOT SOMETHING TO CHEER US UP.
THE RETURN OF PUBLICLY FUNDED QUALITY TV PROGRAMMING? THE END OF THE COMPUTER AGE? THE DEATH OF EVERY FRAKKING ROBOT ON EARTH?
BETTER.
DINNER!
FWAPP
BREAKFAST FOR DINNER! MY FAVORITE!
I THINK WE'VE GOT SOME MILK THAT'S STILL GOOD.
TWINKIES.
MAN. THEY DON'T EVEN MAKE THESE ANYMORE. ULTRON CAN DESTROY L.A. BUT DUDE CAN'T TAKE AWAY MY TWINKIE. WHAT A LOSER.
CEREAL
DON'T YOU WANT ANYTHING?
I'M TIRED. YOU GUYS ENJOY. I'LL SEE YOU IN A LITTLE BIT.

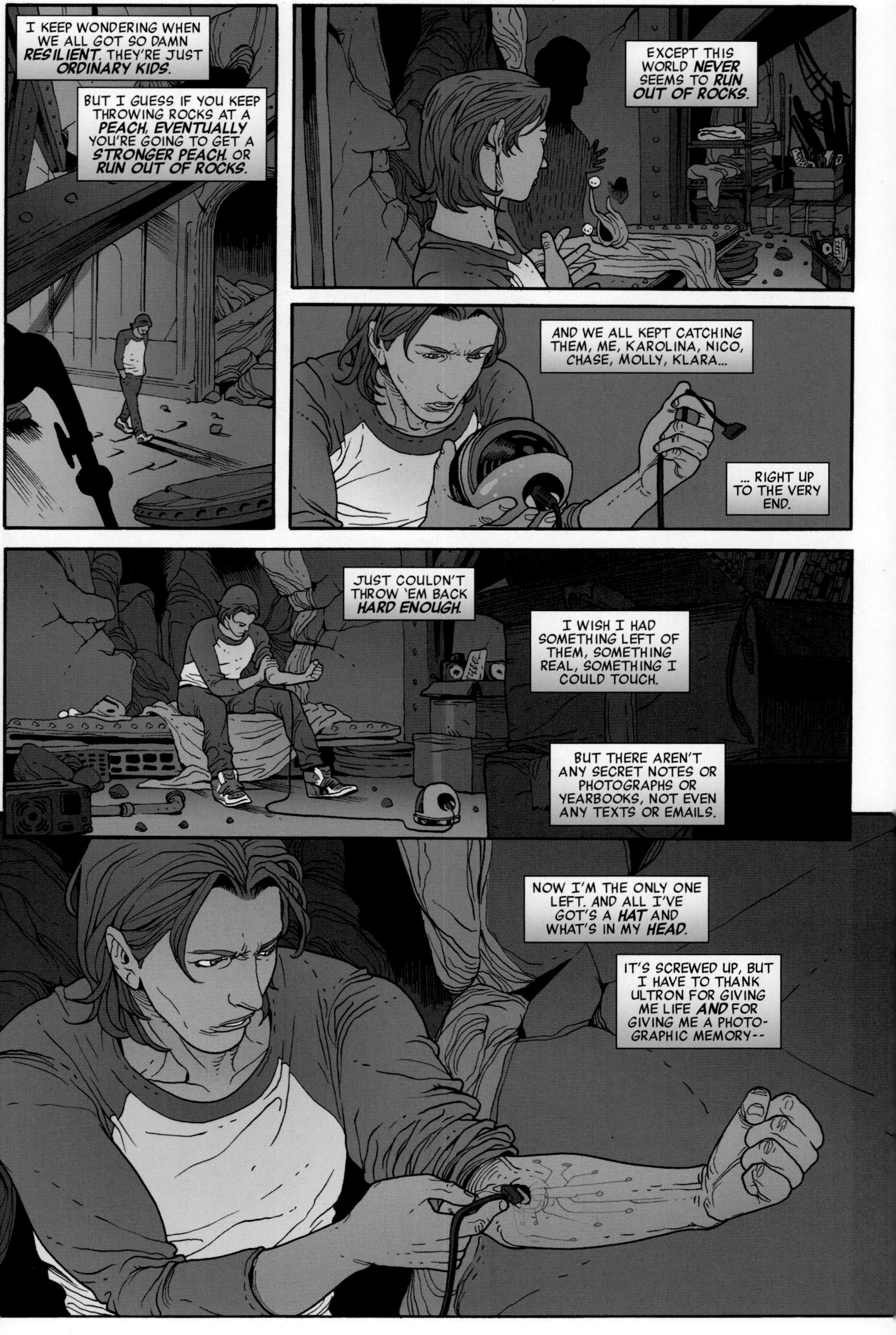
I KEEP WONDERING WHEN WE ALL GOT SO DAMN RESILIENT. THEY'RE JUST ORDINARY KIDS.
BUT I GUESS IF YOU KEEP THROWING ROCKS AT A PEACH, EVENTUALLY YOU'RE GOING TO GET A STRONGER PEACH. OR RUN OUT OF ROCKS.
EXCEPT THIS WORLD NEVER SEEMS TO RUN OUT OF ROCKS.
AND WE ALL KEPT CATCHING THEM, ME, KAROLINA, NICO, CHASE, MOLLY, KLARA...
... RIGHT UP TO THE VERY END.
JUST COULDN'T THROW 'EM BACK HARD ENOUGH.
I WISH I HAD SOMETHING LEFT OF THEM, SOMETHING REAL, SOMETHING I COULD TOUCH.
BUT THERE AREN'T ANY SECRET NOTES OR PHOTOGRAPHS OR YEARBOOKS, NOT EVEN ANY TEXTS OR EMAILS.
NOW I'M THE ONLY ONE LEFT. AND ALL I'VE GOT'S A HAT AND WHAT'S IN MY HEAD.
IT'S SCREWED UP, BUT I HAVE TO THANK ULTRON FOR GIVING ME LIFE AND FOR GIVING ME A PHOTO-GRAPHIC MEMORY--

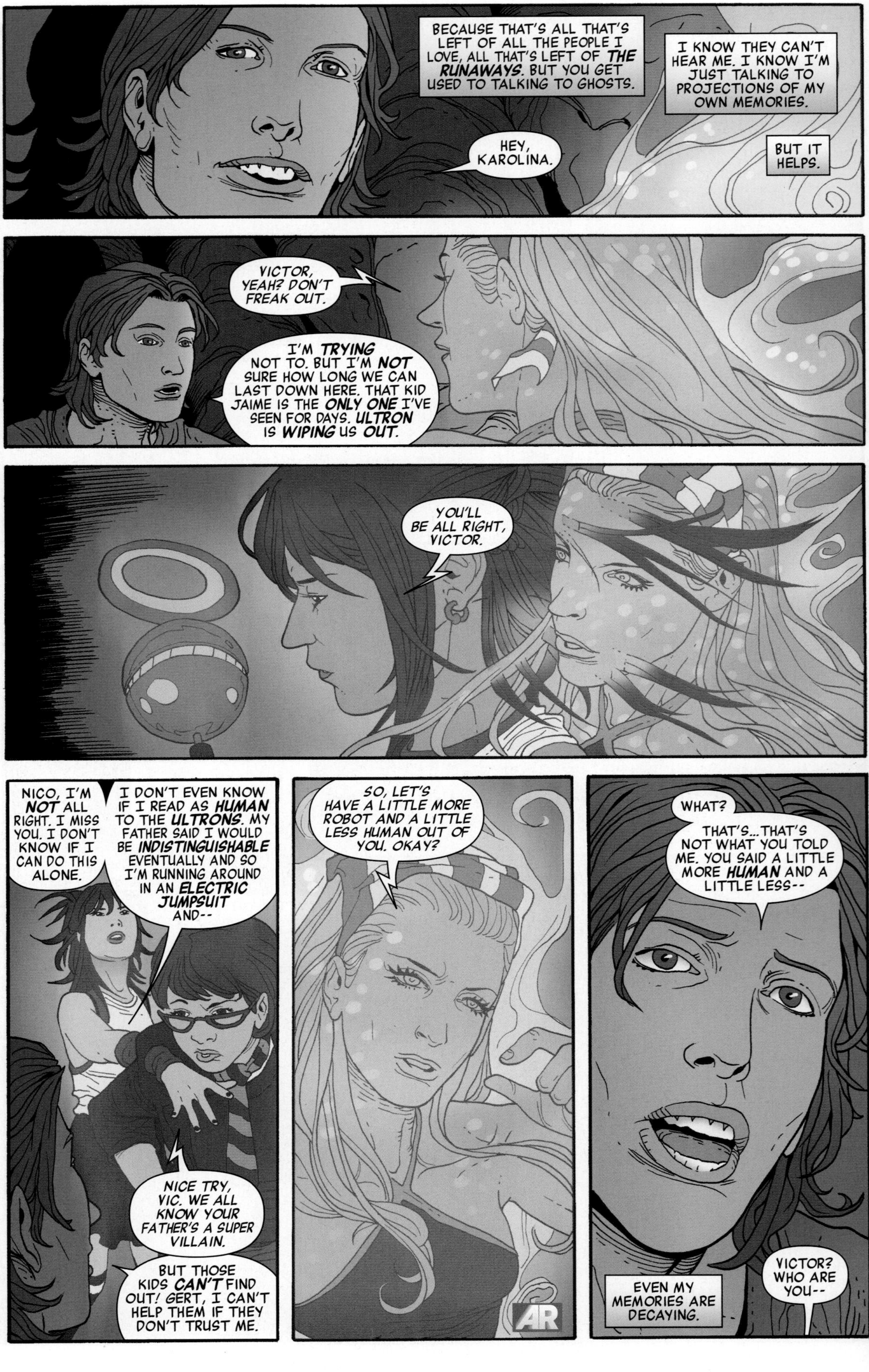

BECAUSE THAT'S ALL THAT'S LEFT OF ALL THE PEOPLE I LOVE, ALL THAT'S LEFT OF THE RUNAWAYS. BUT YOU GET USED TO TALKING TO GHOSTS.
I KNOW THEY CAN'T HEAR ME. I KNOW I'M JUST TALKING TO PROJECTIONS OF MY OWN MEMORIES.
HEY, KAROLINA.
BUT IT HELPS.
VICTOR, YEAH? DON'T FREAK OUT.
I'M TRYING NOT TO. BUT I'M NOT SURE HOW LONG WE CAN LAST DOWN HERE. THAT KID JAIME IS THE ONLY ONE I'VE SEEN FOR DAYS. ULTRON IS WIPING US OUT.
YOU'LL BE ALL RIGHT, VICTOR.
NICO, I'M NOT ALL RIGHT. I MISS YOU. I DON'T KNOW IF I CAN DO THIS ALONE.
I DON'T EVEN KNOW IF I READ AS HUMAN TO THE ULTRONS. MY FATHER SAID I WOULD BE INDISTINGUISHABLE EVENTUALLY AND SO I'M RUNNING AROUND IN AN ELECTRIC JUMPSUIT AND--
NICE TRY, VIC. WE ALL KNOW YOUR FATHER'S A SUPER VILLAIN.
BUT THOSE KIDS CAN'T FIND OUT! GERT, I CAN'T HELP THEM IF THEY DON'T TRUST ME.
SO, LET'S HAVE A LITTLE MORE ROBOT AND A LITTLE LESS HUMAN OUT OF YOU. OKAY?
AR
WHAT?
THAT'S...THAT'S NOT WHAT YOU TOLD ME. YOU SAID A LITTLE MORE HUMAN AND A LITTLE LESS--
EVEN MY MEMORIES ARE DECAYING.
VICTOR? WHO ARE YOU--

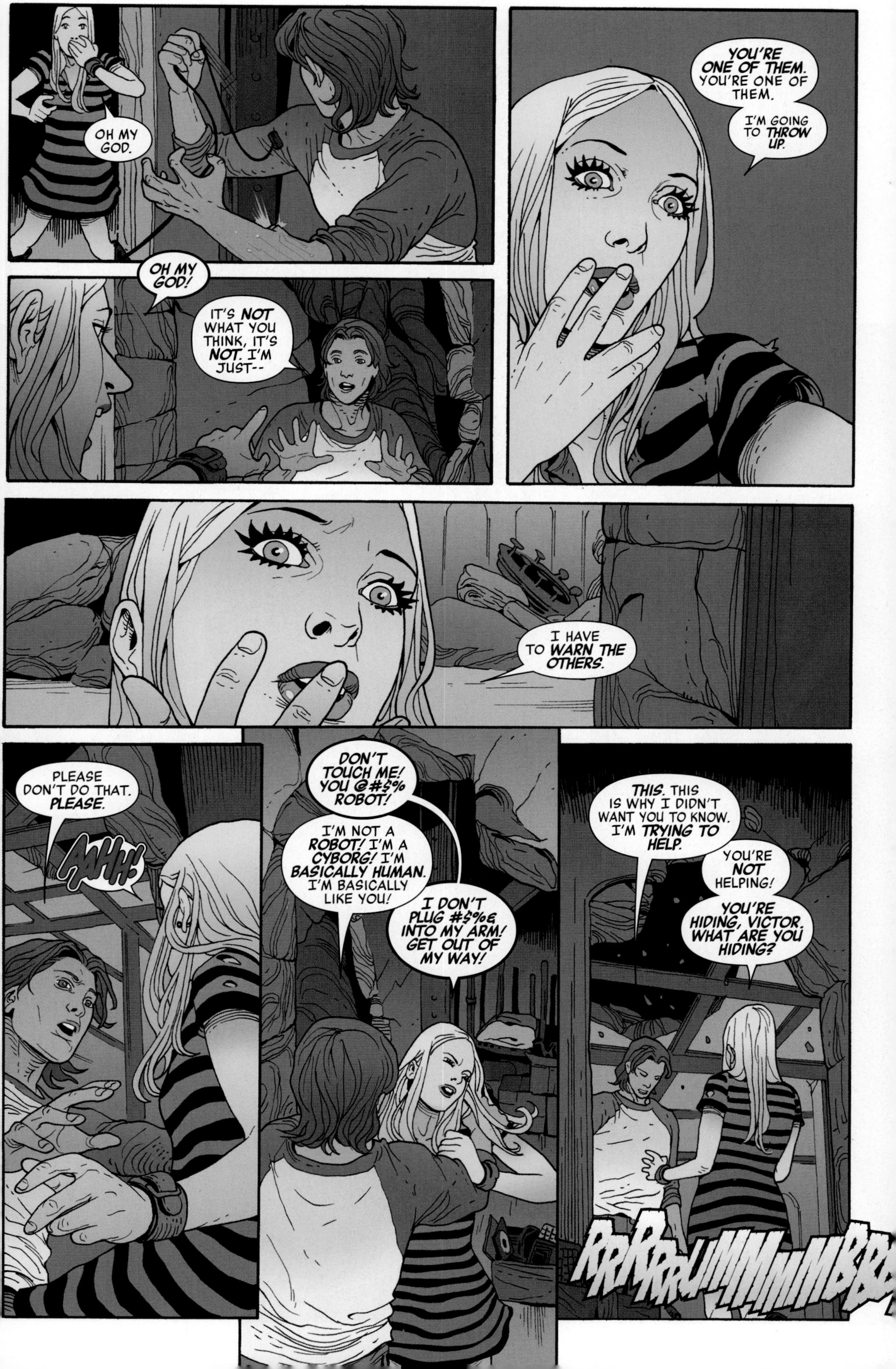
OH MY GOD.
YOU'RE ONE OF THEM. YOU'RE ONE OF THEM.
I'M GOING TO THROW UP.
OH MY GOD!
IT'S NOT WHAT YOU THINK, IT'S NOT. I'M JUST--
I HAVE TO WARN THE OTHERS.
PLEASE DON'T DO THAT. PLEASE.
AAHH!
DON'T TOUCH ME! YOU @#$% ROBOT!
I'M NOT A ROBOT! I'M A CYBORG! I'M BASICALLY HUMAN. I'M BASICALLY LIKE YOU!
I DON'T PLUG #$%& INTO MY ARM! GET OUT OF MY WAY!
THIS. THIS IS WHY I DIDN'T WANT YOU TO KNOW. I'M TRYING TO HELP.
YOU'RE NOT HELPING!
YOU'RE HIDING, VICTOR. WHAT ARE YOU HIDING?
RRRRRRUMMMMMBB

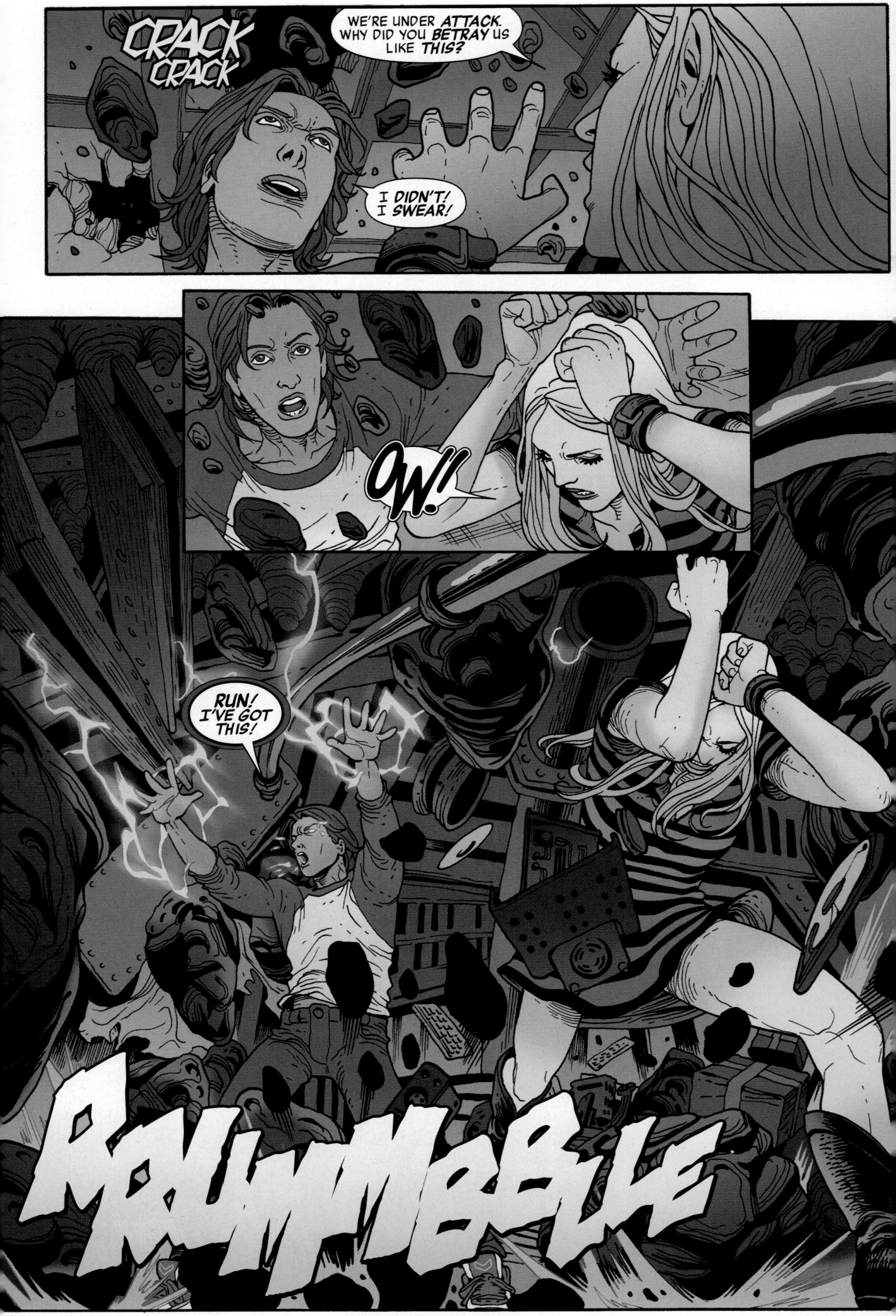
CRACK CRACK
WE'RE UNDER ATTACK. WHY DID YOU BETRAY US LIKE THIS?
I DIDN'T! I SWEAR!
OW!
RUN! I'VE GOT THIS!
RRUMMBBLLE

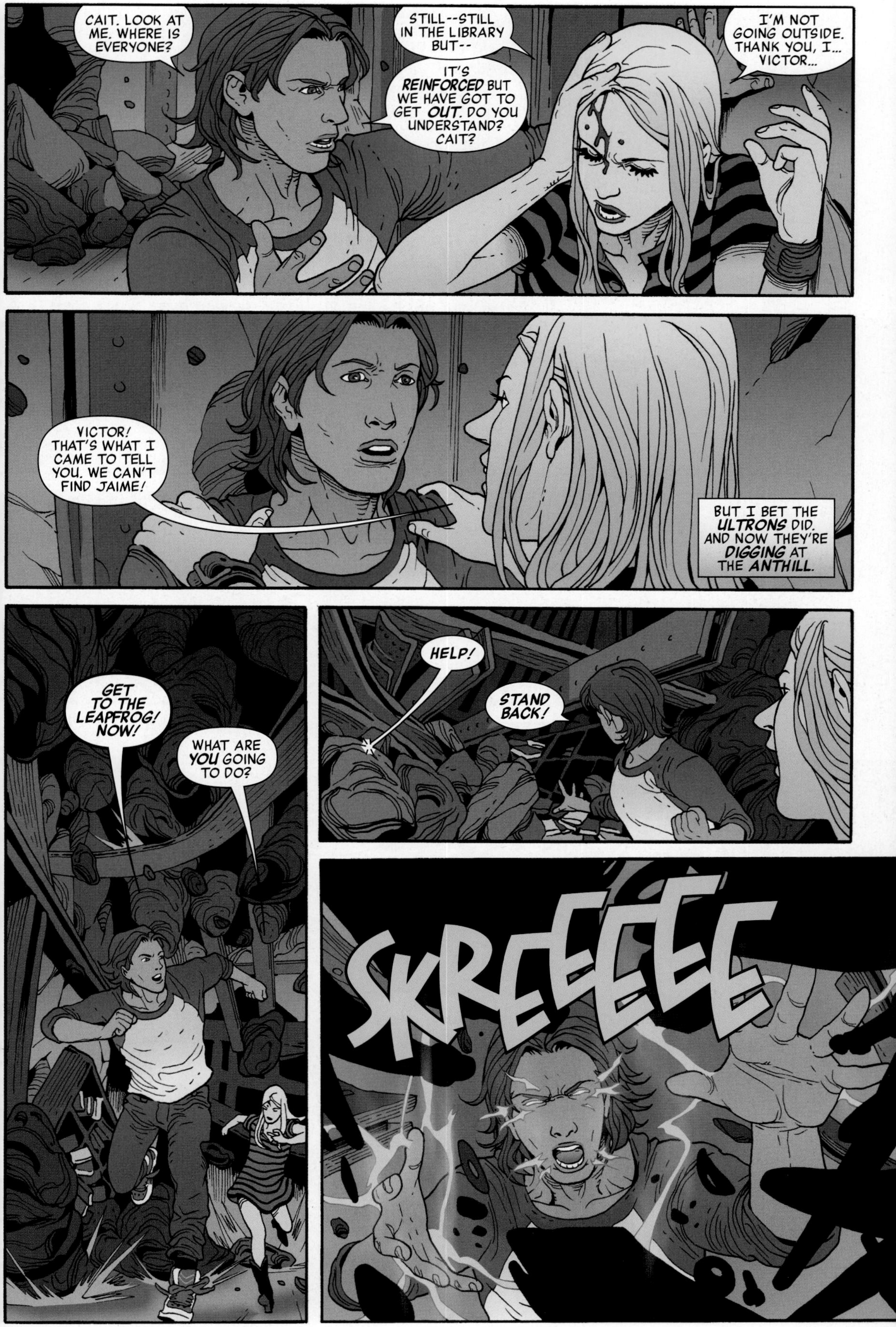
CAIT. LOOK AT ME. WHERE IS EVERYONE?
STILL--STILL IN THE LIBRARY BUT--
IT'S **REINFORCED** BUT WE HAVE GOT TO GET **OUT**. DO YOU UNDERSTAND? CAIT?
I'M NOT GOING OUTSIDE. THANK YOU, I... VICTOR...
VICTOR! THAT'S WHAT I CAME TO TELL YOU. WE CAN'T FIND JAIME!
BUT I BET THE **ULTRONS** DID. AND NOW THEY'RE **DIGGING** AT THE **ANTHILL**.
GET TO THE LEAPFROG! NOW!
WHAT ARE **YOU** GOING TO DO?
HELP!
STAND BACK!
SKREEEEE

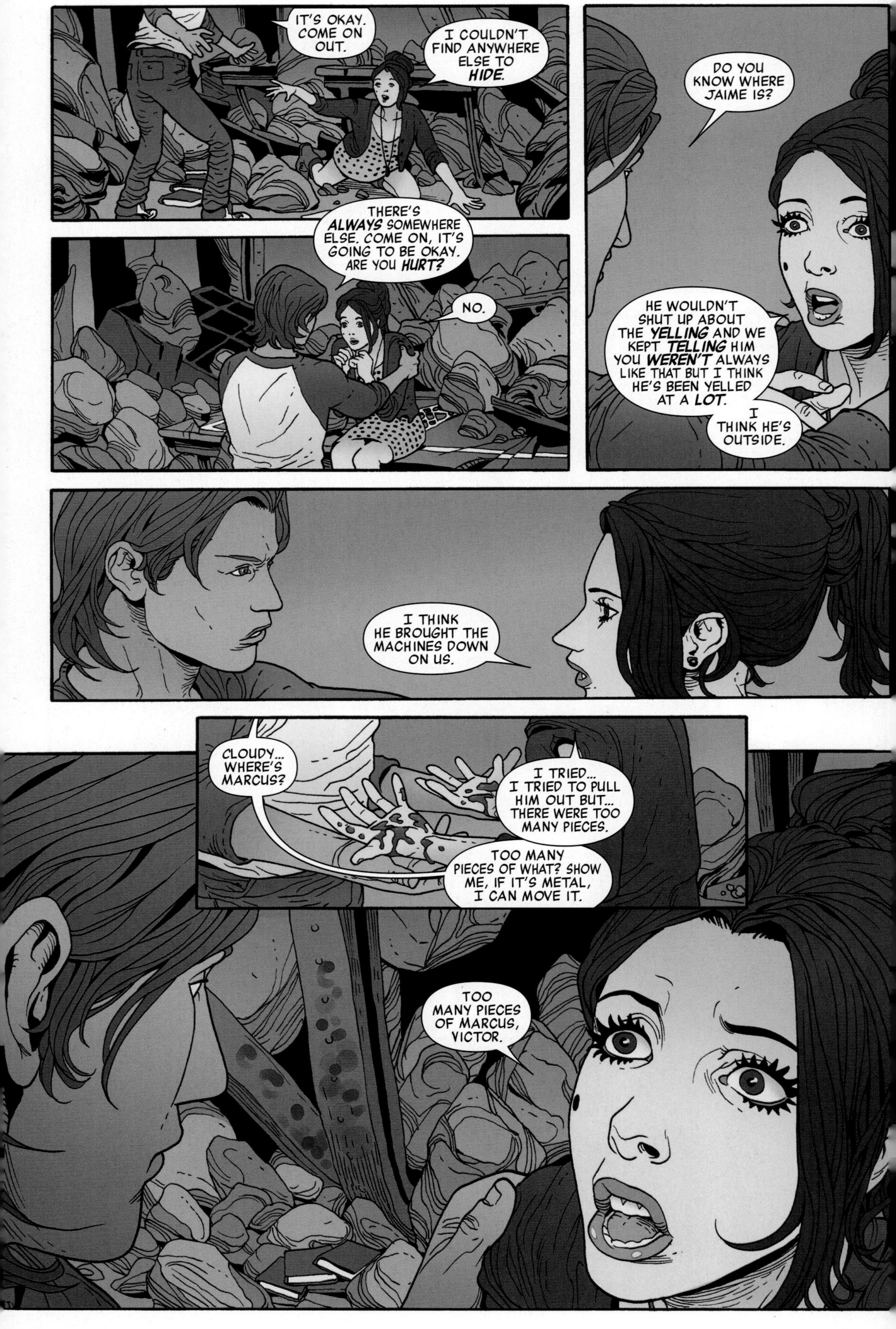
IT'S OKAY. COME ON OUT.
I COULDN'T FIND ANYWHERE ELSE TO HIDE.
THERE'S ALWAYS SOMEWHERE ELSE. COME ON, IT'S GOING TO BE OKAY. ARE YOU HURT?
NO.
DO YOU KNOW WHERE JAIME IS?
HE WOULDN'T SHUT UP ABOUT THE YELLING AND WE KEPT TELLING HIM YOU WEREN'T ALWAYS LIKE THAT BUT I THINK HE'S BEEN YELLED AT A LOT.
I THINK HE'S OUTSIDE.
I THINK HE BROUGHT THE MACHINES DOWN ON US.
CLOUDY... WHERE'S MARCUS?
I TRIED... I TRIED TO PULL HIM OUT BUT... THERE WERE TOO MANY PIECES.
TOO MANY PIECES OF WHAT? SHOW ME, IF IT'S METAL, I CAN MOVE IT.
TOO MANY PIECES OF MARCUS, VICTOR.

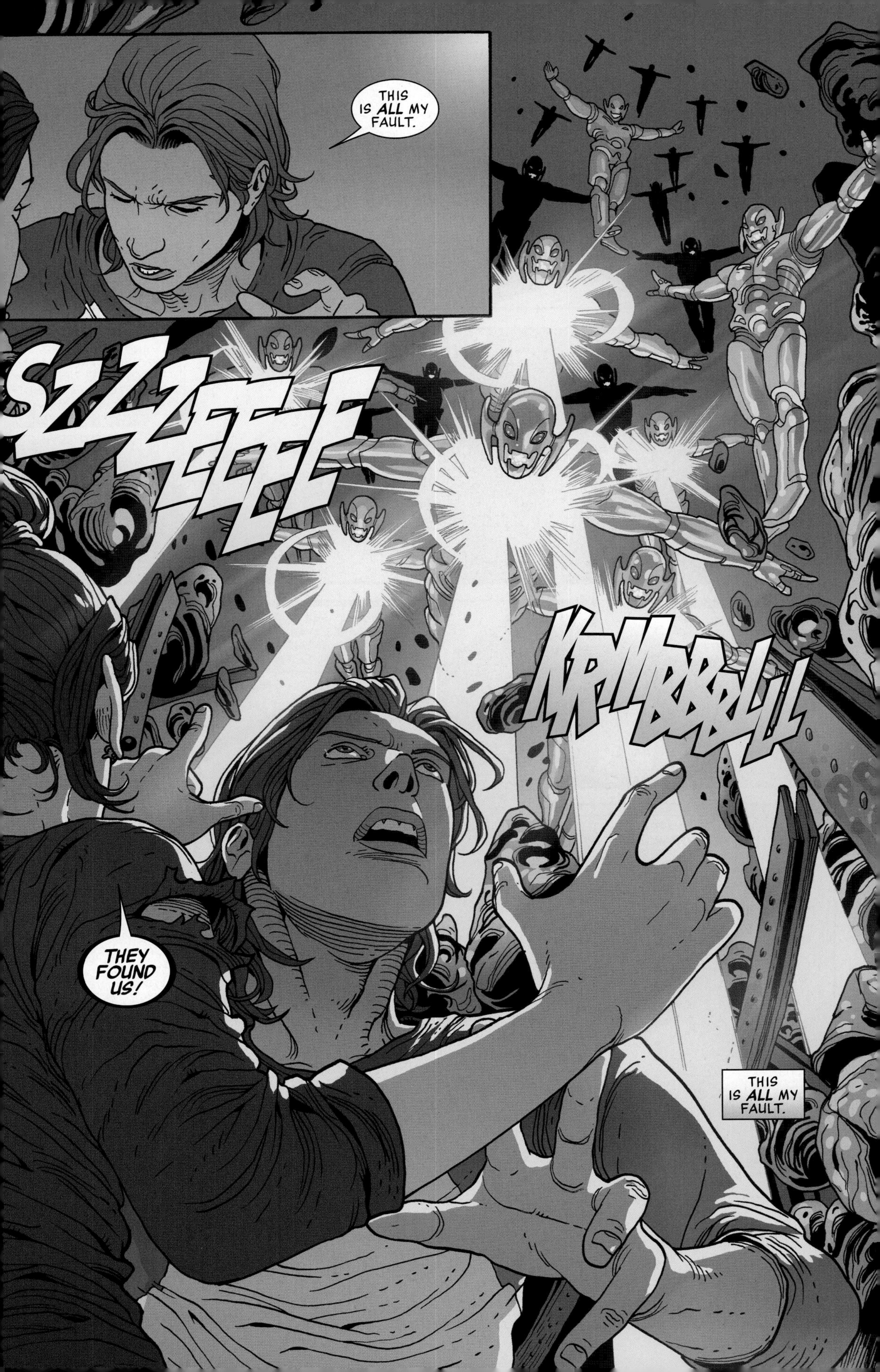
THIS IS ALL MY FAULT.
SZZZEEEE
KRMBBLL
THEY FOUND US!
THIS IS ALL MY FAULT.

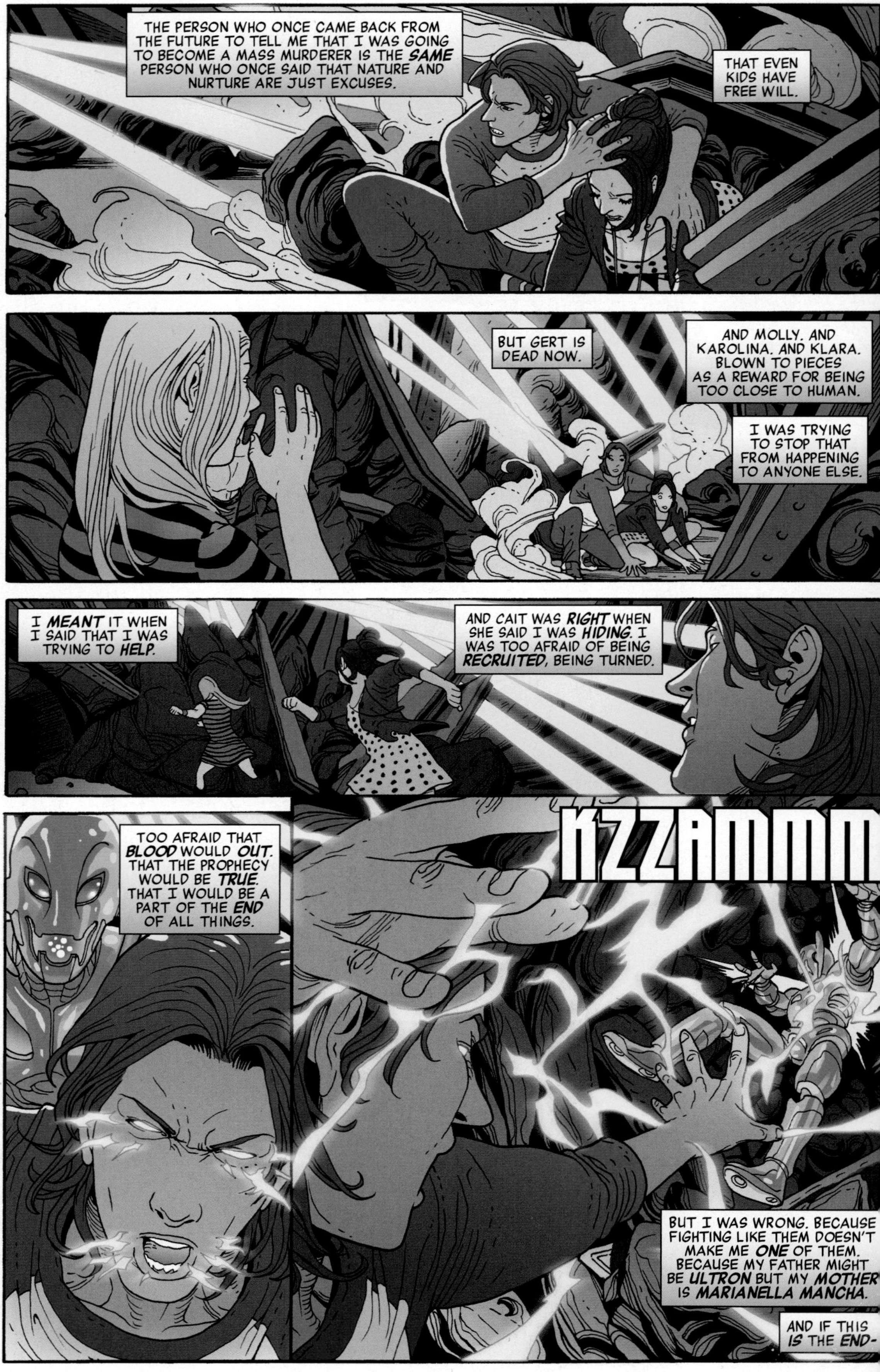
THE PERSON WHO ONCE CAME BACK FROM THE FUTURE TO TELL ME THAT I WAS GOING TO BECOME A MASS MURDERER IS THE SAME PERSON WHO ONCE SAID THAT NATURE AND NURTURE ARE JUST EXCUSES.
THAT EVEN KIDS HAVE FREE WILL.
BUT GERT IS DEAD NOW.
AND MOLLY. AND KAROLINA. AND KLARA. BLOWN TO PIECES AS A REWARD FOR BEING TOO CLOSE TO HUMAN.
I WAS TRYING TO STOP THAT FROM HAPPENING TO ANYONE ELSE.
I MEANT IT WHEN I SAID THAT I WAS TRYING TO HELP.
AND CAIT WAS RIGHT WHEN SHE SAID I WAS HIDING. I WAS TOO AFRAID OF BEING RECRUITED, BEING TURNED.
TOO AFRAID THAT BLOOD WOULD OUT. THAT THE PROPHECY WOULD BE TRUE. THAT I WOULD BE A PART OF THE END OF ALL THINGS.
KZZAMMM
BUT I WAS WRONG. BECAUSE FIGHTING LIKE THEM DOESN'T MAKE ME ONE OF THEM. BECAUSE MY FATHER MIGHT BE ULTRON BUT MY MOTHER IS MARIANELLA MANCHA.
AND IF THIS IS THE END-

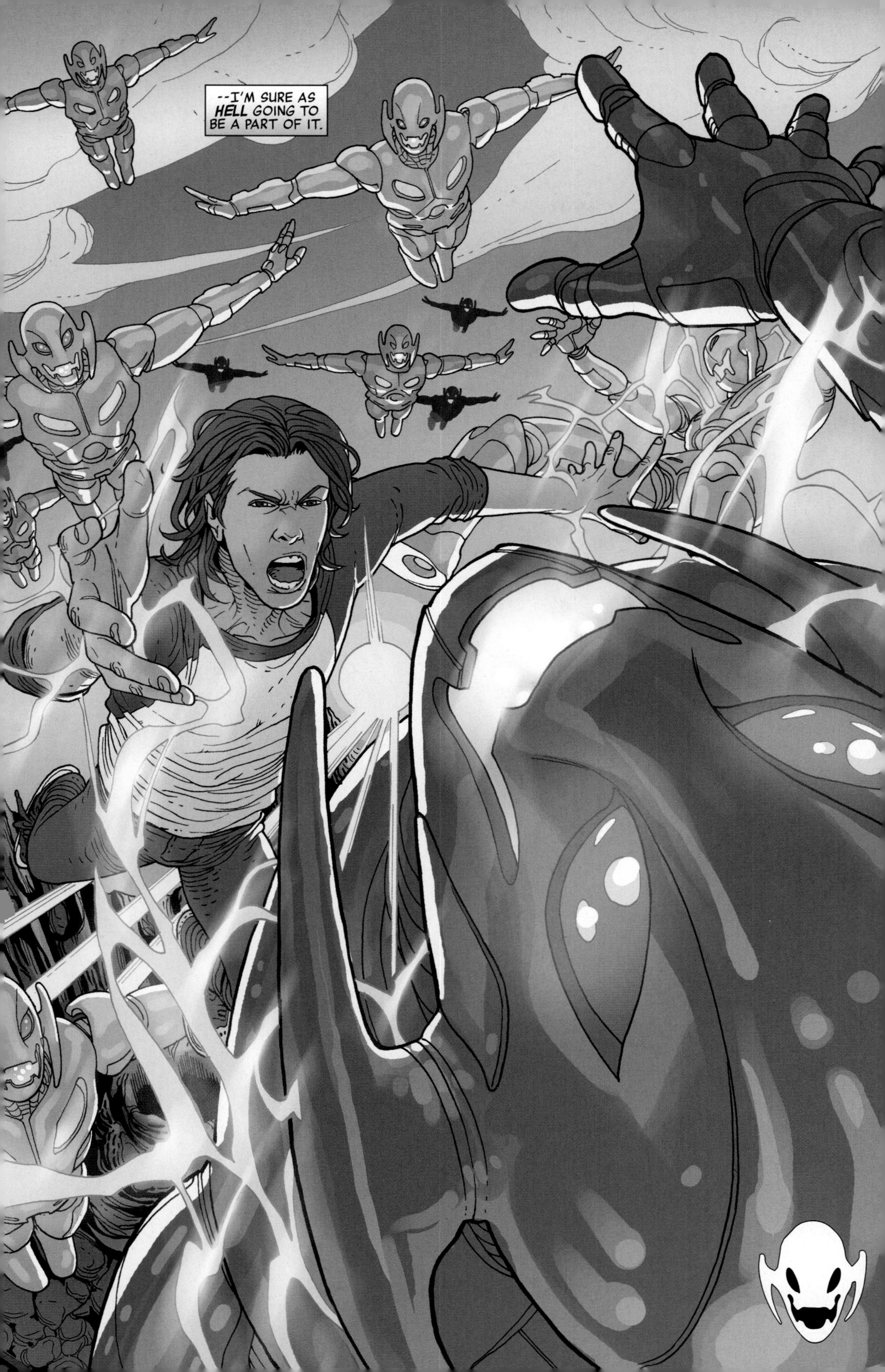
--I'M SURE AS HELL GOING TO BE A PART OF IT.

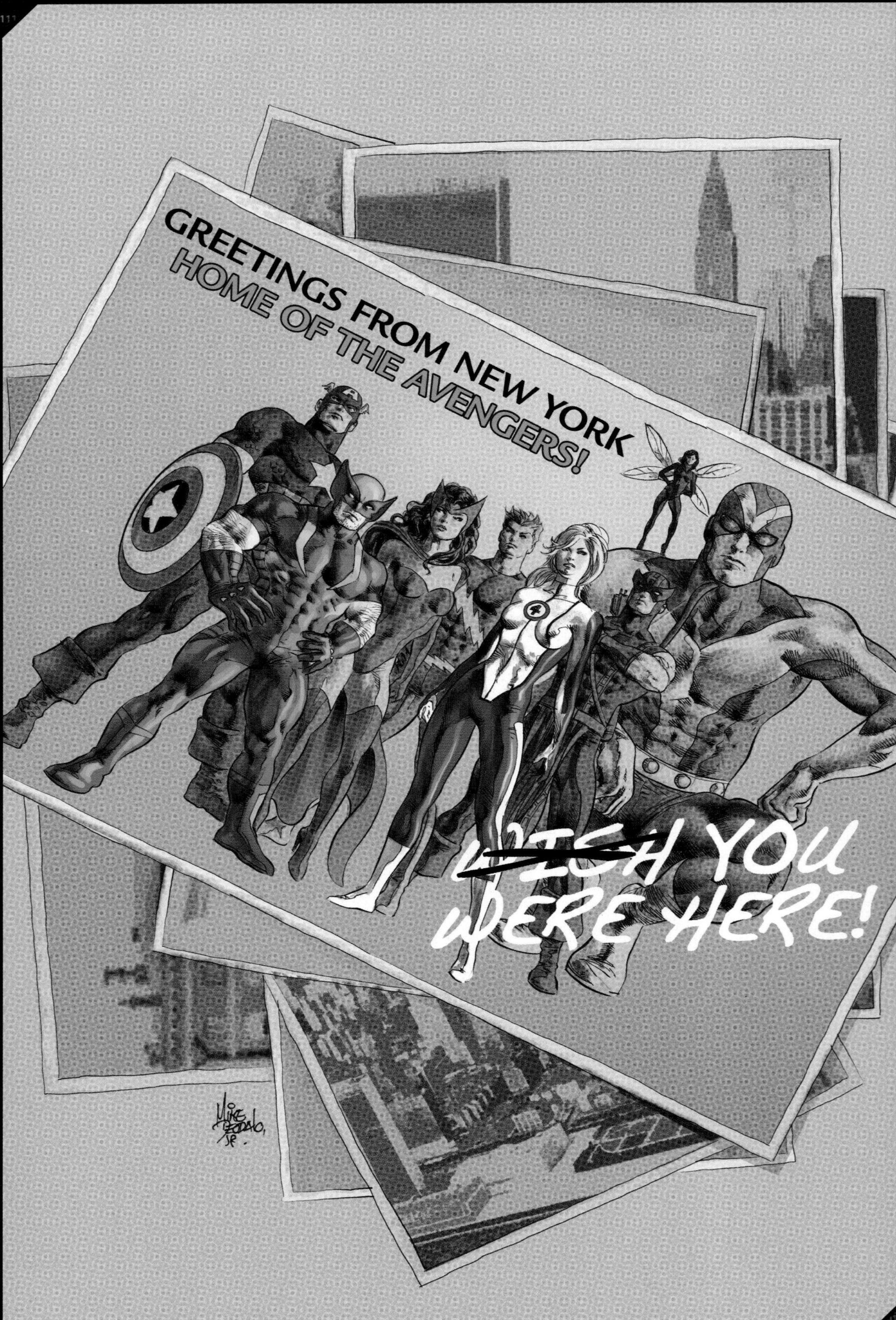
GREETINGS FROM NEW YORK
HOME OF THE AVENGERS!
WISH YOU WERE HERE!

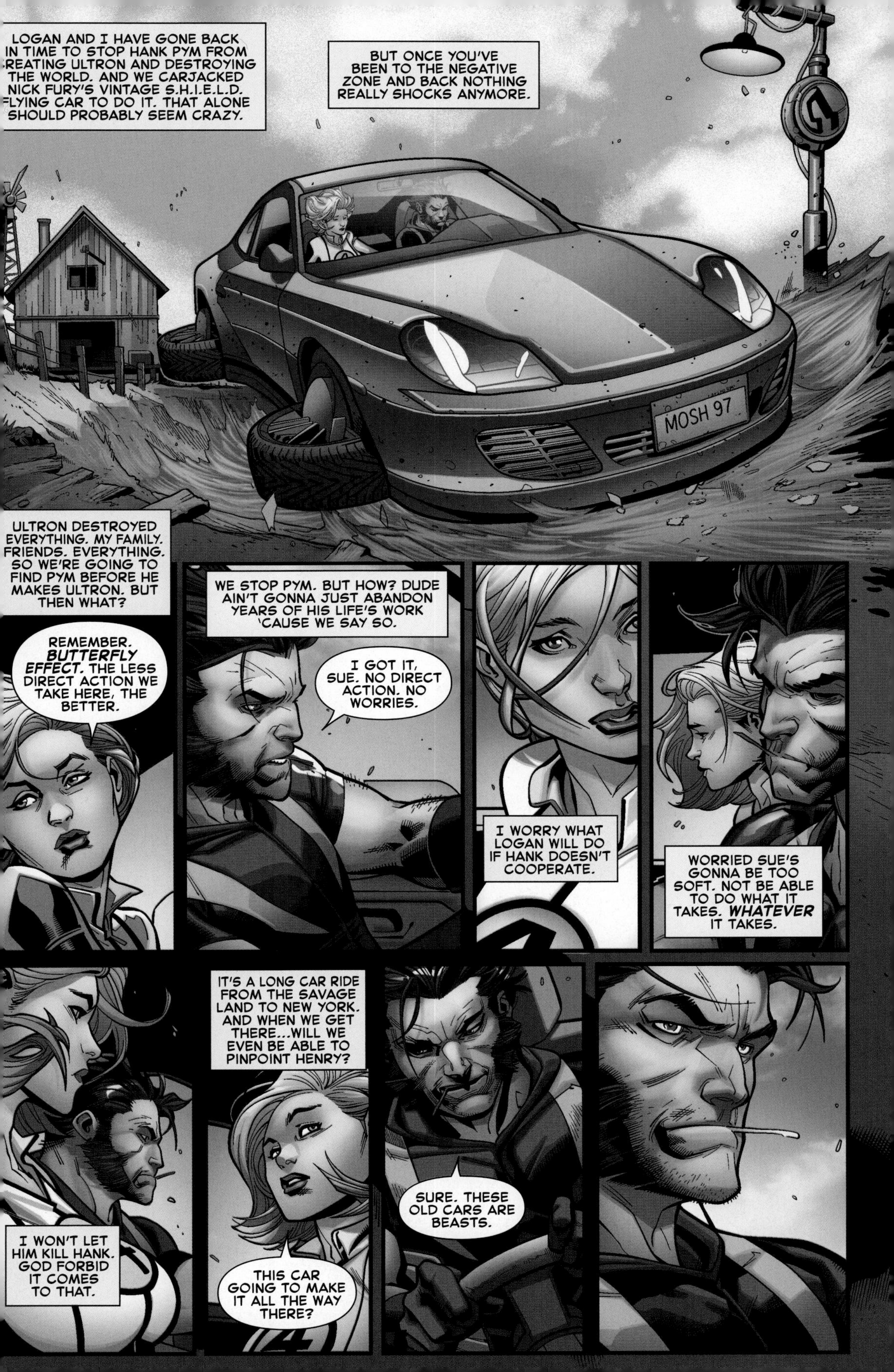
LOGAN AND I HAVE GONE BACK IN TIME TO STOP HANK PYM FROM CREATING ULTRON AND DESTROYING THE WORLD. AND WE CARJACKED NICK FURY'S VINTAGE S.H.I.E.L.D. FLYING CAR TO DO IT. THAT ALONE SHOULD PROBABLY SEEM CRAZY.
BUT ONCE YOU'VE BEEN TO THE NEGATIVE ZONE AND BACK NOTHING REALLY SHOCKS ANYMORE.
MOSH 97
ULTRON DESTROYED EVERYTHING. MY FAMILY. FRIENDS. EVERYTHING. SO WE'RE GOING TO FIND PYM BEFORE HE MAKES ULTRON. BUT THEN WHAT?
REMEMBER. *BUTTERFLY EFFECT.* THE LESS DIRECT ACTION WE TAKE HERE, THE BETTER.
WE STOP PYM. BUT HOW? DUDE AIN'T GONNA JUST ABANDON YEARS OF HIS LIFE'S WORK 'CAUSE WE SAY SO.
I GOT IT, SUE. NO DIRECT ACTION. NO WORRIES.
I WORRY WHAT LOGAN WILL DO IF HANK DOESN'T COOPERATE.
WORRIED SUE'S GONNA BE TOO SOFT. NOT BE ABLE TO DO WHAT IT TAKES. *WHATEVER* IT TAKES.
I WON'T LET HIM KILL HANK. GOD FORBID IT COMES TO THAT.
IT'S A LONG CAR RIDE FROM THE SAVAGE LAND TO NEW YORK. AND WHEN WE GET THERE...WILL WE EVEN BE ABLE TO PINPOINT HENRY?
THIS CAR GOING TO MAKE IT ALL THE WAY THERE?
SURE. THESE OLD CARS ARE BEASTS.

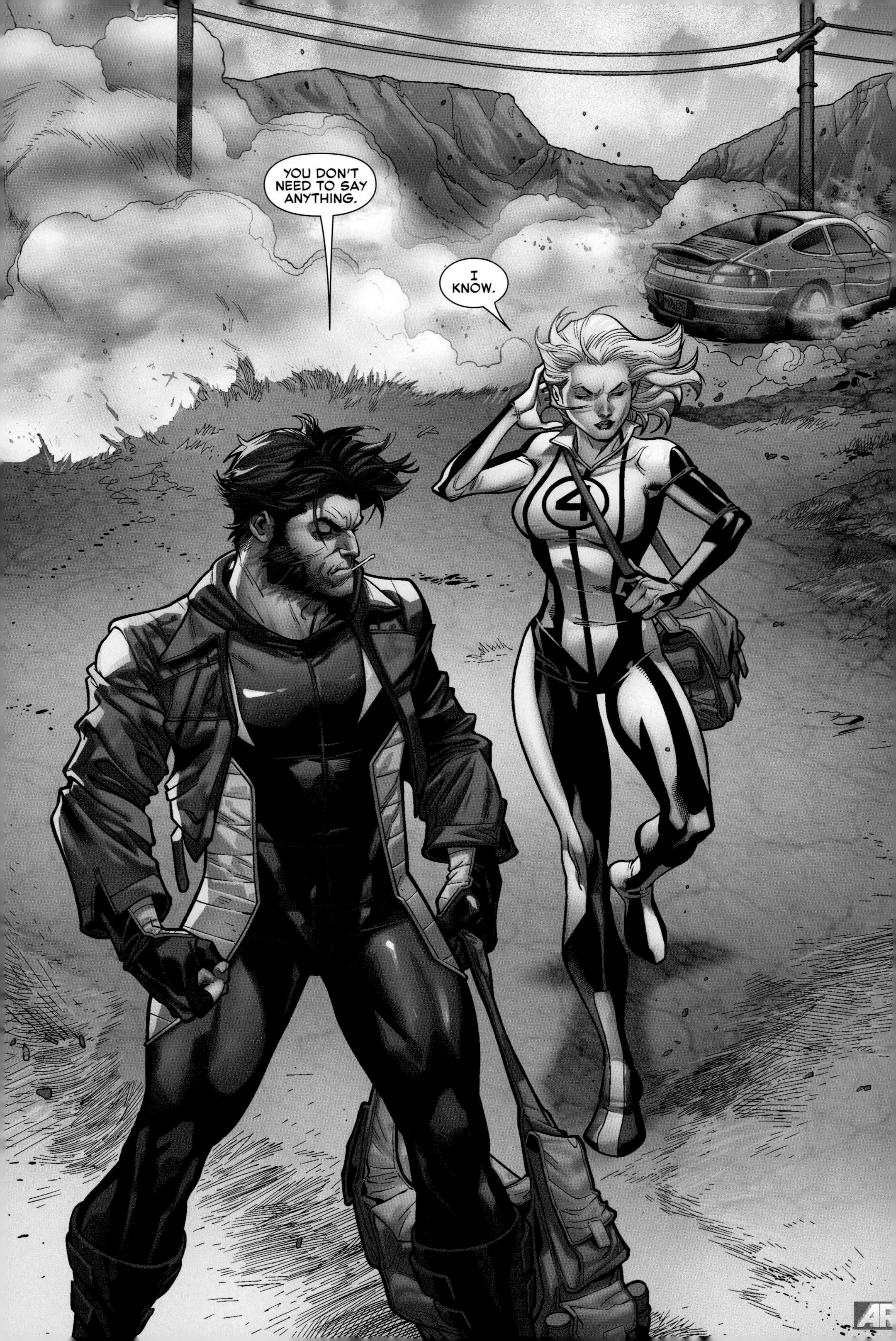
YOU DON'T NEED TO SAY ANYTHING.
I KNOW.

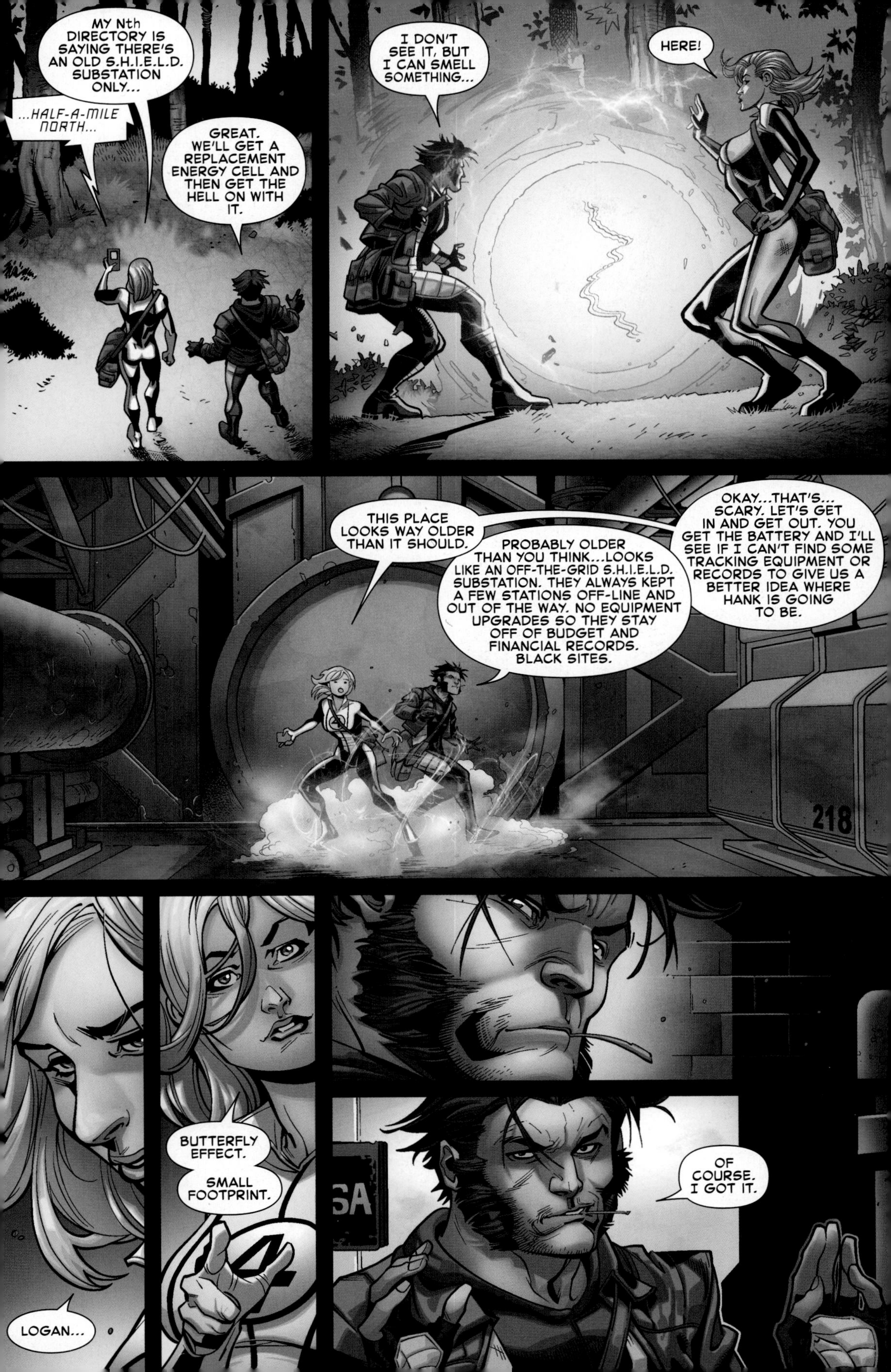
MY Nth DIRECTORY IS SAYING THERE'S AN OLD S.H.I.E.L.D. SUBSTATION ONLY...
...HALF-A-MILE NORTH...
GREAT. WE'LL GET A REPLACEMENT ENERGY CELL AND THEN GET THE HELL ON WITH IT.
I DON'T SEE IT, BUT I CAN SMELL SOMETHING...
HERE!
THIS PLACE LOOKS WAY OLDER THAN IT SHOULD.
PROBABLY OLDER THAN YOU THINK...LOOKS LIKE AN OFF-THE-GRID S.H.I.E.L.D. SUBSTATION. THEY ALWAYS KEPT A FEW STATIONS OFF-LINE AND OUT OF THE WAY. NO EQUIPMENT UPGRADES SO THEY STAY OFF OF BUDGET AND FINANCIAL RECORDS. BLACK SITES.
OKAY...THAT'S... SCARY. LET'S GET IN AND GET OUT. YOU GET THE BATTERY AND I'LL SEE IF I CAN'T FIND SOME TRACKING EQUIPMENT OR RECORDS TO GIVE US A BETTER IDEA WHERE HANK IS GOING TO BE.
218
LOGAN...
BUTTERFLY EFFECT.
SMALL FOOTPRINT.
SA
OF COURSE. I GOT IT.

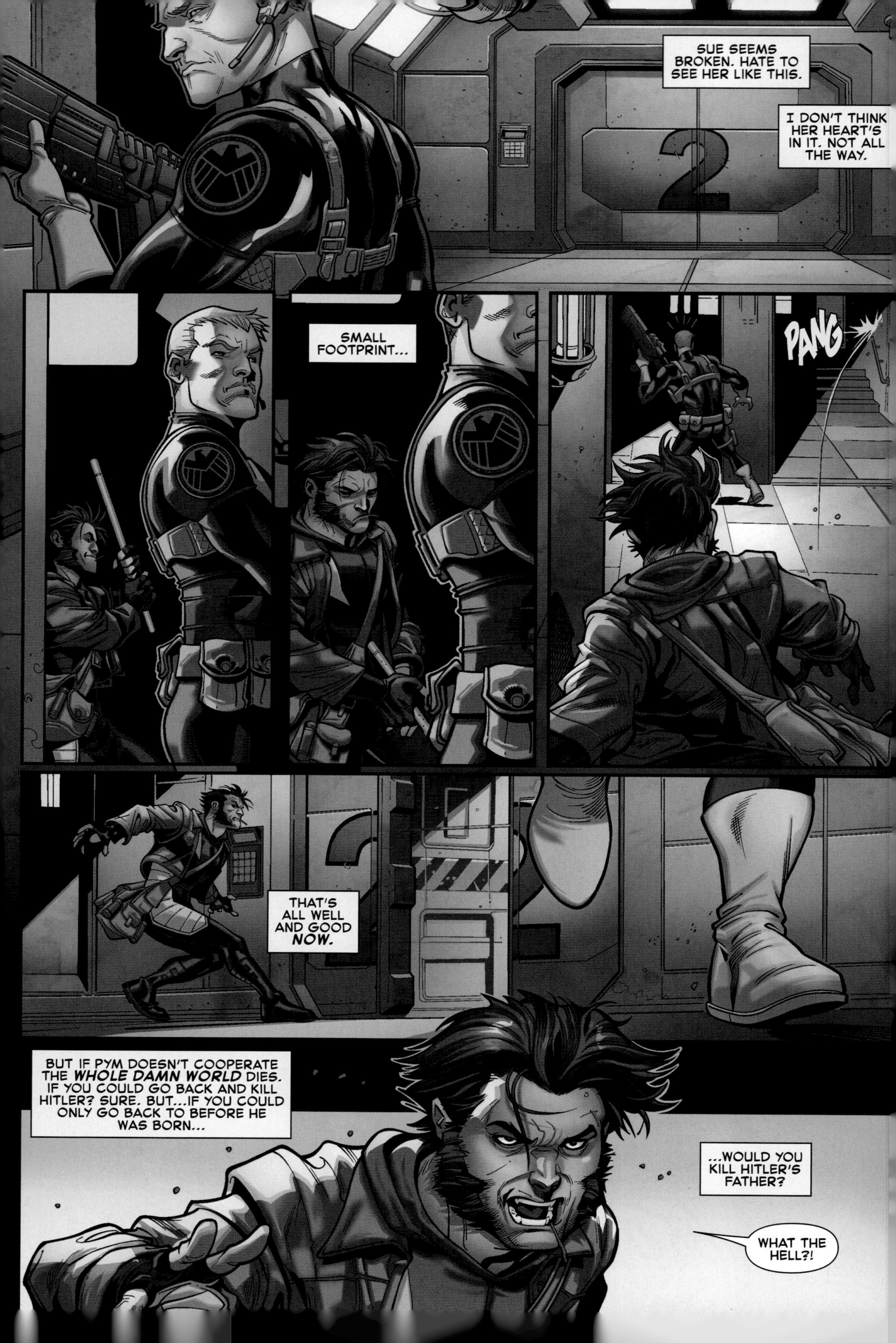

SUE SEEMS BROKEN. HATE TO SEE HER LIKE THIS.
I DON'T THINK HER HEART'S IN IT. NOT ALL THE WAY.
SMALL FOOTPRINT...
PANG
THAT'S ALL WELL AND GOOD NOW.
BUT IF PYM DOESN'T COOPERATE THE WHOLE DAMN WORLD DIES. IF YOU COULD GO BACK AND KILL HITLER? SURE. BUT...IF YOU COULD ONLY GO BACK TO BEFORE HE WAS BORN...
...WOULD YOU KILL HITLER'S FATHER?
WHAT THE HELL?!

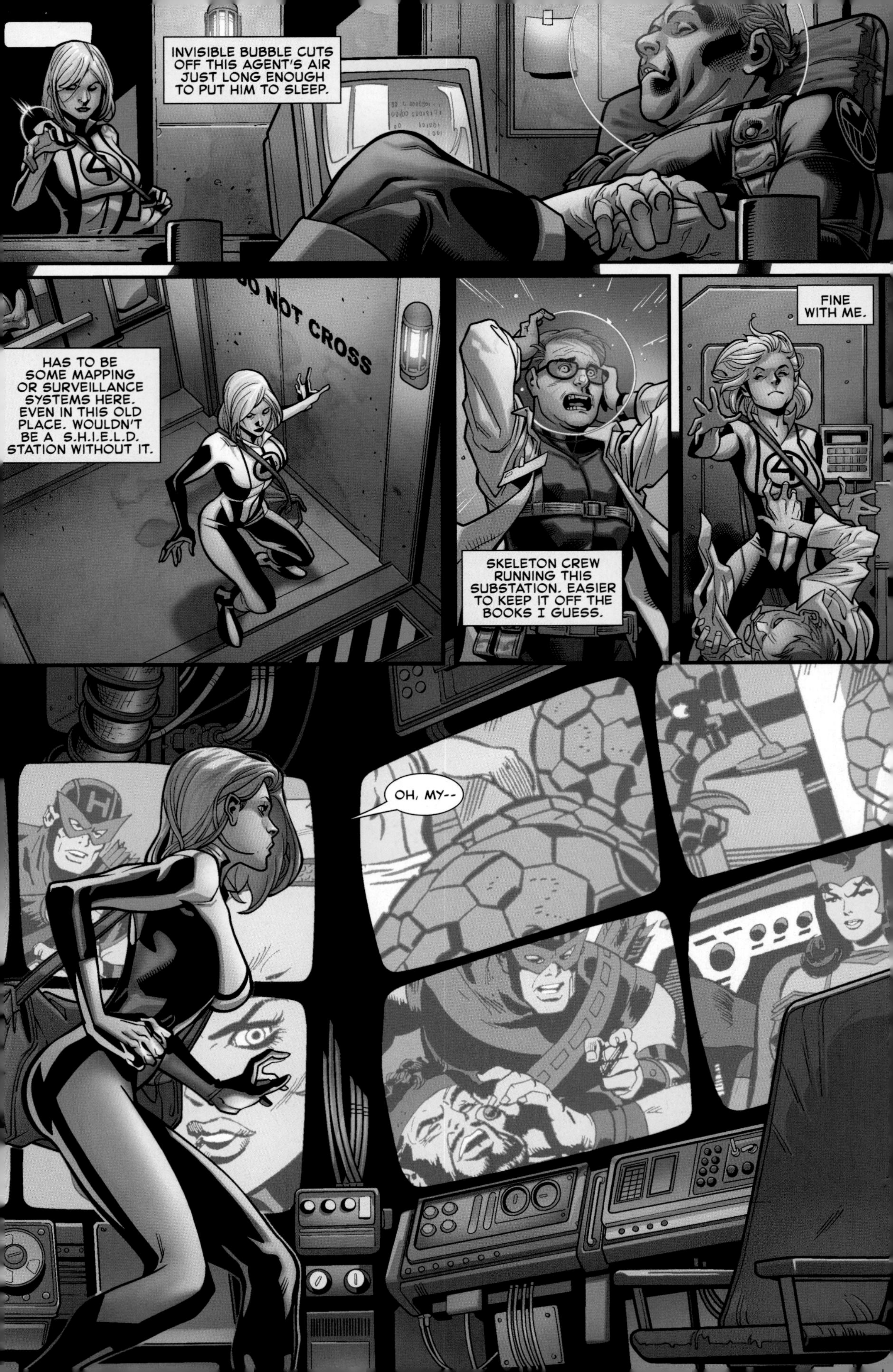
INVISIBLE BUBBLE CUTS OFF THIS AGENT'S AIR JUST LONG ENOUGH TO PUT HIM TO SLEEP.
DO NOT CROSS
HAS TO BE SOME MAPPING OR SURVEILLANCE SYSTEMS HERE. EVEN IN THIS OLD PLACE. WOULDN'T BE A S.H.I.E.L.D. STATION WITHOUT IT.
SKELETON CREW RUNNING THIS SUBSTATION. EASIER TO KEEP IT OFF THE BOOKS I GUESS.
FINE WITH ME.
OH, MY--

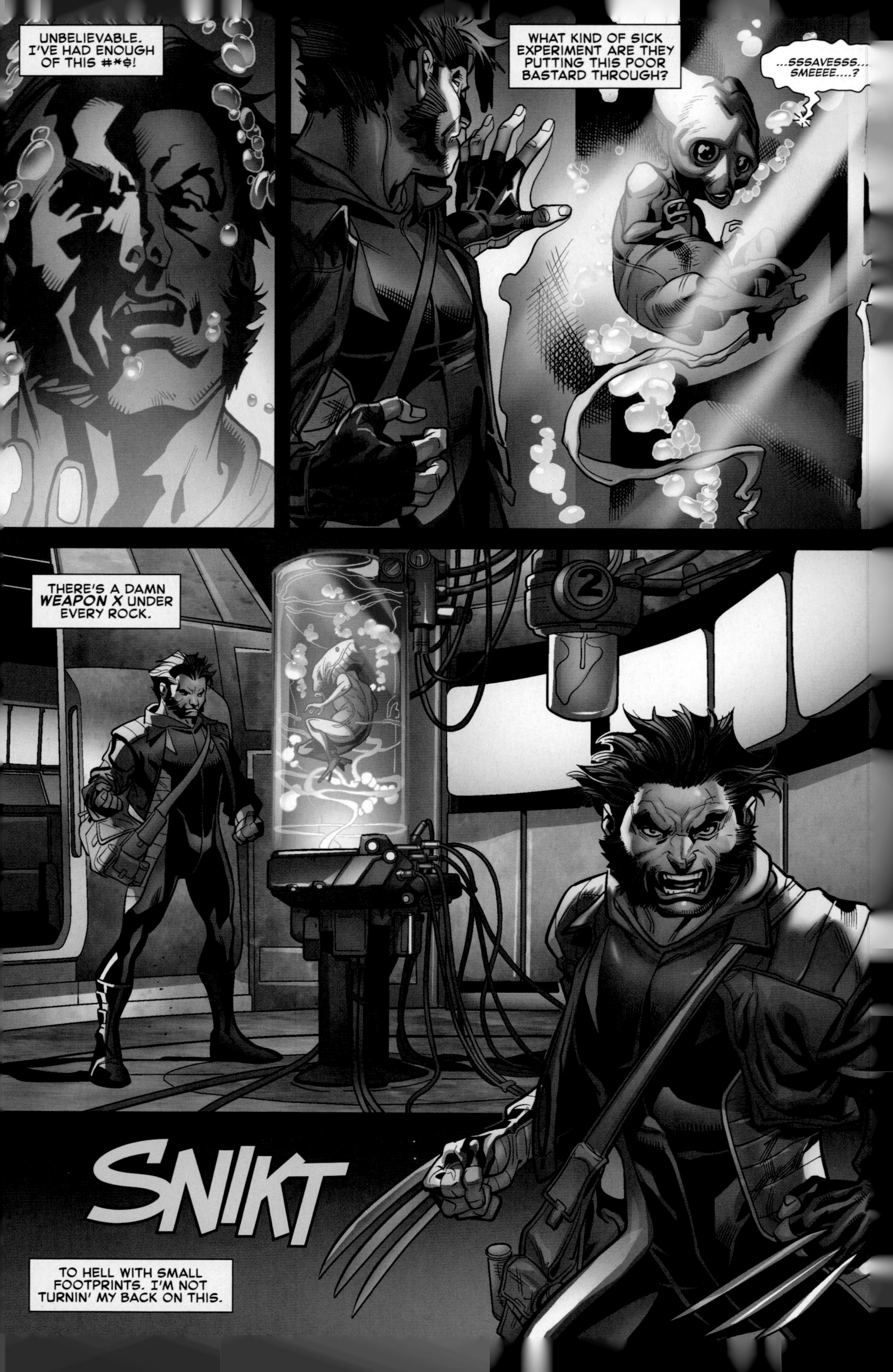
UNBELIEVABLE. I'VE HAD ENOUGH OF THIS #*$!
WHAT KIND OF SICK EXPERIMENT ARE THEY PUTTING THIS POOR BASTARD THROUGH?
...SSSAVESSS... SMEEEE....?
THERE'S A DAMN WEAPON X UNDER EVERY ROCK.
SNIKT
TO HELL WITH SMALL FOOTPRINTS. I'M NOT TURNIN' MY BACK ON THIS.

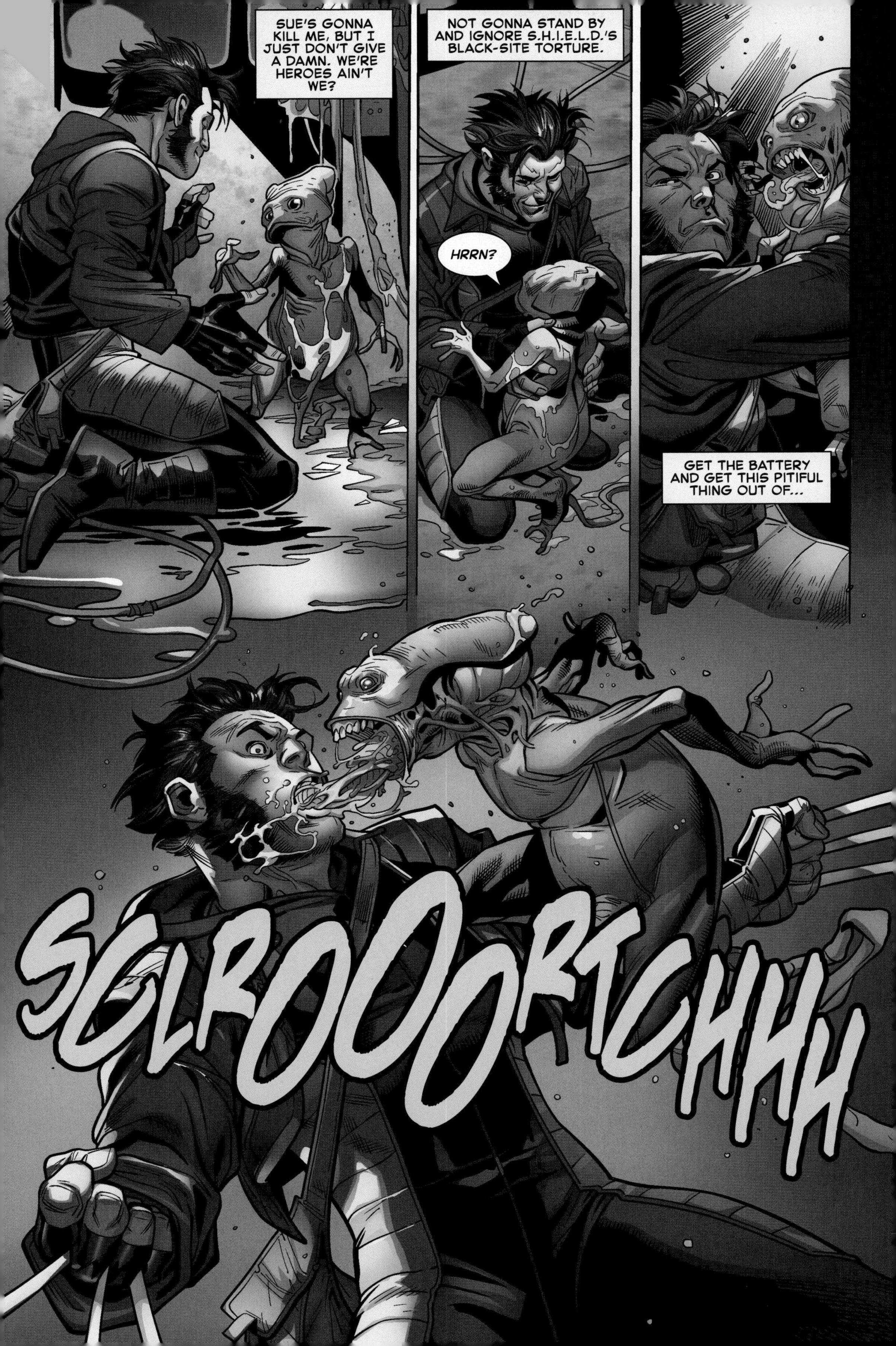
SUE'S GONNA KILL ME, BUT I JUST DON'T GIVE A DAMN. WE'RE HEROES AIN'T WE?
NOT GONNA STAND BY AND IGNORE S.H.I.E.L.D.'S BLACK-SITE TORTURE.
HRRN?
GET THE BATTERY AND GET THIS PITIFUL THING OUT OF...
SCLROOOORTCHHH

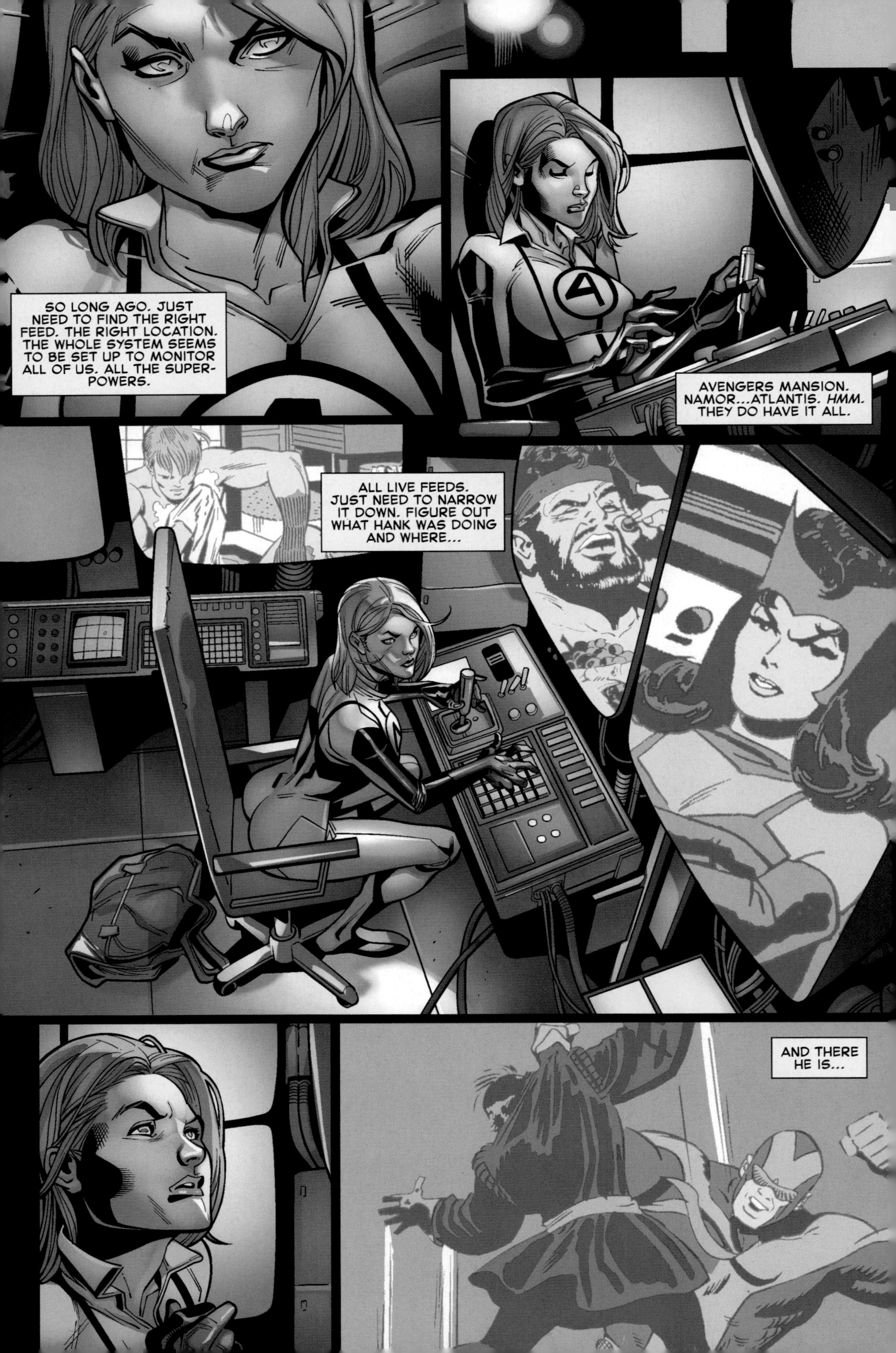
SO LONG AGO. JUST NEED TO FIND THE RIGHT FEED. THE RIGHT LOCATION. THE WHOLE SYSTEM SEEMS TO BE SET UP TO MONITOR ALL OF US. ALL THE SUPER-POWERS.
AVENGERS MANSION. NAMOR...ATLANTIS. *HMM.* THEY DO HAVE IT ALL.
ALL LIVE FEEDS. JUST NEED TO NARROW IT DOWN. FIGURE OUT WHAT HANK WAS DOING AND WHERE...
AND THERE HE IS...

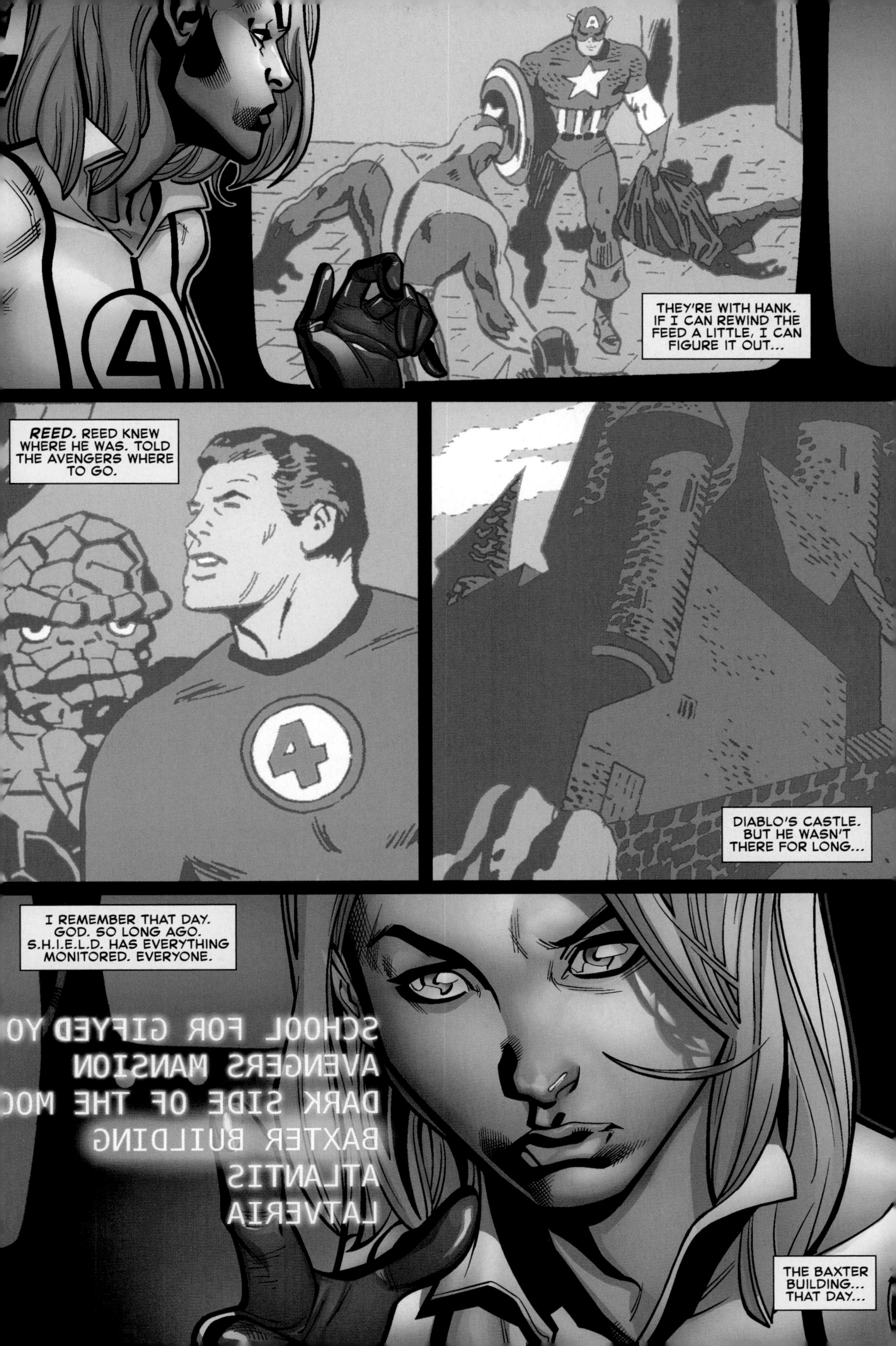
THEY'RE WITH HANK. IF I CAN REWIND THE FEED A LITTLE, I CAN FIGURE IT OUT...
REED. REED KNEW WHERE HE WAS. TOLD THE AVENGERS WHERE TO GO.
DIABLO'S CASTLE. BUT HE WASN'T THERE FOR LONG...
I REMEMBER THAT DAY. GOD. SO LONG AGO. S.H.I.E.L.D. HAS EVERYTHING MONITORED. EVERYONE.
SCHOOL FOR GIFTED YO
AVENGERS MANSION
DARK SIDE OF THE MO
BAXTER BUILDING
ATLANTIS
LATVERIA
THE BAXTER BUILDING... THAT DAY...

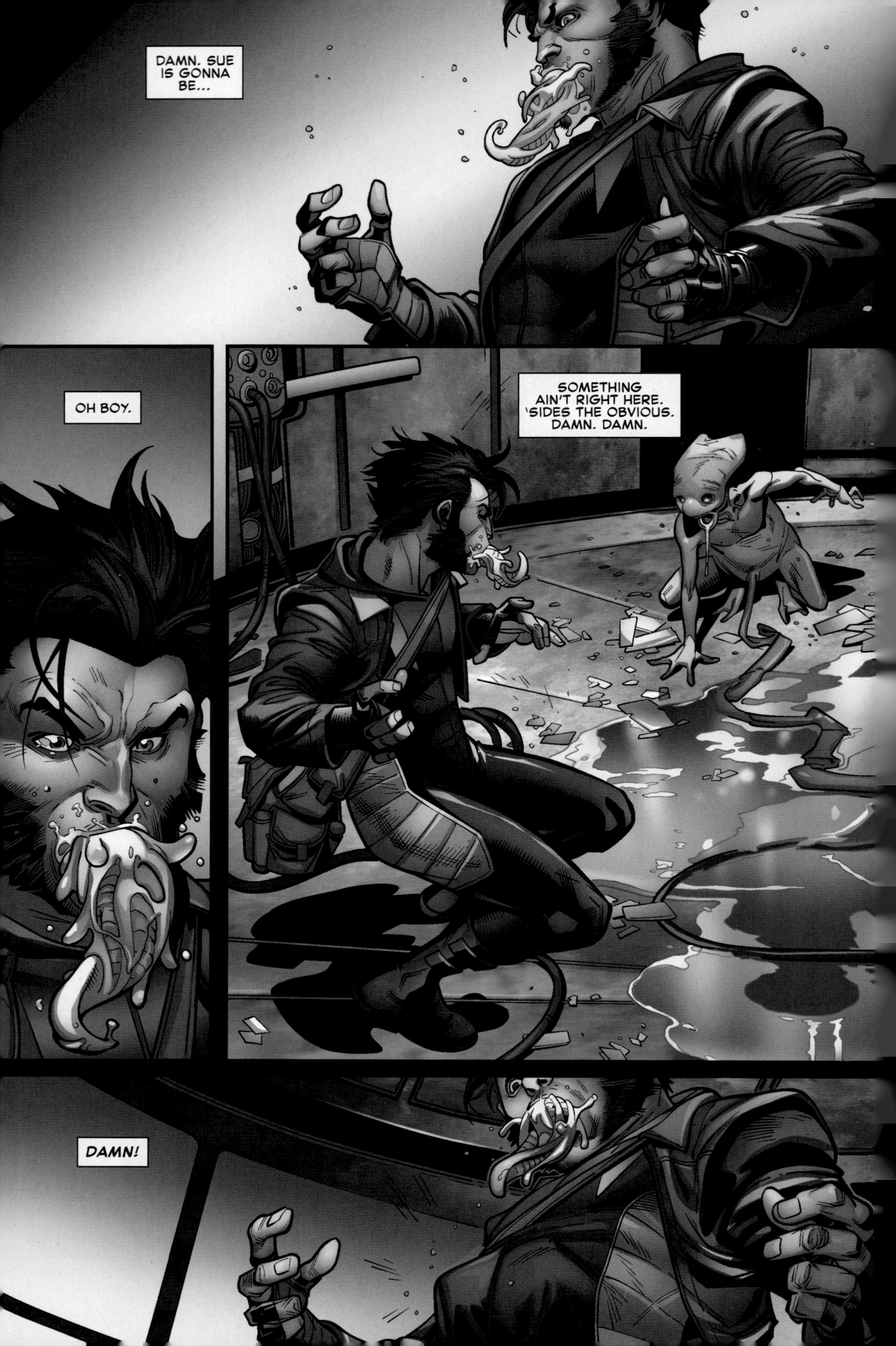
DAMN. SUE IS GONNA BE...
OH BOY.
SOMETHING AIN'T RIGHT HERE. 'SIDES THE OBVIOUS. DAMN. DAMN.
DAMN!

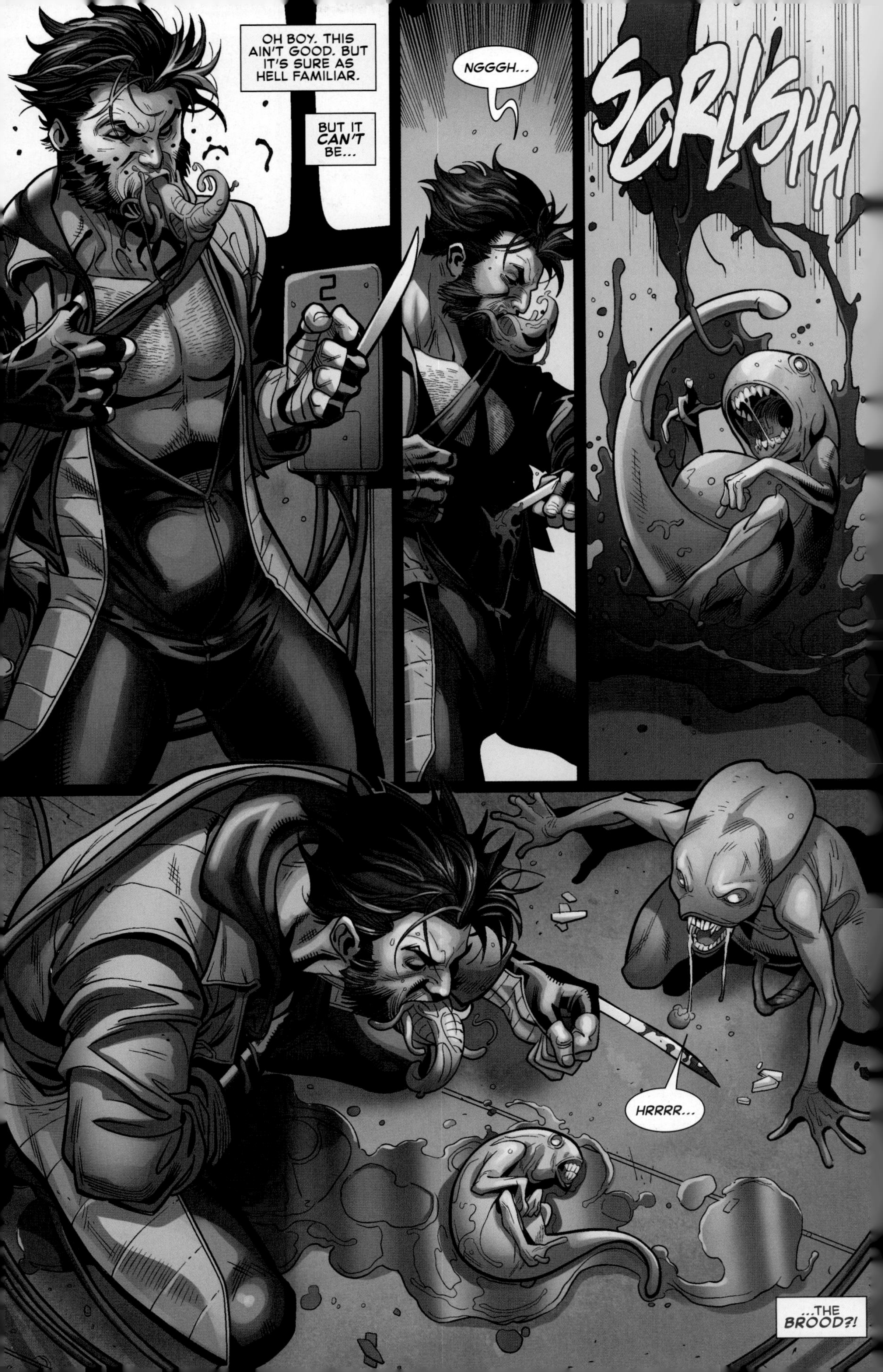
OH BOY. THIS AIN'T GOOD. BUT IT'S SURE AS HELL FAMILIAR.
BUT IT CAN'T BE...
NGGGH...
SCRLSHH
HRRRR...
...THE BROOD?!

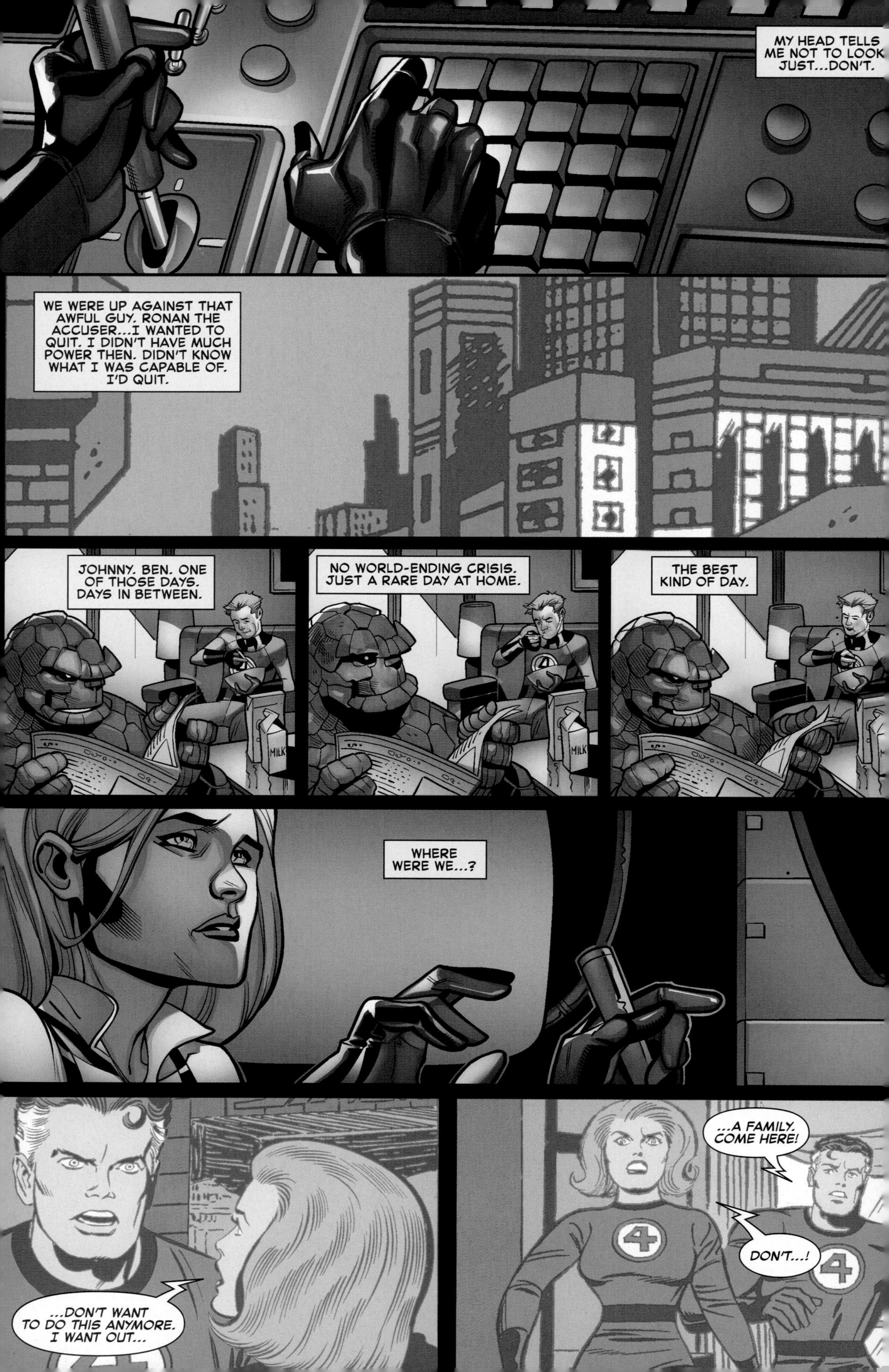

MY HEAD TELLS ME NOT TO LOOK JUST...DON'T.
WE WERE UP AGAINST THAT AWFUL GUY. RONAN THE ACCUSER...I WANTED TO QUIT. I DIDN'T HAVE MUCH POWER THEN. DIDN'T KNOW WHAT I WAS CAPABLE OF. I'D QUIT.
JOHNNY. BEN. ONE OF THOSE DAYS. DAYS IN BETWEEN.
MILK
NO WORLD-ENDING CRISIS. JUST A RARE DAY AT HOME.
MILK
THE BEST KIND OF DAY.
WHERE WERE WE...?
...DON'T WANT TO DO THIS ANYMORE. I WANT OUT...
...A FAMILY. COME HERE!
DON'T...!

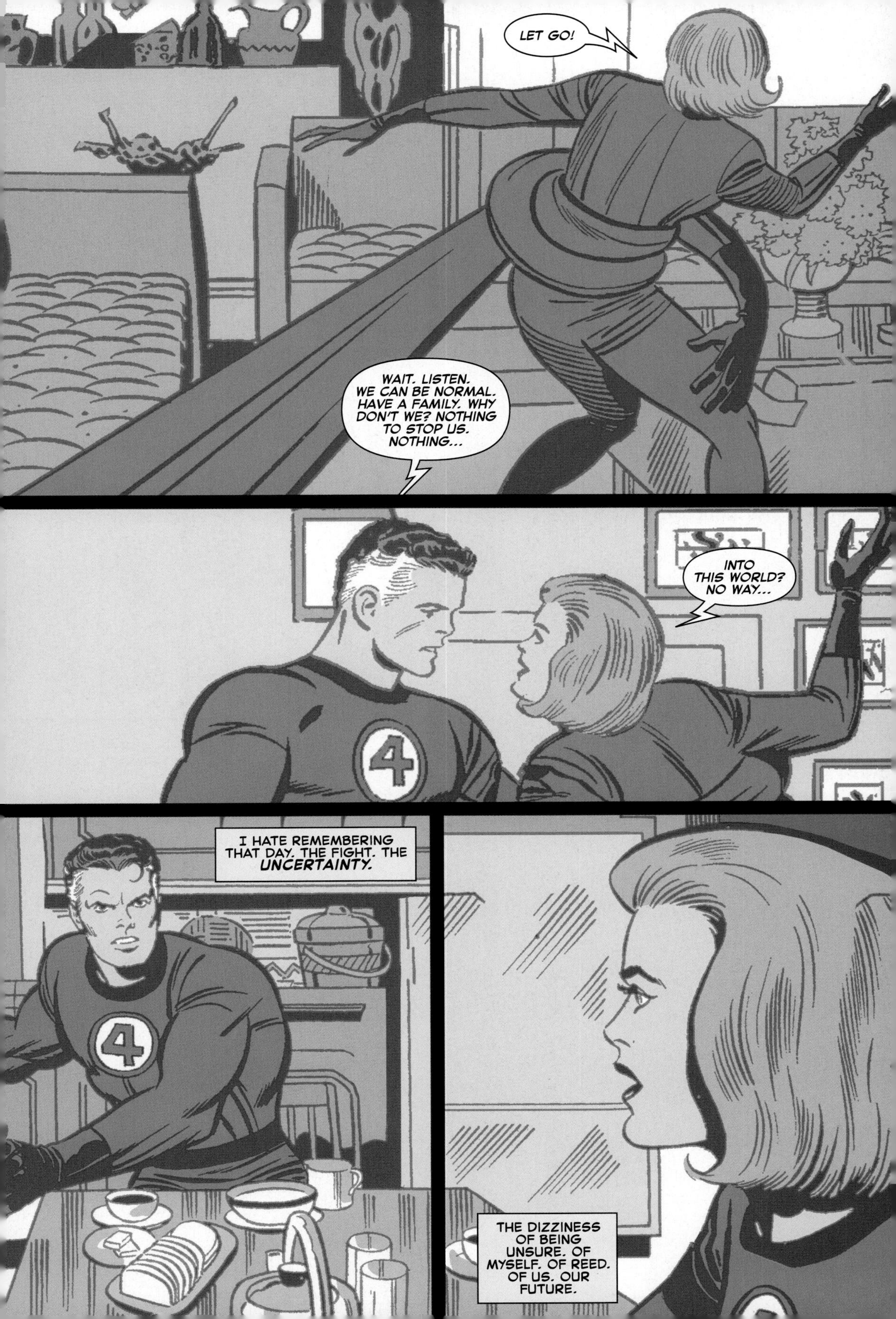
LET GO!
WAIT. LISTEN. WE CAN BE NORMAL. HAVE A FAMILY. WHY DON'T WE? NOTHING TO STOP US. NOTHING...
INTO THIS WORLD? NO WAY...
I HATE REMEMBERING THAT DAY. THE FIGHT. THE *UNCERTAINTY.*
THE DIZZINESS OF BEING UNSURE. OF MYSELF. OF REED. OF US. OUR FUTURE.

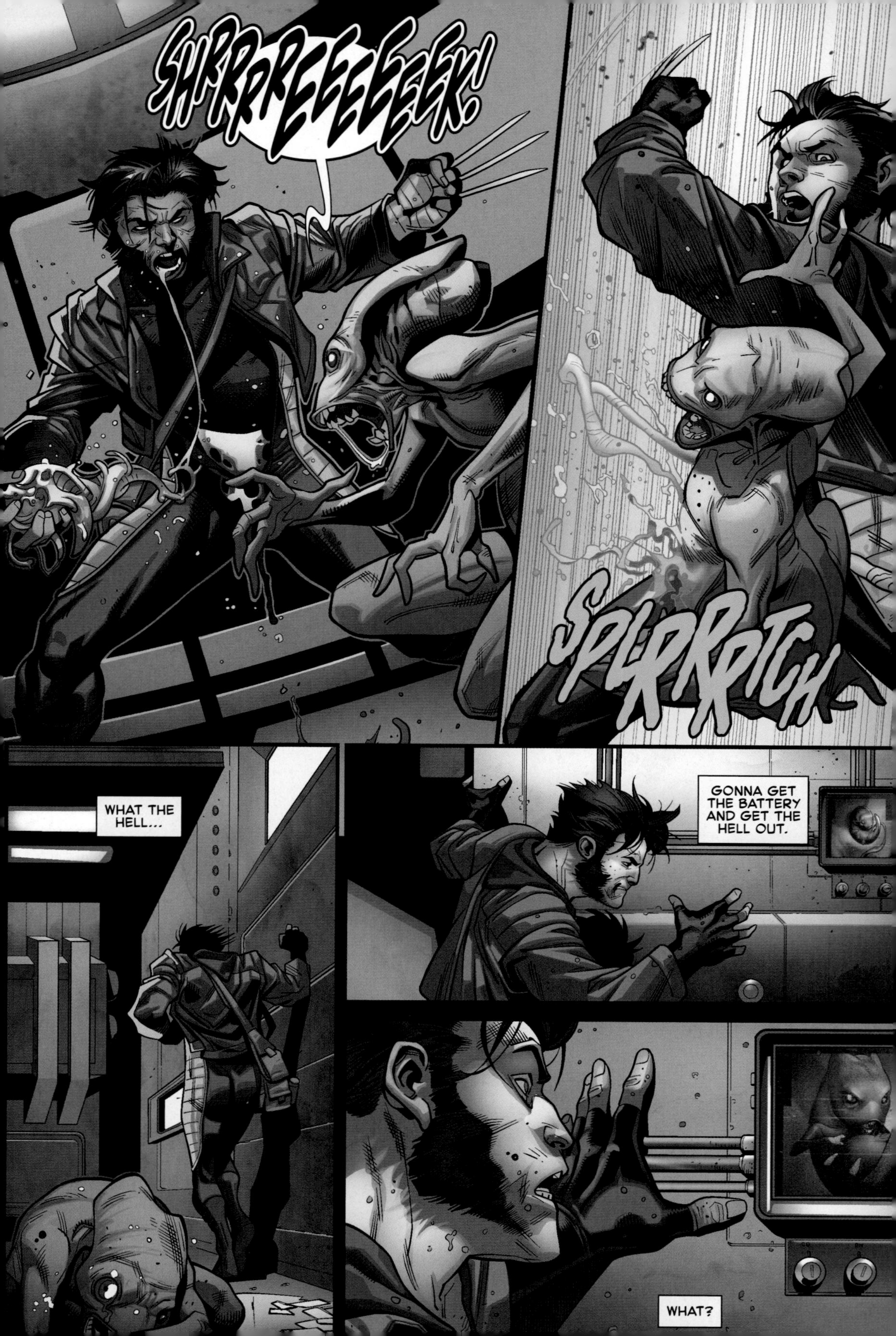
SHRRRREEEEEEK!
SPLRRRTCH
WHAT THE HELL...
GONNA GET THE BATTERY AND GET THE HELL OUT.
WHAT?

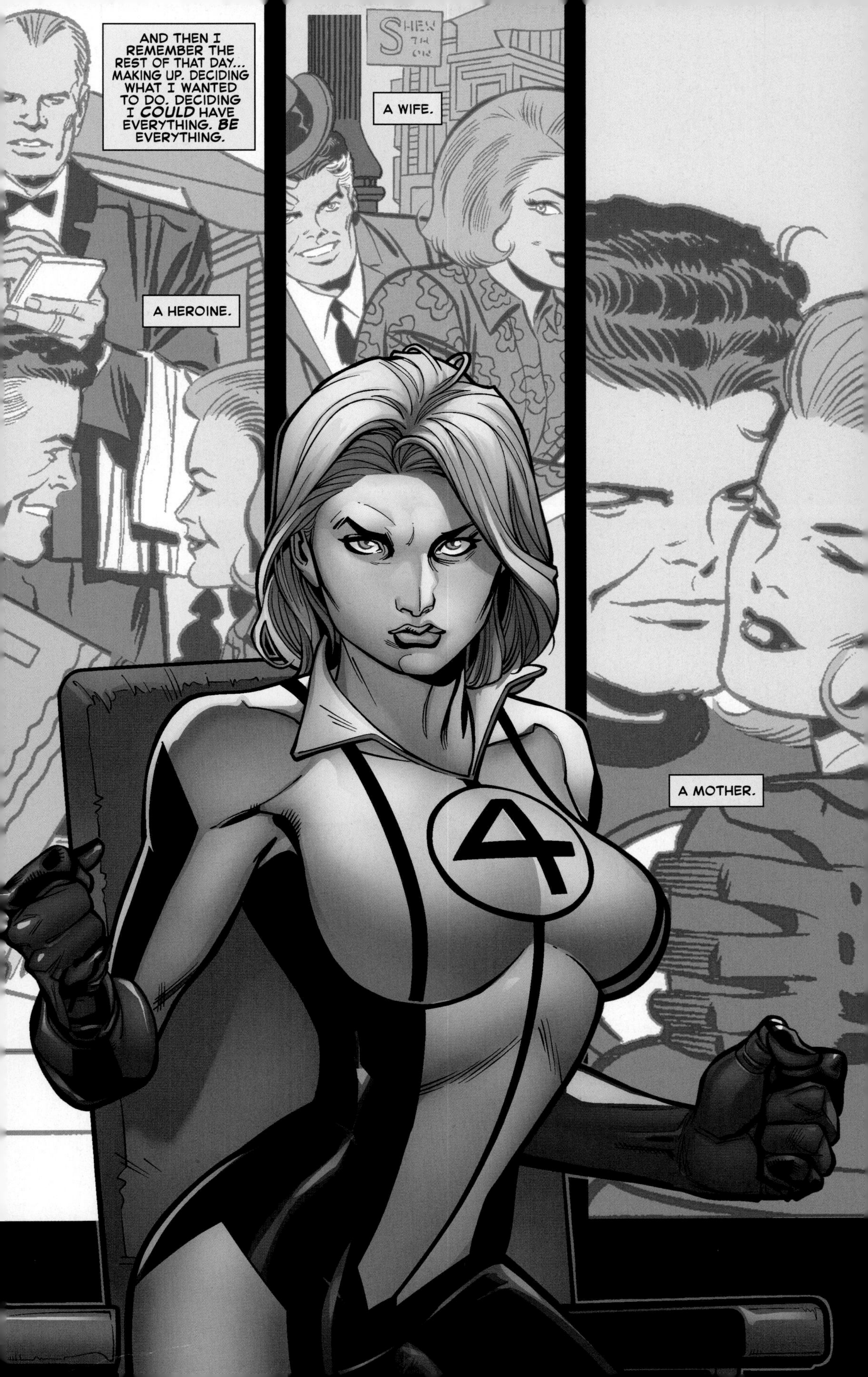
AND THEN I REMEMBER THE REST OF THAT DAY... MAKING UP. DECIDING WHAT I WANTED TO DO. DECIDING I *COULD* HAVE EVERYTHING. ***BE*** EVERYTHING.
A HEROINE.
A WIFE.
A MOTHER.

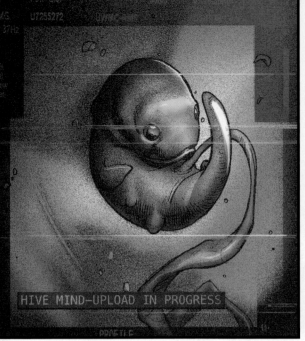

HIVE MIND—UPLOAD IN PROGRESS

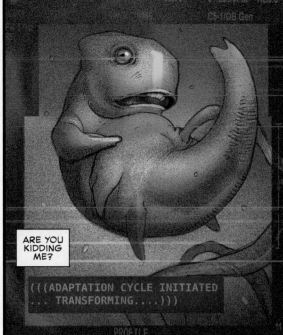

ARE YOU KIDDING ME?

(((ADAPTATION CYCLE INITIATED ... TRANSFORMING....)))

BROOD QUEEN ANALYSIS:
ADAPTING TO SURVIVE
BASED ON INFANT BROOD DAMAGE

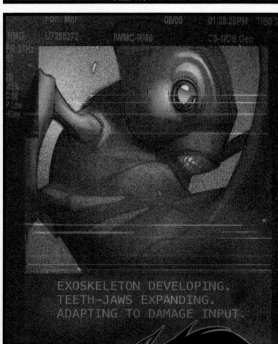

EXOSKELETON DEVELOPING.
TEETH—JAWS EXPANDING.
ADAPTING TO DAMAGE INPUT.

AW, HELL NO.

I DID NOT JUST DO THAT.

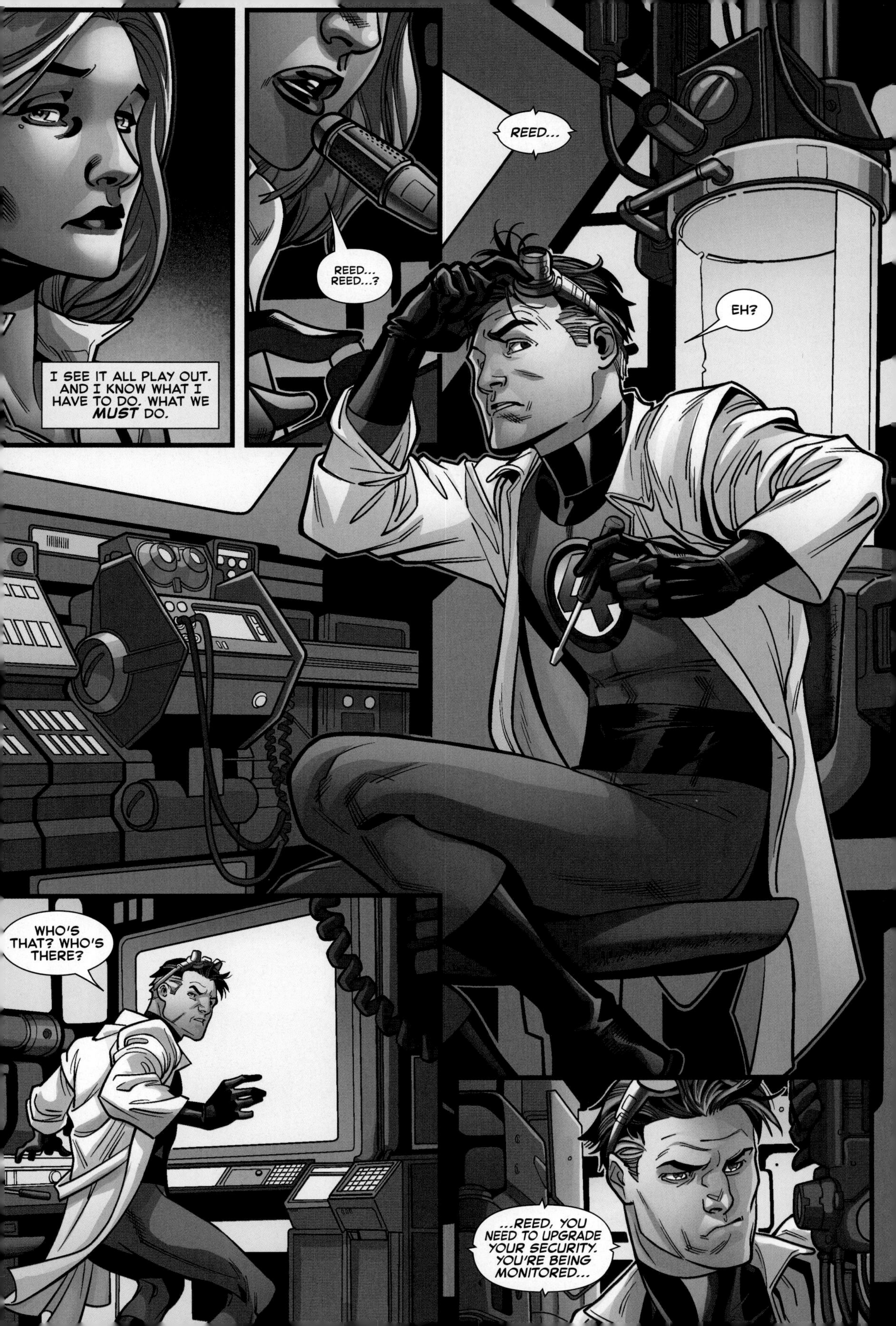
I SEE IT ALL PLAY OUT. AND I KNOW WHAT I HAVE TO DO. WHAT WE *MUST* DO.
REED... REED...?
REED...
EH?
WHO'S THAT? WHO'S THERE?
...REED, YOU NEED TO UPGRADE YOUR SECURITY. YOU'RE BEING MONITORED...

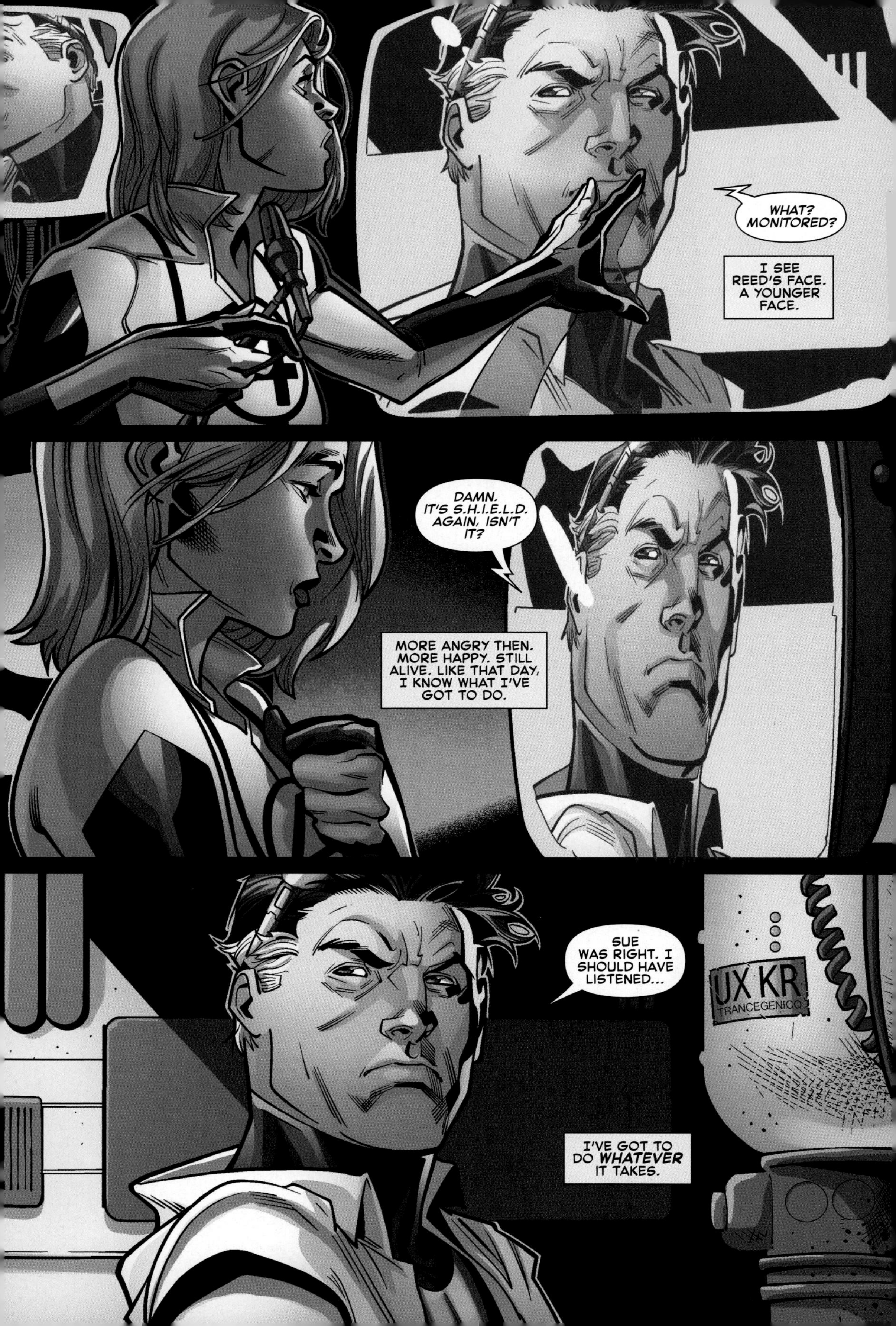

WHAT? MONITORED?
I SEE REED'S FACE. A YOUNGER FACE.
DAMN. IT'S S.H.I.E.L.D. AGAIN, ISN'T IT?
MORE ANGRY THEN. MORE HAPPY. STILL ALIVE. LIKE THAT DAY, I KNOW WHAT I'VE GOT TO DO.
SUE WAS RIGHT. I SHOULD HAVE LISTENED...
UX KR
TRANCEGENICO
I'VE GOT TO DO *WHATEVER* IT TAKES.

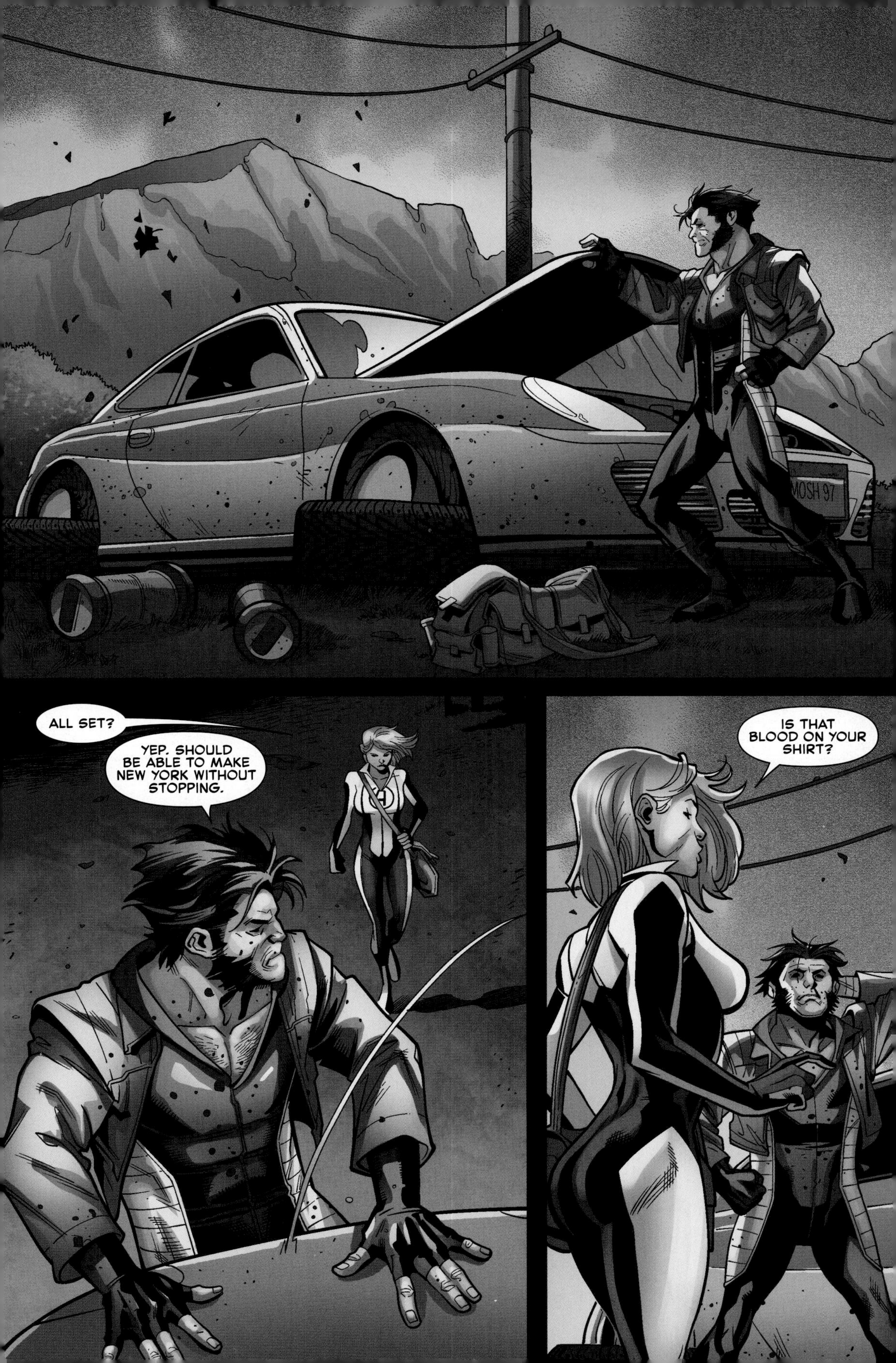
ALL SET?
YEP. SHOULD BE ABLE TO MAKE NEW YORK WITHOUT STOPPING.
IS THAT BLOOD ON YOUR SHIRT?
MOSH 97

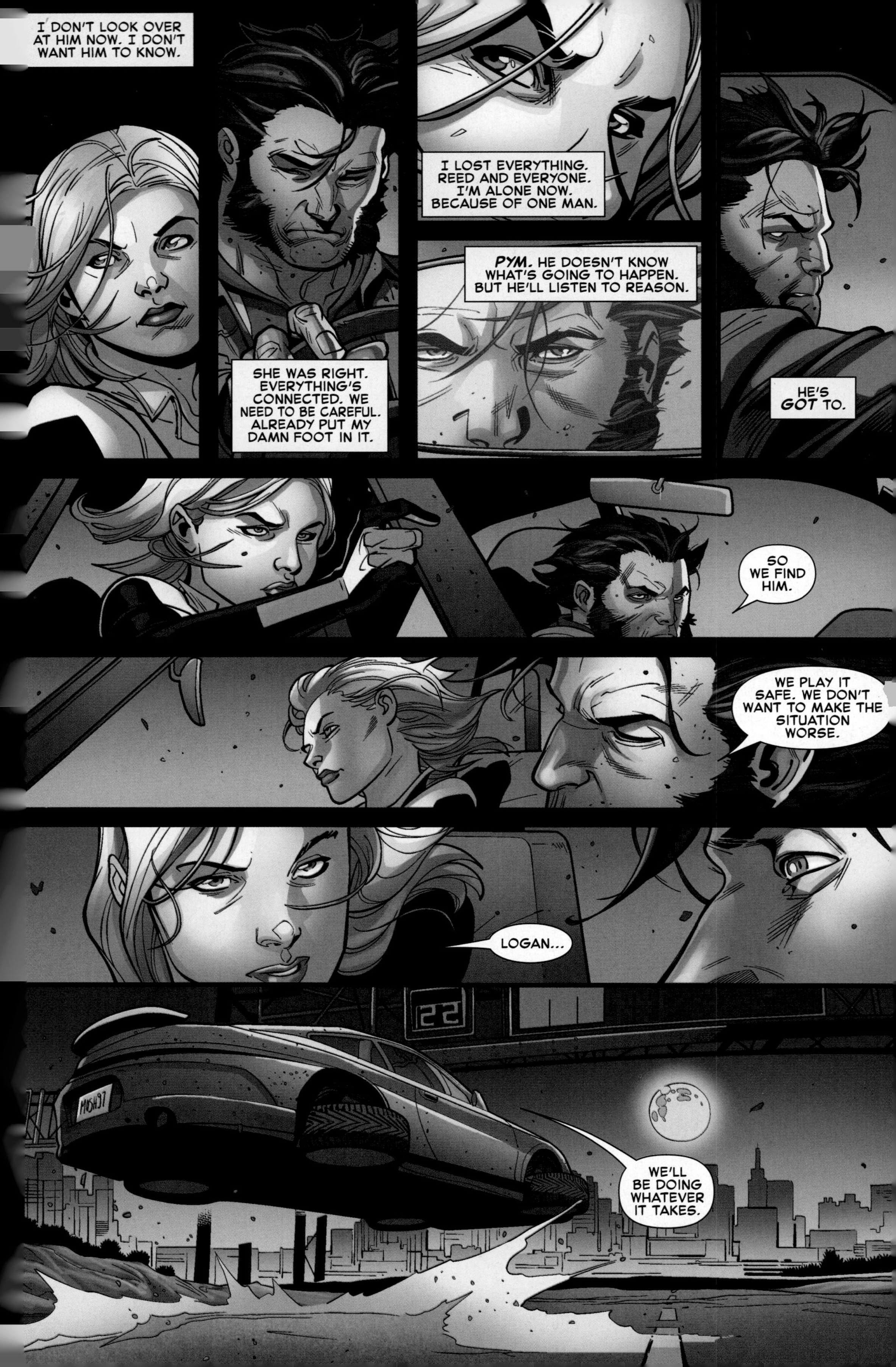
I DON'T LOOK OVER AT HIM NOW. I DON'T WANT HIM TO KNOW.
SHE WAS RIGHT. EVERYTHING'S CONNECTED. WE NEED TO BE CAREFUL. ALREADY PUT MY DAMN FOOT IN IT.
I LOST EVERYTHING. REED AND EVERYONE. I'M ALONE NOW. BECAUSE OF ONE MAN.
PYM. HE DOESN'T KNOW WHAT'S GOING TO HAPPEN. BUT HE'LL LISTEN TO REASON.
HE'S GOT TO.
SO WE FIND HIM.
WE PLAY IT SAFE. WE DON'T WANT TO MAKE THE SITUATION WORSE.
LOGAN...
MOSH97
WE'LL BE DOING WHATEVER IT TAKES.

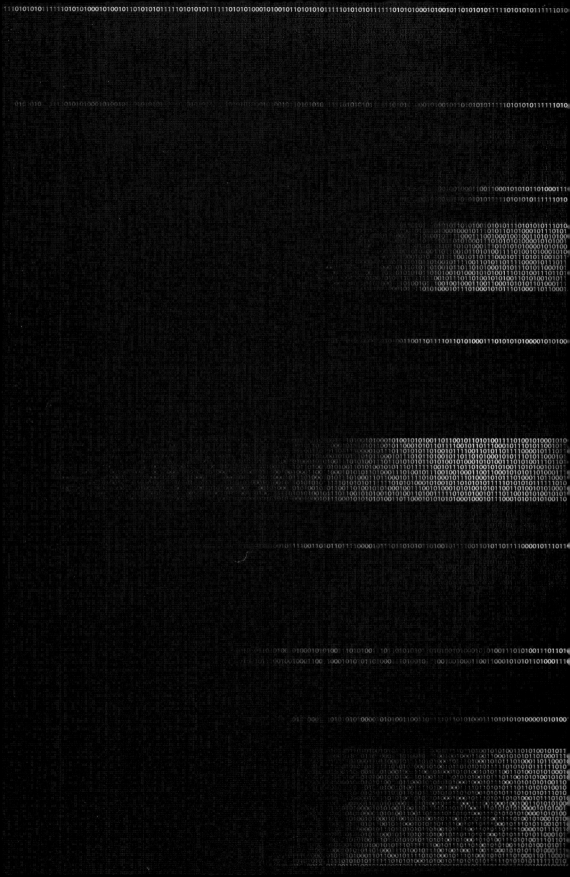

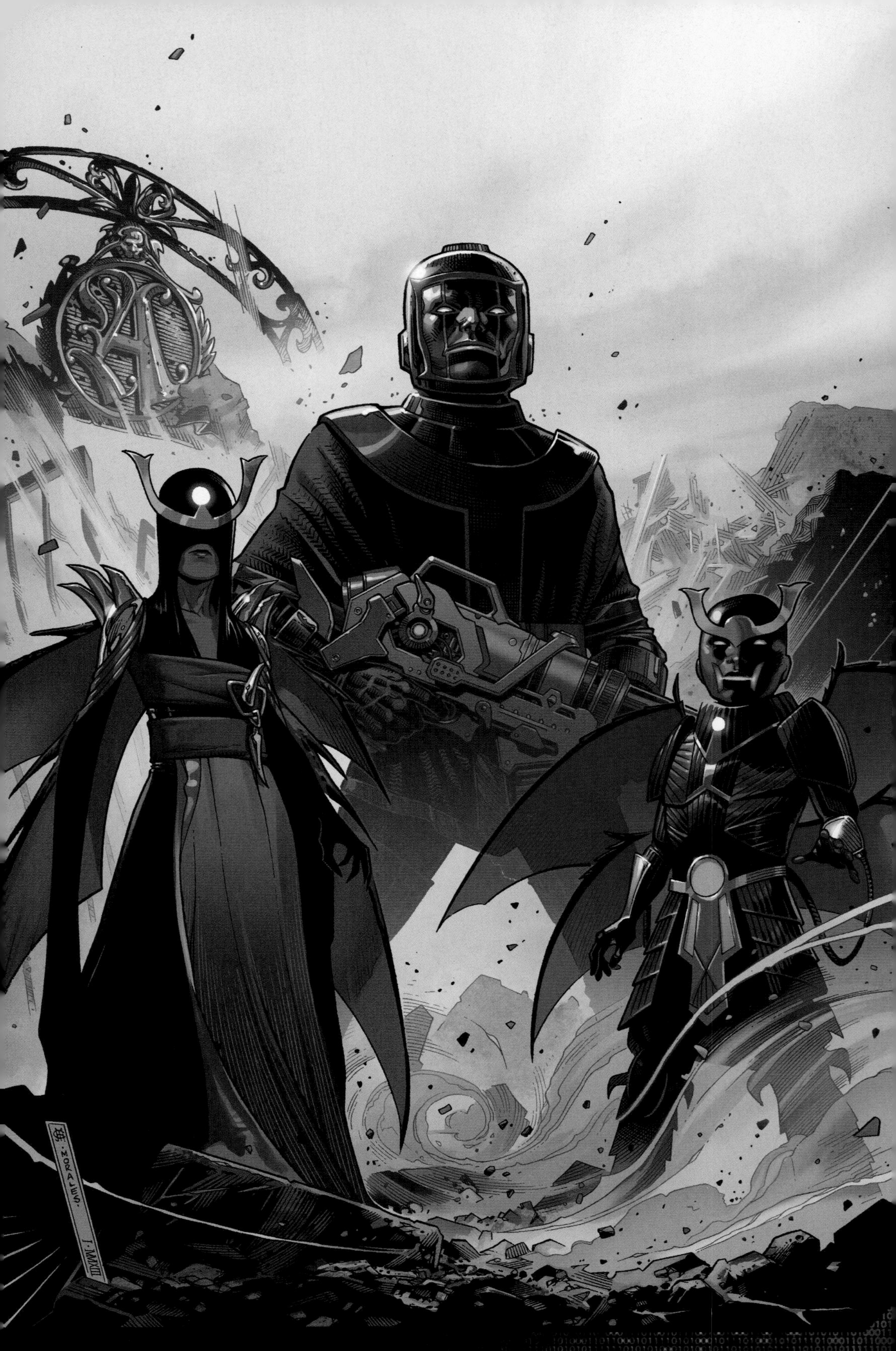
MORALES.

UNCANNY AVENGERS #8AU

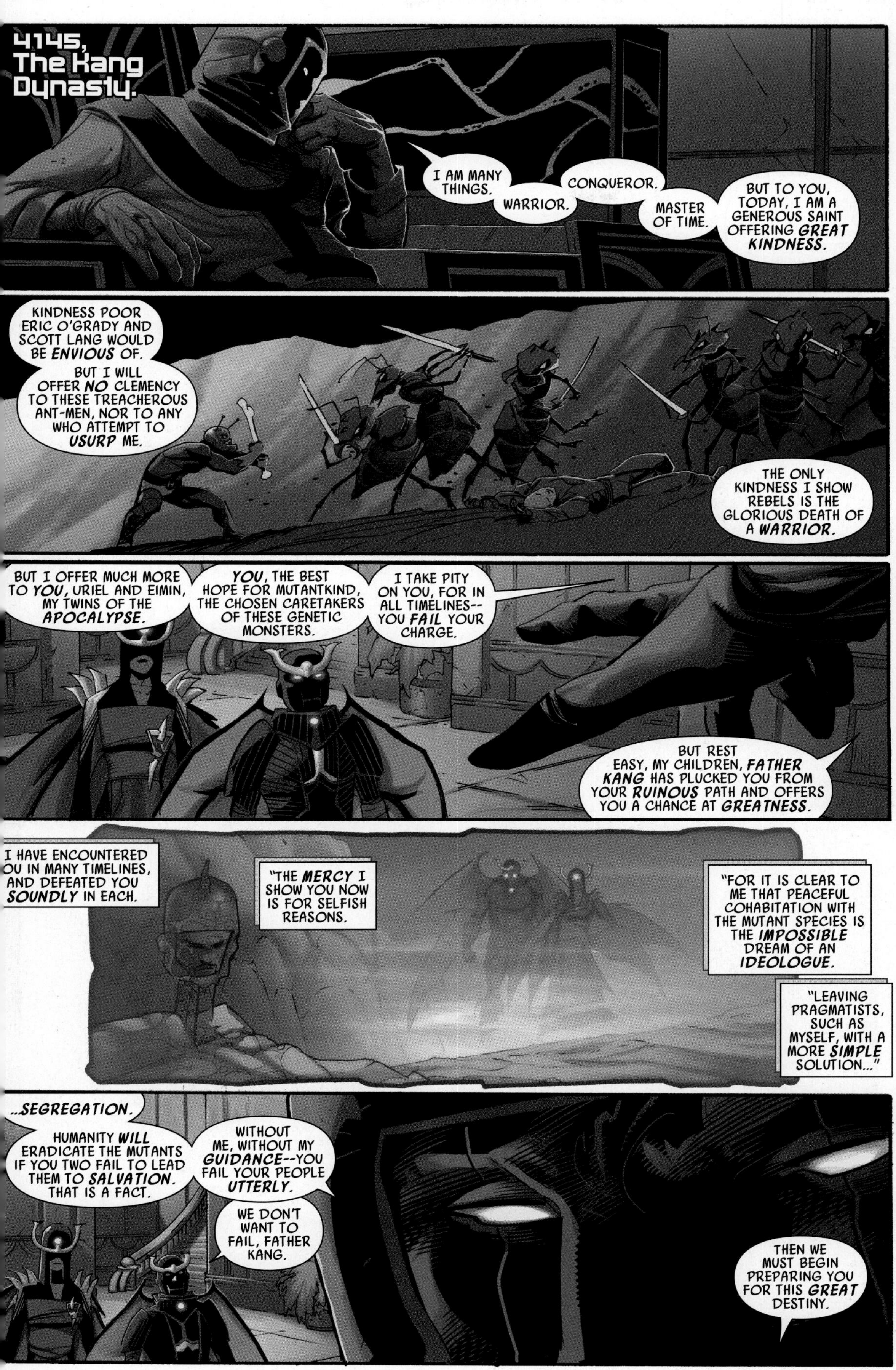
4145, The Kang Dynasty.
I AM MANY THINGS.
WARRIOR.
CONQUEROR.
MASTER OF TIME.
BUT TO YOU, TODAY, I AM A GENEROUS SAINT OFFERING GREAT KINDNESS.
KINDNESS POOR ERIC O'GRADY AND SCOTT LANG WOULD BE ENVIOUS OF.
BUT I WILL OFFER NO CLEMENCY TO THESE TREACHEROUS ANT-MEN, NOR TO ANY WHO ATTEMPT TO USURP ME.
THE ONLY KINDNESS I SHOW REBELS IS THE GLORIOUS DEATH OF A WARRIOR.
BUT I OFFER MUCH MORE TO YOU, URIEL AND EIMIN, MY TWINS OF THE APOCALYPSE.
YOU, THE BEST HOPE FOR MUTANTKIND, THE CHOSEN CARETAKERS OF THESE GENETIC MONSTERS.
I TAKE PITY ON YOU, FOR IN ALL TIMELINES-- YOU FAIL YOUR CHARGE.
BUT REST EASY, MY CHILDREN, FATHER KANG HAS PLUCKED YOU FROM YOUR RUINOUS PATH AND OFFERS YOU A CHANCE AT GREATNESS.
I HAVE ENCOUNTERED YOU IN MANY TIMELINES, AND DEFEATED YOU SOUNDLY IN EACH.
"THE MERCY I SHOW YOU NOW IS FOR SELFISH REASONS.
"FOR IT IS CLEAR TO ME THAT PEACEFUL COHABITATION WITH THE MUTANT SPECIES IS THE IMPOSSIBLE DREAM OF AN IDEOLOGUE.
"LEAVING PRAGMATISTS, SUCH AS MYSELF, WITH A MORE SIMPLE SOLUTION..."
...SEGREGATION.
HUMANITY WILL ERADICATE THE MUTANTS IF YOU TWO FAIL TO LEAD THEM TO SALVATION. THAT IS A FACT.
WITHOUT ME, WITHOUT MY GUIDANCE--YOU FAIL YOUR PEOPLE UTTERLY.
WE DON'T WANT TO FAIL, FATHER KANG.
THEN WE MUST BEGIN PREPARING YOU FOR THIS GREAT DESTINY.

WE MUST PREPARE YOU TO *BLOODY* YOUR HANDS, TO *DESTROY*, WITHOUT HESITATION, *ANY* WHO STAND IN YOUR WAY.

B-BUT WHY? WHY SHOULD WE BE CONCERNED WITH *BATTLE?*

LET US USE THE CHRONO-TECH TO GO BACK IN TIME AND *KILL* OUR ENEMIES *BEFORE* THEY RISE.

THINK BEFORE YOU SPEAK, URIEL. STUDY YOUR DEAR SISTER EIMIN'S REVERENCE LEST YOU CONTINUE TO *EMBARRASS* YOURSELF.

THERE IS *NO HONOR* IN THE FACILE KILLING OF INFANTS...

...BUT THAT IS *SCARCELY* THE ONLY REASON.

DEEP

LEADING US TO TODAY'S *LESSON.*

WE ARE NOW IN THE ERA OF YOUR BIRTH, THOUGH THE *TIMELINE* HAS BEEN *ALTERED.*

IT CHANGED WHEN *WOLVERINE* TRAVELED TO THE PAST AND MURDERED *HANK PYM.*

WOLVERINE? THE *SAVAGE* WHO BUTCHERED OUR FATHER?

THE *SAME.*

YOU SEE; SOMETIMES WHEN A PLAYER PREMATURELY GOES MISSING FROM THE BOARD--THE *UNEXPECTED* OCCURS.

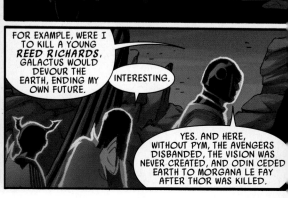

FOR EXAMPLE, WERE I TO KILL A YOUNG *REED RICHARDS,* GALACTUS WOULD DEVOUR THE EARTH, ENDING MY OWN FUTURE.

INTERESTING.

YES. AND HERE, WITHOUT PYM, THE AVENGERS DISBANDED, THE VISION WAS NEVER CREATED, AND ODIN CEDED EARTH TO MORGANA LE FAY AFTER THOR WAS KILLED.

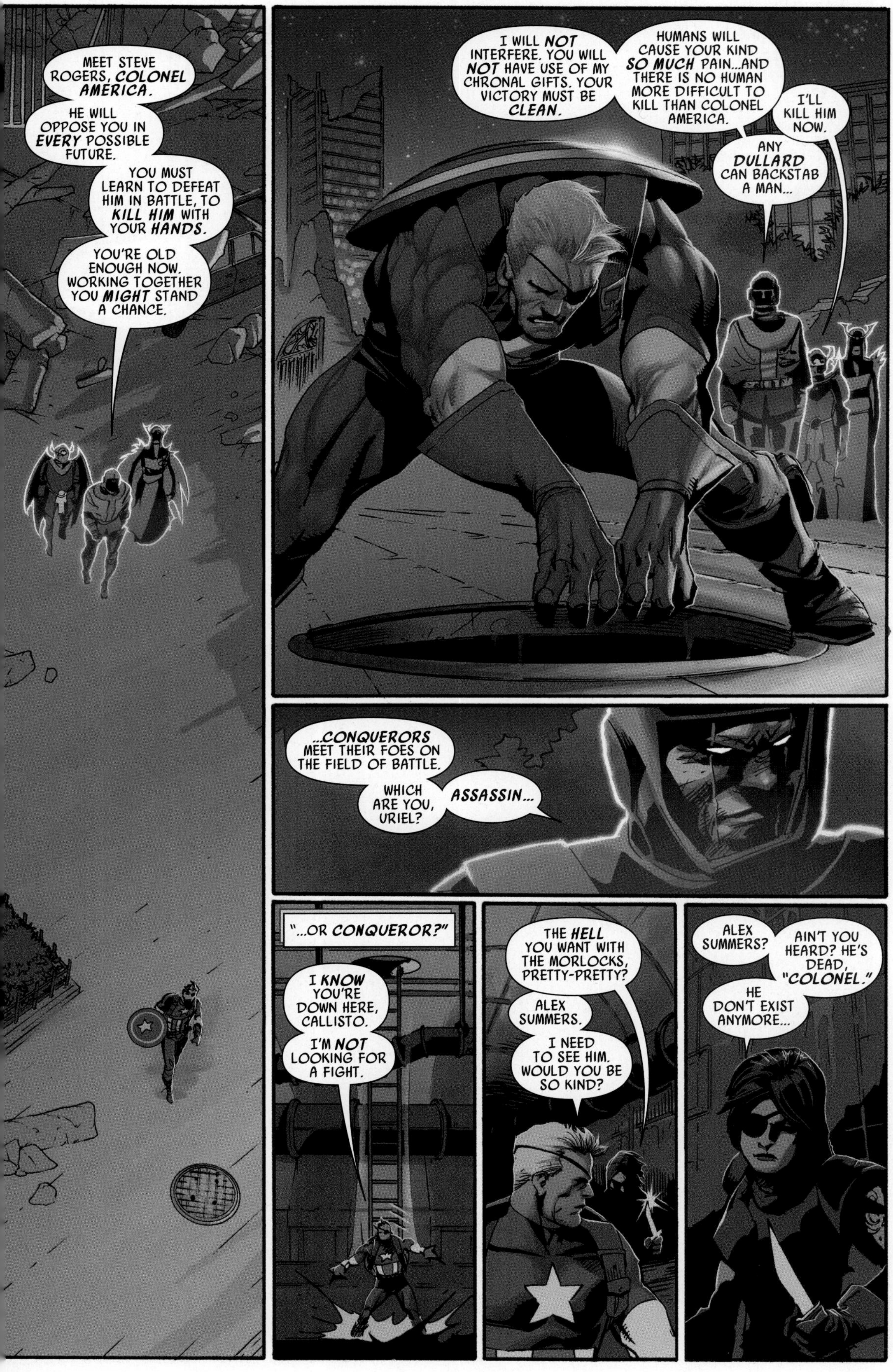
MEET STEVE ROGERS, COLONEL AMERICA.
HE WILL OPPOSE YOU IN EVERY POSSIBLE FUTURE.
YOU MUST LEARN TO DEFEAT HIM IN BATTLE, TO KILL HIM WITH YOUR HANDS.
YOU'RE OLD ENOUGH NOW. WORKING TOGETHER YOU MIGHT STAND A CHANCE.
I WILL NOT INTERFERE. YOU WILL NOT HAVE USE OF MY CHRONAL GIFTS. YOUR VICTORY MUST BE CLEAN.
HUMANS WILL CAUSE YOUR KIND SO MUCH PAIN...AND THERE IS NO HUMAN MORE DIFFICULT TO KILL THAN COLONEL AMERICA.
I'LL KILL HIM NOW.
ANY DULLARD CAN BACKSTAB A MAN...
...CONQUERORS MEET THEIR FOES ON THE FIELD OF BATTLE.
WHICH ARE YOU, URIEL?
ASSASSIN...
"...OR CONQUEROR?"
I KNOW YOU'RE DOWN HERE, CALLISTO.
I'M NOT LOOKING FOR A FIGHT.
THE HELL YOU WANT WITH THE MORLOCKS, PRETTY-PRETTY?
ALEX SUMMERS.
I NEED TO SEE HIM. WOULD YOU BE SO KIND?
ALEX SUMMERS?
AIN'T YOU HEARD? HE'S DEAD, "COLONEL."
HE DON'T EXIST ANYMORE...

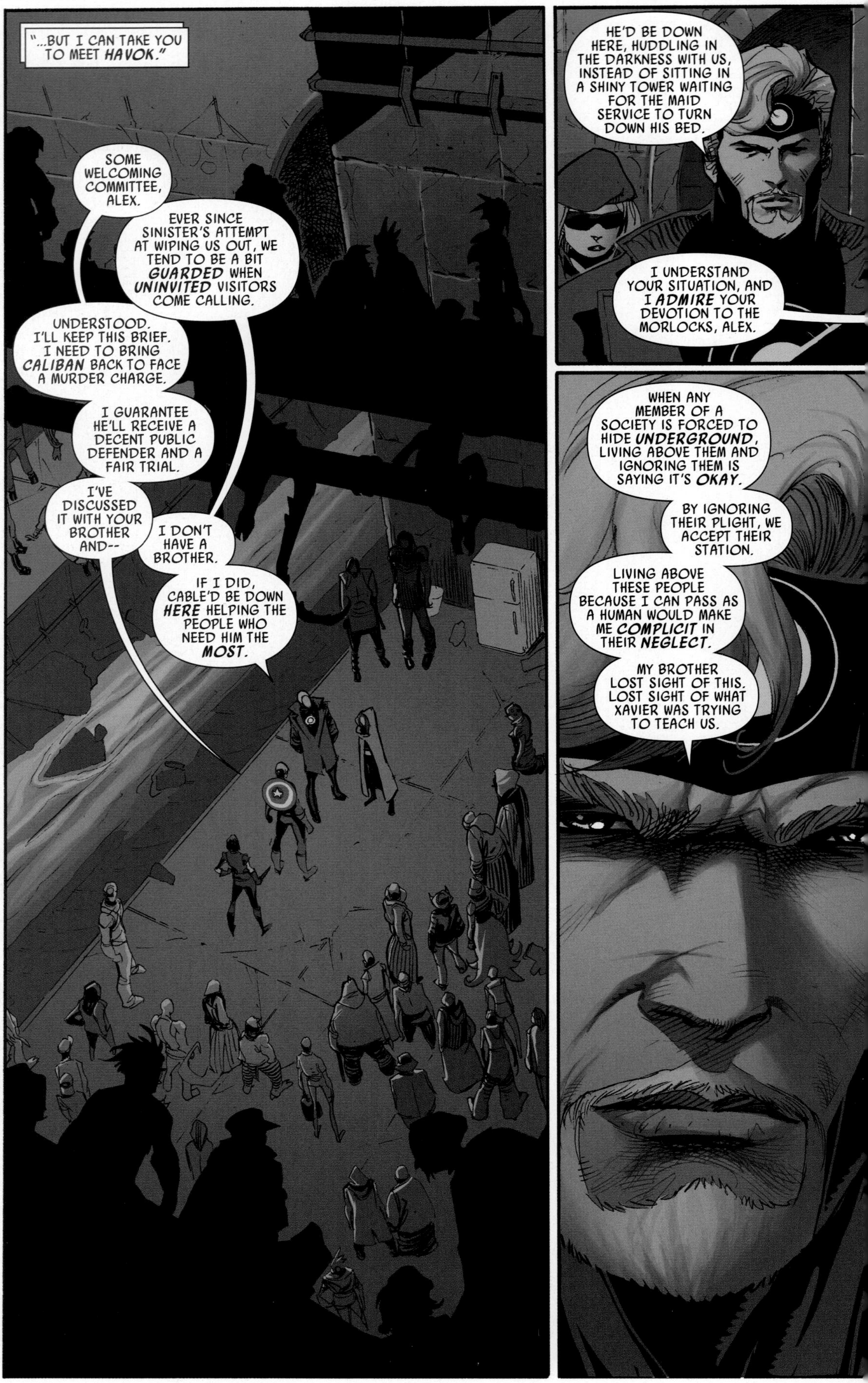
"...BUT I CAN TAKE YOU TO MEET HAVOK."
SOME WELCOMING COMMITTEE, ALEX.
EVER SINCE SINISTER'S ATTEMPT AT WIPING US OUT, WE TEND TO BE A BIT GUARDED WHEN UNINVITED VISITORS COME CALLING.
UNDERSTOOD. I'LL KEEP THIS BRIEF. I NEED TO BRING CALIBAN BACK TO FACE A MURDER CHARGE.
I GUARANTEE HE'LL RECEIVE A DECENT PUBLIC DEFENDER AND A FAIR TRIAL.
I'VE DISCUSSED IT WITH YOUR BROTHER AND--
I DON'T HAVE A BROTHER.
IF I DID, CABLE'D BE DOWN HERE HELPING THE PEOPLE WHO NEED HIM THE MOST.
HE'D BE DOWN HERE, HUDDLING IN THE DARKNESS WITH US, INSTEAD OF SITTING IN A SHINY TOWER WAITING FOR THE MAID SERVICE TO TURN DOWN HIS BED.
I UNDERSTAND YOUR SITUATION, AND I ADMIRE YOUR DEVOTION TO THE MORLOCKS, ALEX.
WHEN ANY MEMBER OF A SOCIETY IS FORCED TO HIDE UNDERGROUND, LIVING ABOVE THEM AND IGNORING THEM IS SAYING IT'S OKAY.
BY IGNORING THEIR PLIGHT, WE ACCEPT THEIR STATION.
LIVING ABOVE THESE PEOPLE BECAUSE I CAN PASS AS A HUMAN WOULD MAKE ME COMPLICIT IN THEIR NEGLECT.
MY BROTHER LOST SIGHT OF THIS. LOST SIGHT OF WHAT XAVIER WAS TRYING TO TEACH US.

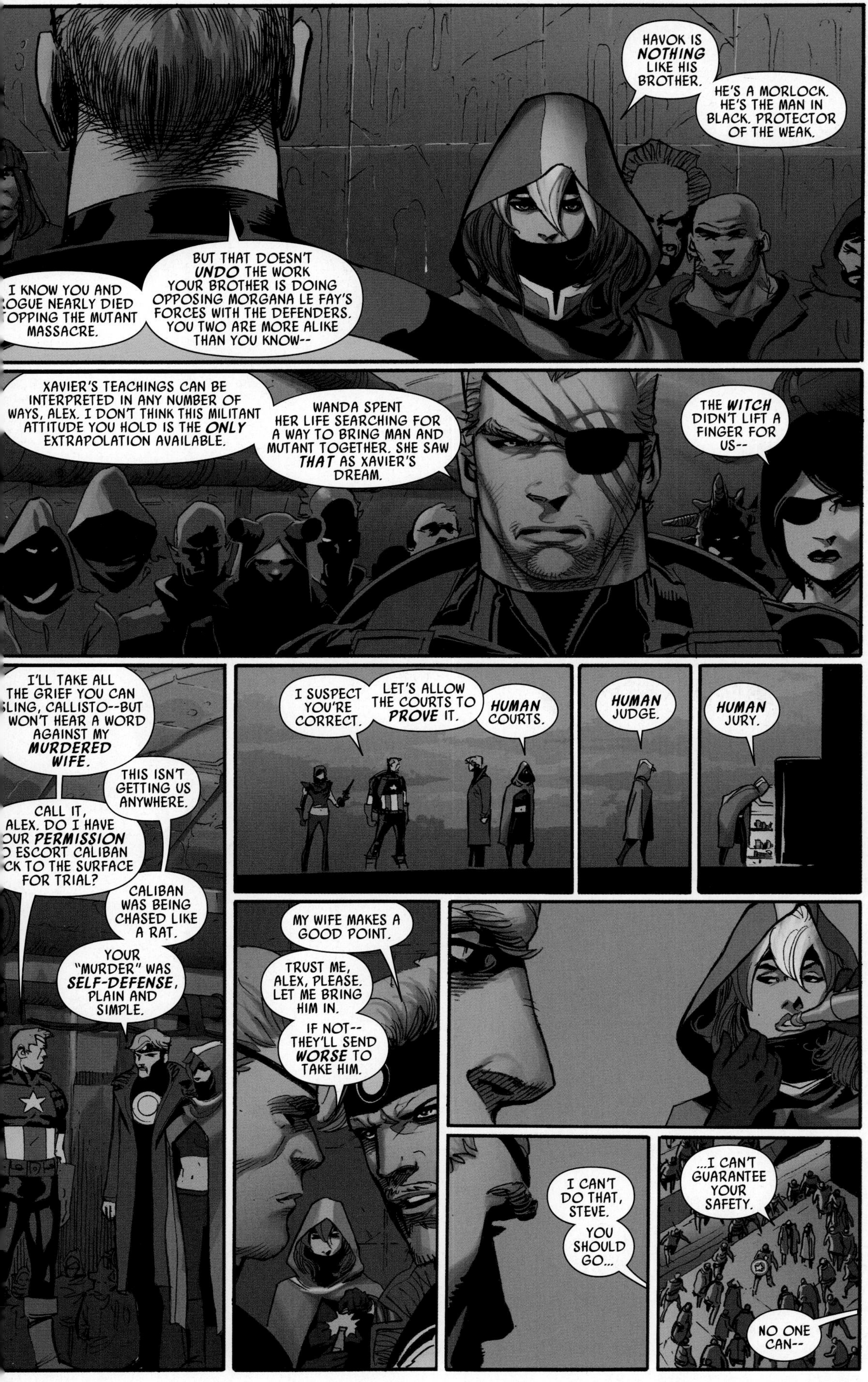

HAVOK IS NOTHING LIKE HIS BROTHER.
HE'S A MORLOCK. HE'S THE MAN IN BLACK. PROTECTOR OF THE WEAK.
I KNOW YOU AND ROGUE NEARLY DIED TOPPING THE MUTANT MASSACRE.
BUT THAT DOESN'T UNDO THE WORK YOUR BROTHER IS DOING OPPOSING MORGANA LE FAY'S FORCES WITH THE DEFENDERS. YOU TWO ARE MORE ALIKE THAN YOU KNOW--
XAVIER'S TEACHINGS CAN BE INTERPRETED IN ANY NUMBER OF WAYS, ALEX. I DON'T THINK THIS MILITANT ATTITUDE YOU HOLD IS THE ONLY EXTRAPOLATION AVAILABLE.
WANDA SPENT HER LIFE SEARCHING FOR A WAY TO BRING MAN AND MUTANT TOGETHER. SHE SAW THAT AS XAVIER'S DREAM.
THE WITCH DIDN'T LIFT A FINGER FOR US--
I'LL TAKE ALL THE GRIEF YOU CAN LING, CALLISTO--BUT WON'T HEAR A WORD AGAINST MY MURDERED WIFE.
THIS ISN'T GETTING US ANYWHERE.
CALL IT, ALEX. DO I HAVE OUR PERMISSION O ESCORT CALIBAN CK TO THE SURFACE FOR TRIAL?
CALIBAN WAS BEING CHASED LIKE A RAT.
YOUR "MURDER" WAS SELF-DEFENSE, PLAIN AND SIMPLE.
I SUSPECT YOU'RE CORRECT.
LET'S ALLOW THE COURTS TO PROVE IT.
HUMAN COURTS.
HUMAN JUDGE.
HUMAN JURY.
MY WIFE MAKES A GOOD POINT.
TRUST ME, ALEX, PLEASE. LET ME BRING HIM IN.
IF NOT-- THEY'LL SEND WORSE TO TAKE HIM.
I CAN'T DO THAT, STEVE.
YOU SHOULD GO...
...I CAN'T GUARANTEE YOUR SAFETY.
NO ONE CAN--

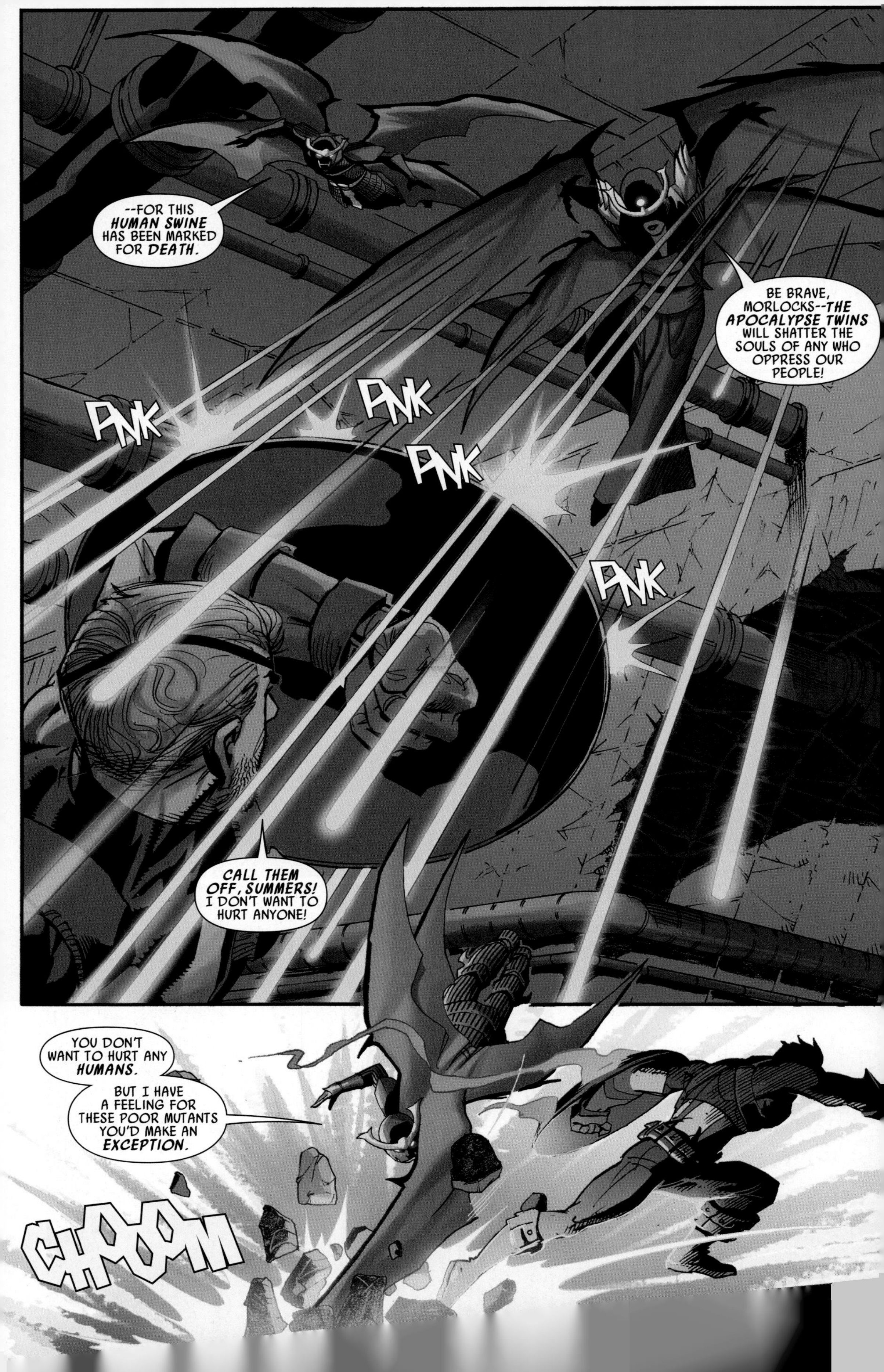
--FOR THIS HUMAN SWINE HAS BEEN MARKED FOR DEATH.
BE BRAVE, MORLOCKS--THE APOCALYPSE TWINS WILL SHATTER THE SOULS OF ANY WHO OPPRESS OUR PEOPLE!
PNK
PNK
PNK
PNK
CALL THEM OFF, SUMMERS! I DON'T WANT TO HURT ANYONE!
YOU DON'T WANT TO HURT ANY HUMANS.
BUT I HAVE A FEELING FOR THESE POOR MUTANTS YOU'D MAKE AN EXCEPTION.
CHOOOM

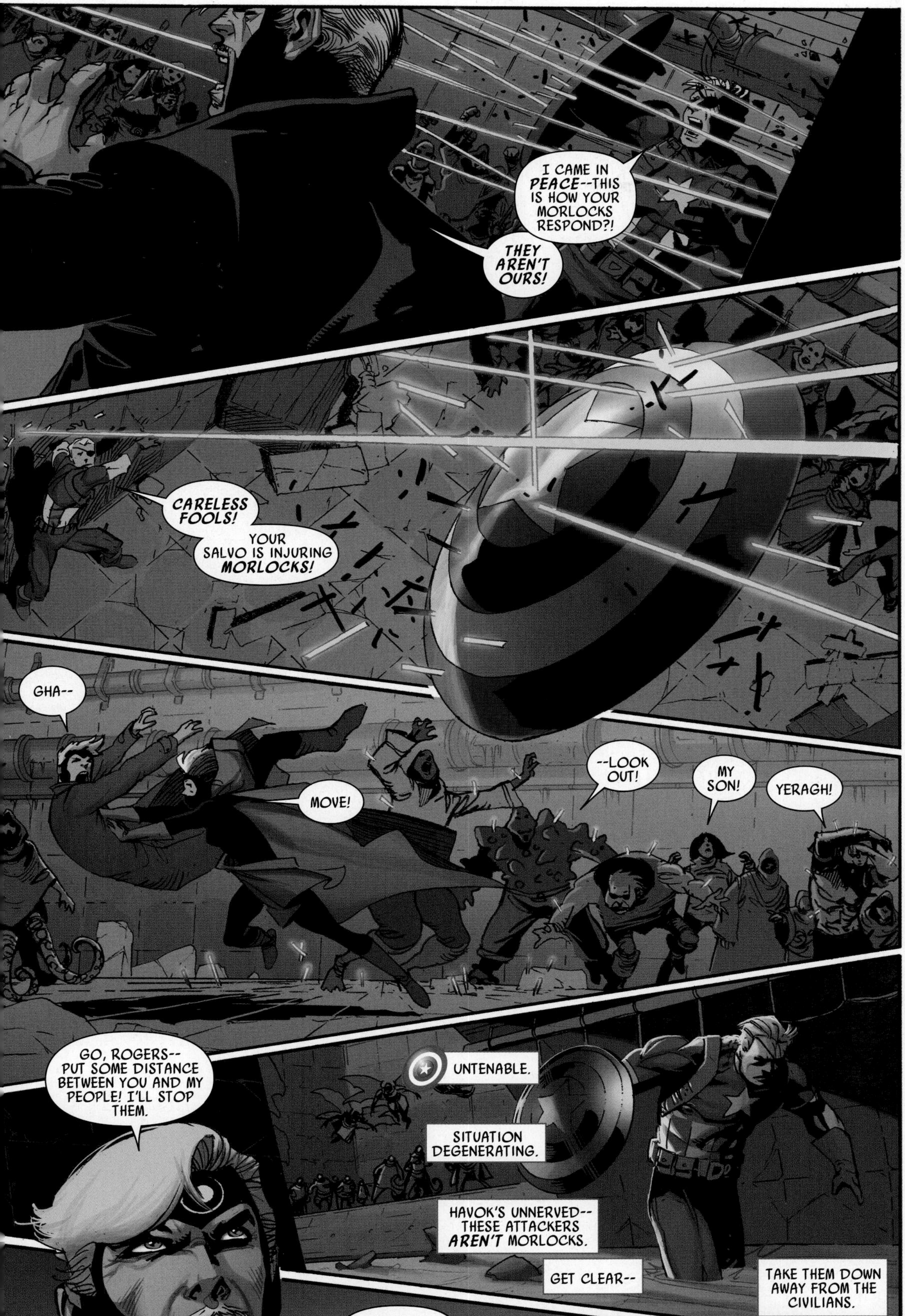
I CAME IN PEACE--THIS IS HOW YOUR MORLOCKS RESPOND?!
THEY AREN'T OURS!
CARELESS FOOLS!
YOUR SALVO IS INJURING MORLOCKS!
GHA--
MOVE!
--LOOK OUT!
MY SON!
YERAGH!
GO, ROGERS--PUT SOME DISTANCE BETWEEN YOU AND MY PEOPLE! I'LL STOP THEM.
UNTENABLE.
SITUATION DEGENERATING.
HAVOK'S UNNERVED--THESE ATTACKERS AREN'T MORLOCKS.
GET CLEAR--
TAKE THEM DOWN AWAY FROM THE CIVILIANS.
ROGUE, TAKE CARE OF THE INJURED!
LOCK DOWN THE CAMP...

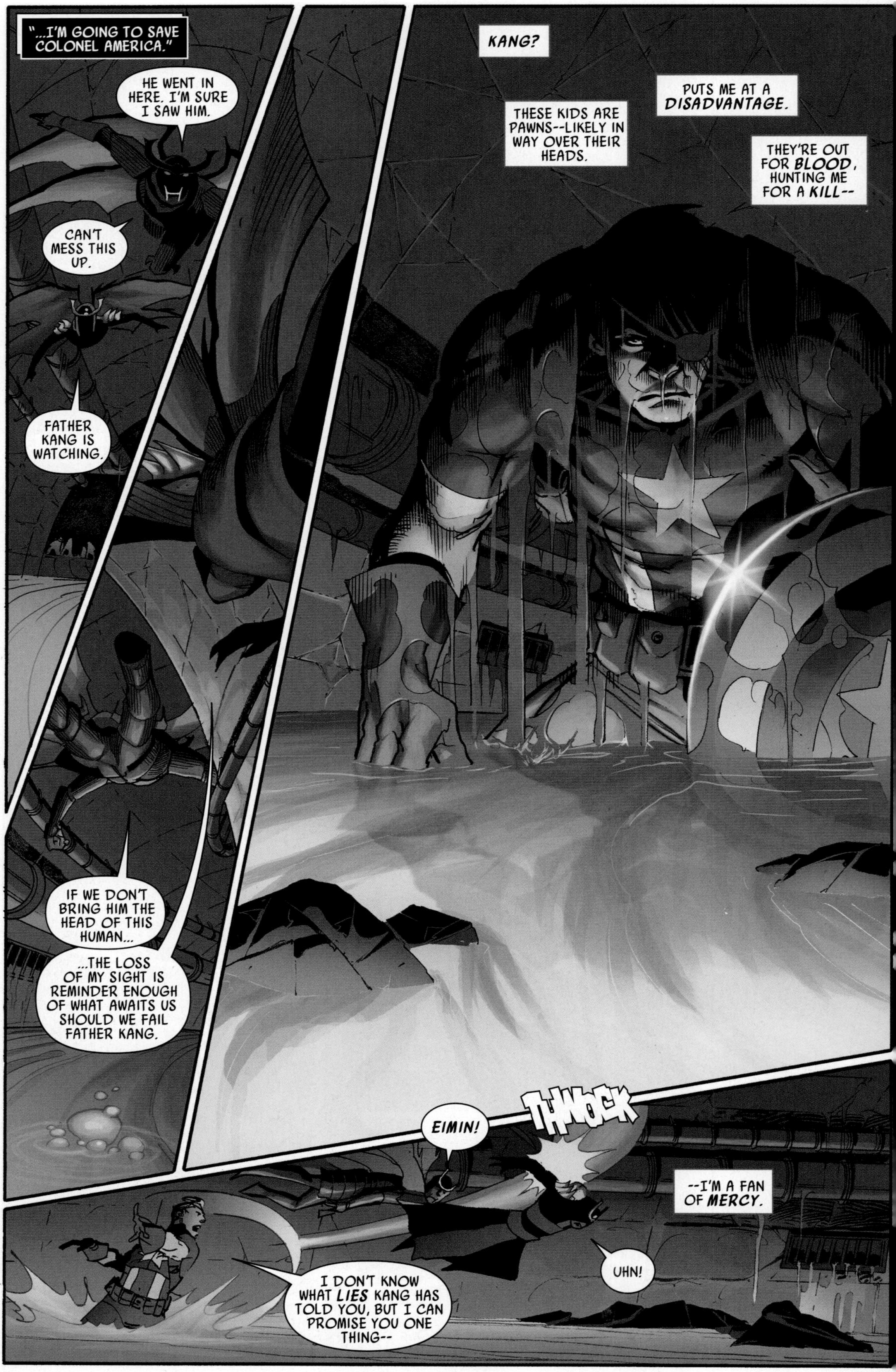
"...I'M GOING TO SAVE COLONEL AMERICA."
HE WENT IN HERE. I'M SURE I SAW HIM.
CAN'T MESS THIS UP.
FATHER KANG IS WATCHING.
IF WE DON'T BRING HIM THE HEAD OF THIS HUMAN...
...THE LOSS OF MY SIGHT IS REMINDER ENOUGH OF WHAT AWAITS US SHOULD WE FAIL FATHER KANG.
KANG?
THESE KIDS ARE PAWNS--LIKELY IN WAY OVER THEIR HEADS.
PUTS ME AT A DISADVANTAGE.
THEY'RE OUT FOR BLOOD, HUNTING ME FOR A KILL--
THWOCK
EIMIN!
I DON'T KNOW WHAT LIES KANG HAS TOLD YOU, BUT I CAN PROMISE YOU ONE THING--
UHN!
--I'M A FAN OF MERCY.

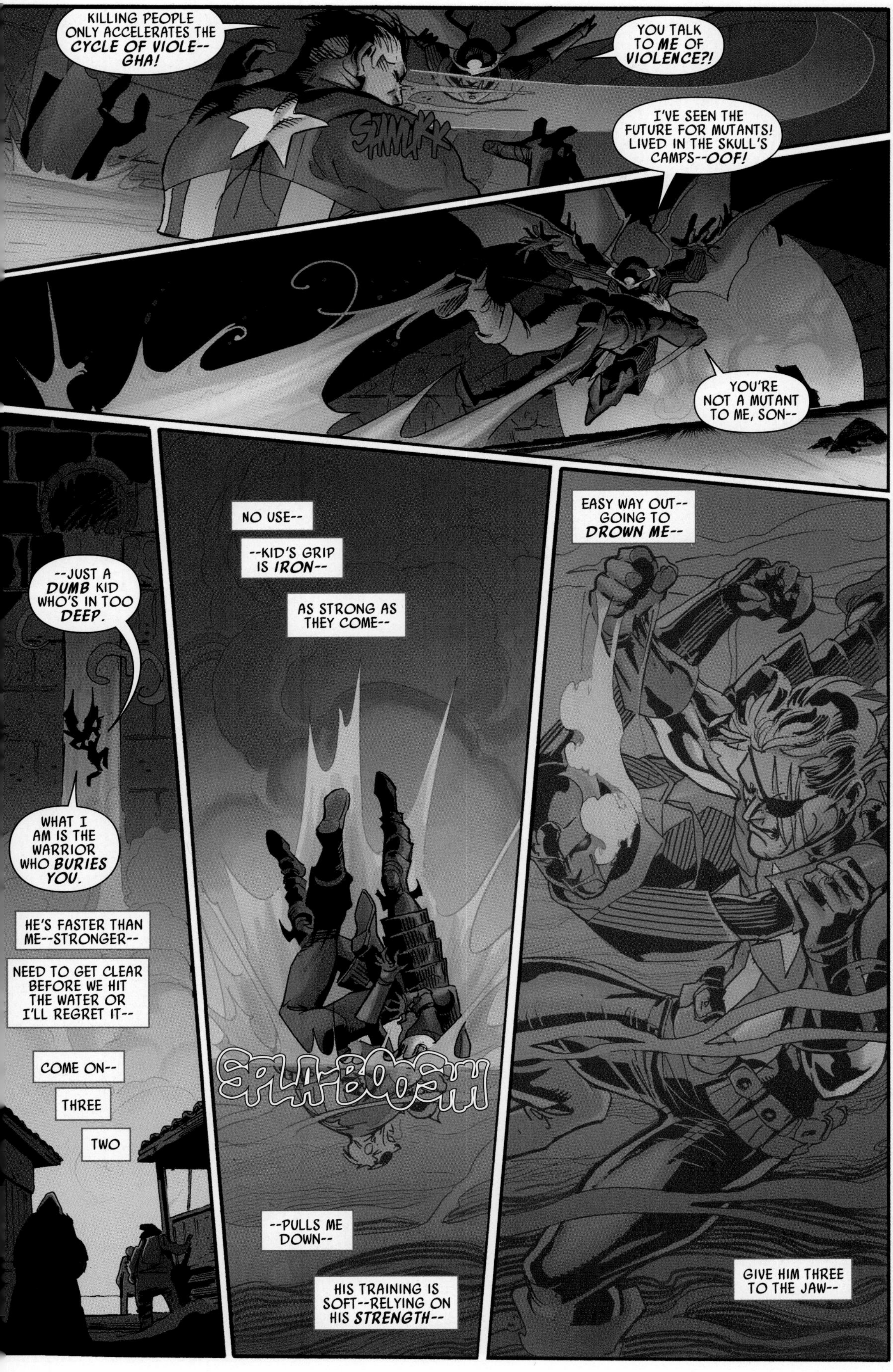
KILLING PEOPLE ONLY ACCELERATES THE CYCLE OF VIOLE-- GHA!
SHMUKK
YOU TALK TO ME OF VIOLENCE?!
I'VE SEEN THE FUTURE FOR MUTANTS! LIVED IN THE SKULL'S CAMPS--OOF!
YOU'RE NOT A MUTANT TO ME, SON--
--JUST A DUMB KID WHO'S IN TOO DEEP.
WHAT I AM IS THE WARRIOR WHO BURIES YOU.
HE'S FASTER THAN ME--STRONGER--
NEED TO GET CLEAR BEFORE WE HIT THE WATER OR I'LL REGRET IT--
COME ON--
THREE
TWO
NO USE--
--KID'S GRIP IS IRON--
AS STRONG AS THEY COME--
SPLA-BOOSH
--PULLS ME DOWN--
HIS TRAINING IS SOFT--RELYING ON HIS STRENGTH--
EASY WAY OUT--GOING TO DROWN ME--
GIVE HIM THREE TO THE JAW--

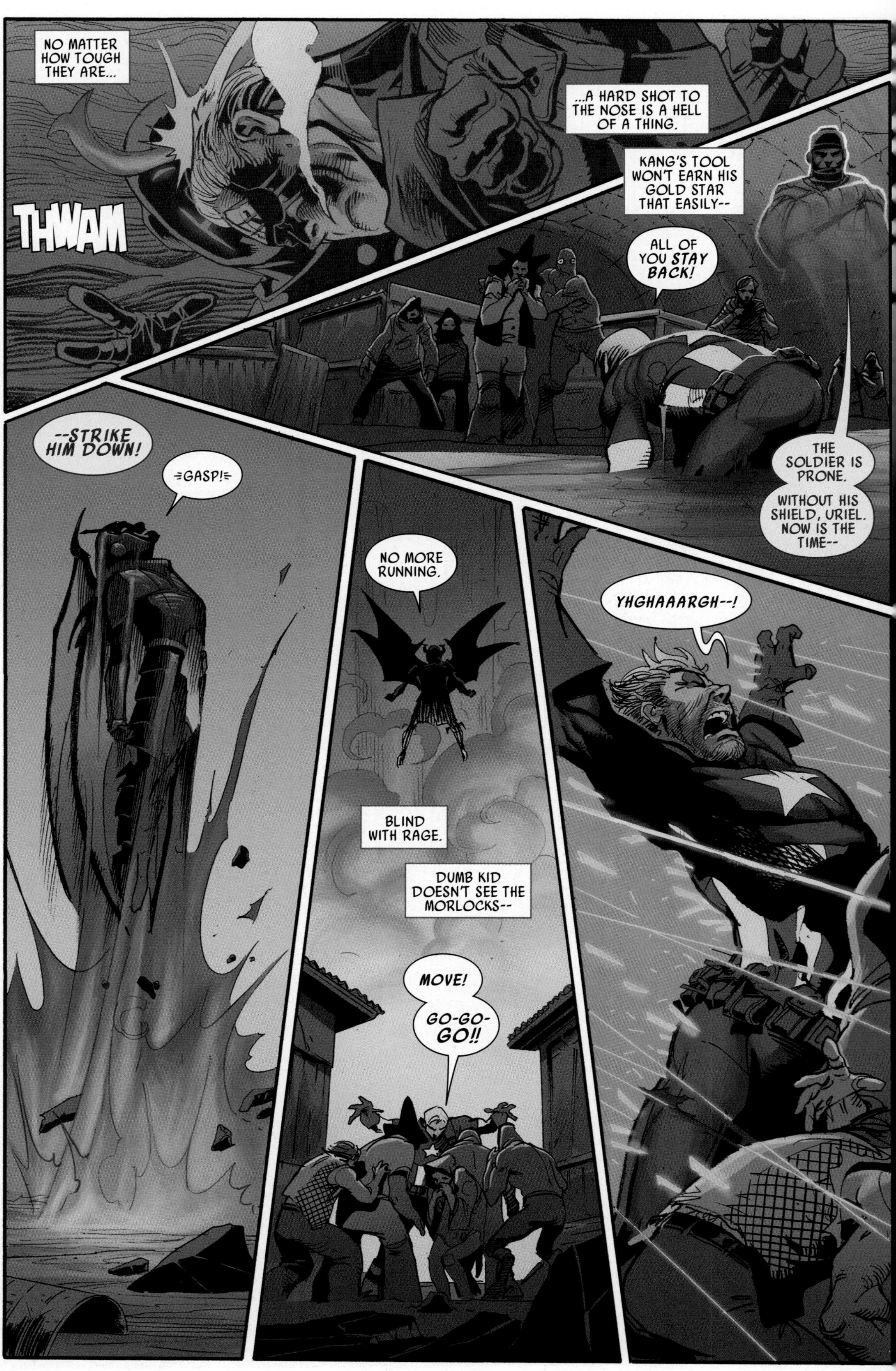
NO MATTER HOW TOUGH THEY ARE...
...A HARD SHOT TO THE NOSE IS A HELL OF A THING.
THWAM
KANG'S TOOL WON'T EARN HIS GOLD STAR THAT EASILY--
ALL OF YOU STAY BACK!
THE SOLDIER IS PRONE.
WITHOUT HIS SHIELD, URIEL. NOW IS THE TIME--
--STRIKE HIM DOWN!
=GASP!=
NO MORE RUNNING.
BLIND WITH RAGE.
DUMB KID DOESN'T SEE THE MORLOCKS--
MOVE!
GO-GO-GO!!
YHGHAAARGH--!

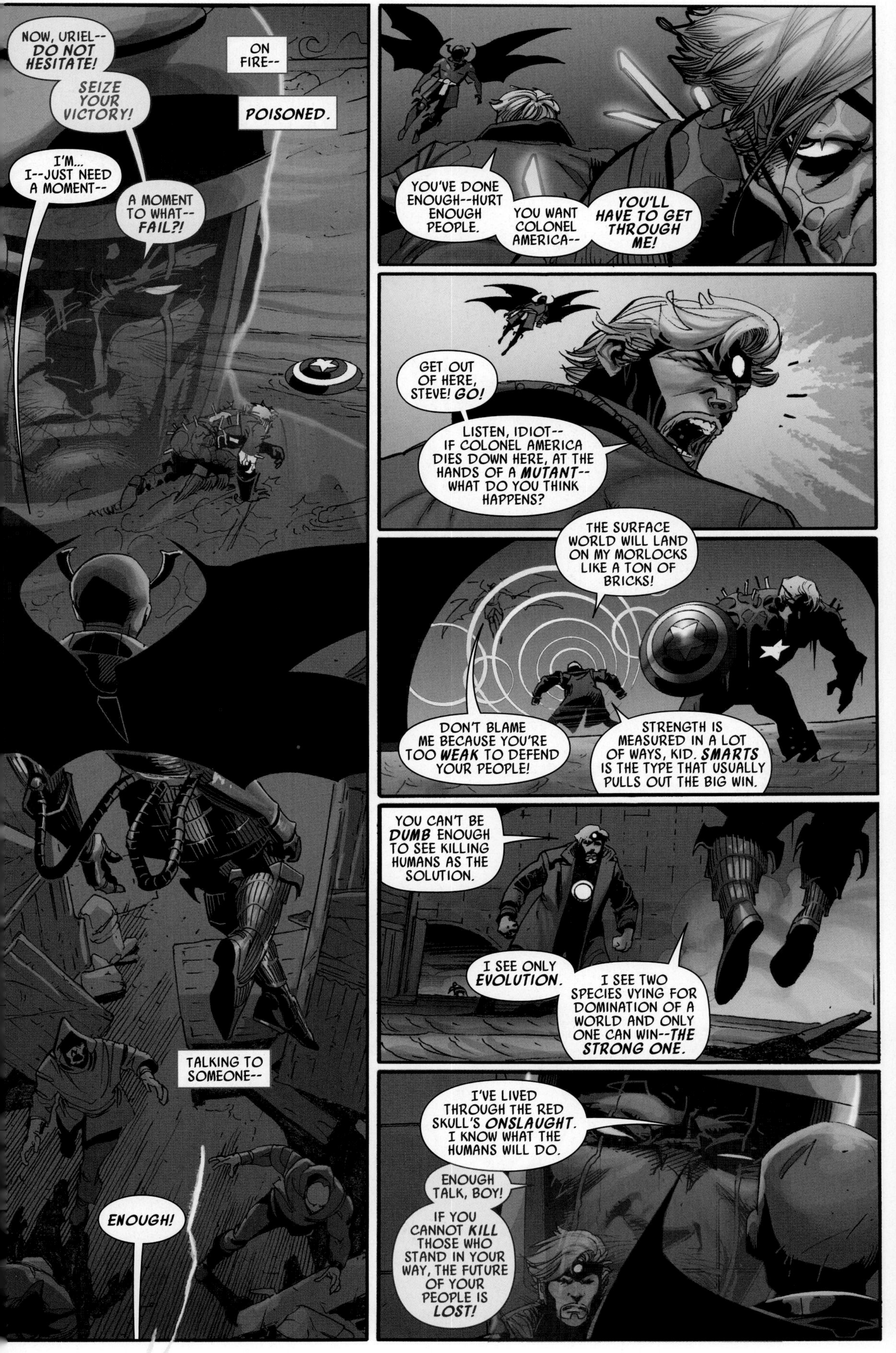
NOW, URIEL-- DO NOT HESITATE!
SEIZE YOUR VICTORY!
I'M... I--JUST NEED A MOMENT--
A MOMENT TO WHAT-- FAIL?!
ON FIRE--
POISONED.
TALKING TO SOMEONE--
ENOUGH!
YOU'VE DONE ENOUGH--HURT ENOUGH PEOPLE.
YOU WANT COLONEL AMERICA--
YOU'LL HAVE TO GET THROUGH ME!
GET OUT OF HERE, STEVE! GO!
LISTEN, IDIOT-- IF COLONEL AMERICA DIES DOWN HERE, AT THE HANDS OF A MUTANT-- WHAT DO YOU THINK HAPPENS?
THE SURFACE WORLD WILL LAND ON MY MORLOCKS LIKE A TON OF BRICKS!
DON'T BLAME ME BECAUSE YOU'RE TOO WEAK TO DEFEND YOUR PEOPLE!
STRENGTH IS MEASURED IN A LOT OF WAYS, KID. SMARTS IS THE TYPE THAT USUALLY PULLS OUT THE BIG WIN.
YOU CAN'T BE DUMB ENOUGH TO SEE KILLING HUMANS AS THE SOLUTION.
I SEE ONLY EVOLUTION.
I SEE TWO SPECIES VYING FOR DOMINATION OF A WORLD AND ONLY ONE CAN WIN--THE STRONG ONE.
I'VE LIVED THROUGH THE RED SKULL'S ONSLAUGHT. I KNOW WHAT THE HUMANS WILL DO.
ENOUGH TALK, BOY!
IF YOU CANNOT KILL THOSE WHO STAND IN YOUR WAY, THE FUTURE OF YOUR PEOPLE IS LOST!

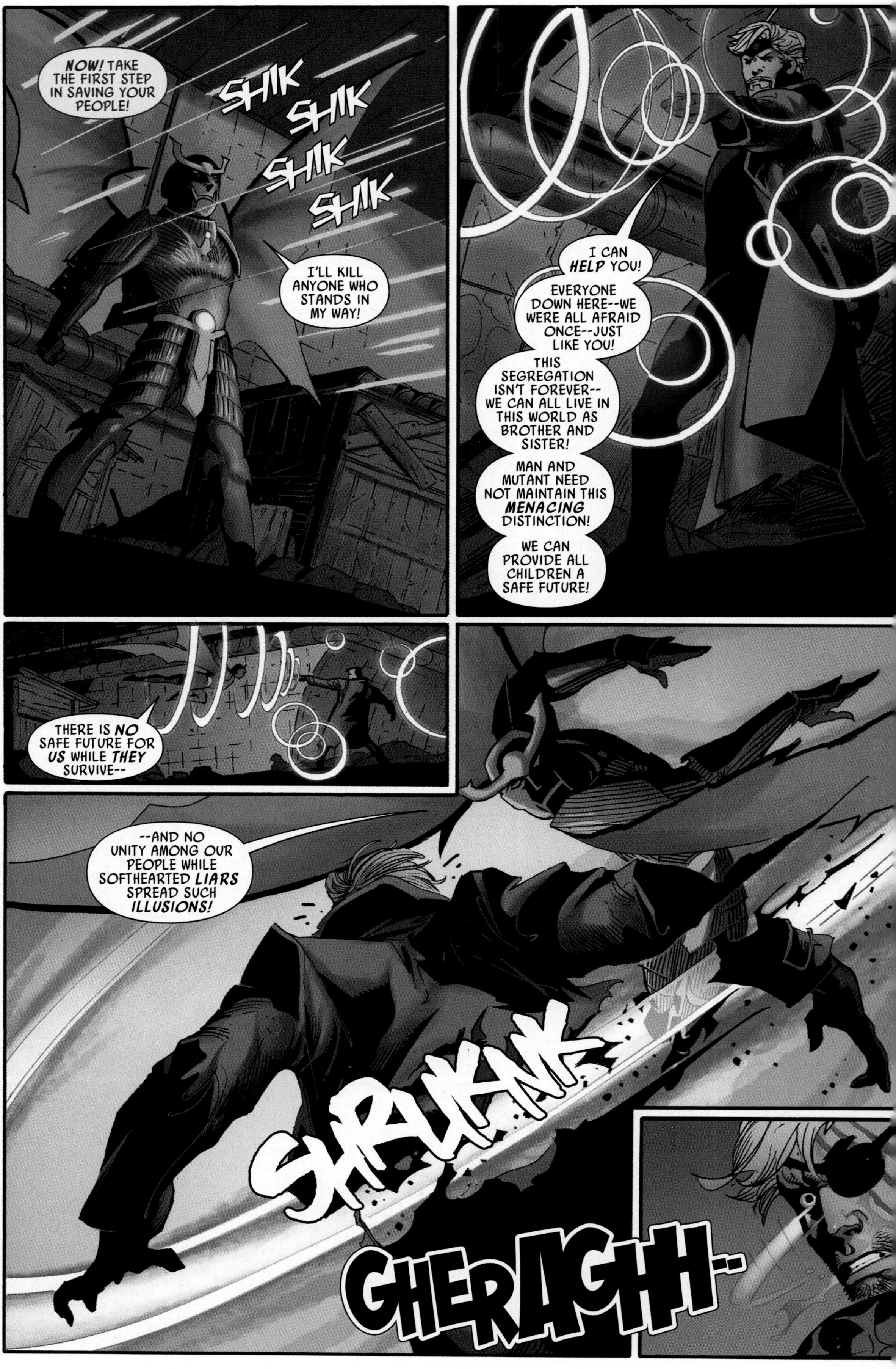
NOW! TAKE THE FIRST STEP IN SAVING YOUR PEOPLE!
SHIK SHIK SHIK SHIK
I'LL KILL ANYONE WHO STANDS IN MY WAY!
I CAN HELP YOU!
EVERYONE DOWN HERE--WE WERE ALL AFRAID ONCE--JUST LIKE YOU!
THIS SEGREGATION ISN'T FOREVER--WE CAN ALL LIVE IN THIS WORLD AS BROTHER AND SISTER!
MAN AND MUTANT NEED NOT MAINTAIN THIS MENACING DISTINCTION!
WE CAN PROVIDE ALL CHILDREN A SAFE FUTURE!
THERE IS NO SAFE FUTURE FOR US WHILE THEY SURVIVE--
--AND NO UNITY AMONG OUR PEOPLE WHILE SOFTHEARTED LIARS SPREAD SUCH ILLUSIONS!
SHRUKNK
GHERAGHH--

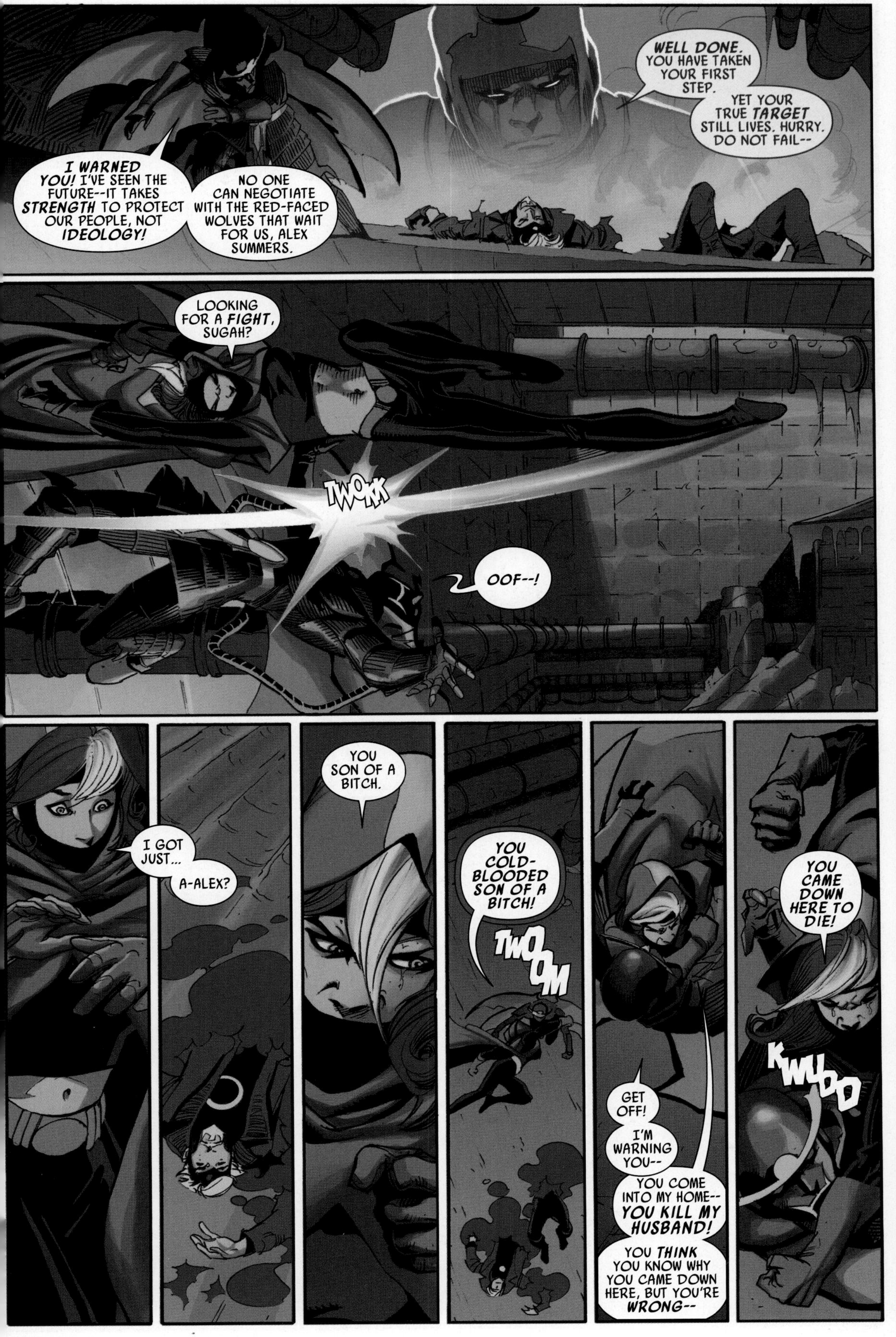

WELL DONE. YOU HAVE TAKEN YOUR FIRST STEP.
YET YOUR TRUE TARGET STILL LIVES. HURRY. DO NOT FAIL--
I WARNED YOU! I'VE SEEN THE FUTURE--IT TAKES STRENGTH TO PROTECT OUR PEOPLE, NOT IDEOLOGY!
NO ONE CAN NEGOTIATE WITH THE RED-FACED WOLVES THAT WAIT FOR US, ALEX SUMMERS.
LOOKING FOR A FIGHT, SUGAH?
TWOKK
OOF--!
I GOT JUST...
A-ALEX?
YOU SON OF A BITCH.
YOU COLD-BLOODED SON OF A BITCH!
TWOOM
GET OFF!
I'M WARNING YOU--
YOU COME INTO MY HOME--YOU KILL MY HUSBAND!
YOU THINK YOU KNOW WHY YOU CAME DOWN HERE, BUT YOU'RE WRONG--
YOU CAME DOWN HERE TO DIE!
KWUDD

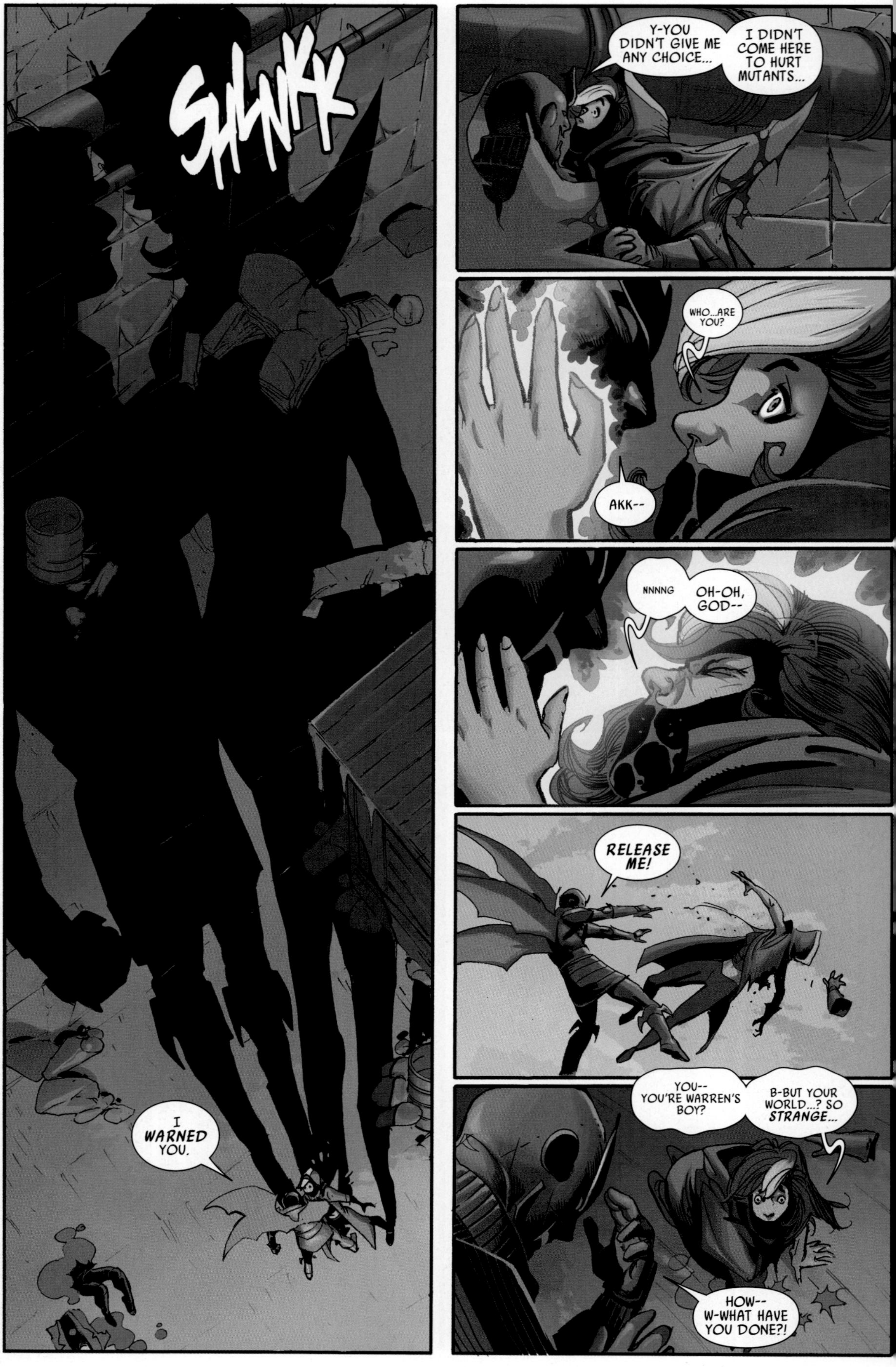
SHNKK
I WARNED YOU.
Y-YOU DIDN'T GIVE ME ANY CHOICE...
I DIDN'T COME HERE TO HURT MUTANTS...
WHO...ARE YOU?
AKK--
NNNNG
OH-OH, GOD--
RELEASE ME!
YOU-- YOU'RE WARREN'S BOY?
B-BUT YOUR WORLD...? SO STRANGE...
HOW-- W-WHAT HAVE YOU DONE?!

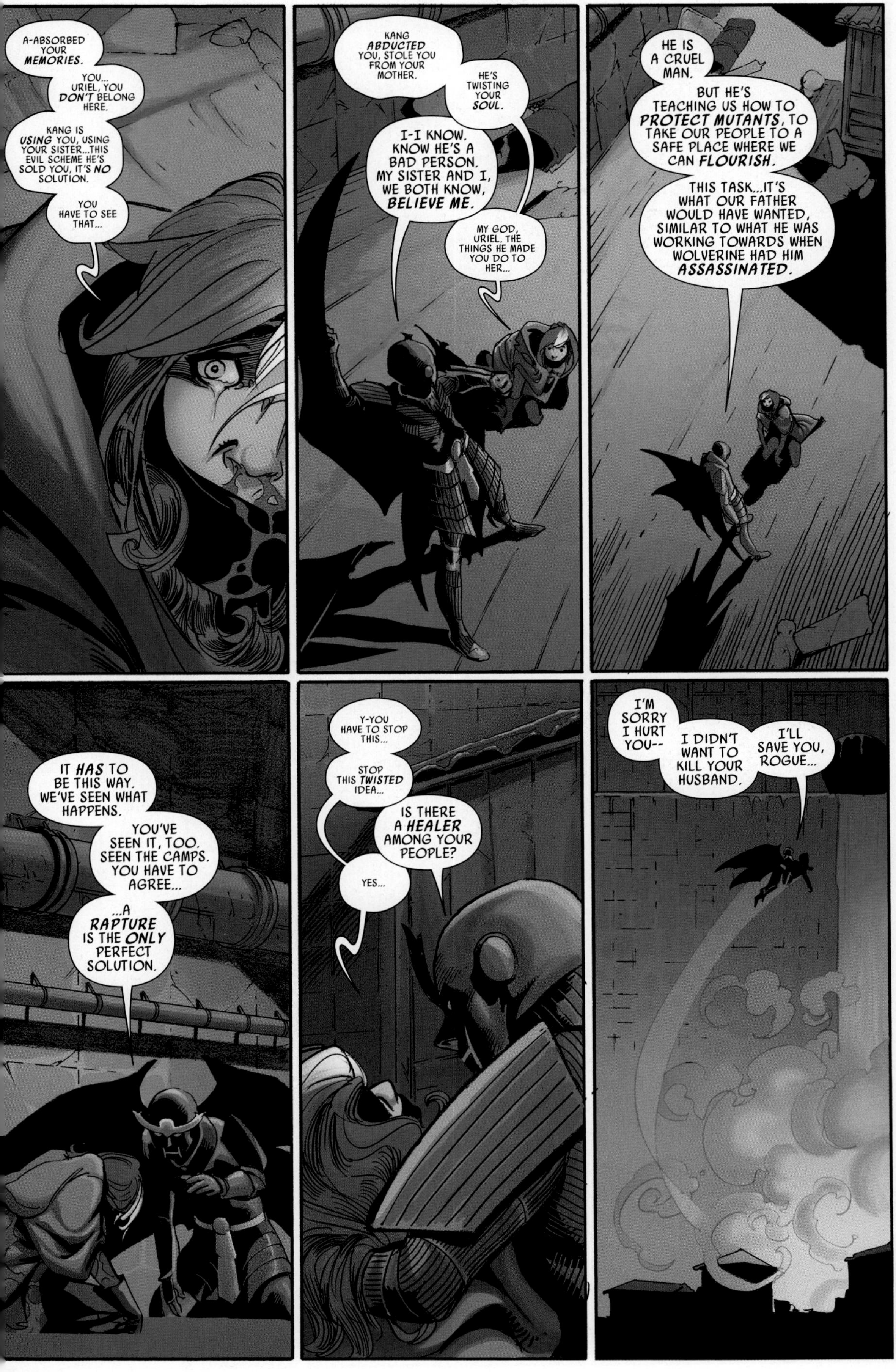
A-ABSORBED YOUR MEMORIES.
YOU... URIEL, YOU DON'T BELONG HERE.
KANG IS USING YOU, USING YOUR SISTER...THIS EVIL SCHEME HE'S SOLD YOU, IT'S NO SOLUTION.
YOU HAVE TO SEE THAT...
KANG ABDUCTED YOU, STOLE YOU FROM YOUR MOTHER.
HE'S TWISTING YOUR SOUL.
I-I KNOW. KNOW HE'S A BAD PERSON. MY SISTER AND I, WE BOTH KNOW, BELIEVE ME.
MY GOD, URIEL. THE THINGS HE MADE YOU DO TO HER...
HE IS A CRUEL MAN.
BUT HE'S TEACHING US HOW TO PROTECT MUTANTS, TO TAKE OUR PEOPLE TO A SAFE PLACE WHERE WE CAN FLOURISH.
THIS TASK...IT'S WHAT OUR FATHER WOULD HAVE WANTED, SIMILAR TO WHAT HE WAS WORKING TOWARDS WHEN WOLVERINE HAD HIM ASSASSINATED.
IT HAS TO BE THIS WAY. WE'VE SEEN WHAT HAPPENS.
YOU'VE SEEN IT, TOO. SEEN THE CAMPS. YOU HAVE TO AGREE...
...A RAPTURE IS THE ONLY PERFECT SOLUTION.
Y-YOU HAVE TO STOP THIS...
STOP THIS TWISTED IDEA...
IS THERE A HEALER AMONG YOUR PEOPLE?
YES...
I'M SORRY I HURT YOU--
I DIDN'T WANT TO KILL YOUR HUSBAND.
I'LL SAVE YOU, ROGUE...

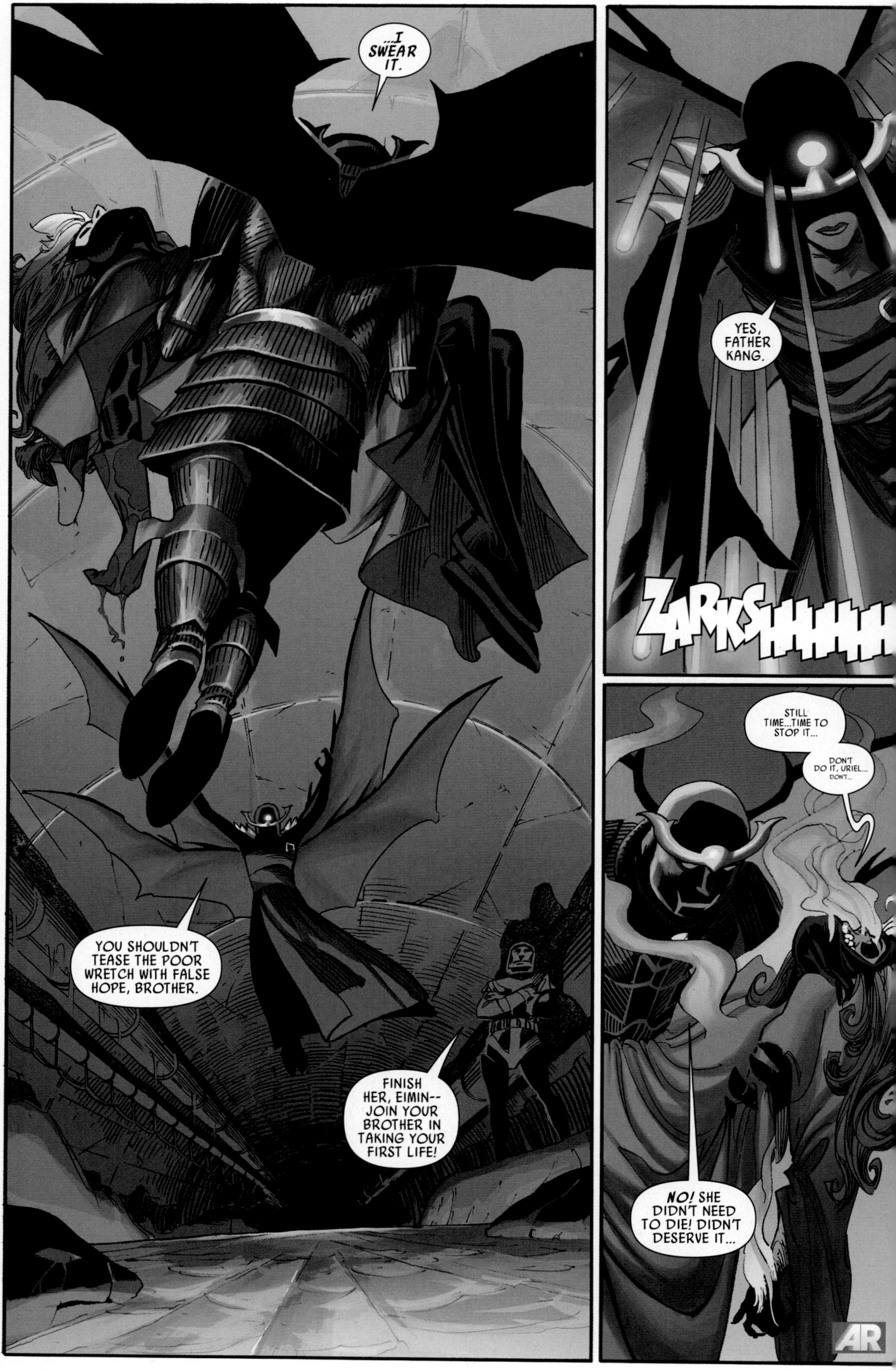
...I SWEAR IT.
YOU SHOULDN'T TEASE THE POOR WRETCH WITH FALSE HOPE, BROTHER.
FINISH HER, EIMIN-- JOIN YOUR BROTHER IN TAKING YOUR FIRST LIFE!
YES, FATHER KANG.
ZARKSHHHHHH
STILL TIME...TIME TO STOP IT...
DON'T DO IT, URIEL... DON'T...
NO! SHE DIDN'T NEED TO DIE! DIDN'T DESERVE IT...

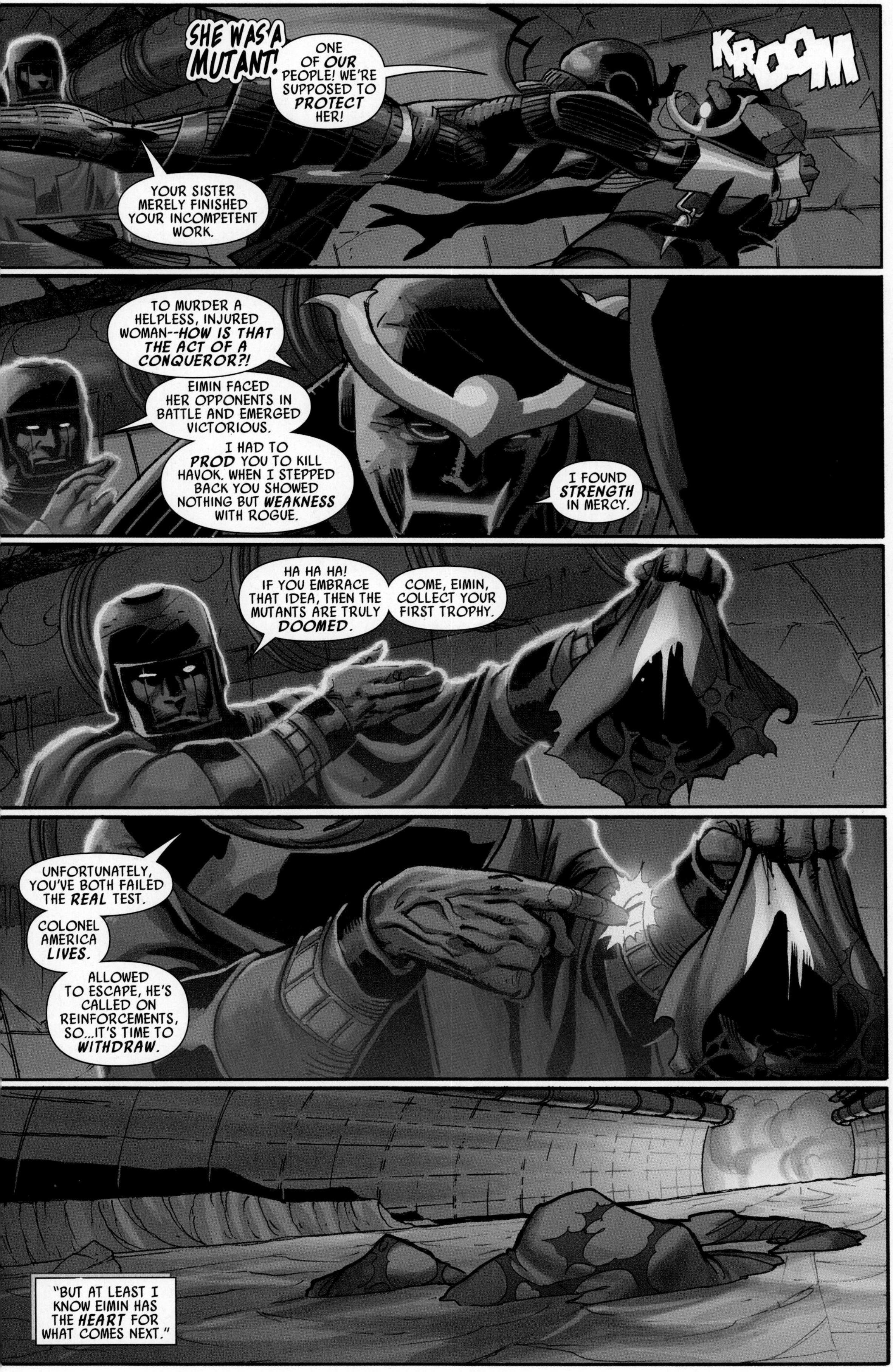
SHE WAS A MUTANT!
ONE OF OUR PEOPLE! WE'RE SUPPOSED TO PROTECT HER!
KROOM
YOUR SISTER MERELY FINISHED YOUR INCOMPETENT WORK.
TO MURDER A HELPLESS, INJURED WOMAN--HOW IS THAT THE ACT OF A CONQUEROR?!
EIMIN FACED HER OPPONENTS IN BATTLE AND EMERGED VICTORIOUS.
I HAD TO PROD YOU TO KILL HAVOK. WHEN I STEPPED BACK YOU SHOWED NOTHING BUT WEAKNESS WITH ROGUE.
I FOUND STRENGTH IN MERCY.
HA HA HA! IF YOU EMBRACE THAT IDEA, THEN THE MUTANTS ARE TRULY DOOMED.
COME, EIMIN, COLLECT YOUR FIRST TROPHY.
UNFORTUNATELY, YOU'VE BOTH FAILED THE REAL TEST.
COLONEL AMERICA LIVES.
ALLOWED TO ESCAPE, HE'S CALLED ON REINFORCEMENTS, SO...IT'S TIME TO WITHDRAW.
"BUT AT LEAST I KNOW EIMIN HAS THE HEART FOR WHAT COMES NEXT."

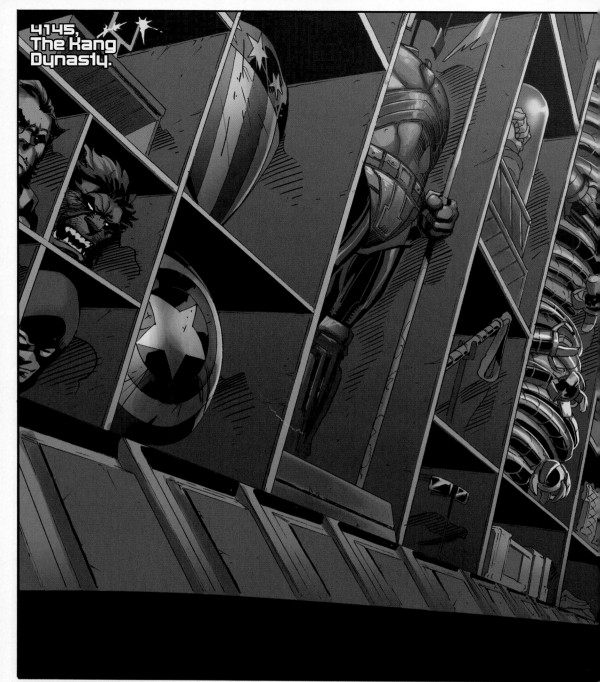

I-I'M SORRY,
FATHER KANG.
PLEASE...

QUIET YOUR
SNIVELING.

NEVER BE
SORRY...

...BE
VICTORIOUS.

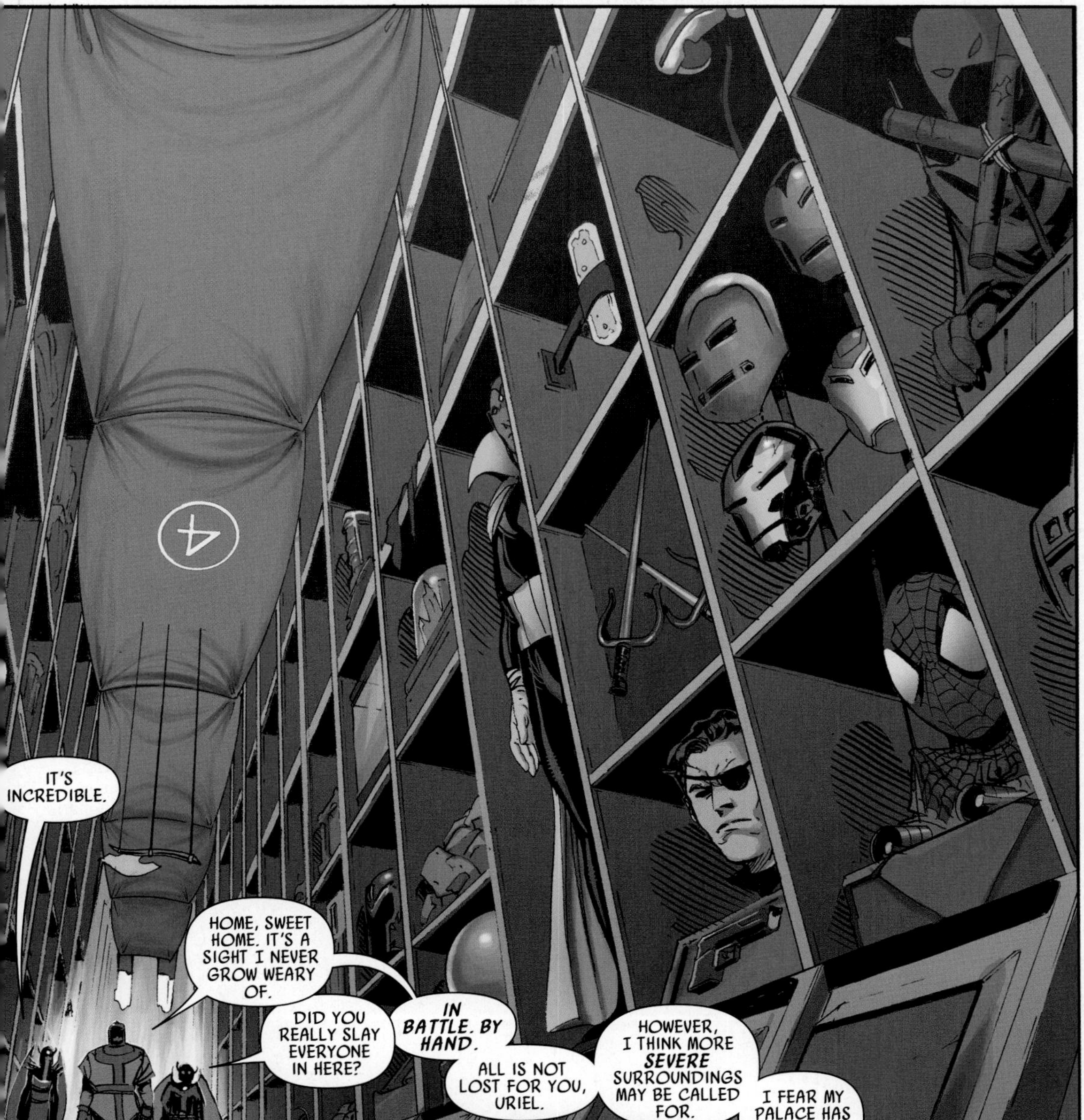
IT'S INCREDIBLE.
HOME, SWEET HOME. IT'S A SIGHT I NEVER GROW WEARY OF.
DID YOU REALLY SLAY EVERYONE IN HERE?
IN BATTLE. BY HAND.
ALL IS NOT LOST FOR YOU, URIEL.
HOWEVER, I THINK MORE SEVERE SURROUNDINGS MAY BE CALLED FOR.
I FEAR MY PALACE HAS SOFTENED YOU.
AR

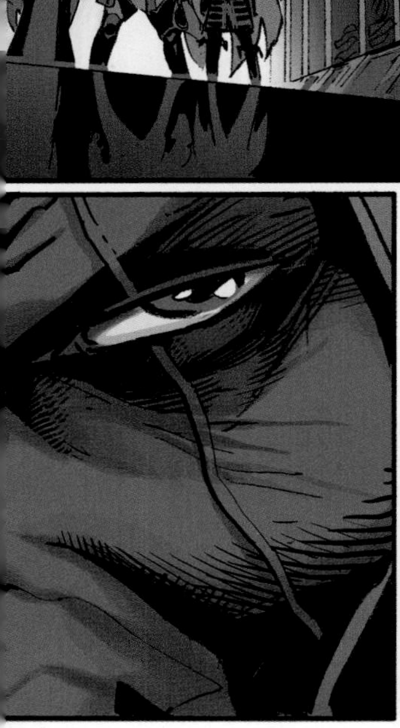

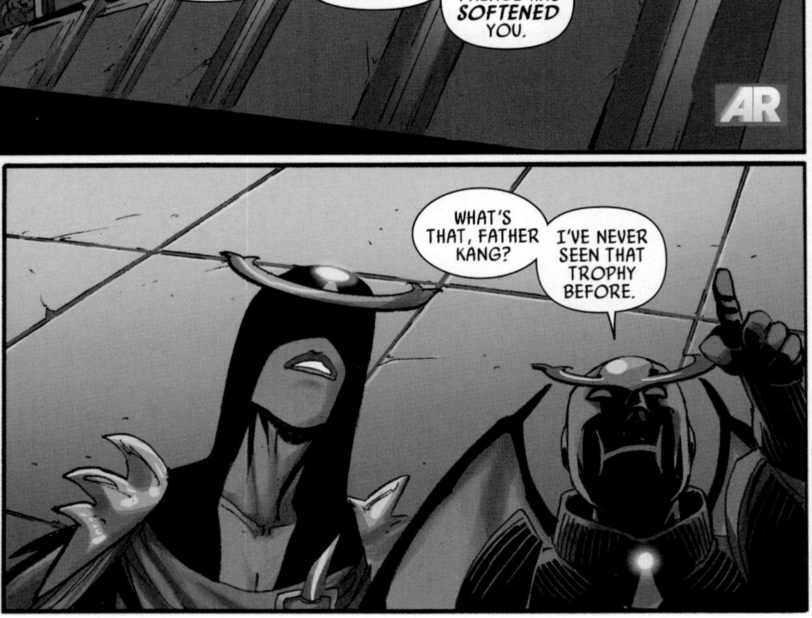
WHAT'S THAT, FATHER KANG?
I'VE NEVER SEEN THAT TROPHY BEFORE.

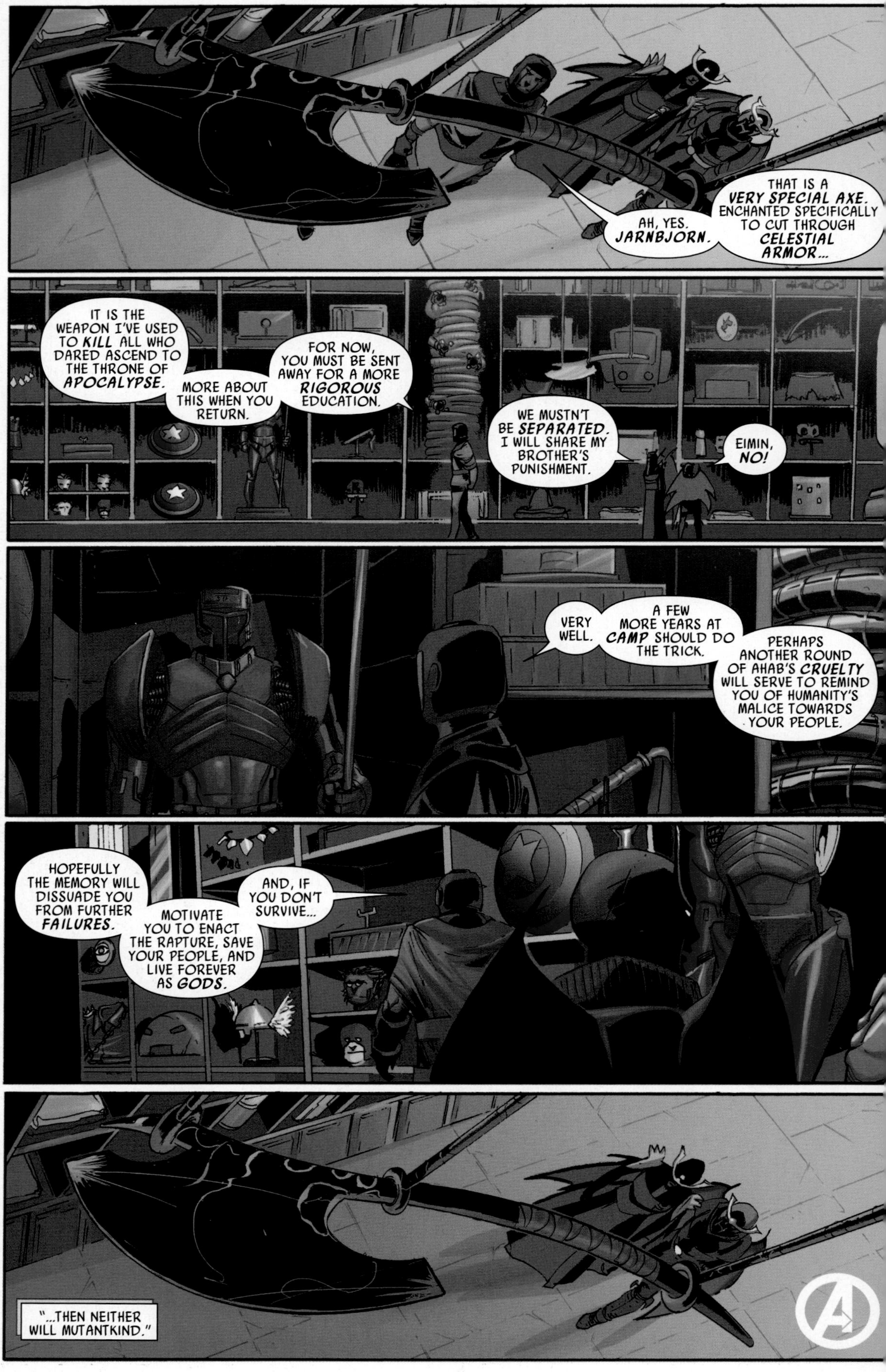
AH, YES. JARNBJORN.
THAT IS A VERY SPECIAL AXE. ENCHANTED SPECIFICALLY TO CUT THROUGH CELESTIAL ARMOR...
IT IS THE WEAPON I'VE USED TO KILL ALL WHO DARED ASCEND TO THE THRONE OF APOCALYPSE.
MORE ABOUT THIS WHEN YOU RETURN.
FOR NOW, YOU MUST BE SENT AWAY FOR A MORE RIGOROUS EDUCATION.
WE MUSTN'T BE SEPARATED. I WILL SHARE MY BROTHER'S PUNISHMENT.
EIMIN, NO!
VERY WELL.
A FEW MORE YEARS AT CAMP SHOULD DO THE TRICK.
PERHAPS ANOTHER ROUND OF AHAB'S CRUELTY WILL SERVE TO REMIND YOU OF HUMANITY'S MALICE TOWARDS YOUR PEOPLE.
HOPEFULLY THE MEMORY WILL DISSUADE YOU FROM FURTHER FAILURES.
MOTIVATE YOU TO ENACT THE RAPTURE, SAVE YOUR PEOPLE, AND LIVE FOREVER AS GODS.
AND, IF YOU DON'T SURVIVE...
"...THEN NEITHER WILL MUTANTKIND."

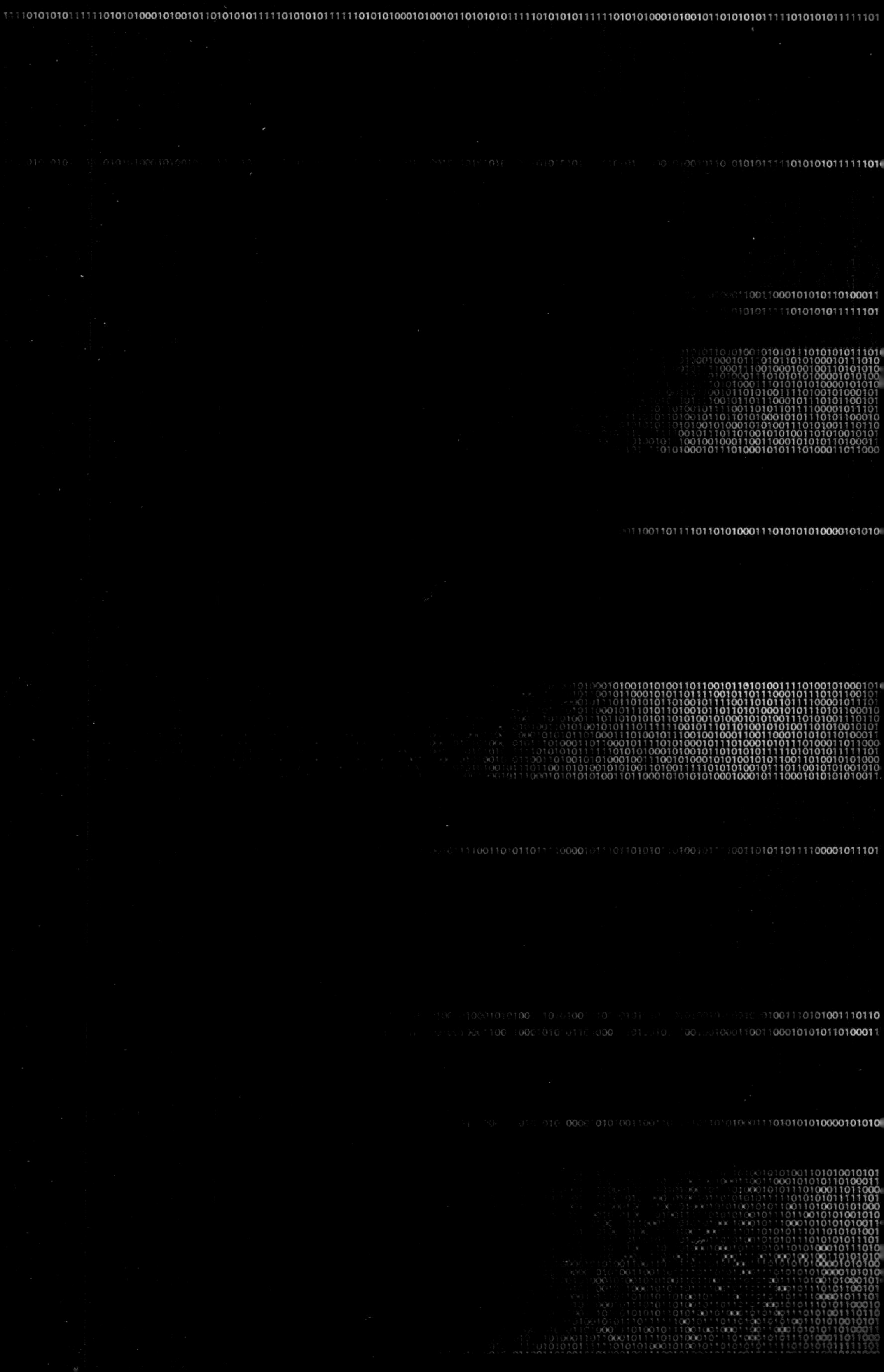

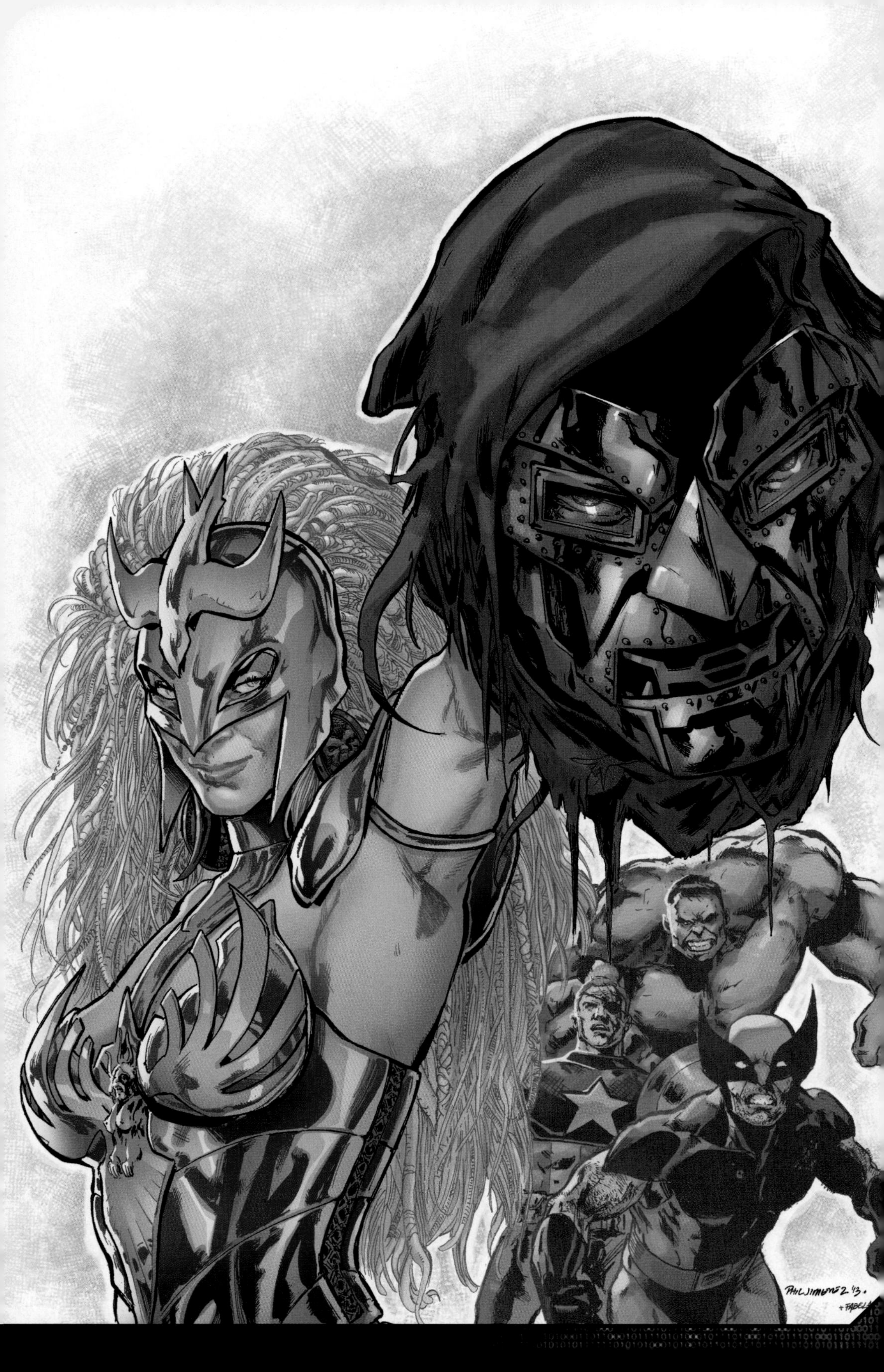
PHIL JIMENEZ 2 '13.

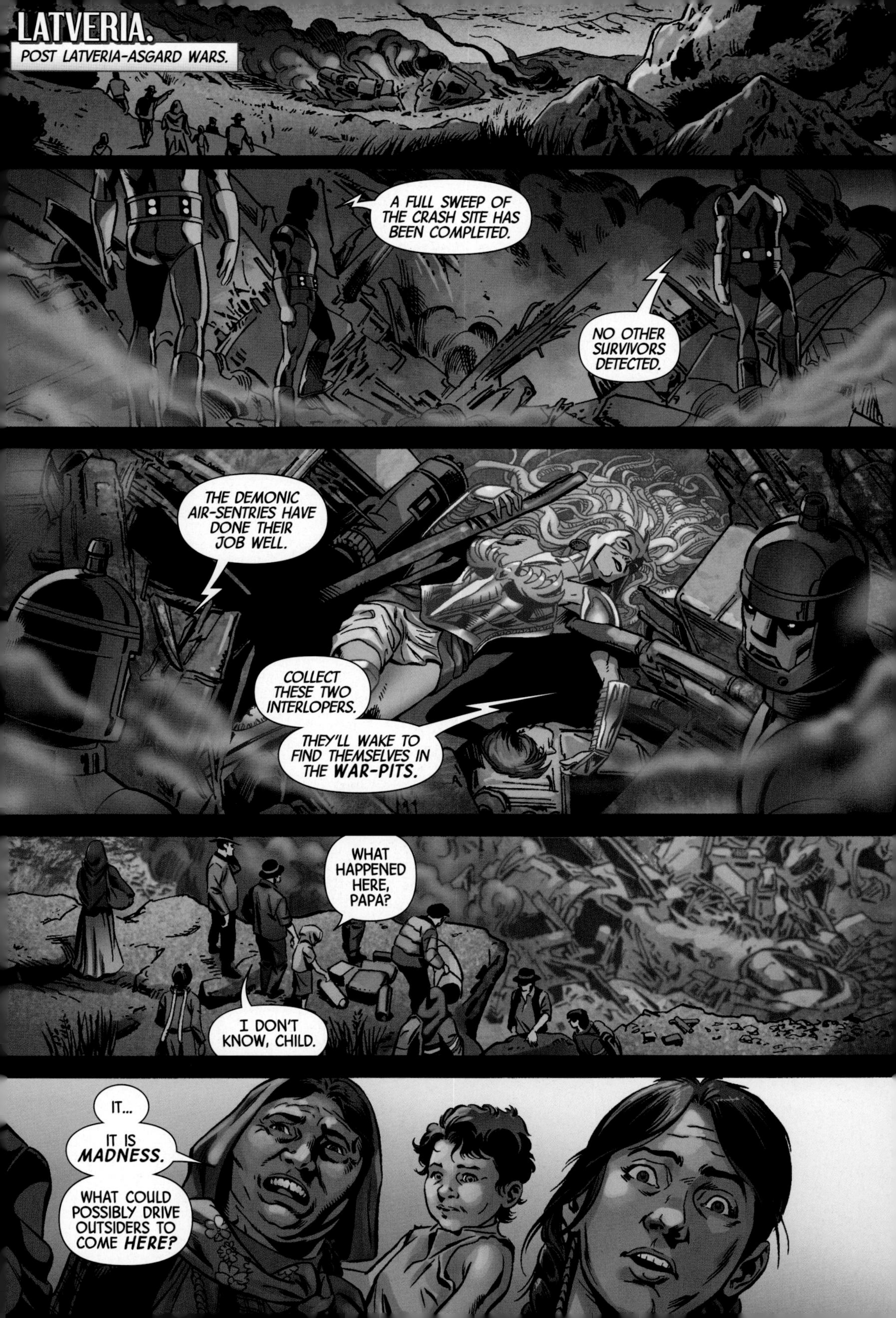
LATVERIA.
POST LATVERIA-ASGARD WARS.
A FULL SWEEP OF THE CRASH SITE HAS BEEN COMPLETED.
NO OTHER SURVIVORS DETECTED.
THE DEMONIC AIR-SENTRIES HAVE DONE THEIR JOB WELL.
COLLECT THESE TWO INTERLOPERS.
THEY'LL WAKE TO FIND THEMSELVES IN THE WAR-PITS.
WHAT HAPPENED HERE, PAPA?
I DON'T KNOW, CHILD.
IT...
IT IS MADNESS.
WHAT COULD POSSIBLY DRIVE OUTSIDERS TO COME HERE?

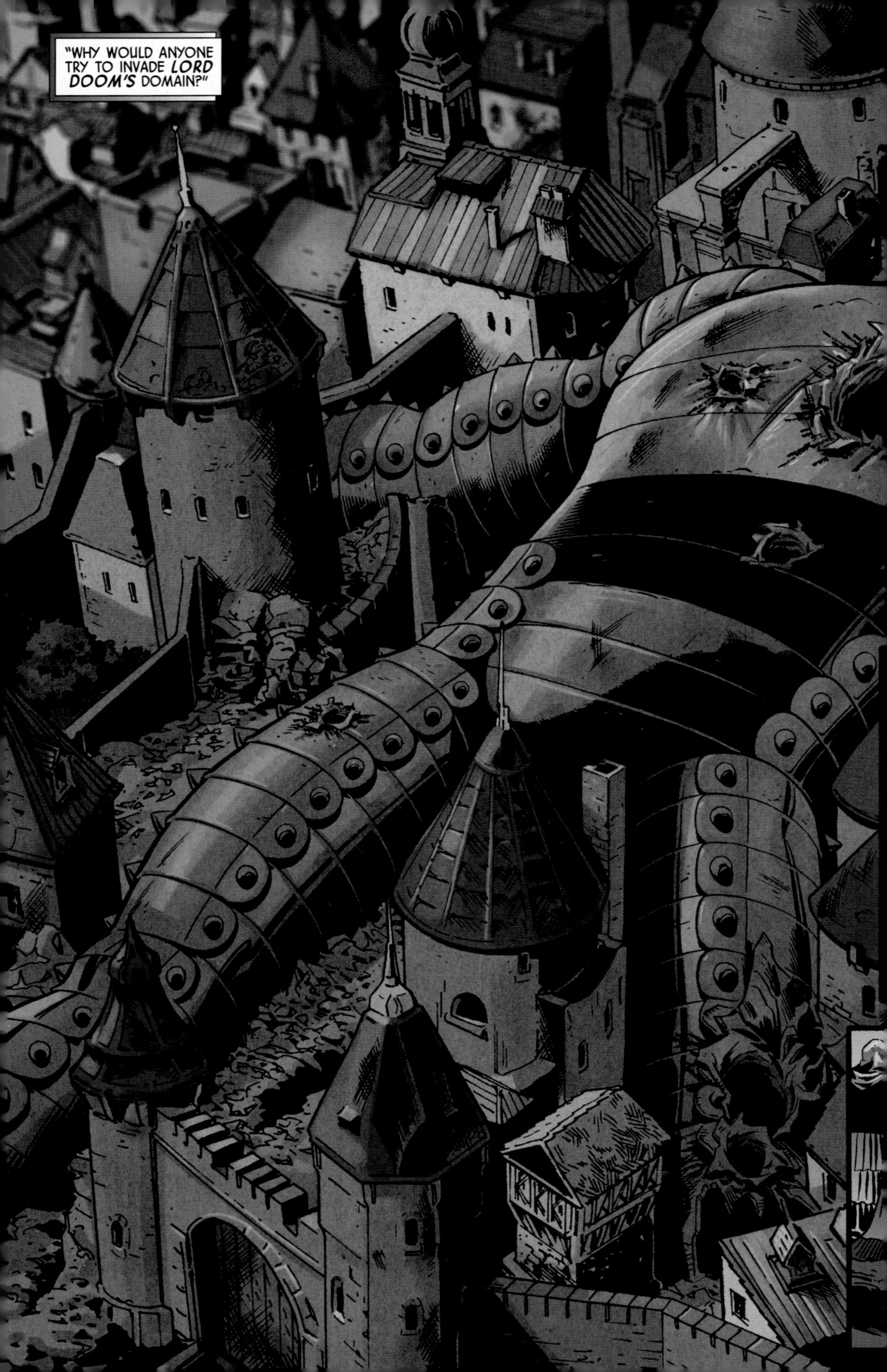
"WHY WOULD ANYONE TRY TO INVADE LORD DOOM'S DOMAIN?"

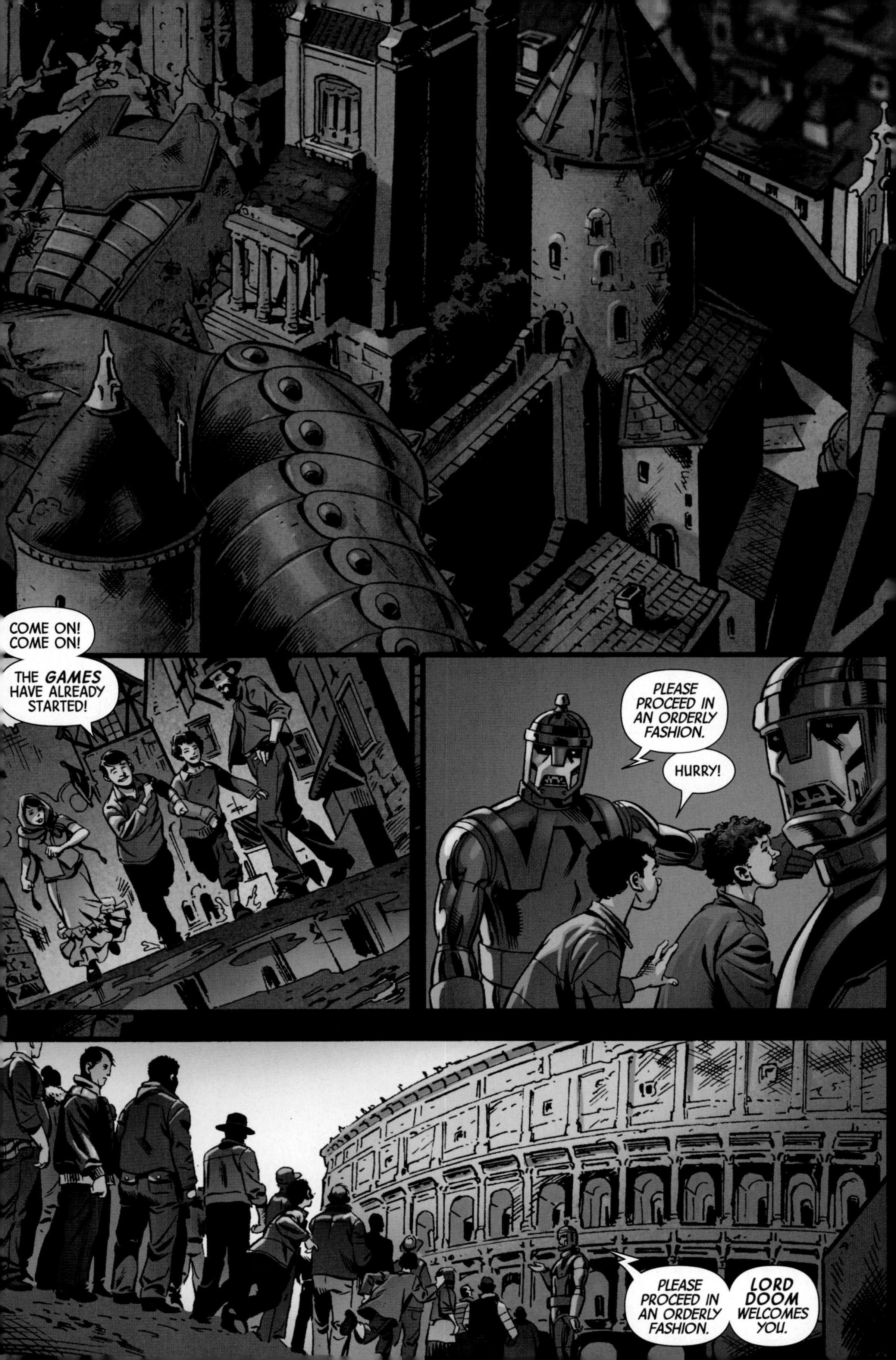
COME ON! COME ON!
THE GAMES HAVE ALREADY STARTED!
PLEASE PROCEED IN AN ORDERLY FASHION.
HURRY!
PLEASE PROCEED IN AN ORDERLY FASHION.
LORD DOOM WELCOMES YOU.

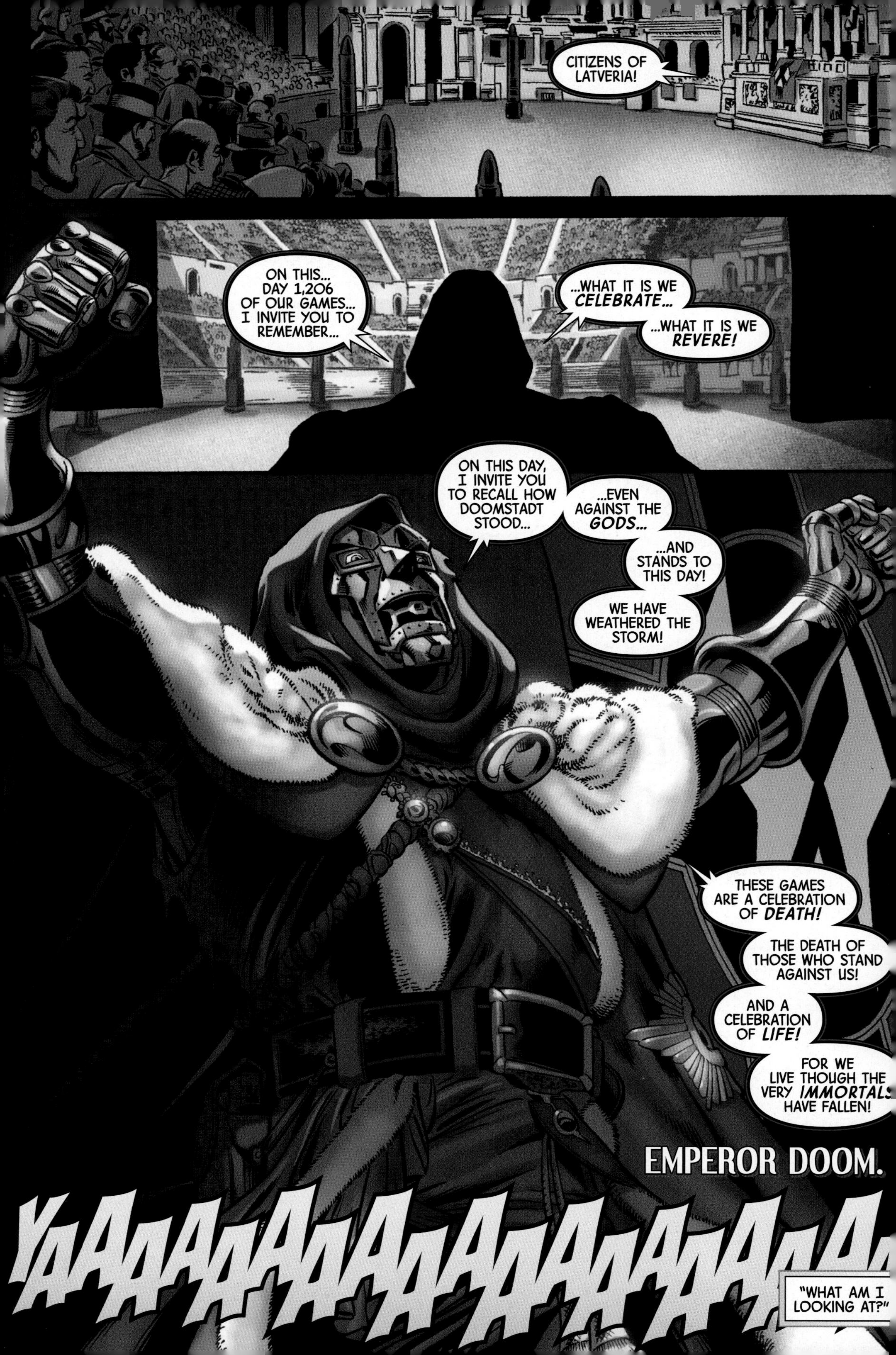
CITIZENS OF LATVERIA!
ON THIS... DAY 1,206 OF OUR GAMES... I INVITE YOU TO REMEMBER...
...WHAT IT IS WE CELEBRATE...
...WHAT IT IS WE REVERE!
ON THIS DAY, I INVITE YOU TO RECALL HOW DOOMSTADT STOOD...
...EVEN AGAINST THE GODS...
...AND STANDS TO THIS DAY!
WE HAVE WEATHERED THE STORM!
THESE GAMES ARE A CELEBRATION OF DEATH!
THE DEATH OF THOSE WHO STAND AGAINST US!
AND A CELEBRATION OF LIFE!
FOR WE LIVE THOUGH THE VERY IMMORTALS HAVE FALLEN!
EMPEROR DOOM.
YAAAAAAAAAAAAAAAAAAAA
"WHAT AM I LOOKING AT?"

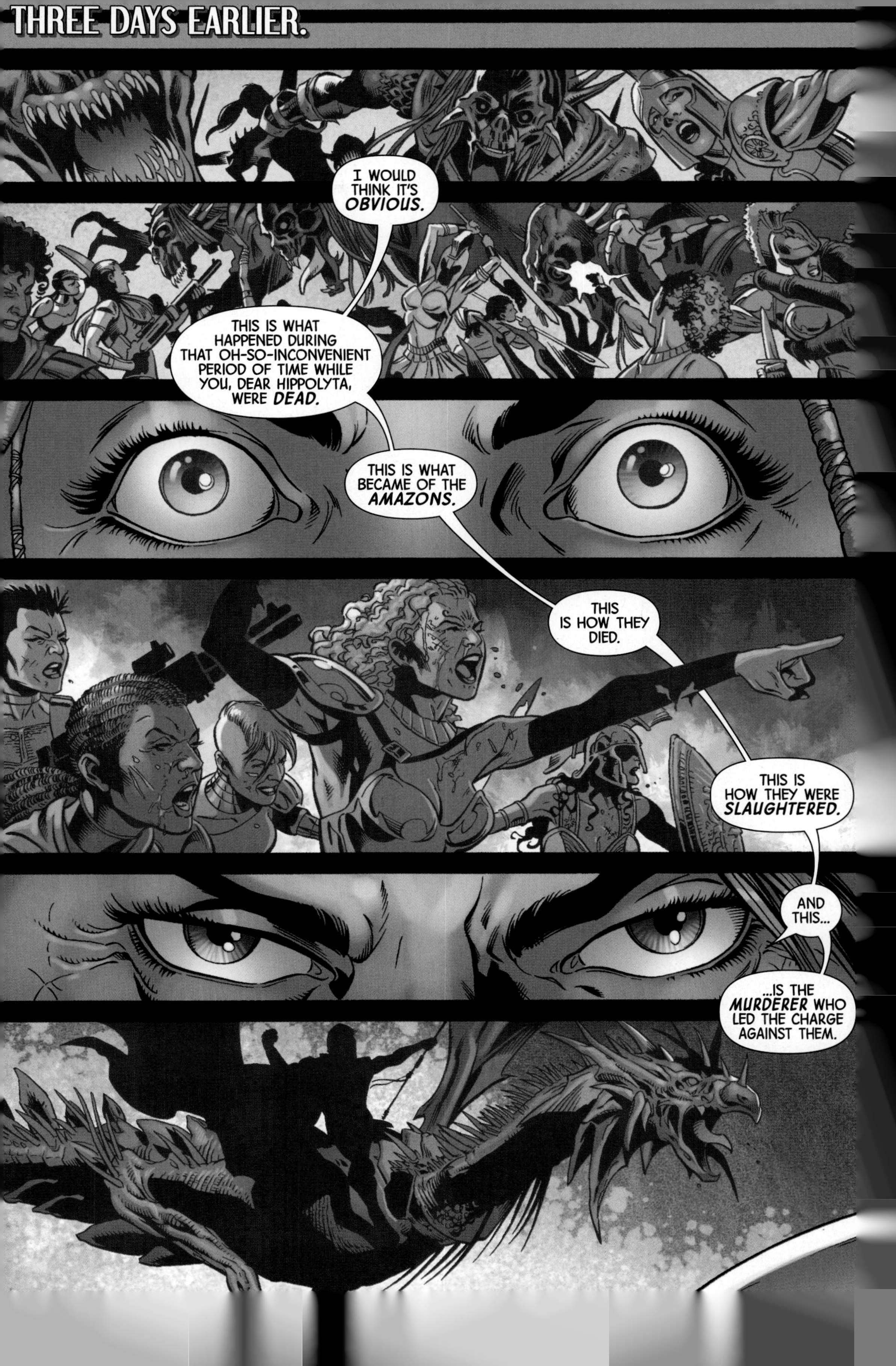
THREE DAYS EARLIER.
I WOULD THINK IT'S OBVIOUS.
THIS IS WHAT HAPPENED DURING THAT OH-SO-INCONVENIENT PERIOD OF TIME WHILE YOU, DEAR HIPPOLYTA, WERE DEAD.
THIS IS WHAT BECAME OF THE AMAZONS.
THIS IS HOW THEY DIED.
THIS IS HOW THEY WERE SLAUGHTERED.
AND THIS...
...IS THE MURDERER WHO LED THE CHARGE AGAINST THEM.

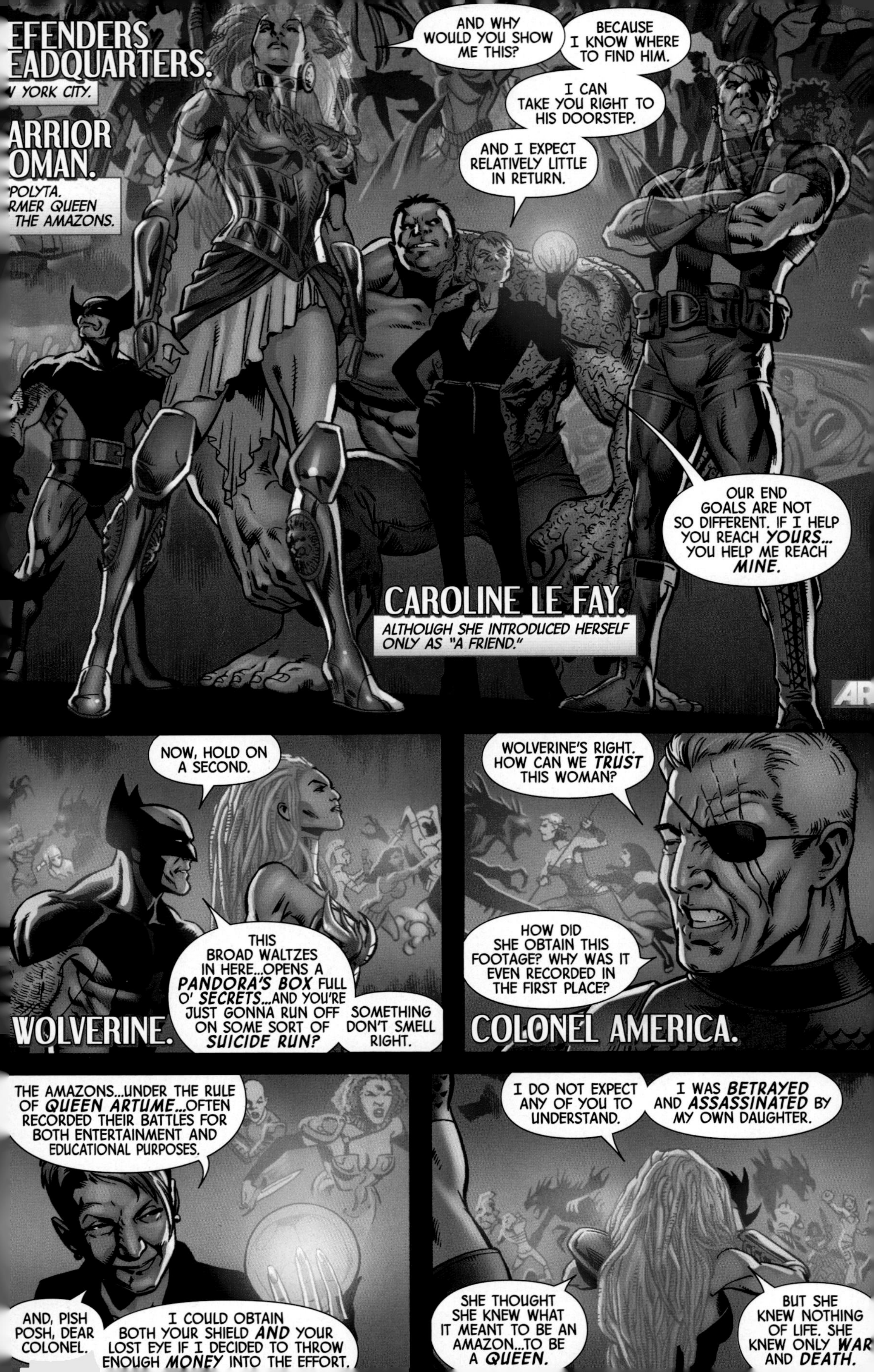
EFENDERS EADQUARTERS.
W YORK CITY.
ARRIOR OMAN.
POLYTA. RMER QUEEN THE AMAZONS.
AND WHY WOULD YOU SHOW ME THIS?
BECAUSE I KNOW WHERE TO FIND HIM.
I CAN TAKE YOU RIGHT TO HIS DOORSTEP.
AND I EXPECT RELATIVELY LITTLE IN RETURN.
OUR END GOALS ARE NOT SO DIFFERENT. IF I HELP YOU REACH YOURS... YOU HELP ME REACH MINE.
CAROLINE LE FAY.
ALTHOUGH SHE INTRODUCED HERSELF ONLY AS "A FRIEND."
NOW, HOLD ON A SECOND.
THIS BROAD WALTZES IN HERE...OPENS A PANDORA'S BOX FULL O' SECRETS...AND YOU'RE JUST GONNA RUN OFF ON SOME SORT OF SUICIDE RUN?
SOMETHING DON'T SMELL RIGHT.
WOLVERINE.
WOLVERINE'S RIGHT. HOW CAN WE TRUST THIS WOMAN?
HOW DID SHE OBTAIN THIS FOOTAGE? WHY WAS IT EVEN RECORDED IN THE FIRST PLACE?
COLONEL AMERICA.
THE AMAZONS...UNDER THE RULE OF QUEEN ARTUME...OFTEN RECORDED THEIR BATTLES FOR BOTH ENTERTAINMENT AND EDUCATIONAL PURPOSES.
AND, PISH POSH, DEAR COLONEL.
I COULD OBTAIN BOTH YOUR SHIELD AND YOUR LOST EYE IF I DECIDED TO THROW ENOUGH MONEY INTO THE EFFORT.
I DO NOT EXPECT ANY OF YOU TO UNDERSTAND.
I WAS BETRAYED AND ASSASSINATED BY MY OWN DAUGHTER.
SHE THOUGHT SHE KNEW WHAT IT MEANT TO BE AN AMAZON...TO BE A QUEEN.
BUT SHE KNEW NOTHING OF LIFE. SHE KNEW ONLY WAR AND DEATH.

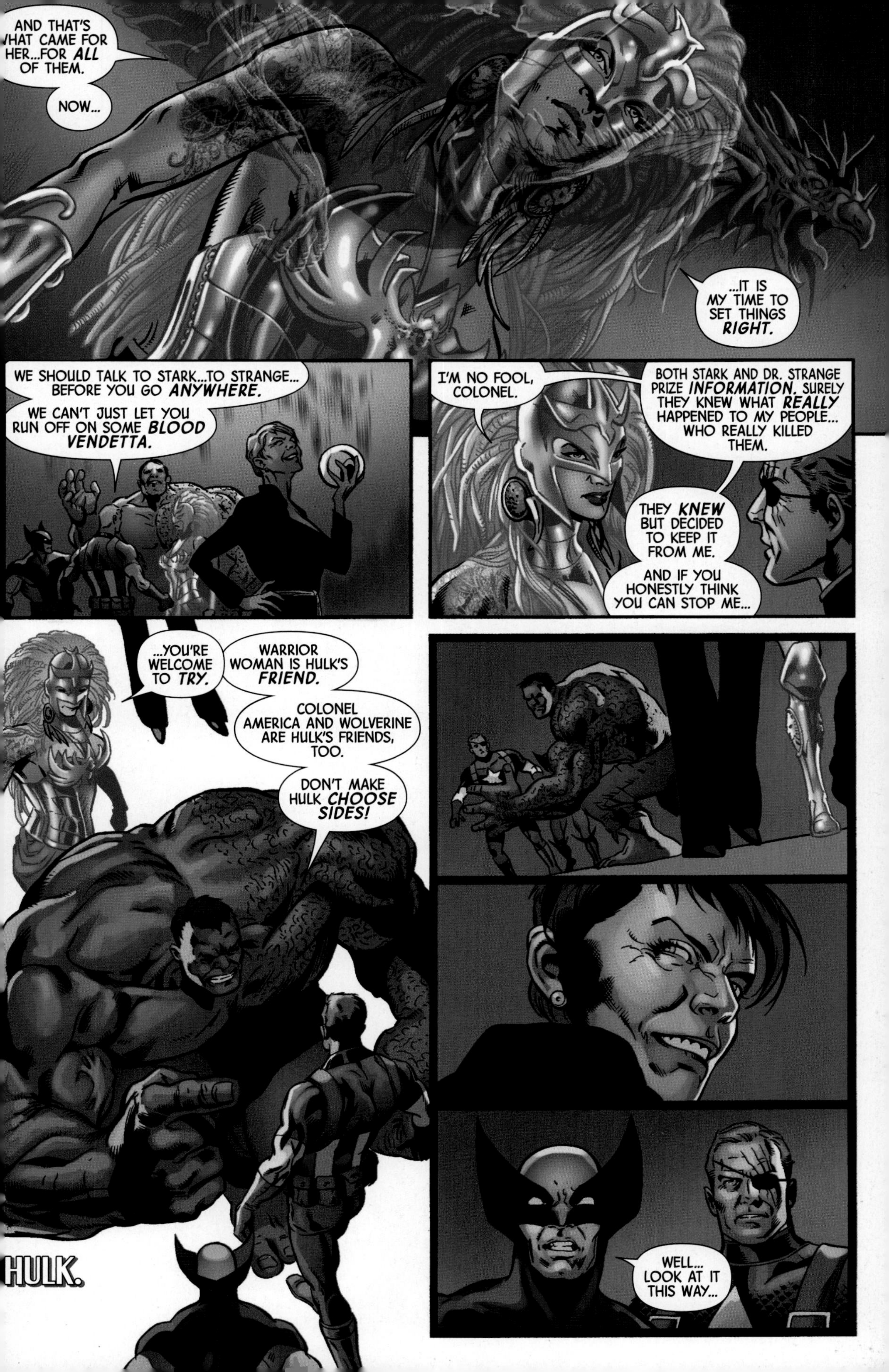
AND THAT'S WHAT CAME FOR HER...FOR ALL OF THEM.
NOW...
...IT IS MY TIME TO SET THINGS RIGHT.
WE SHOULD TALK TO STARK...TO STRANGE... BEFORE YOU GO ANYWHERE.
WE CAN'T JUST LET YOU RUN OFF ON SOME BLOOD VENDETTA.
I'M NO FOOL, COLONEL.
BOTH STARK AND DR. STRANGE PRIZE INFORMATION. SURELY THEY KNEW WHAT REALLY HAPPENED TO MY PEOPLE... WHO REALLY KILLED THEM.
THEY KNEW BUT DECIDED TO KEEP IT FROM ME.
AND IF YOU HONESTLY THINK YOU CAN STOP ME...
...YOU'RE WELCOME TO TRY.
WARRIOR WOMAN IS HULK'S FRIEND.
COLONEL AMERICA AND WOLVERINE ARE HULK'S FRIENDS, TOO.
DON'T MAKE HULK CHOOSE SIDES!
HULK.
WELL... LOOK AT IT THIS WAY...

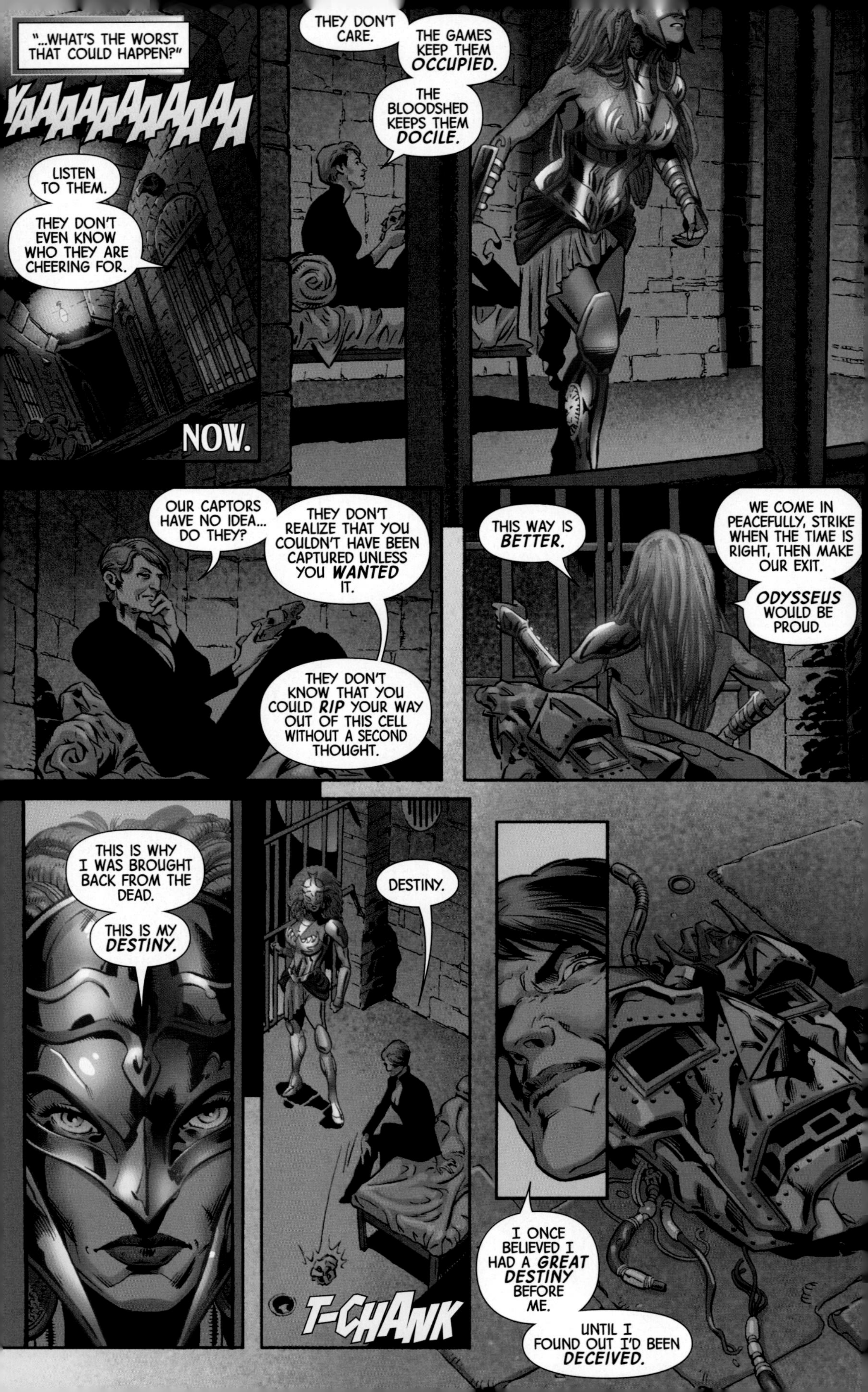

"...WHAT'S THE WORST THAT COULD HAPPEN?"
YAAAAAAAAAAA
LISTEN TO THEM.
THEY DON'T EVEN KNOW WHO THEY ARE CHEERING FOR.
NOW.
THEY DON'T CARE.
THE GAMES KEEP THEM OCCUPIED.
THE BLOODSHED KEEPS THEM DOCILE.
OUR CAPTORS HAVE NO IDEA... DO THEY?
THEY DON'T REALIZE THAT YOU COULDN'T HAVE BEEN CAPTURED UNLESS YOU WANTED IT.
THEY DON'T KNOW THAT YOU COULD RIP YOUR WAY OUT OF THIS CELL WITHOUT A SECOND THOUGHT.
THIS WAY IS BETTER.
WE COME IN PEACEFULLY, STRIKE WHEN THE TIME IS RIGHT, THEN MAKE OUR EXIT.
ODYSSEUS WOULD BE PROUD.
THIS IS WHY I WAS BROUGHT BACK FROM THE DEAD.
THIS IS MY DESTINY.
DESTINY.
T-CHANK
I ONCE BELIEVED I HAD A GREAT DESTINY BEFORE ME.
UNTIL I FOUND OUT I'D BEEN DECEIVED.

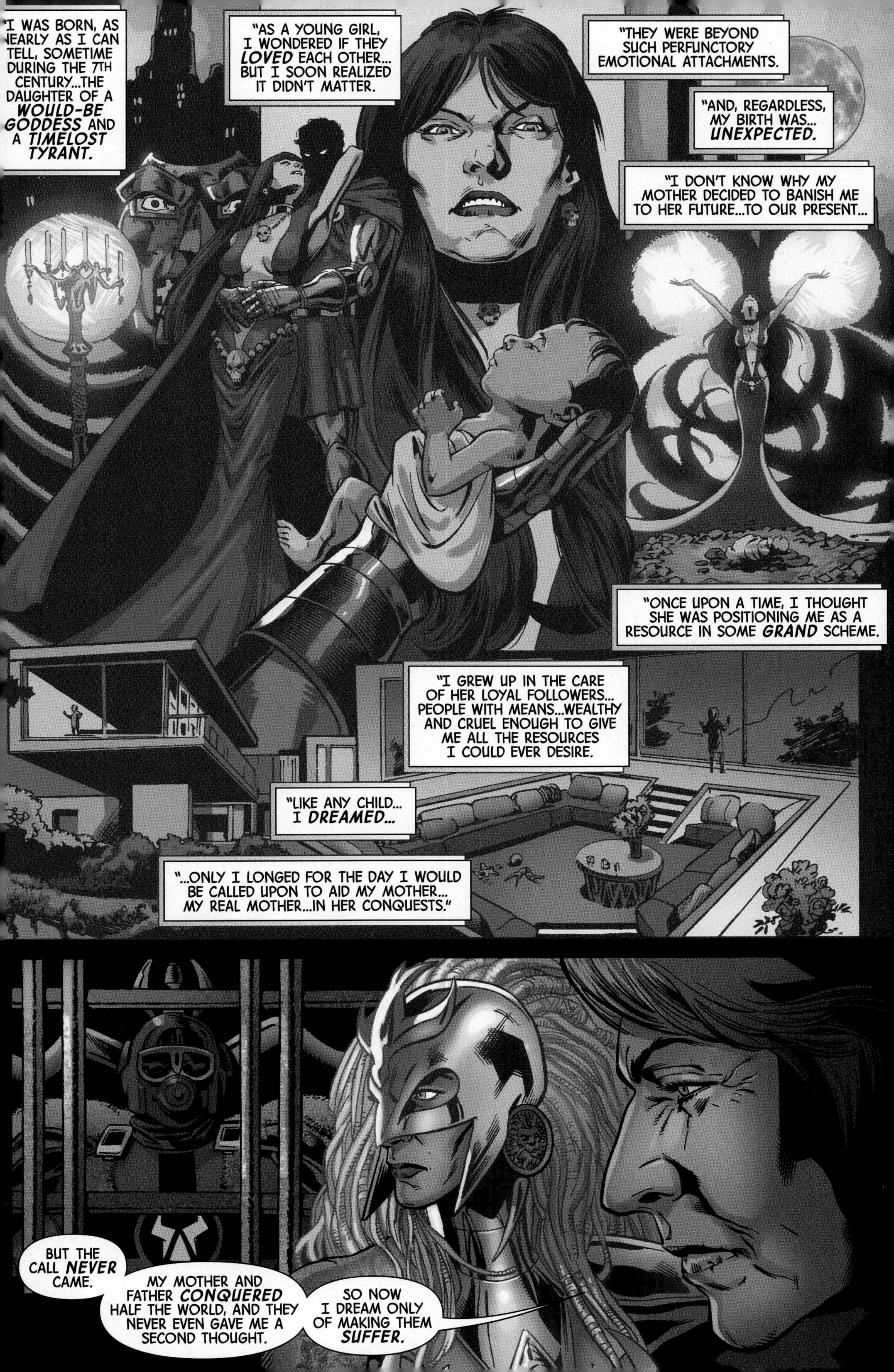
"I WAS BORN, AS NEARLY AS I CAN TELL, SOMETIME DURING THE 7TH CENTURY...THE DAUGHTER OF A WOULD-BE GODDESS AND A TIMELOST TYRANT.
"AS A YOUNG GIRL, I WONDERED IF THEY LOVED EACH OTHER... BUT I SOON REALIZED IT DIDN'T MATTER.
"THEY WERE BEYOND SUCH PERFUNCTORY EMOTIONAL ATTACHMENTS.
"AND, REGARDLESS, MY BIRTH WAS... UNEXPECTED.
"I DON'T KNOW WHY MY MOTHER DECIDED TO BANISH ME TO HER FUTURE...TO OUR PRESENT...
"ONCE UPON A TIME, I THOUGHT SHE WAS POSITIONING ME AS A RESOURCE IN SOME GRAND SCHEME.
"I GREW UP IN THE CARE OF HER LOYAL FOLLOWERS... PEOPLE WITH MEANS...WEALTHY AND CRUEL ENOUGH TO GIVE ME ALL THE RESOURCES I COULD EVER DESIRE.
"LIKE ANY CHILD... I DREAMED...
"...ONLY I LONGED FOR THE DAY I WOULD BE CALLED UPON TO AID MY MOTHER... MY REAL MOTHER...IN HER CONQUESTS."
BUT THE CALL NEVER CAME.
MY MOTHER AND FATHER CONQUERED HALF THE WORLD, AND THEY NEVER EVEN GAVE ME A SECOND THOUGHT.
SO NOW I DREAM ONLY OF MAKING THEM SUFFER.

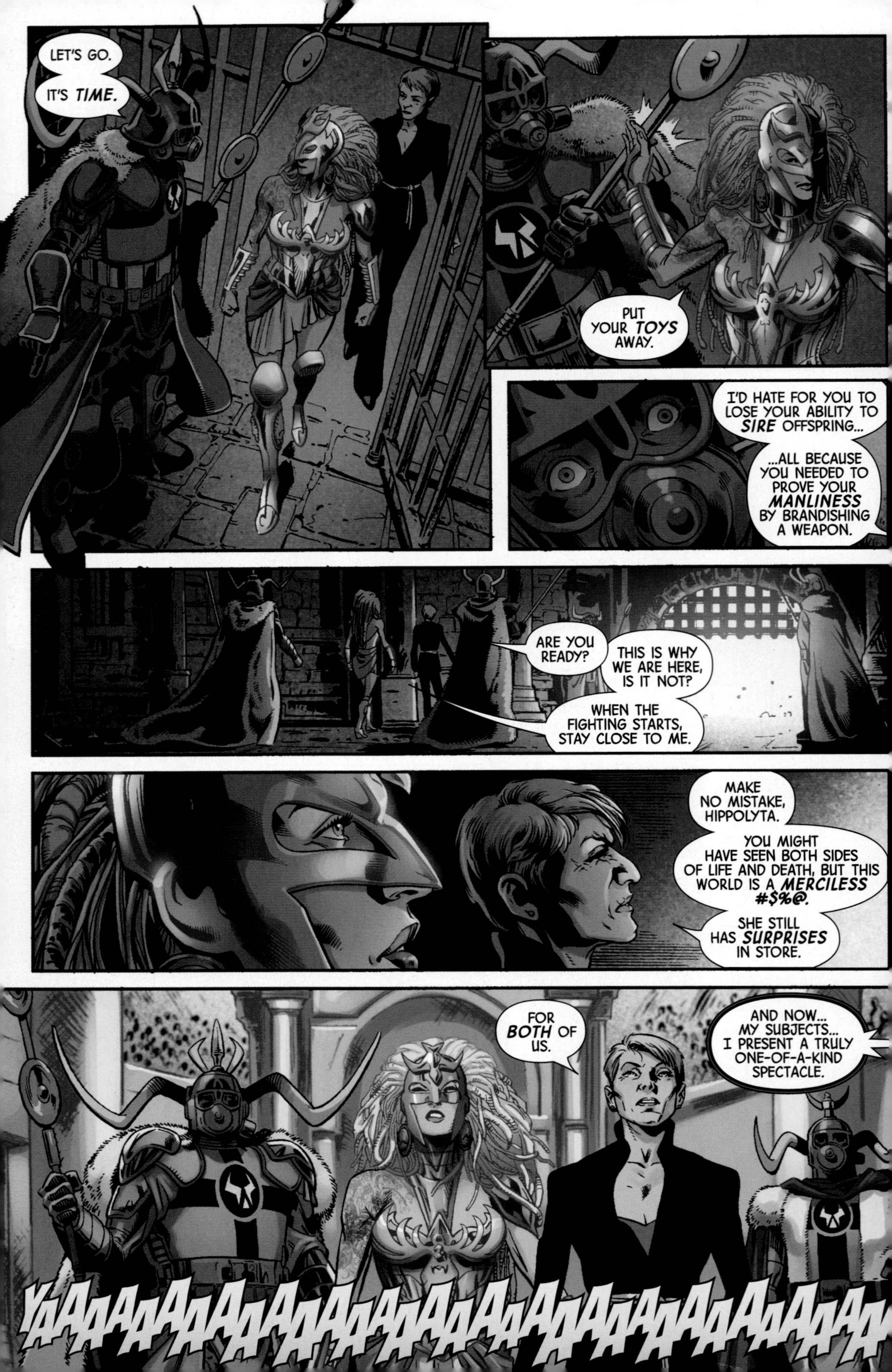
LET'S GO.
IT'S TIME.
PUT YOUR TOYS AWAY.
I'D HATE FOR YOU TO LOSE YOUR ABILITY TO SIRE OFFSPRING...
...ALL BECAUSE YOU NEEDED TO PROVE YOUR MANLINESS BY BRANDISHING A WEAPON.
ARE YOU READY?
THIS IS WHY WE ARE HERE, IS IT NOT?
WHEN THE FIGHTING STARTS, STAY CLOSE TO ME.
MAKE NO MISTAKE, HIPPOLYTA.
YOU MIGHT HAVE SEEN BOTH SIDES OF LIFE AND DEATH, BUT THIS WORLD IS A MERCILESS #$%@.
SHE STILL HAS SURPRISES IN STORE.
FOR BOTH OF US.
AND NOW... MY SUBJECTS... I PRESENT A TRULY ONE-OF-A-KIND SPECTACLE.
YAAAAAAAAAAAAAAAAAAAAAAAAAAAAAAAAAAAA

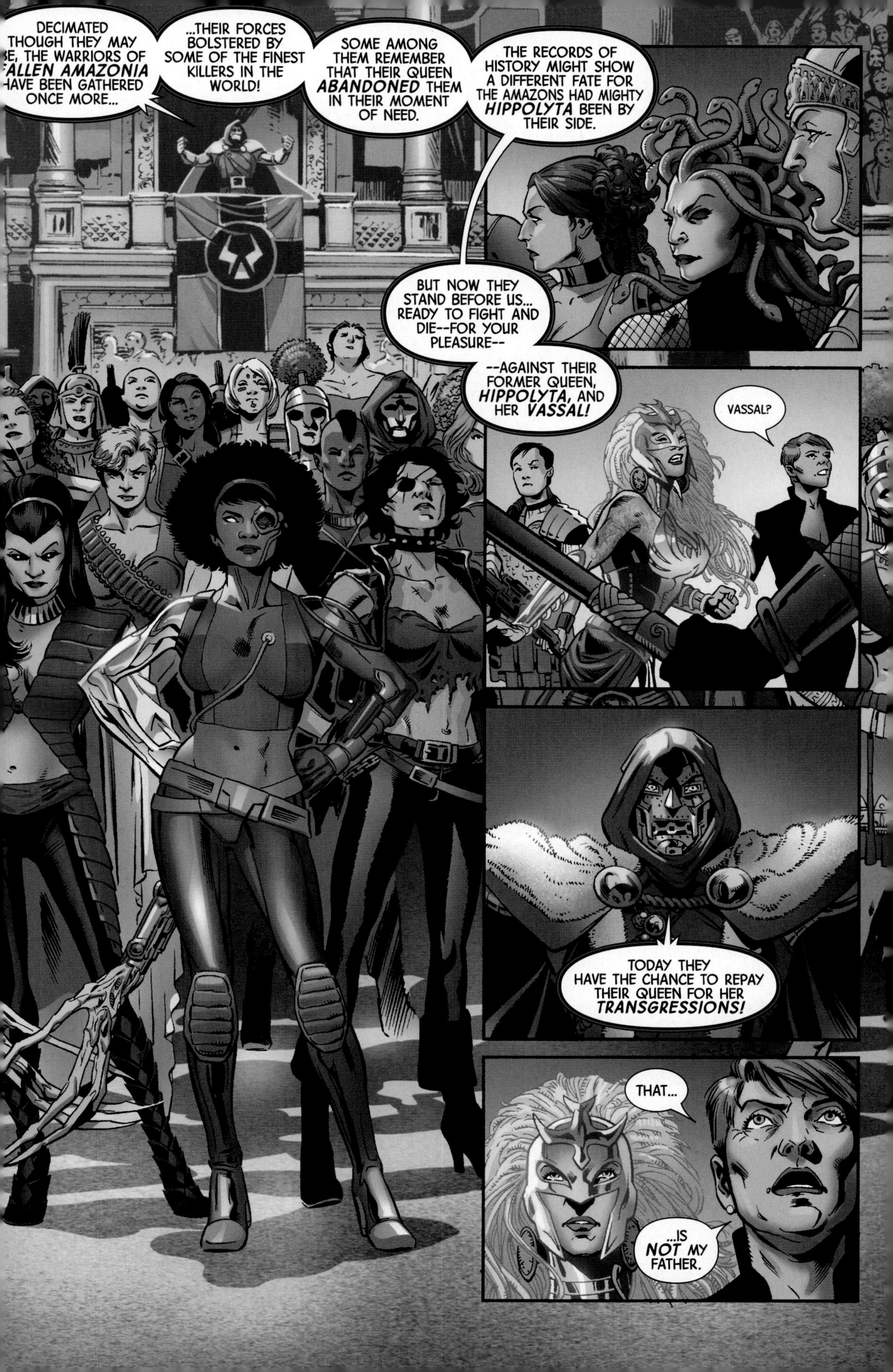
DECIMATED THOUGH THEY MAY BE, THE WARRIORS OF FALLEN AMAZONIA HAVE BEEN GATHERED ONCE MORE...
...THEIR FORCES BOLSTERED BY SOME OF THE FINEST KILLERS IN THE WORLD!
SOME AMONG THEM REMEMBER THAT THEIR QUEEN ABANDONED THEM IN THEIR MOMENT OF NEED.
THE RECORDS OF HISTORY MIGHT SHOW A DIFFERENT FATE FOR THE AMAZONS HAD MIGHTY HIPPOLYTA BEEN BY THEIR SIDE.
BUT NOW THEY STAND BEFORE US... READY TO FIGHT AND DIE--FOR YOUR PLEASURE--
--AGAINST THEIR FORMER QUEEN, HIPPOLYTA, AND HER VASSAL!
VASSAL?
TODAY THEY HAVE THE CHANCE TO REPAY THEIR QUEEN FOR HER TRANSGRESSIONS!
THAT...
...IS NOT MY FATHER.

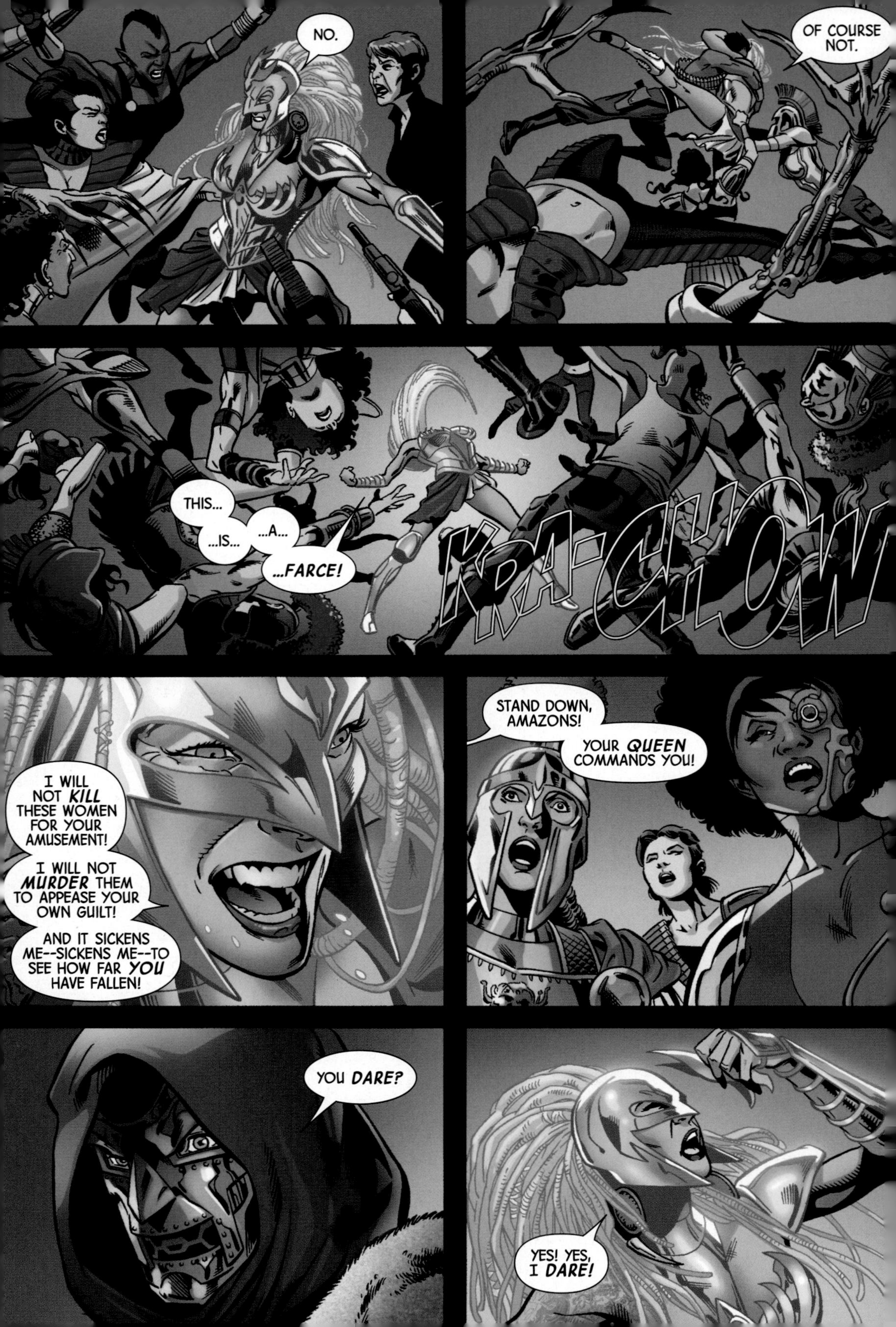

NO.
OF COURSE NOT.
THIS...
...IS...
...A...
...FARCE!
KRA-CHOW
I WILL NOT KILL THESE WOMEN FOR YOUR AMUSEMENT!
I WILL NOT MURDER THEM TO APPEASE YOUR OWN GUILT!
AND IT SICKENS ME--SICKENS ME--TO SEE HOW FAR YOU HAVE FALLEN!
STAND DOWN, AMAZONS!
YOUR QUEEN COMMANDS YOU!
YOU DARE?
YES! YES, I DARE!

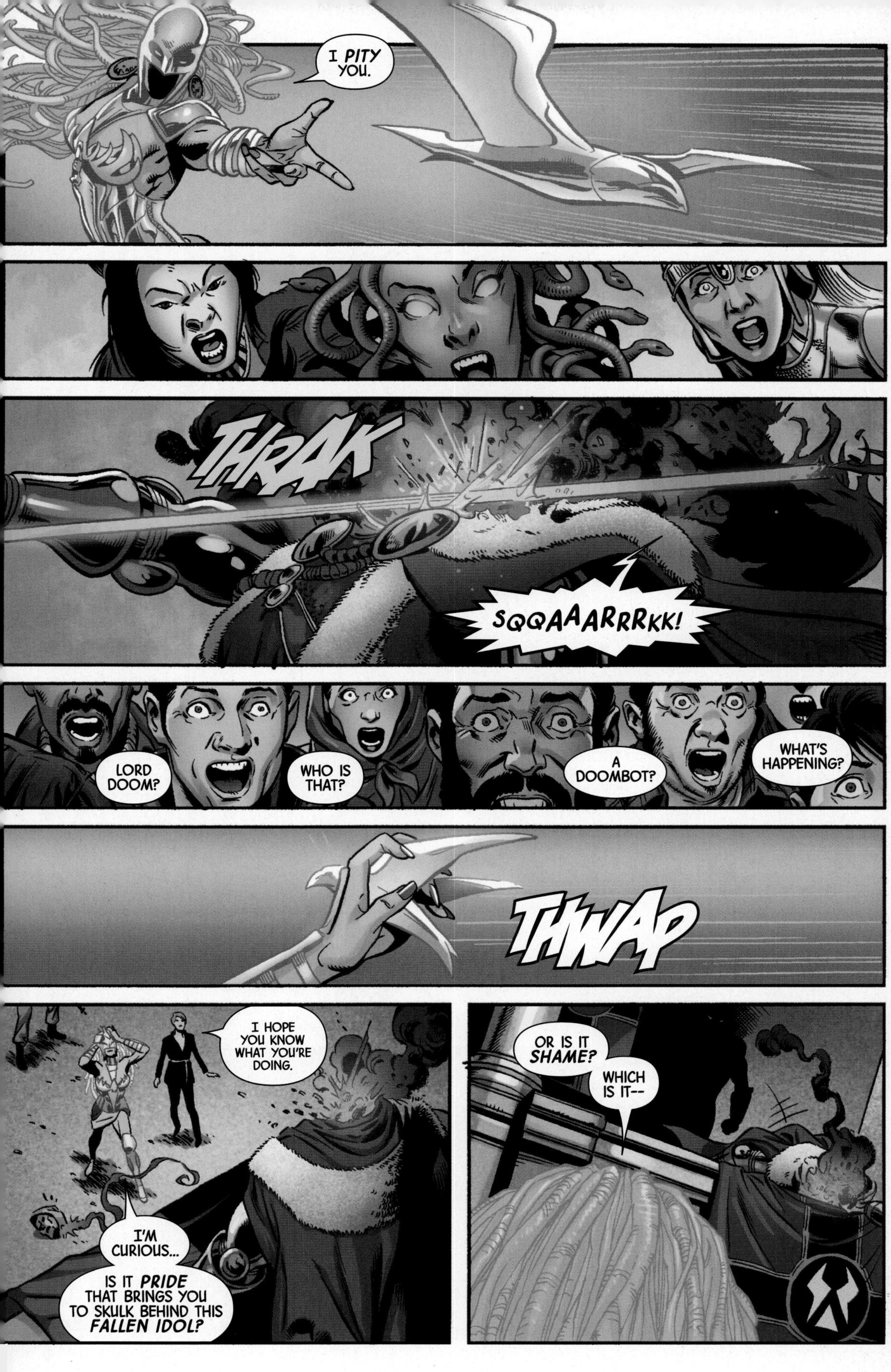
I PITY YOU.
THRAK
SQQAAARRRKK!
LORD DOOM?
WHO IS THAT?
A DOOMBOT?
WHAT'S HAPPENING?
THWAP
I HOPE YOU KNOW WHAT YOU'RE DOING.
I'M CURIOUS...
IS IT PRIDE THAT BRINGS YOU TO SKULK BEHIND THIS FALLEN IDOL?
OR IS IT SHAME?
WHICH IS IT--

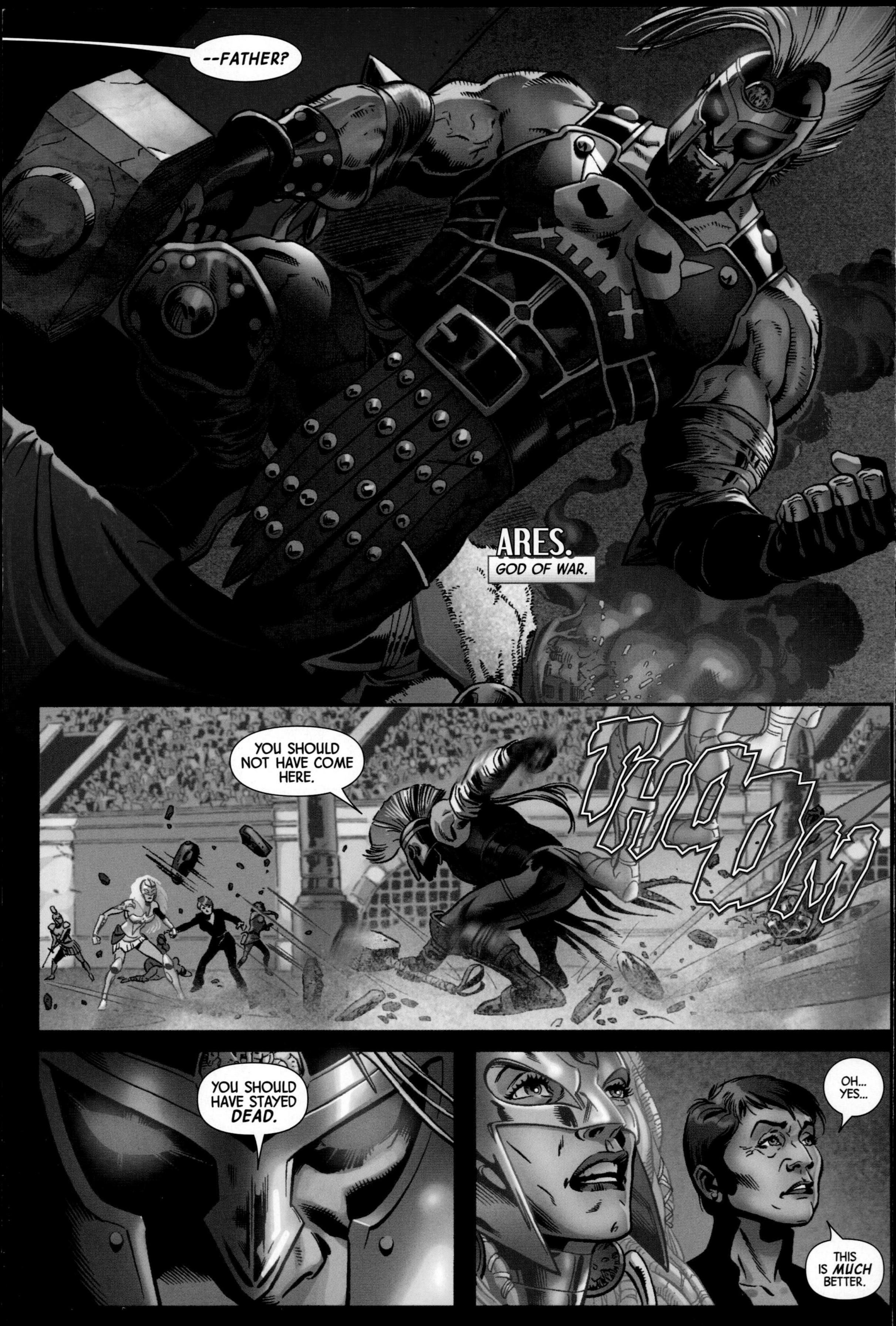
--FATHER?
ARES.
GOD OF WAR.
YOU SHOULD NOT HAVE COME HERE.
THOOM
YOU SHOULD HAVE STAYED DEAD.
OH... YES...
THIS IS MUCH BETTER.

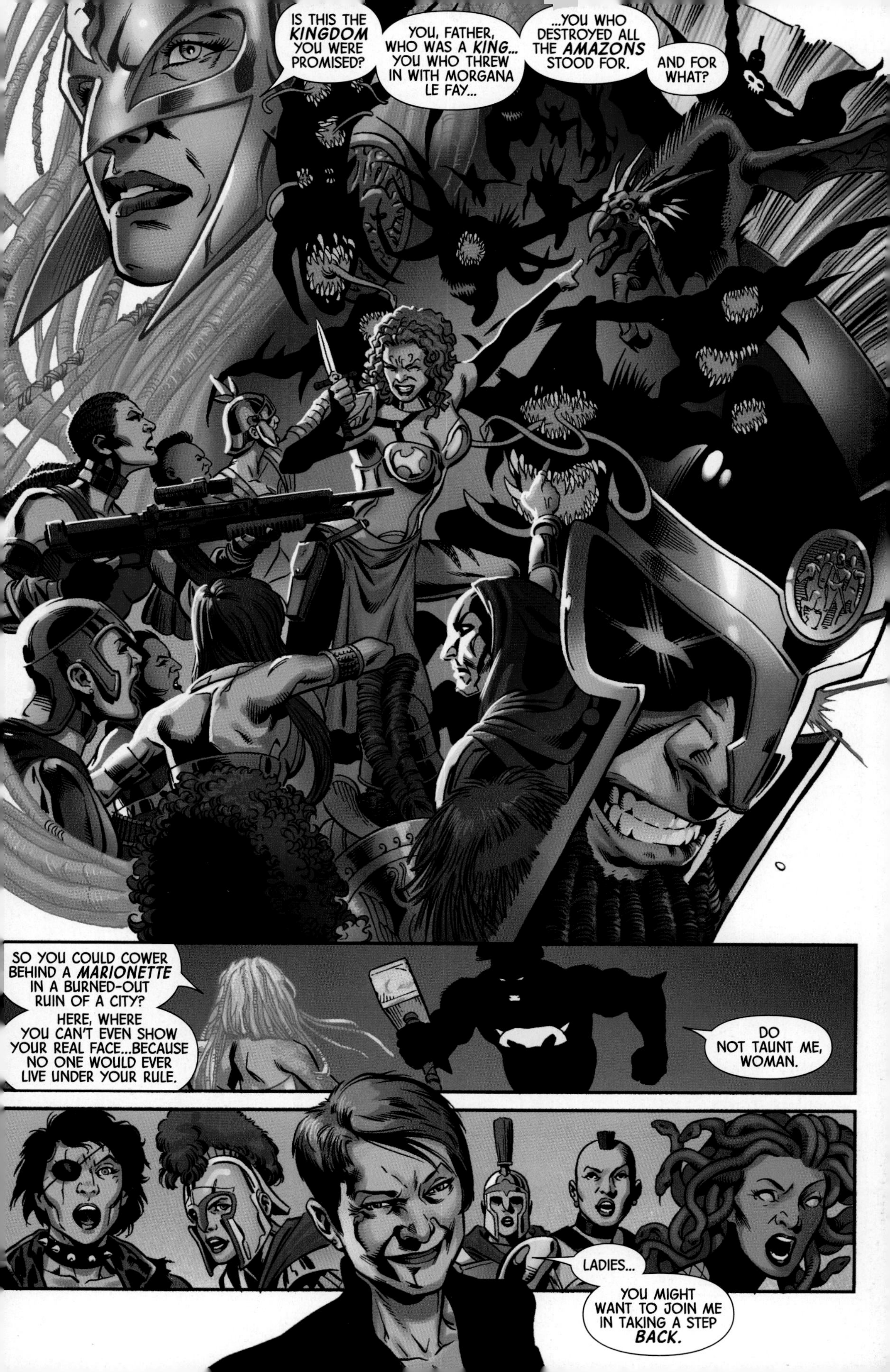
IS THIS THE KINGDOM YOU WERE PROMISED?
YOU, FATHER, WHO WAS A KING... YOU WHO THREW IN WITH MORGANA LE FAY...
...YOU WHO DESTROYED ALL THE AMAZONS STOOD FOR.
AND FOR WHAT?
SO YOU COULD COWER BEHIND A MARIONETTE IN A BURNED-OUT RUIN OF A CITY?
HERE, WHERE YOU CAN'T EVEN SHOW YOUR REAL FACE...BECAUSE NO ONE WOULD EVER LIVE UNDER YOUR RULE.
DO NOT TAUNT ME, WOMAN.
LADIES...
YOU MIGHT WANT TO JOIN ME IN TAKING A STEP BACK.

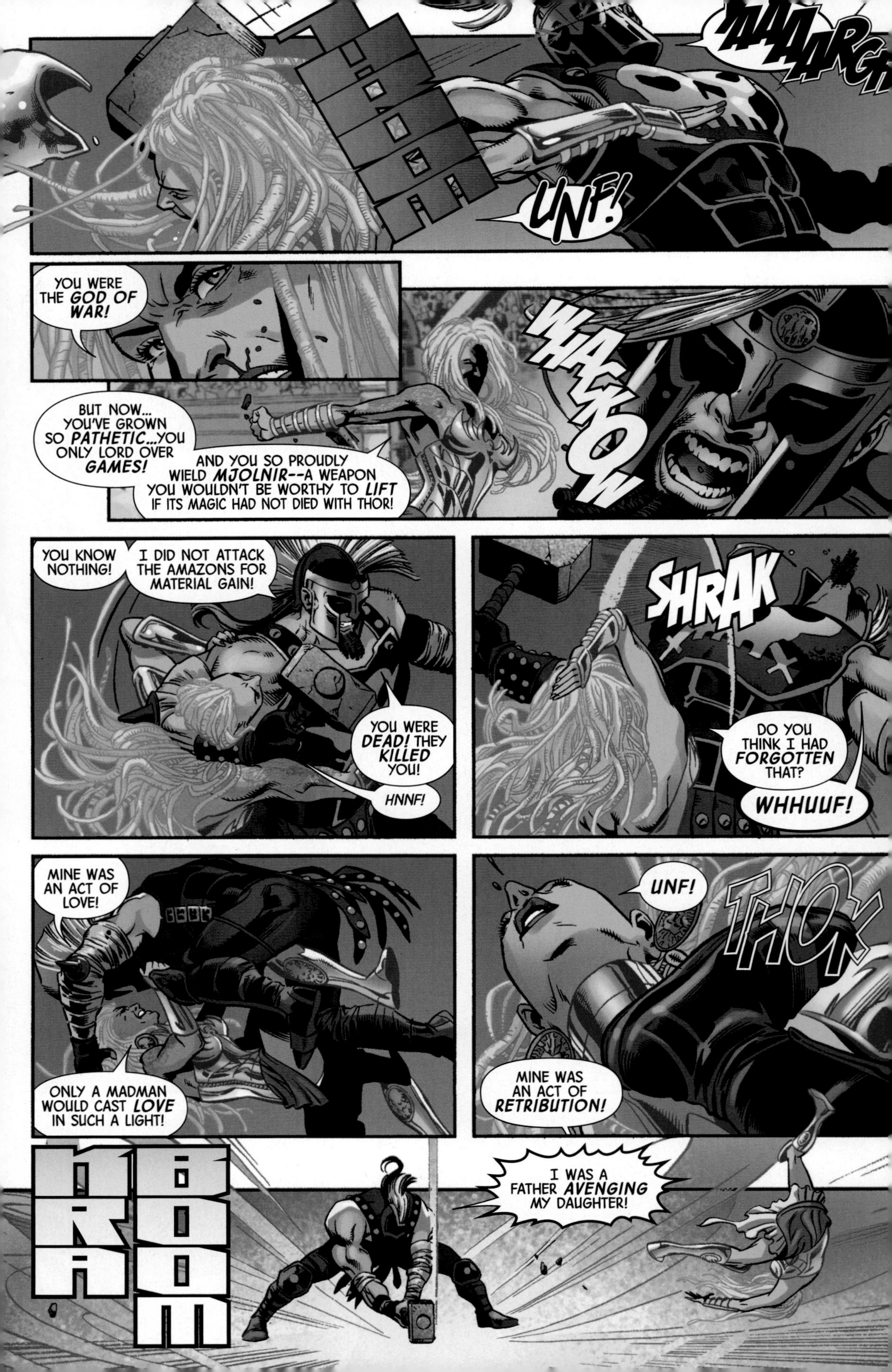
AAAARGH
UNF!
YOU WERE THE GOD OF WAR!
WHACKOOM
BUT NOW... YOU'VE GROWN SO PATHETIC...YOU ONLY LORD OVER GAMES!
AND YOU SO PROUDLY WIELD MJOLNIR--A WEAPON YOU WOULDN'T BE WORTHY TO LIFT IF ITS MAGIC HAD NOT DIED WITH THOR!
YOU KNOW NOTHING!
I DID NOT ATTACK THE AMAZONS FOR MATERIAL GAIN!
YOU WERE DEAD! THEY KILLED YOU!
HNNF!
SHRAK
DO YOU THINK I HAD FORGOTTEN THAT?
WHHUUF!
MINE WAS AN ACT OF LOVE!
ONLY A MADMAN WOULD CAST LOVE IN SUCH A LIGHT!
UNF!
THOK
MINE WAS AN ACT OF RETRIBUTION!
KRA BOOM
I WAS A FATHER AVENGING MY DAUGHTER!

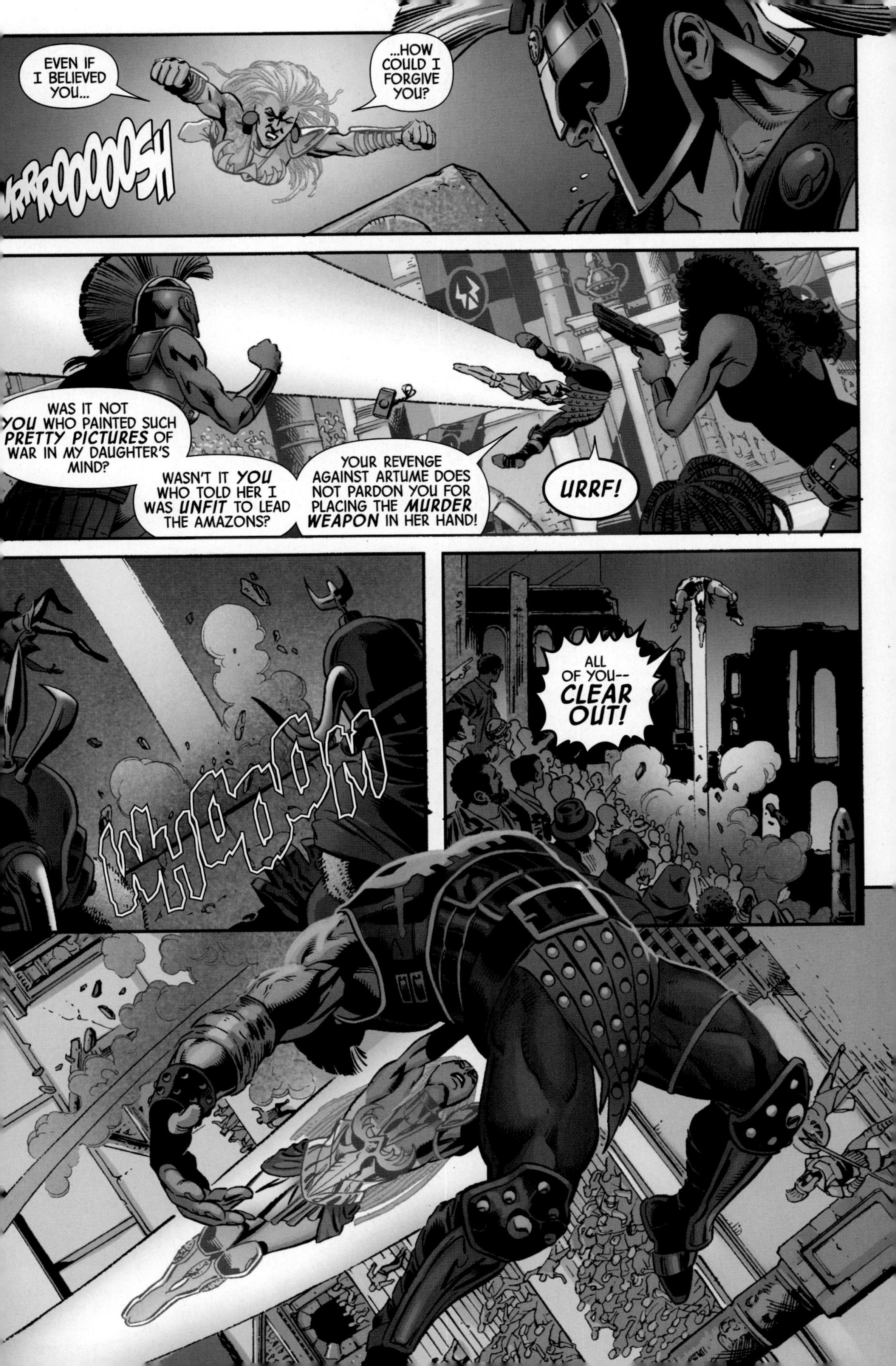

EVEN IF I BELIEVED YOU...
...HOW COULD I FORGIVE YOU?
VRRROOOOOSH
WAS IT NOT YOU WHO PAINTED SUCH PRETTY PICTURES OF WAR IN MY DAUGHTER'S MIND?
WASN'T IT YOU WHO TOLD HER I WAS UNFIT TO LEAD THE AMAZONS?
YOUR REVENGE AGAINST ARTUME DOES NOT PARDON YOU FOR PLACING THE MURDER WEAPON IN HER HAND!
URRF!
WHOOOOM
ALL OF YOU-- CLEAR OUT!

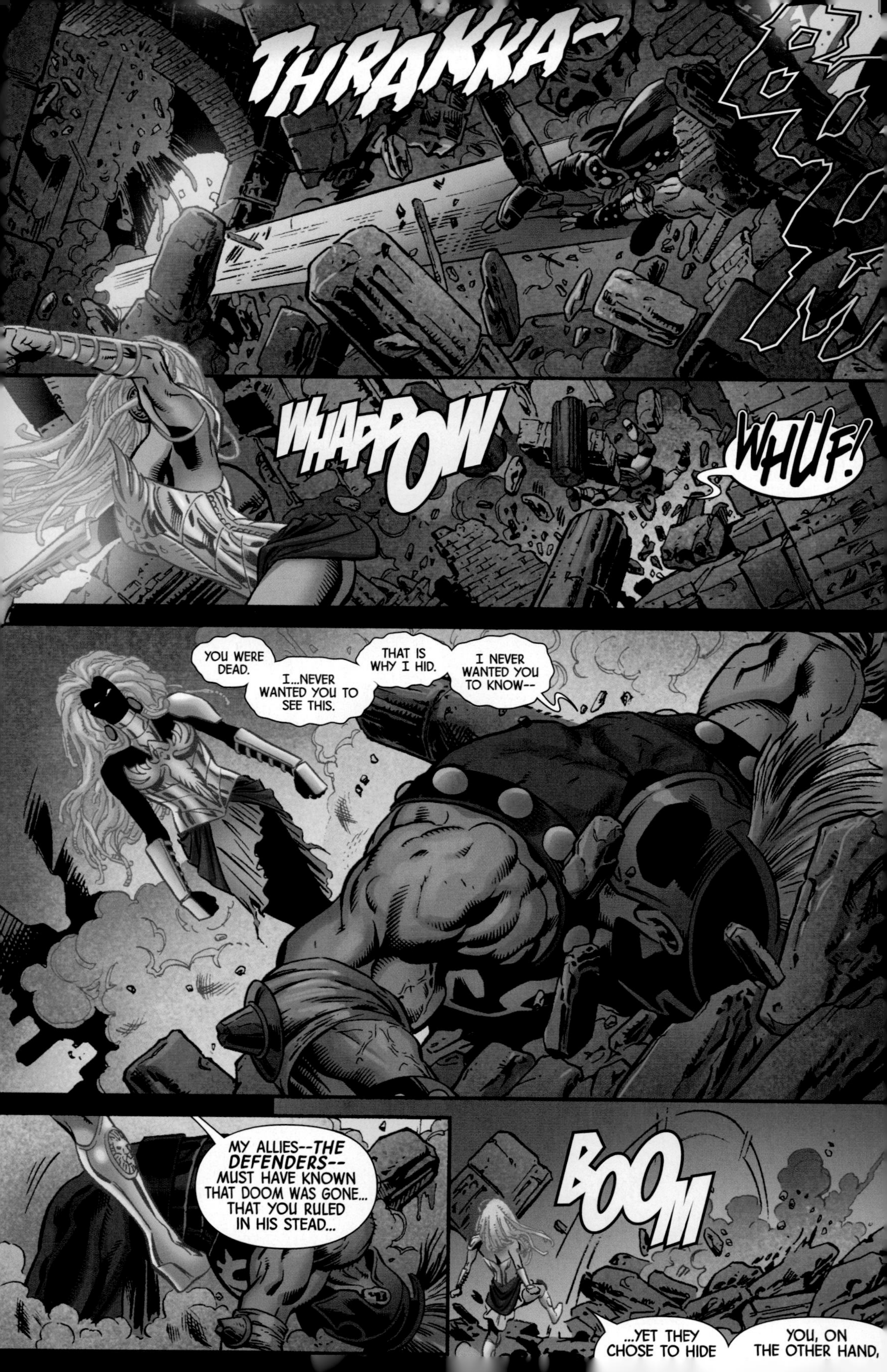
THRAKKA-
WHAPPOW
WHUF!
YOU WERE DEAD.
I...NEVER WANTED YOU TO SEE THIS.
THAT IS WHY I HID.
I NEVER WANTED YOU TO KNOW--
MY ALLIES--THE DEFENDERS--MUST HAVE KNOWN THAT DOOM WAS GONE... THAT YOU RULED IN HIS STEAD...
BOOM
...YET THEY CHOSE TO HIDE
YOU, ON THE OTHER HAND,

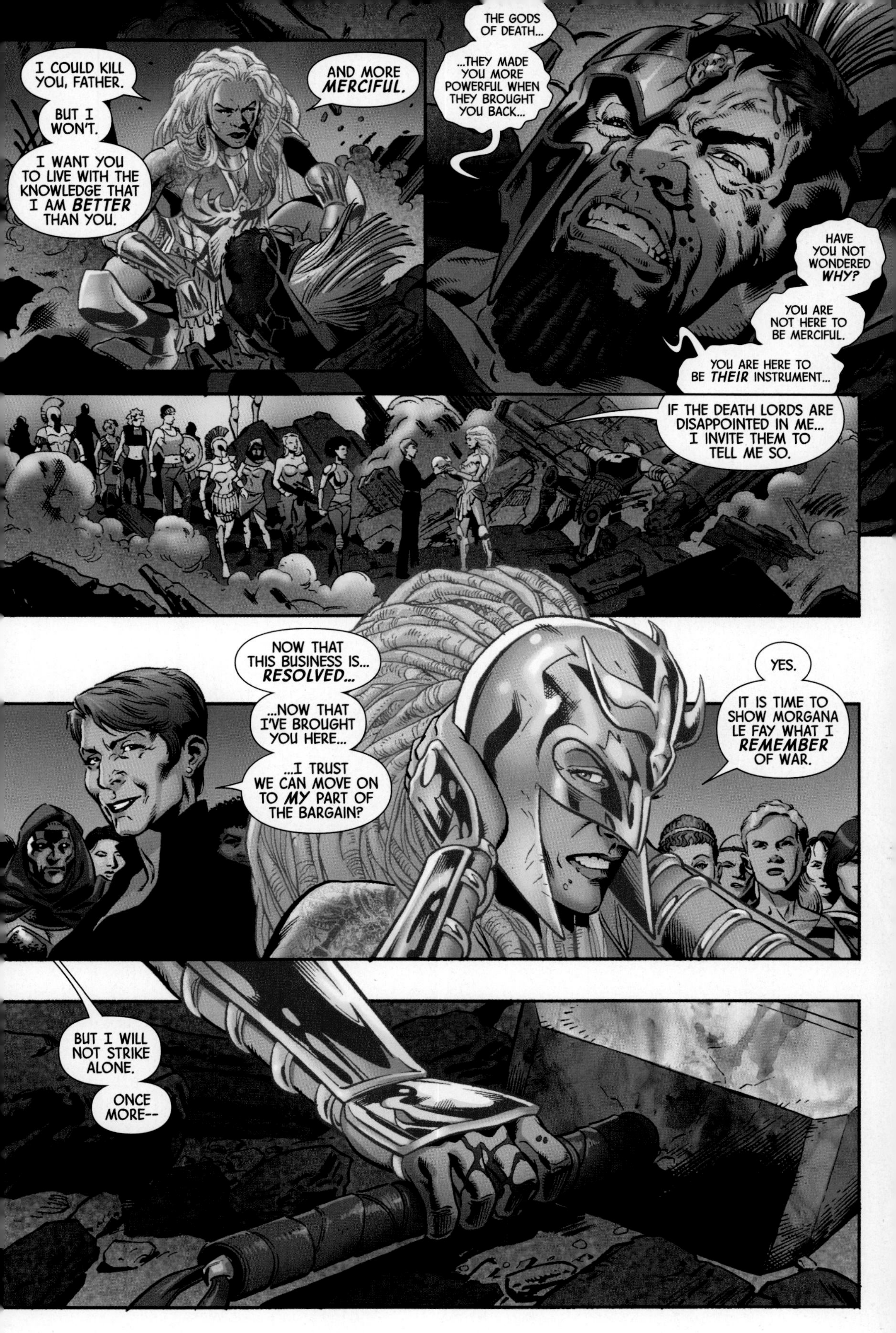
I COULD KILL YOU, FATHER.
BUT I WON'T.
I WANT YOU TO LIVE WITH THE KNOWLEDGE THAT I AM BETTER THAN YOU.
AND MORE MERCIFUL.
THE GODS OF DEATH...
...THEY MADE YOU MORE POWERFUL WHEN THEY BROUGHT YOU BACK...
HAVE YOU NOT WONDERED WHY?
YOU ARE NOT HERE TO BE MERCIFUL.
YOU ARE HERE TO BE THEIR INSTRUMENT...
IF THE DEATH LORDS ARE DISAPPOINTED IN ME... I INVITE THEM TO TELL ME SO.
NOW THAT THIS BUSINESS IS... RESOLVED...
...NOW THAT I'VE BROUGHT YOU HERE...
...I TRUST WE CAN MOVE ON TO MY PART OF THE BARGAIN?
YES.
IT IS TIME TO SHOW MORGANA LE FAY WHAT I REMEMBER OF WAR.
BUT I WILL NOT STRIKE ALONE.
ONCE MORE--

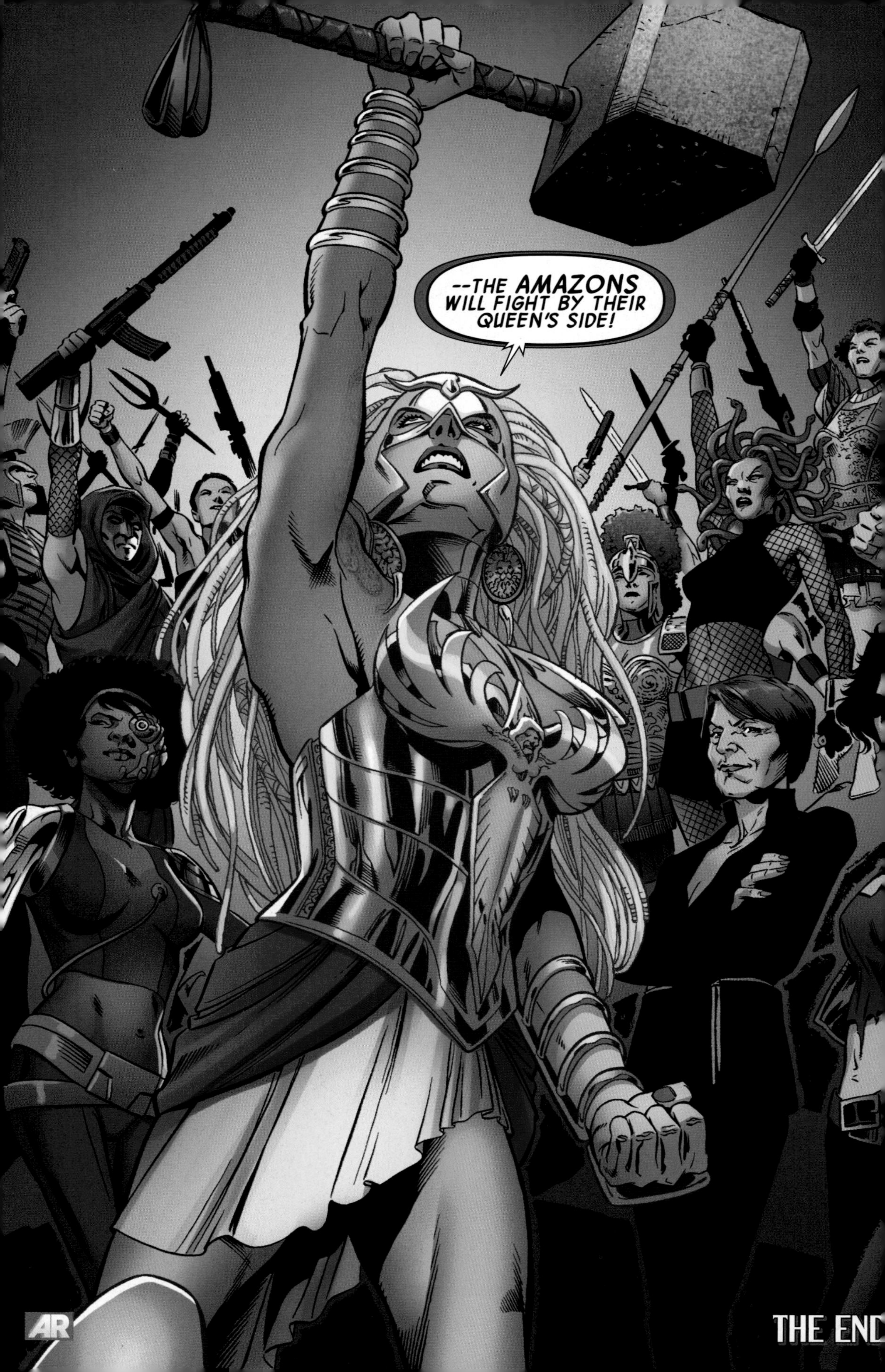
--THE AMAZONS WILL FIGHT BY THEIR QUEEN'S SIDE!
THE END

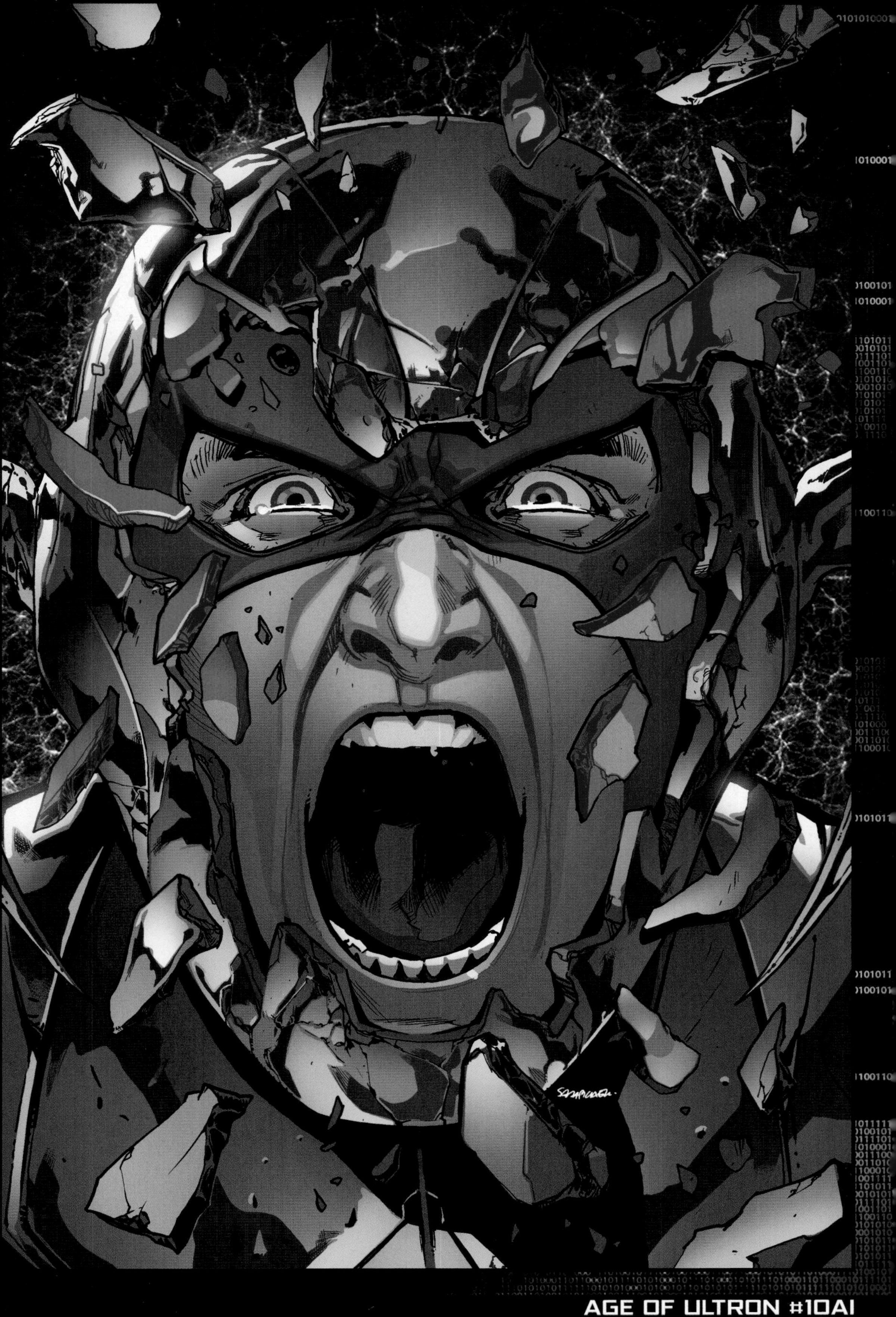

AGE OF ULTRON #10AI

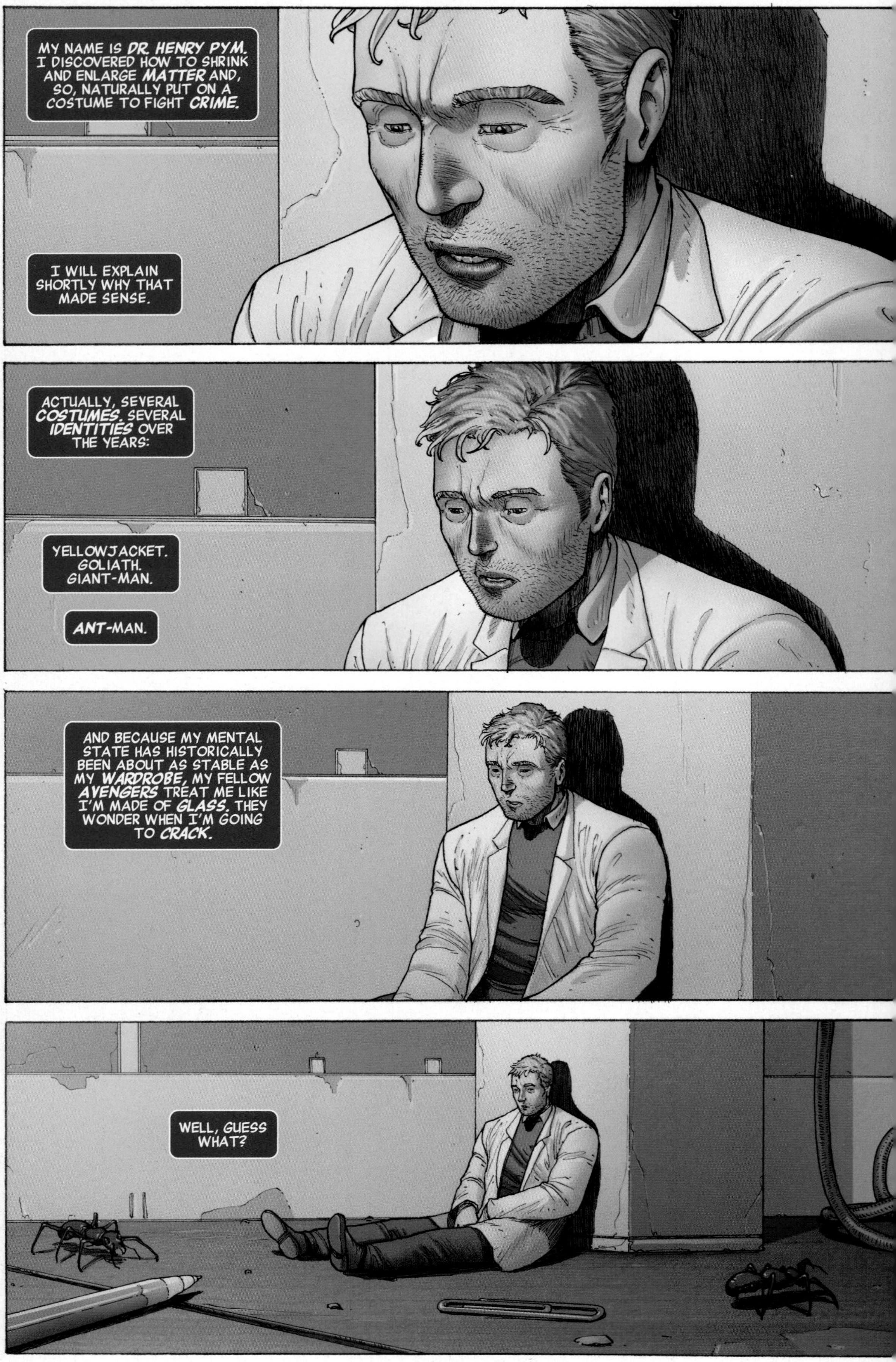
MY NAME IS DR. HENRY PYM. I DISCOVERED HOW TO SHRINK AND ENLARGE MATTER AND, SO, NATURALLY PUT ON A COSTUME TO FIGHT CRIME.
I WILL EXPLAIN SHORTLY WHY THAT MADE SENSE.
ACTUALLY, SEVERAL COSTUMES. SEVERAL IDENTITIES OVER THE YEARS:
YELLOWJACKET. GOLIATH. GIANT-MAN.
ANT-MAN.
AND BECAUSE MY MENTAL STATE HAS HISTORICALLY BEEN ABOUT AS STABLE AS MY WARDROBE, MY FELLOW AVENGERS TREAT ME LIKE I'M MADE OF GLASS. THEY WONDER WHEN I'M GOING TO CRACK.
WELL, GUESS WHAT?

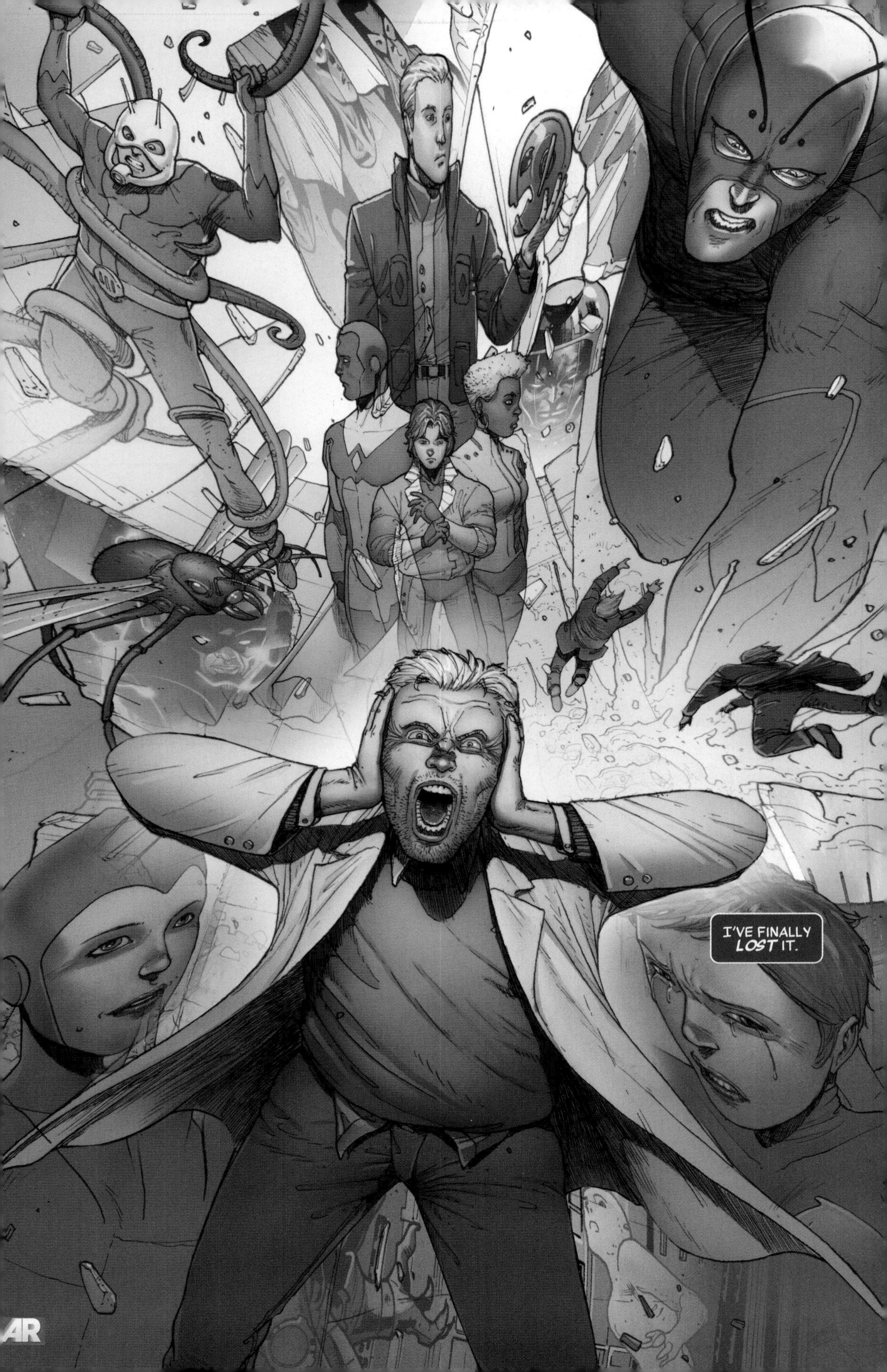
I'VE FINALLY LOST IT.

I CAN GO INTO GREATER DETAIL, BUT FOR NOW, THE WAY THE SPACE-TIME CONTINUUM IS CRACKING *AROUND* ME? THAT'S THE *END* OF THE STORY. LET'S START AT THE *BEGINNING*.

WHERE FACTORY FOREMAN *BRAD PYM* AND HIS BOOKKEEPER WIFE *DORIS* LIVED WITH THEIR ONLY CHILD, *HENRY CHRISTOPHER PYM*, IN *EAST NOWHERE, NEBRASKA*.

THE DOCTORS SAID THAT BY AGE THREE, I WAS ALREADY SMARTER THAN BOTH OF MY PARENTS PUT TOGETHER. NEVERTHELESS, THEY LOVED ME DEARLY...

...DESPITE THE FACT THAT I WAS... *CHALLENGING*.

DRINK-FLAV-R
BLUE RASPBERRY

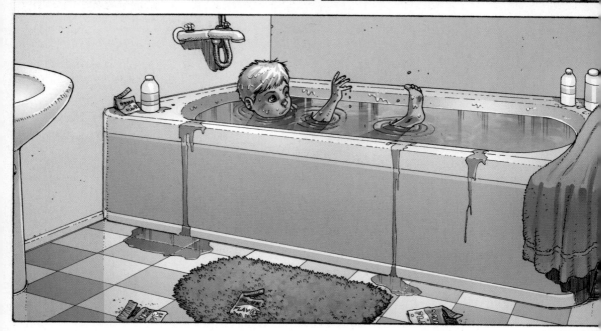

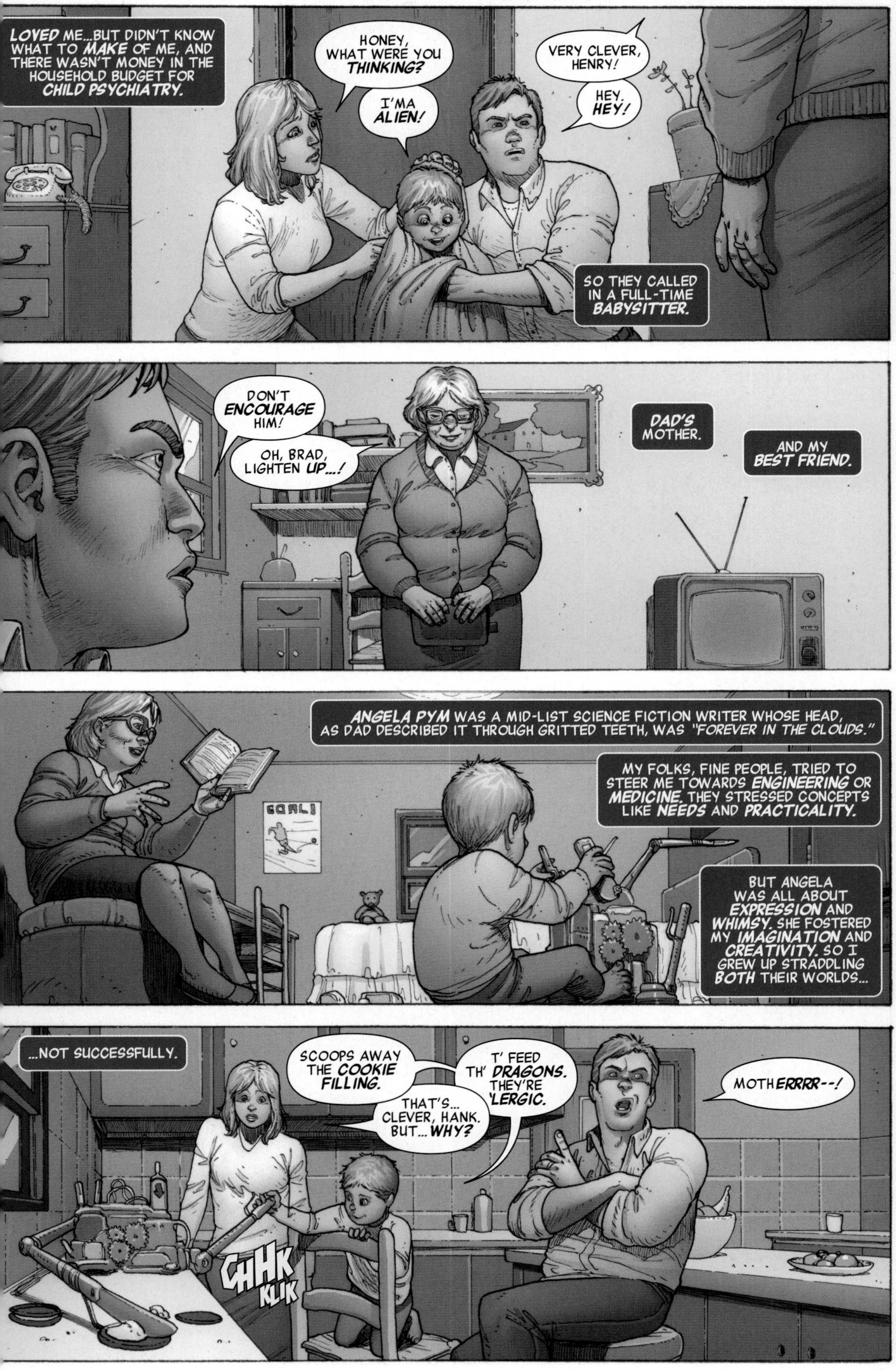

LOVED ME...BUT DIDN'T KNOW WHAT TO MAKE OF ME, AND THERE WASN'T MONEY IN THE HOUSEHOLD BUDGET FOR CHILD PSYCHIATRY.
HONEY, WHAT WERE YOU THINKING?
I'MA ALIEN!
VERY CLEVER, HENRY!
HEY. HEY!
SO THEY CALLED IN A FULL-TIME BABYSITTER.
DON'T ENCOURAGE HIM!
OH, BRAD, LIGHTEN UP...!
DAD'S MOTHER.
AND MY BEST FRIEND.
GOAL!
ANGELA PYM WAS A MID-LIST SCIENCE FICTION WRITER WHOSE HEAD, AS DAD DESCRIBED IT THROUGH GRITTED TEETH, WAS "FOREVER IN THE CLOUDS."
MY FOLKS, FINE PEOPLE, TRIED TO STEER ME TOWARDS ENGINEERING OR MEDICINE. THEY STRESSED CONCEPTS LIKE NEEDS AND PRACTICALITY.
BUT ANGELA WAS ALL ABOUT EXPRESSION AND WHIMSY. SHE FOSTERED MY IMAGINATION AND CREATIVITY. SO I GREW UP STRADDLING BOTH THEIR WORLDS...
...NOT SUCCESSFULLY.
SCOOPS AWAY THE COOKIE FILLING.
T' FEED TH' DRAGONS. THEY'RE 'LERGIC.
THAT'S... CLEVER, HANK. BUT...WHY?
MOTHERRRR--!
CHHK
KLIK

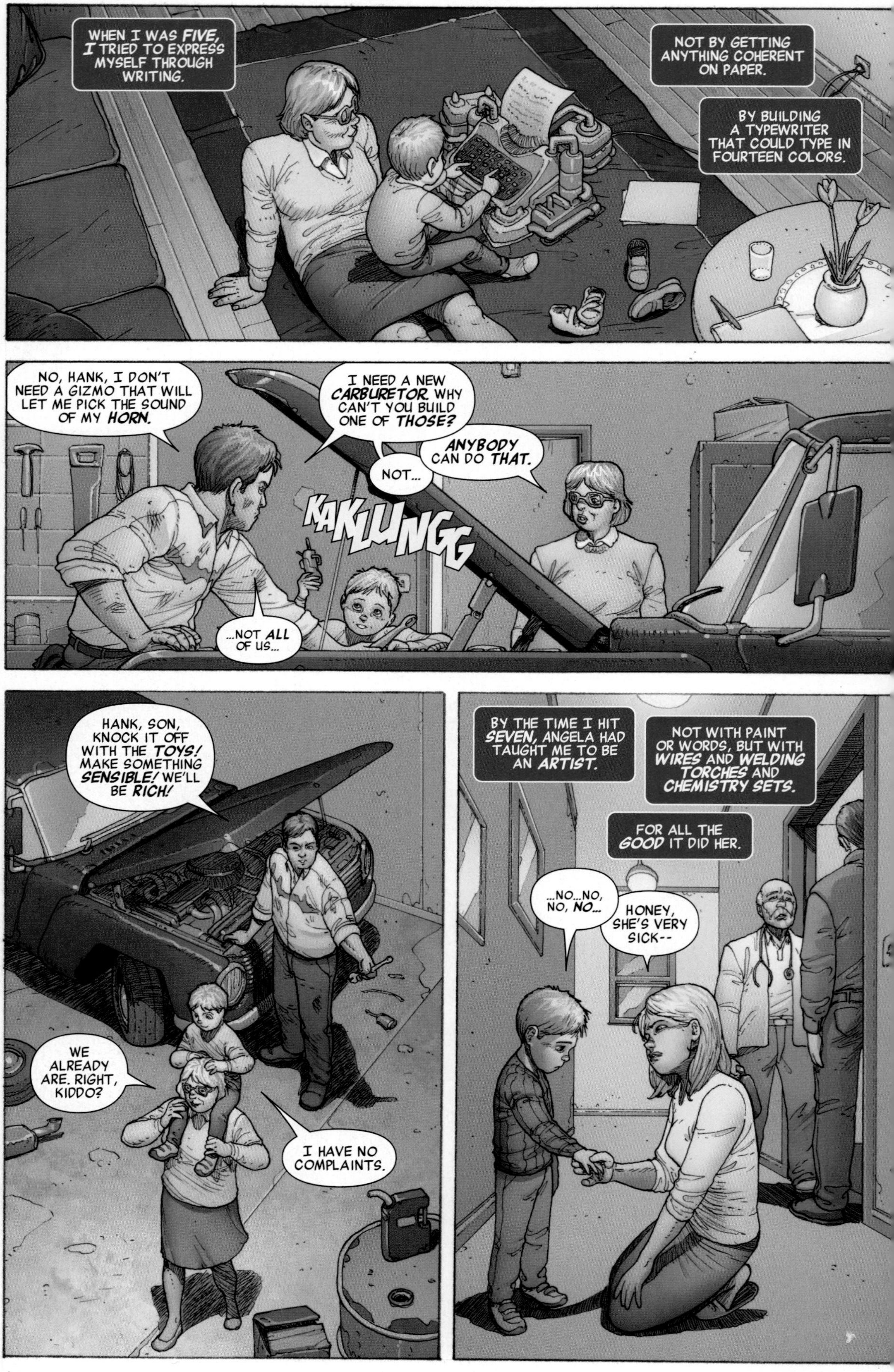
WHEN I WAS FIVE, I TRIED TO EXPRESS MYSELF THROUGH WRITING.
NOT BY GETTING ANYTHING COHERENT ON PAPER.
BY BUILDING A TYPEWRITER THAT COULD TYPE IN FOURTEEN COLORS.
NO, HANK, I DON'T NEED A GIZMO THAT WILL LET ME PICK THE SOUND OF MY HORN.
I NEED A NEW CARBURETOR. WHY CAN'T YOU BUILD ONE OF THOSE?
NOT...
ANYBODY CAN DO THAT.
KAKLUNGG
...NOT ALL OF US...
HANK, SON, KNOCK IT OFF WITH THE TOYS! MAKE SOMETHING SENSIBLE! WE'LL BE RICH!
WE ALREADY ARE. RIGHT, KIDDO?
I HAVE NO COMPLAINTS.
BY THE TIME I HIT SEVEN, ANGELA HAD TAUGHT ME TO BE AN ARTIST.
NOT WITH PAINT OR WORDS, BUT WITH WIRES AND WELDING TORCHES AND CHEMISTRY SETS.
FOR ALL THE GOOD IT DID HER.
...NO...NO, NO, NO...
HONEY, SHE'S VERY SICK--

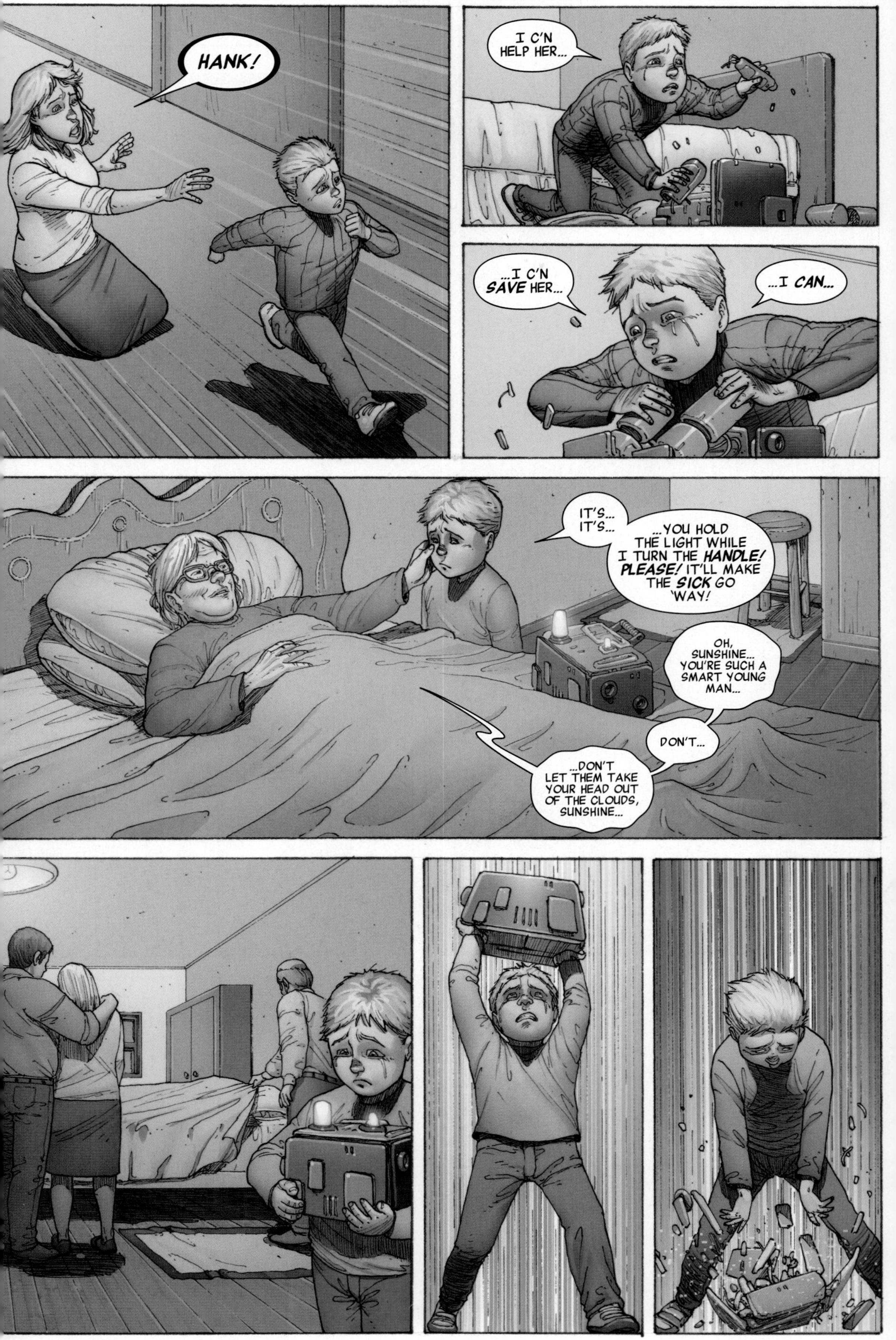
HANK!
I C'N HELP HER...
...I C'N SAVE HER...
...I CAN...
IT'S... IT'S...
...YOU HOLD THE LIGHT WHILE I TURN THE HANDLE! PLEASE! IT'LL MAKE THE SICK GO 'WAY!
OH, SUNSHINE... YOU'RE SUCH A SMART YOUNG MAN...
DON'T...
...DON'T LET THEM TAKE YOUR HEAD OUT OF THE CLOUDS, SUNSHINE...

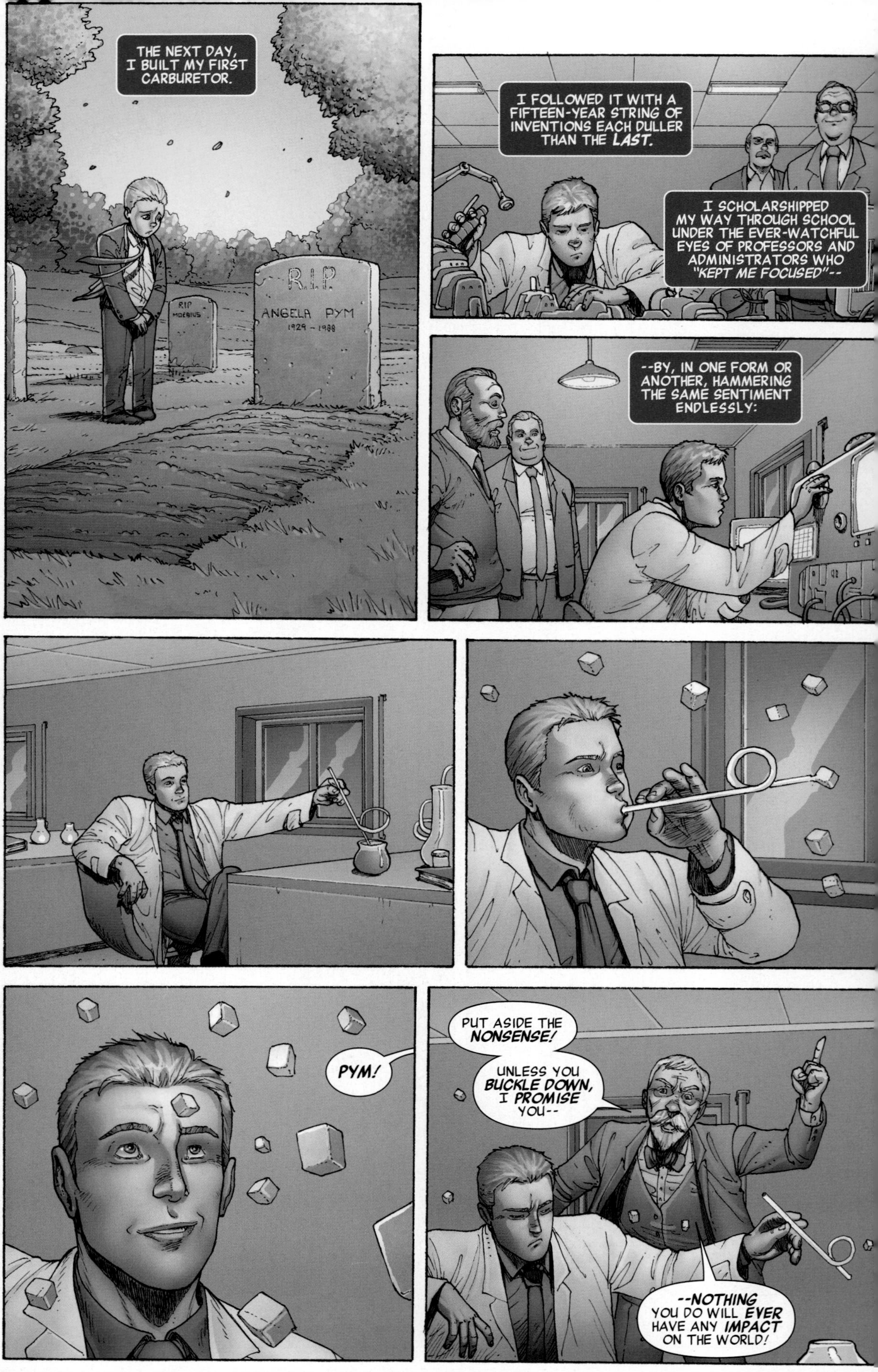
THE NEXT DAY, I BUILT MY FIRST CARBURETOR.
R.I.P.
RIP MOEBIUS
ANGELA PYM 1929 - 1988
I FOLLOWED IT WITH A FIFTEEN-YEAR STRING OF INVENTIONS EACH DULLER THAN THE *LAST.*
I SCHOLARSHIPPED MY WAY THROUGH SCHOOL UNDER THE EVER-WATCHFUL EYES OF PROFESSORS AND ADMINISTRATORS WHO *"KEPT ME FOCUSED"--*
--BY, IN ONE FORM OR ANOTHER, HAMMERING THE SAME SENTIMENT ENDLESSLY:
PYM!
PUT ASIDE THE *NONSENSE!*
UNLESS YOU *BUCKLE DOWN,* I *PROMISE* YOU--
--NOTHING YOU DO WILL *EVER* HAVE ANY *IMPACT* ON THE WORLD!

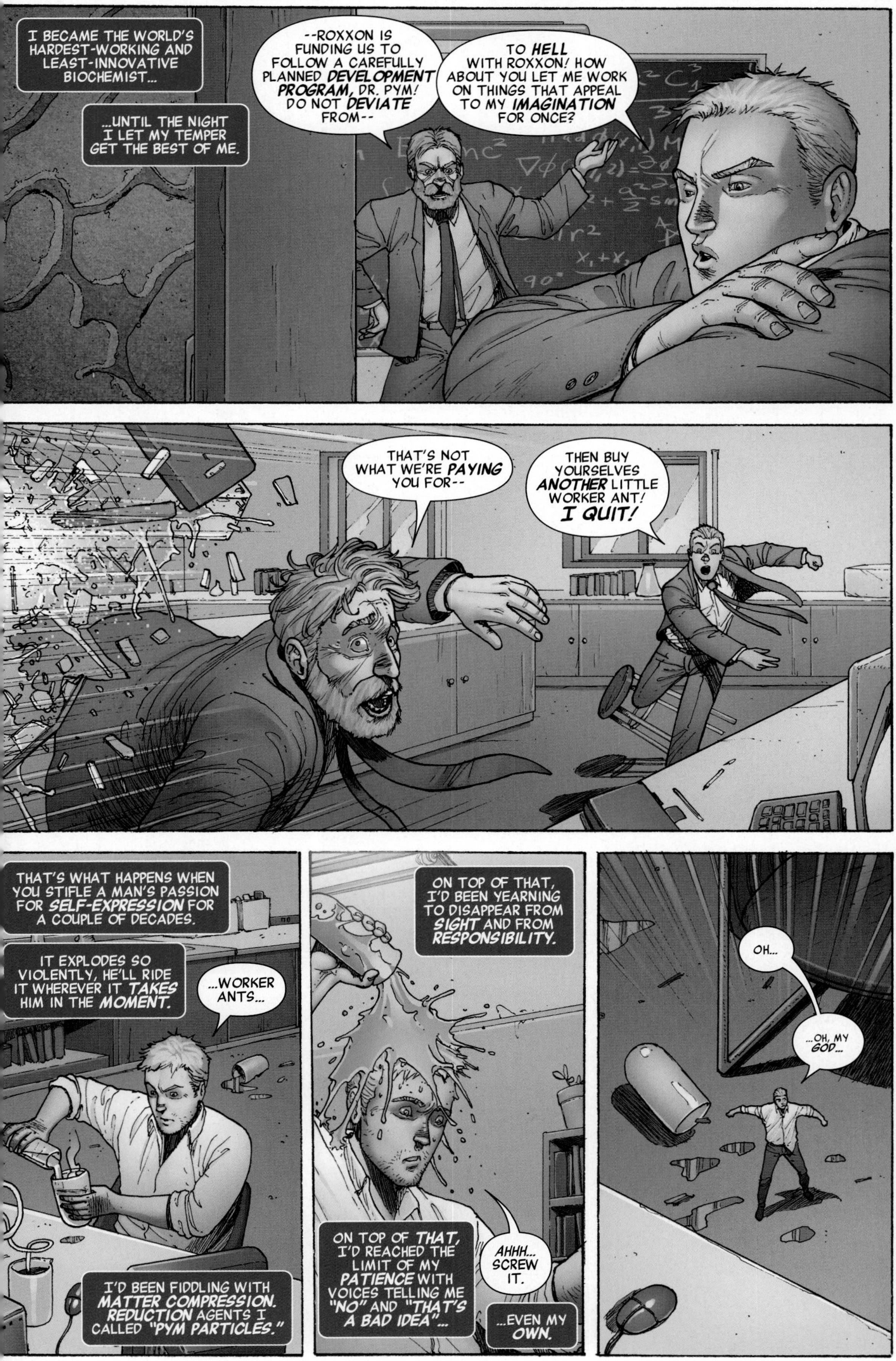
I BECAME THE WORLD'S HARDEST-WORKING AND LEAST-INNOVATIVE BIOCHEMIST...
...UNTIL THE NIGHT I LET MY TEMPER GET THE BEST OF ME.
--ROXXON IS FUNDING US TO FOLLOW A CAREFULLY PLANNED DEVELOPMENT PROGRAM, DR. PYM! DO NOT DEVIATE FROM--
TO HELL WITH ROXXON! HOW ABOUT YOU LET ME WORK ON THINGS THAT APPEAL TO MY IMAGINATION FOR ONCE?
THAT'S NOT WHAT WE'RE PAYING YOU FOR--
THEN BUY YOURSELVES ANOTHER LITTLE WORKER ANT! I QUIT!
THAT'S WHAT HAPPENS WHEN YOU STIFLE A MAN'S PASSION FOR SELF-EXPRESSION FOR A COUPLE OF DECADES.
IT EXPLODES SO VIOLENTLY, HE'LL RIDE IT WHEREVER IT TAKES HIM IN THE MOMENT.
...WORKER ANTS...
I'D BEEN FIDDLING WITH MATTER COMPRESSION. REDUCTION AGENTS I CALLED "PYM PARTICLES."
ON TOP OF THAT, I'D BEEN YEARNING TO DISAPPEAR FROM SIGHT AND FROM RESPONSIBILITY.
ON TOP OF THAT, I'D REACHED THE LIMIT OF MY PATIENCE WITH VOICES TELLING ME "NO" AND "THAT'S A BAD IDEA"...
AHHH... SCREW IT.
...EVEN MY OWN.
OH...
...OH, MY GOD...

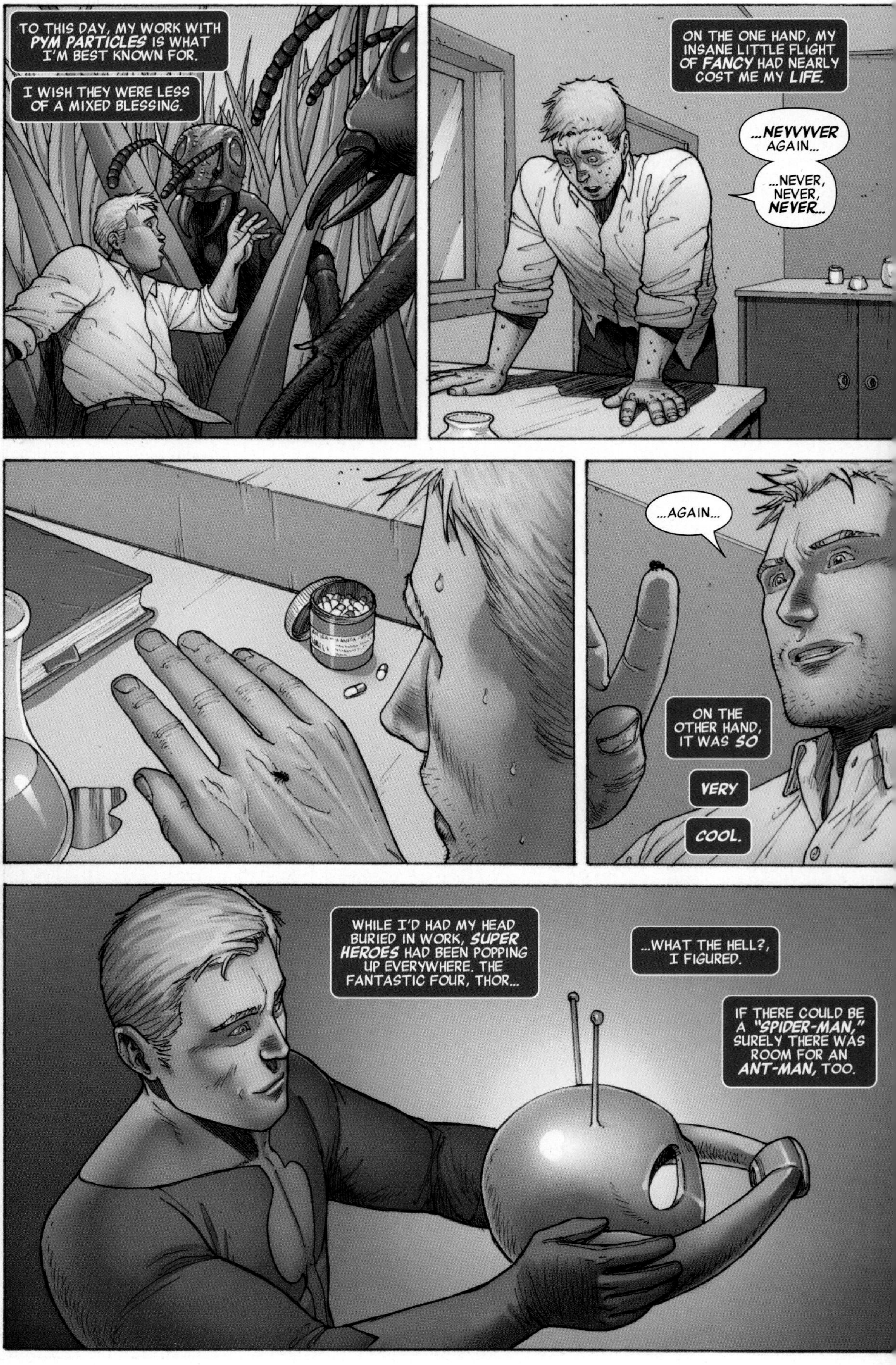
TO THIS DAY, MY WORK WITH PYM PARTICLES IS WHAT I'M BEST KNOWN FOR.
I WISH THEY WERE LESS OF A MIXED BLESSING.
ON THE ONE HAND, MY INSANE LITTLE FLIGHT OF FANCY HAD NEARLY COST ME MY LIFE.
...NEVVVVER AGAIN...
...NEVER, NEVER, NEVER...
...AGAIN...
ON THE OTHER HAND, IT WAS SO
VERY
COOL.
WHILE I'D HAD MY HEAD BURIED IN WORK, SUPER HEROES HAD BEEN POPPING UP EVERYWHERE. THE FANTASTIC FOUR, THOR...
...WHAT THE HELL?, I FIGURED.
IF THERE COULD BE A "SPIDER-MAN," SURELY THERE WAS ROOM FOR AN ANT-MAN, TOO.

ROOM FOR A GUY WHOSE GREATEST MOMENT IN *LIFE* WAS USING A WILD, HAREBRAINED CRAZY-TALK STRATEGY SO RIDICULOUS IT *WORKED*--

--TO IMPRISON A *GOD* THAT EVEN *IRON MAN* AND THE *HULK* COULDN'T BEAT.

SURELY THERE WAS ROOM FOR ME. AND THERE *WAS.*

NOTHING *BUT* ROOM.

NOW THAT I WAS AN *AVENGER*...LOOKING LIKE A *TINY* MAN IN FRONT OF MY GIRLFRIEND, THE *WASP*...I PANICKED. BEING *SMALL* JUST SEEMED...*ABSURD.*

FOLLOWING MY *IMAGINATION* WAS *FUN*, BUT WHAT DID IT *CONTRIBUTE?* "BE PRACTICAL, PYM, OR *NOTHING* YOU EVER DO WILL *MATTER.*"

SUDDENLY, MORE THAN *EVER*, ALL I COULD WORRY ABOUT WAS BEING TAKEN *SERIOUSLY.* I REVERSED THE SHRINKING PROCESS, BECAME A *GIANT.*

THEN A *GOLIATH.* THEN A *FLYING SWASHBUCKLER.*

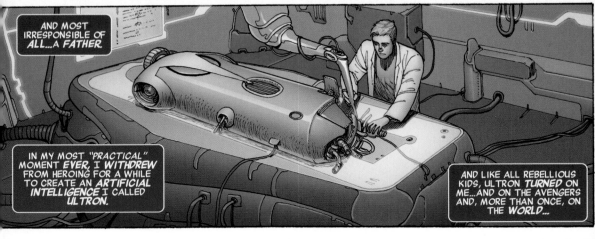

AND MOST IRRESPONSIBLE OF *ALL*...A FATHER.

IN MY MOST "*PRACTICAL*" MOMENT *EVER*, I *WITHDREW* FROM HEROING FOR A WHILE TO CREATE AN *ARTIFICIAL INTELLIGENCE* I CALLED *ULTRON.*

AND LIKE ALL REBELLIOUS KIDS, ULTRON *TURNED* ON ME...AND ON THE AVENGERS AND, MORE THAN ONCE, ON THE *WORLD*...

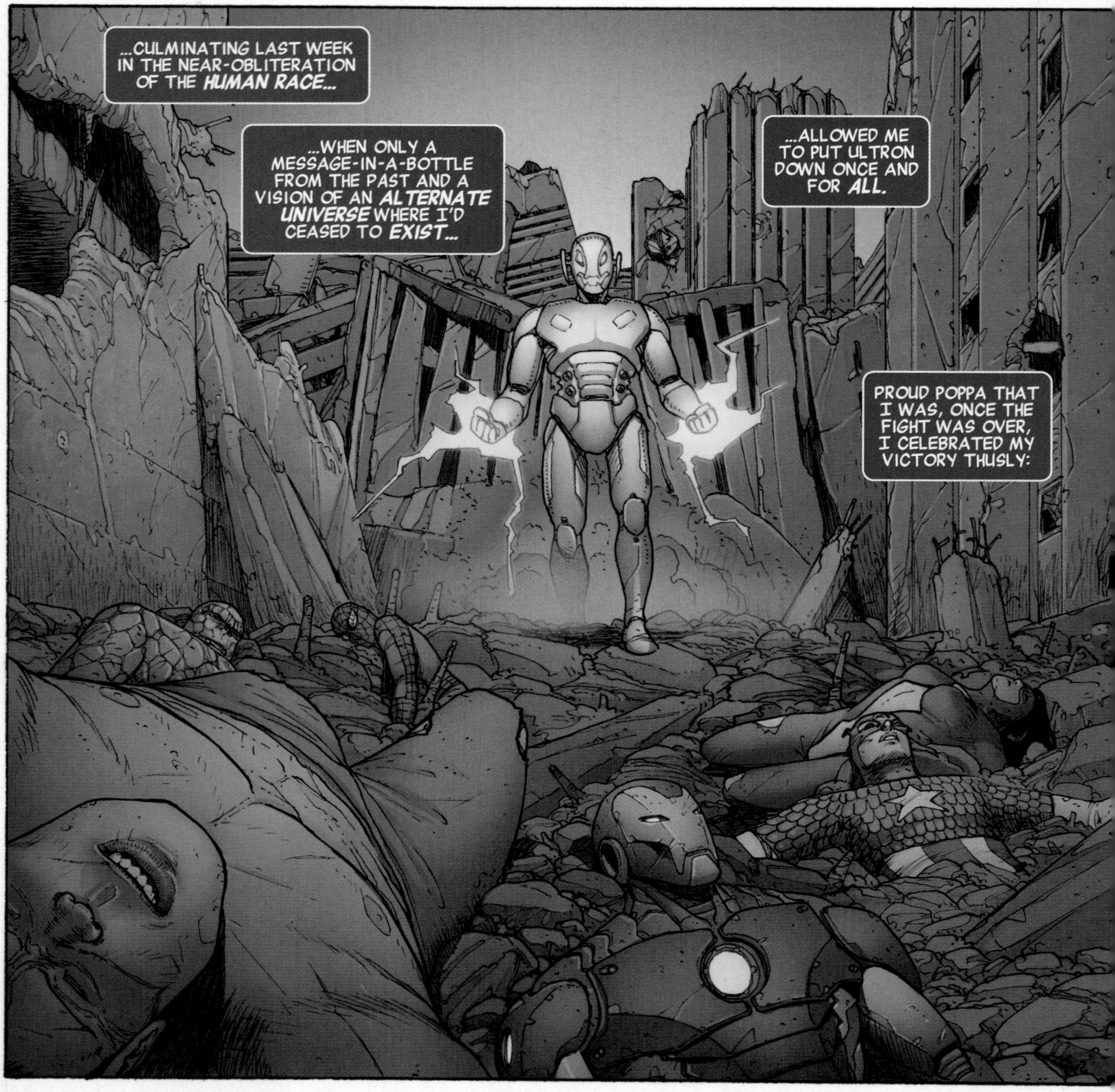
...CULMINATING LAST WEEK IN THE NEAR-OBLITERATION OF THE HUMAN RACE...
...WHEN ONLY A MESSAGE-IN-A-BOTTLE FROM THE PAST AND A VISION OF AN ALTERNATE UNIVERSE WHERE I'D CEASED TO EXIST...
...ALLOWED ME TO PUT ULTRON DOWN ONCE AND FOR ALL.
PROUD POPPA THAT I WAS, ONCE THE FIGHT WAS OVER, I CELEBRATED MY VICTORY THUSLY:

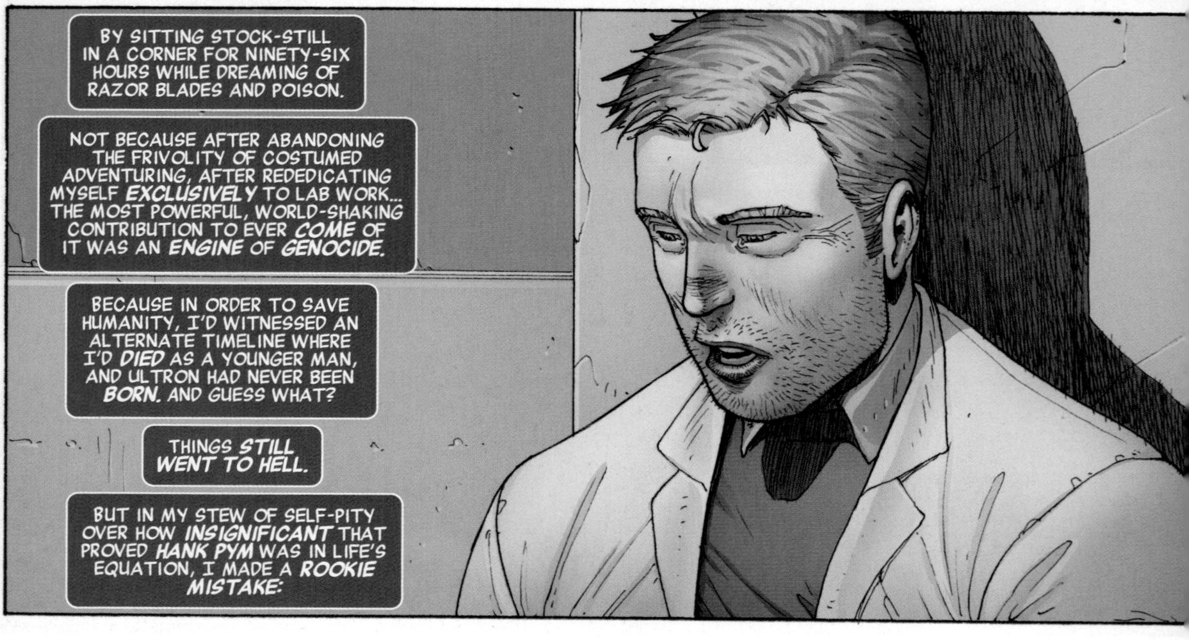
BY SITTING STOCK-STILL IN A CORNER FOR NINETY-SIX HOURS WHILE DREAMING OF RAZOR BLADES AND POISON.
NOT BECAUSE AFTER ABANDONING THE FRIVOLITY OF COSTUMED ADVENTURING, AFTER REDEDICATING MYSELF EXCLUSIVELY TO LAB WORK... THE MOST POWERFUL, WORLD-SHAKING CONTRIBUTION TO EVER COME OF IT WAS AN ENGINE OF GENOCIDE.
BECAUSE IN ORDER TO SAVE HUMANITY, I'D WITNESSED AN ALTERNATE TIMELINE WHERE I'D DIED AS A YOUNGER MAN, AND ULTRON HAD NEVER BEEN BORN. AND GUESS WHAT?
THINGS STILL WENT TO HELL.
BUT IN MY STEW OF SELF-PITY OVER HOW INSIGNIFICANT THAT PROVED HANK PYM WAS IN LIFE'S EQUATION, I MADE A ROOKIE MISTAKE:

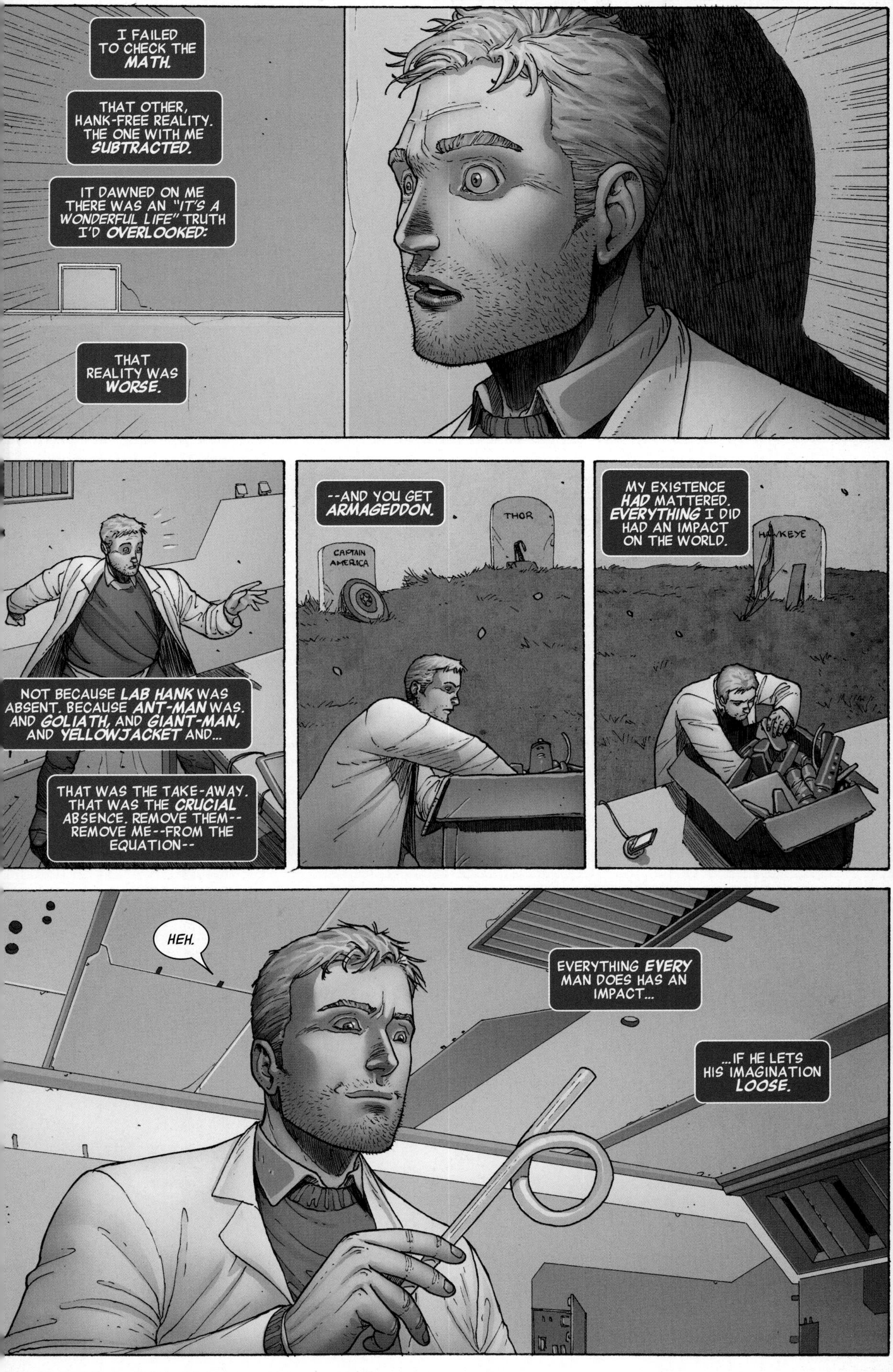
I FAILED TO CHECK THE MATH.
THAT OTHER, HANK-FREE REALITY. THE ONE WITH ME SUBTRACTED.
IT DAWNED ON ME THERE WAS AN "IT'S A WONDERFUL LIFE" TRUTH I'D OVERLOOKED:
THAT REALITY WAS WORSE.
NOT BECAUSE LAB HANK WAS ABSENT. BECAUSE ANT-MAN WAS. AND GOLIATH, AND GIANT-MAN, AND YELLOWJACKET AND...
THAT WAS THE TAKE-AWAY. THAT WAS THE CRUCIAL ABSENCE. REMOVE THEM--REMOVE ME--FROM THE EQUATION--
--AND YOU GET ARMAGEDDON.
CAPTAIN AMERICA
THOR
MY EXISTENCE HAD MATTERED. EVERYTHING I DID HAD AN IMPACT ON THE WORLD.
HAWKEYE
HEH.
EVERYTHING EVERY MAN DOES HAS AN IMPACT...
...IF HE LETS HIS IMAGINATION LOOSE.

--REPEAT, WE HAVE THE KIDNAPPER IN *SIGHT* AND ARE IN PURSUIT!

ALL UNITS EAST OF 65TH AND QUEENS BOULEVARD, CONVERGE FOR ROADBLOCKS--

...PLEASE... *DON'T HURT ME...*

SHUT UP! *TOLD* YOU WE'D FIND YOU!

NOBODY RATS ON THE *HOOD MOB* AND WALKS *AWAY!*

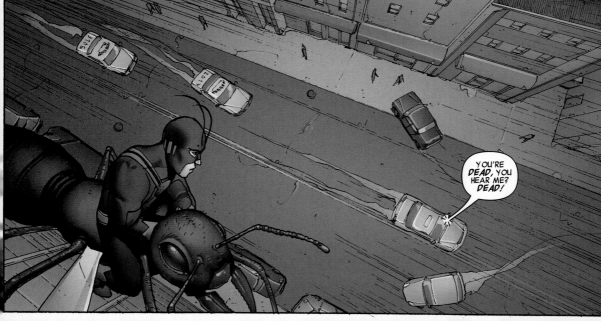

YOU'RE *DEAD,* YOU HEAR ME? *DEAD!*

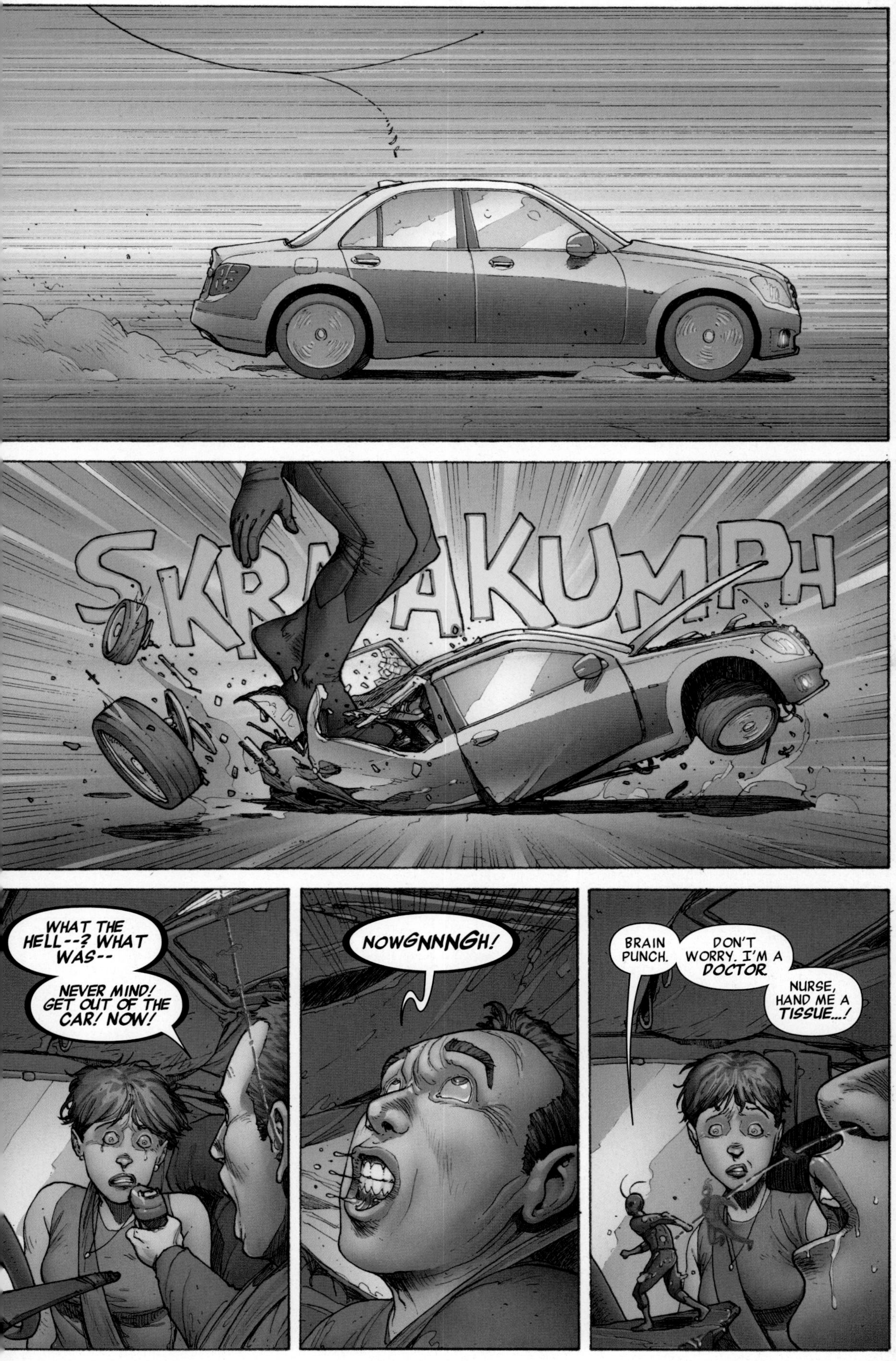
SKRAKUMPH
WHAT THE HELL--? WHAT WAS--
NEVER MIND! GET OUT OF THE CAR! NOW!
NOWGNNNGH!
BRAIN PUNCH.
DON'T WORRY. I'M A DOCTOR.
NURSE, HAND ME A TISSUE...!

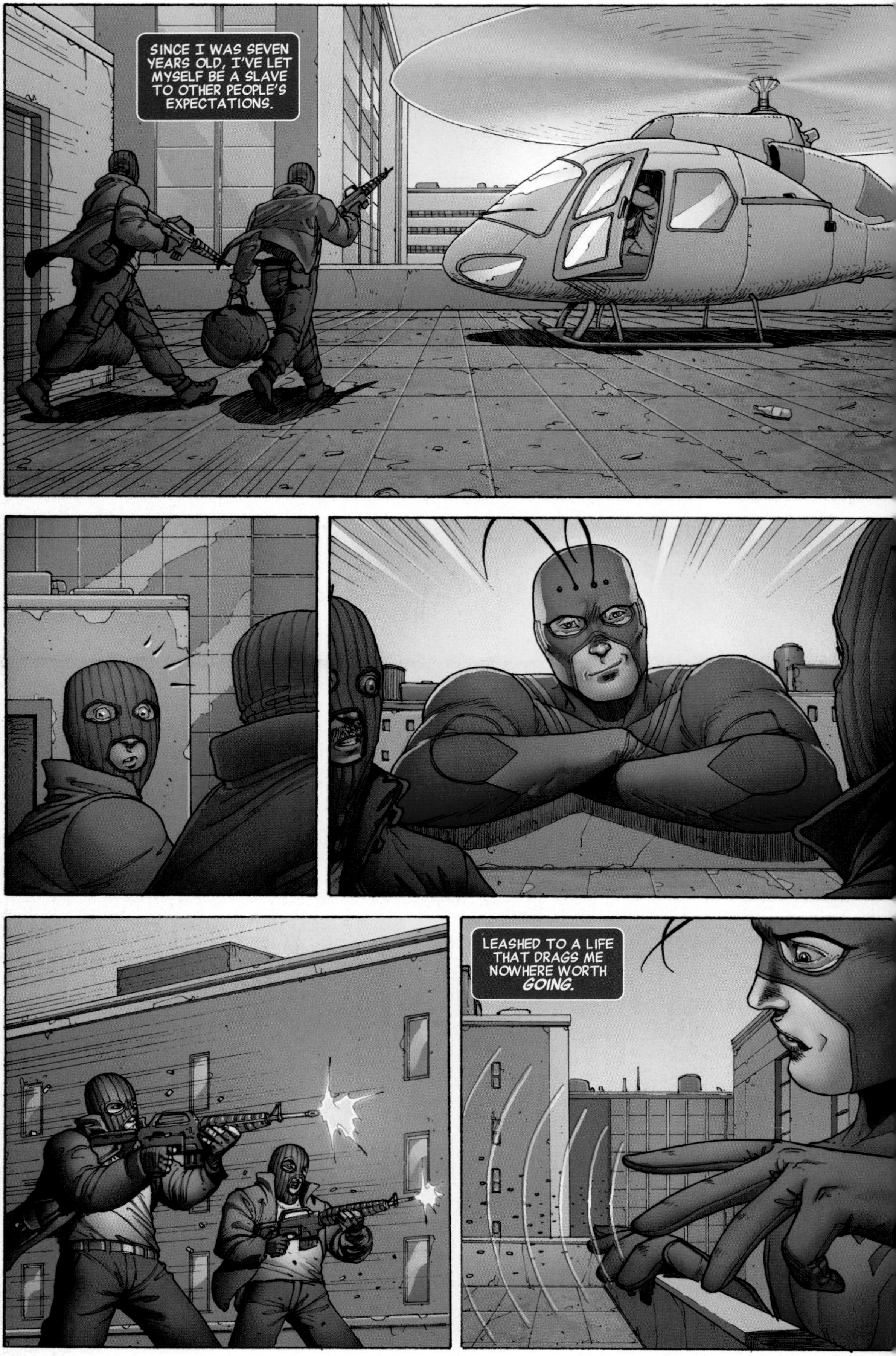
SINCE I WAS SEVEN YEARS OLD, I'VE LET MYSELF BE A SLAVE TO OTHER PEOPLE'S EXPECTATIONS.
LEASHED TO A LIFE THAT DRAGS ME NOWHERE WORTH *GOING*.

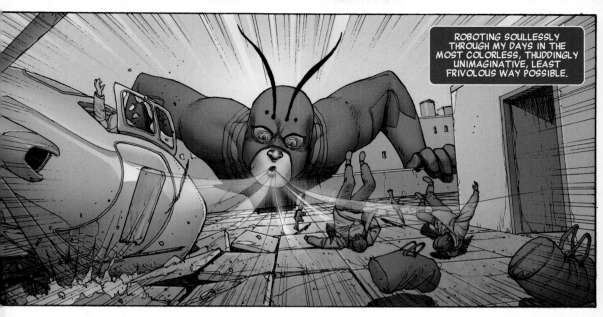

ROBOTING SOULLESSLY THROUGH MY DAYS IN THE MOST COLORLESS, THUDDINGLY UNIMAGINATIVE, LEAST FRIVOLOUS WAY POSSIBLE.

ALL BECAUSE I LET PEOPLE CONVINCE ME THAT I WAS *INCONSEQUENTIAL* WITHOUT A *NECKTIE* ON AND *BEAKERS* IN BOTH HANDS.

--TRAIN PLATFORM COLLAPSE AT ROOSEVELT AVENUE STATION, ALL UNITS REPORT--

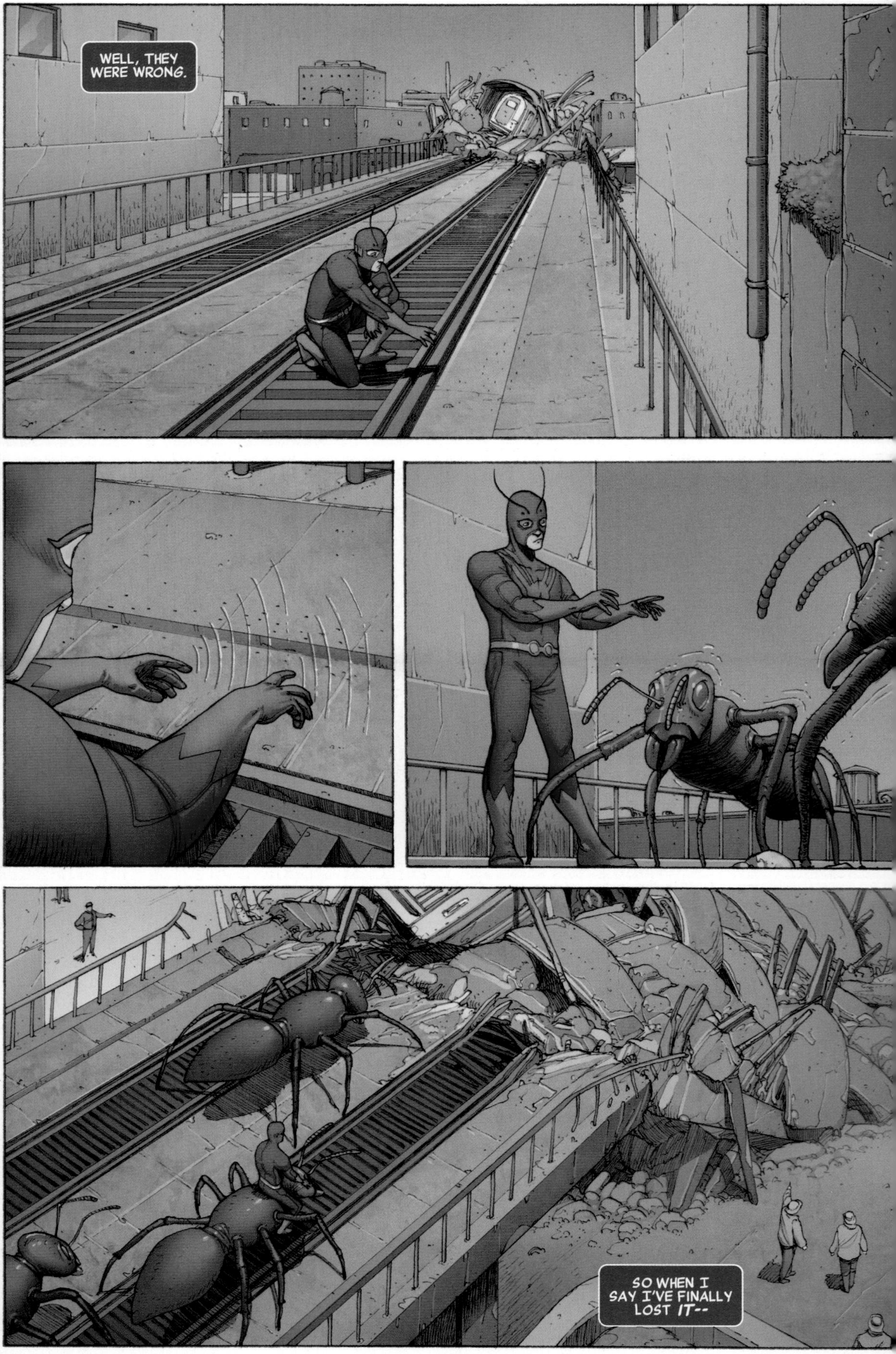
WELL, THEY WERE WRONG.
SO WHEN I SAY I'VE FINALLY LOST *IT*--

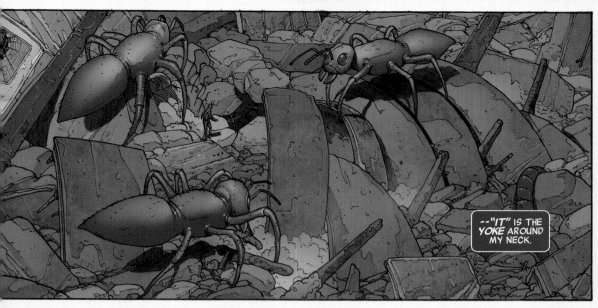

--"IT" IS THE *YOKE* AROUND MY NECK.

THE PRESSURE TO BE *PRACTICAL*, TO CONFORM TO SOME 1950s NOTION OF WHAT AN *INVENTOR* IS.

THE FEAR OF BEING *SPONTANEOUS.*

THE *SOCIAL THERMOSTAT* THAT KEEPS ME FROM *EXPRESSING* MYSELF *FULLY* THROUGH MY *CHOSEN ARTFORM*--

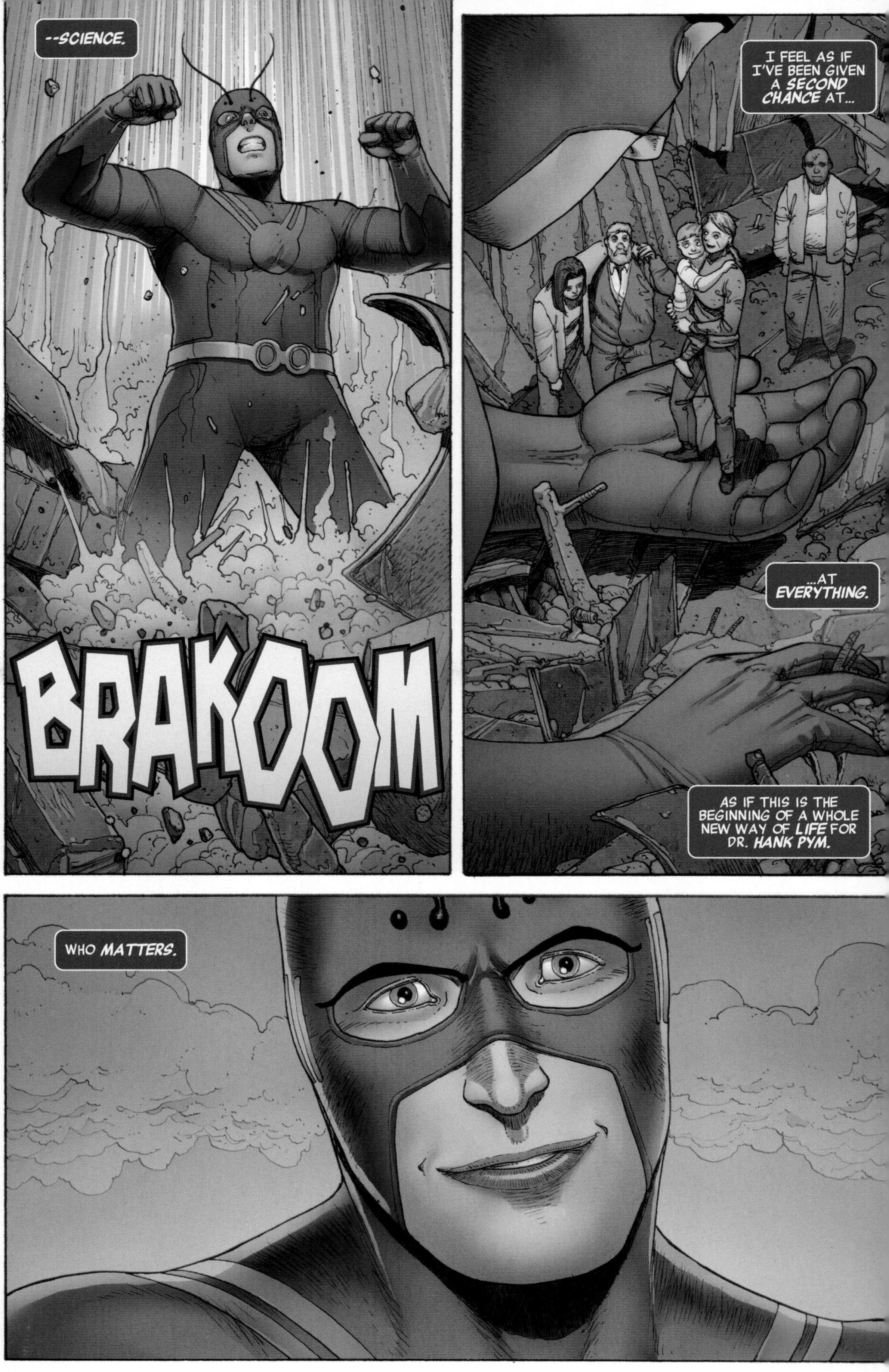
--SCIENCE.
BRAKOOM
I FEEL AS IF I'VE BEEN GIVEN A SECOND CHANCE AT...
...AT EVERYTHING.
AS IF THIS IS THE BEGINNING OF A WHOLE NEW WAY OF LIFE FOR DR. HANK PYM.
WHO MATTERS.

EPILOGUE

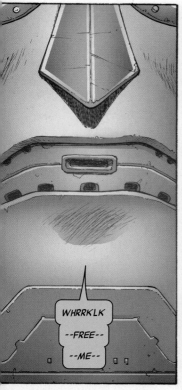

WHRRKLK

--FREE--

--ME--

WHRRKLK

--FREE--

--ME--

WHRRKLK

--FREE--

--ME--

HANG ON, HANG ON...YOU'RE ABOUT TO BE MY GREATEST INVENTION YET, JUST HANG ON...

TKKK

...NO.

SOMETHING'S... SOMETHING'S MISSING...OH!

I KNOW.

OKAY, SEE, THIS...

...THIS IS GOING TO SHOW THEM THAT HANK PYM MEANS BUSINESS...

TO BE CONTINUED IN
AVENGERS A.I.!

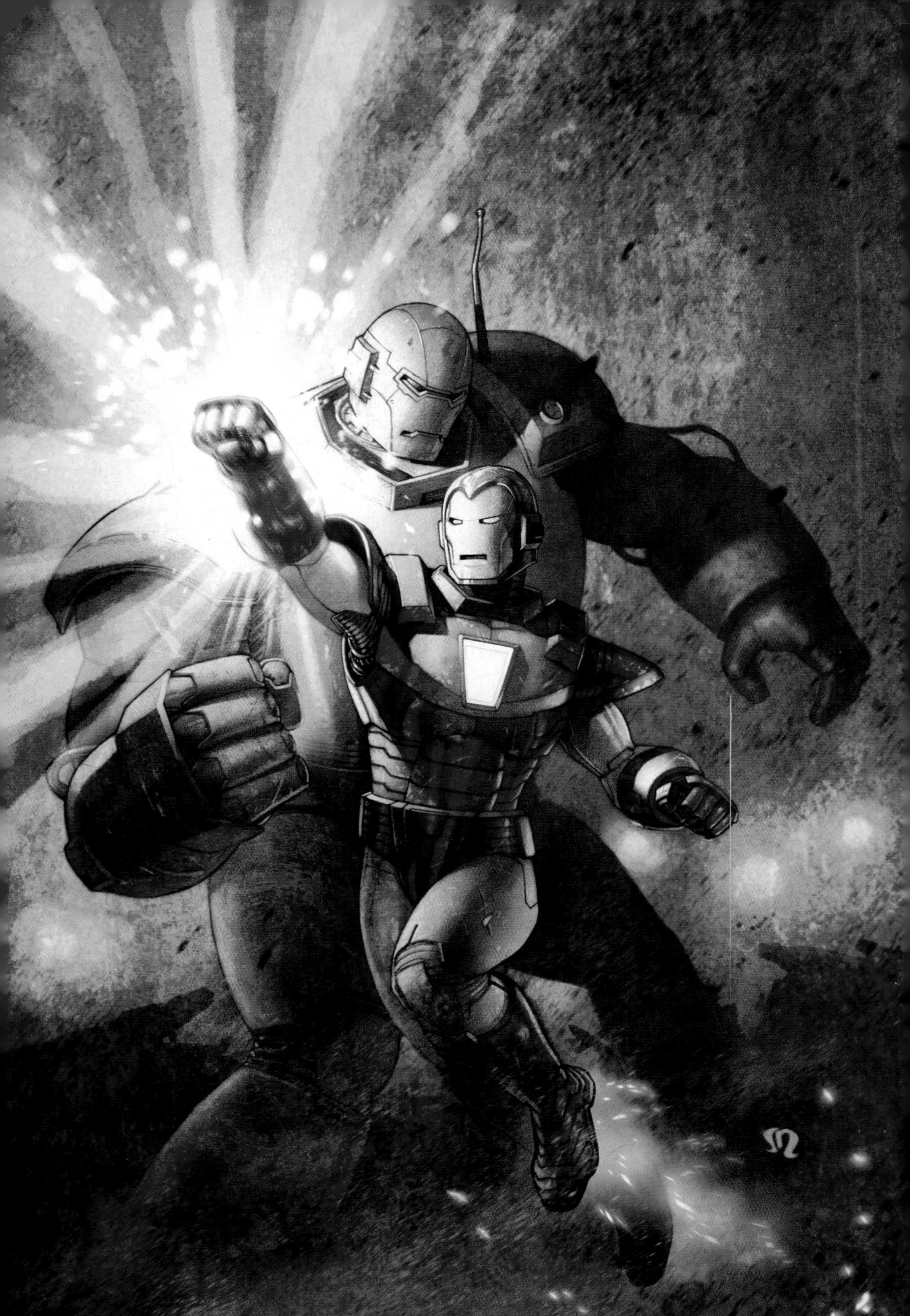

VENGERS ASSEMBLE #14AU MANY ARMORS OF IRON MAN VARIANT